DOSKO PANDA

尾田栄一郎

Some phrases just have a nice ring to them,
y'know? Like, "The water sprite goes flowing down
the river." Or, "Ahh, spring." "It's totally autumn."
"Drop dead." "Stiff roundhouse kick." Or, "Thick
soy broth flavor." See? Let's begin Volume 20.

-Eiichiro Oda, 2001

E iichiro Oda began his manga career at the age of
17, when his one-shot cowboy manga **Wanted!**
won second place in the coveted Tezuka manga
awards. Oda went on to work as an assistant to
some of the biggest manga artists in the industry,
including Nobuhiro Watsuki, before winning the
Hop Step Award for new artists. His pirate
adventure **One Piece**, which debuted in **Weekly
Shonen Jump** in 1997, quickly became one of the
most popular manga in Japan.

P9-EJS-674

ONE PIECE VOL. 20
BAROQUE WORKS PART 9

SHONEN JUMP Manga Edition

This volume contains material that was originally published in English
SHONEN JUMP #70–73. Artwork in the magazine may have been
slightly altered from that presented here.

STORY AND ART BY EIICHIRO ODA

English Adaptation/Lance Caselman
Translation/JN Productions
Touch-up Art & Lettering/Vanessa Satone
Additional Touch-up/Rachel Lightfoot
Design/Sean Lee
Editor/ Yuki Murashige

ONE PIECE © 1997 by Eiichiro Oda. All rights reserved.
First published in Japan in 1997 by SHUEISHA Inc., Tokyo.
English translation rights arranged by SHUEISHA Inc.

The rights of the author(s) of the work(s) in this publication to be so
identified have been asserted in accordance with the Copyright, Designs
and Patents Act 1988. A CIP catalogue record for this book is available
from the British Library.

The stories, characters and incidents mentioned in this publication
are entirely fictional.

No portion of this book may be reproduced or transmitted in any form
or by any means without written permission from the copyright holders.

Printed in the U.S.A.

Published by VIZ Media, LLC
P.O. Box 77010
San Francisco, CA 94107

10 9 8 7 6 5 4
First printing, February 2009
Fourth printing, January 2012

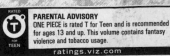

PARENTAL ADVISORY
ONE PIECE is rated T for Teen and is recommended
for ages 13 and up. This volume contains fantasy
violence and tobacco usage.
ratings.viz.com

www.viz.com

SHONEN JUMP MANGA

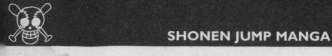

ONE PIECE

Vol. 20
SHOWDOWN AT ALUBARNA

STORY AND ART BY
EIICHIRO ODA

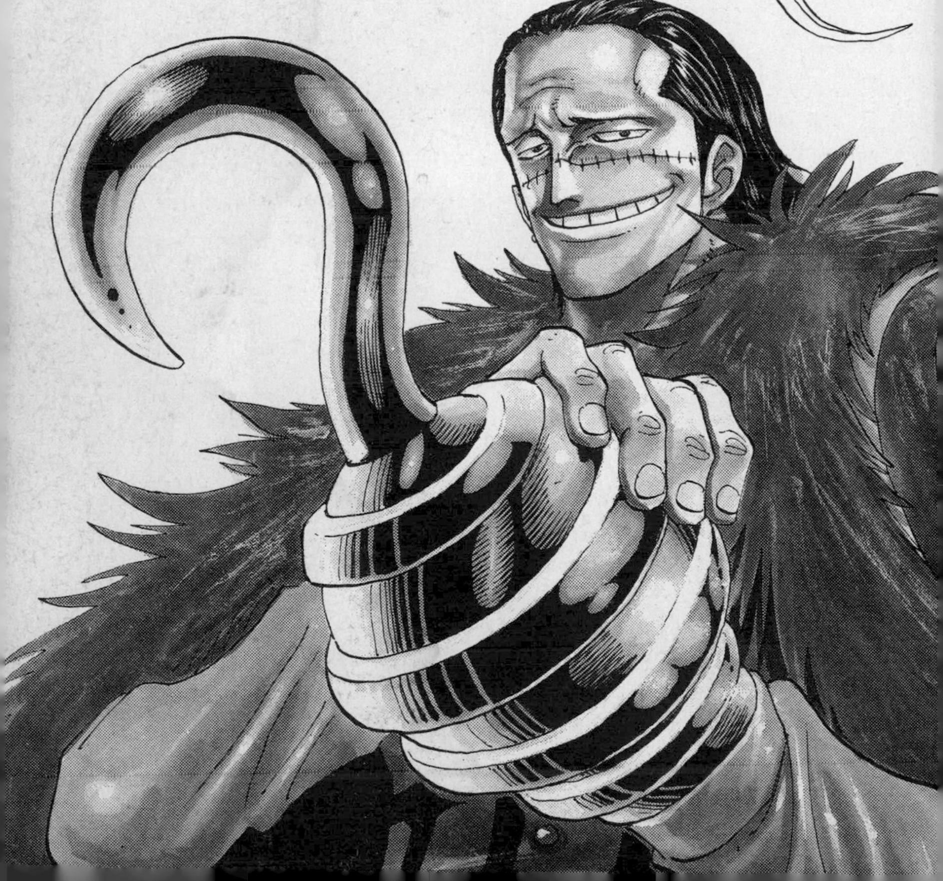

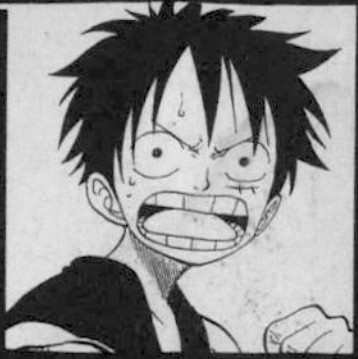

Monkey D. Luffy
Boundlessly optimistic and able to stretch like rubber, he is determined to become King of the Pirates.

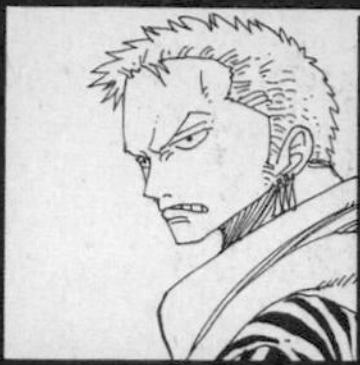

Roronoa Zolo
A former bounty hunter and master of the "three-sword" style. He aspires to be the world's greatest swordsman.

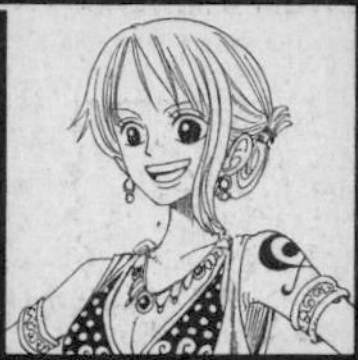

Nami
A thief who specializes in robbing pirates. Nami hates pirates, but Luffy convinced her to be his navigator.

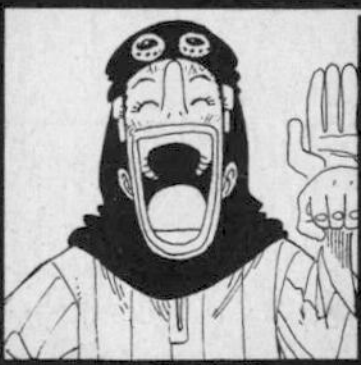

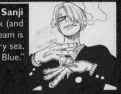

Usopp
A village boy with a talent for telling tall tales. His father, Yasopp, is a member of Shanks's crew.

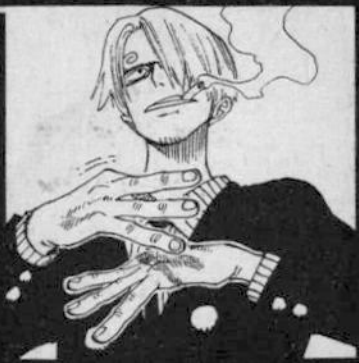

Sanji
The big-hearted cook (and ladies' man) whose dream is to find the legendary sea, the "All Blue."

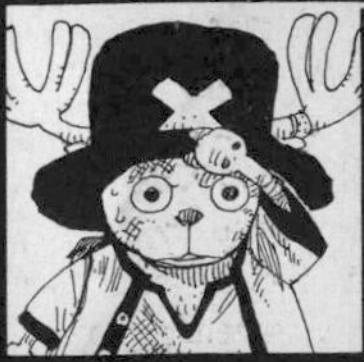

Tony Tony Chopper
A blue-nosed man-reindeer and the ship's doctor.

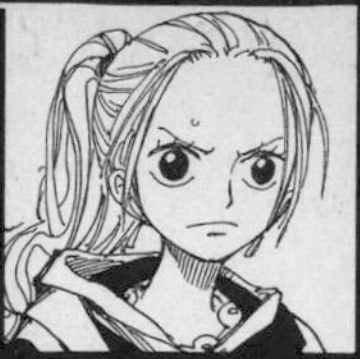

Vivi

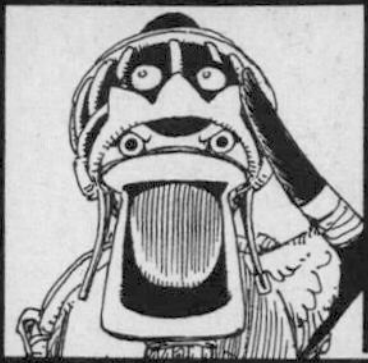

Karoo

—— Royal Forces ——

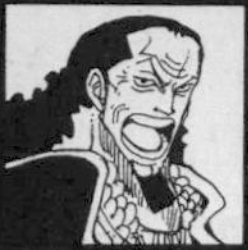

Nefeltari Cobra (King of Alabasta)

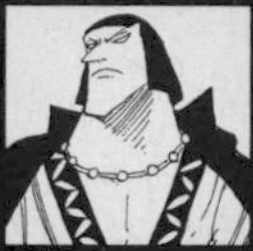

Chaka

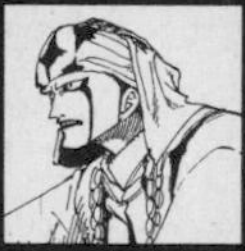

Pell

—— Rebel Forces ——

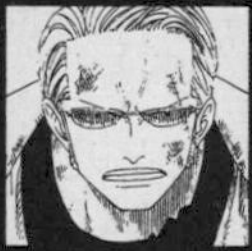

Koza

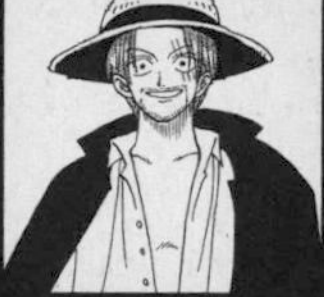

"Red-Haired" Shanks
A pirate that Luffy idolizes. Shanks gave Luffy his trademark straw hat.

Volume 20 THE STORY OF

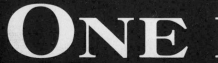

ONE PIECE

Navy

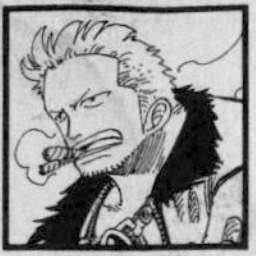

Captain Smoker

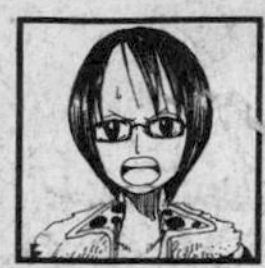

Tashigi

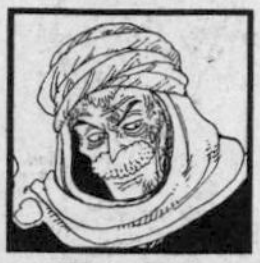

Toh-Toh

BAROQUE WORKS

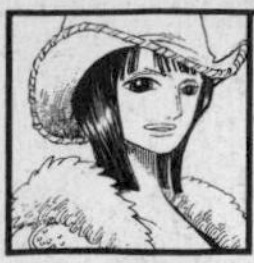

Ms. All Sunday

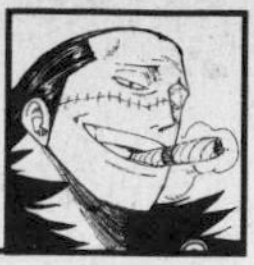

Mr. Zero (Sir Crocodile)

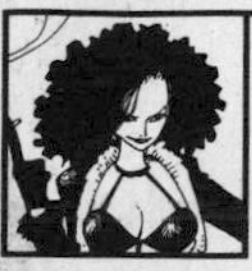

Ms. Doublefinger

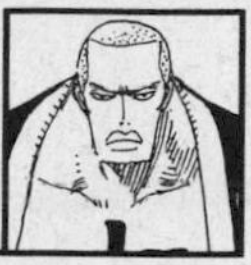

Mr. 1

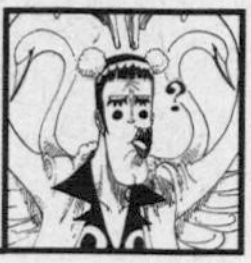

Mr. 2 Bon Clay

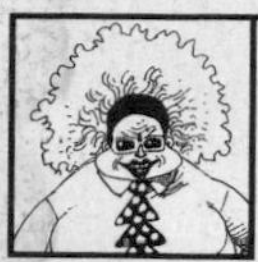

Ms. Merry Christmas

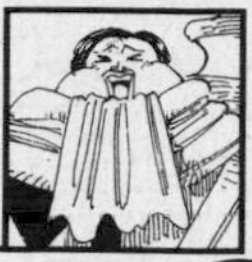

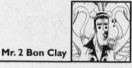

Mr. 4

Monkey D. Luffy started out as just a kid with a dream—to become the greatest pirate in history! Stirred by the tales of pirate "Red-Haired" Shanks, Luffy vowed to become a pirate himself. That was before the enchanted Devil Fruit gave Luffy the power to stretch like rubber, at the cost of being unable to swim—a serious handicap for an aspiring sea dog. Undeterred, Luffy set out to sea and recruited some crewmates—master swordsman Zolo, treasure-hunting thief Nami, lying sharpshooter Usopp, the high-kicking chef Sanji, and the latest addition, Chopper—the walkin' talkin' reindeer doctor.

On the Grand Line, Luffy and crew struggle to help Princess Vivi save her war-torn and drought-ravaged kingdom from the evil Sir Crocodile and his secret criminal organization, the Baroque Works. But, having trekked to Rainbase to confront the villain, Luffy instead finds himself imprisoned in Sir Crocodile's hideout—with Captain Smoker of the Navy! Meanwhile, the rebels and the royal army head for a catastrophic clash, and Vivi must choose between going to Alubarna to stop it or saving her friends from the gigantic Bananagators. Only Sanji's unexpected arrival saves the day, and the crew races to Alubarna in hopes of stopping the war. But even as they set out, Sir Crododile's sudden appearance forces Luffy into a showdown!!

BAROQUE WORKS

ONE PIECE

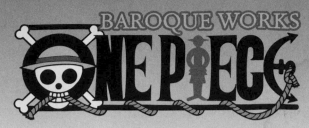

Vol. 20

Showdown at Alubarna

CONTENTS

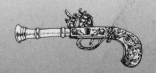

Chapter 177:
30 MILLION VS. 81 MILLION

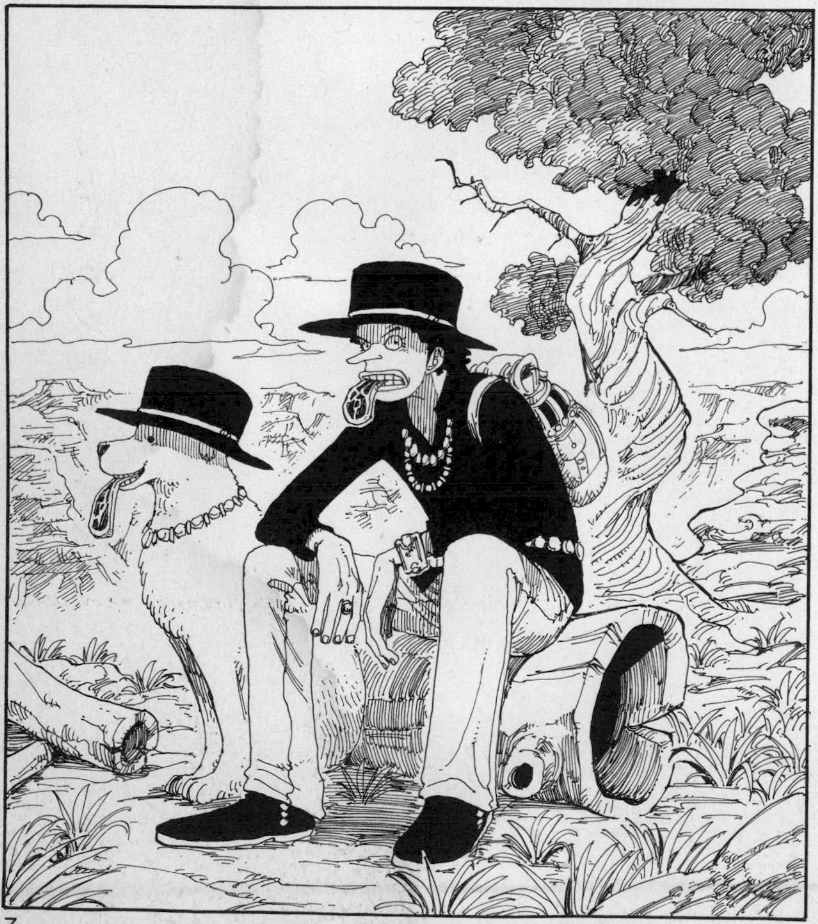

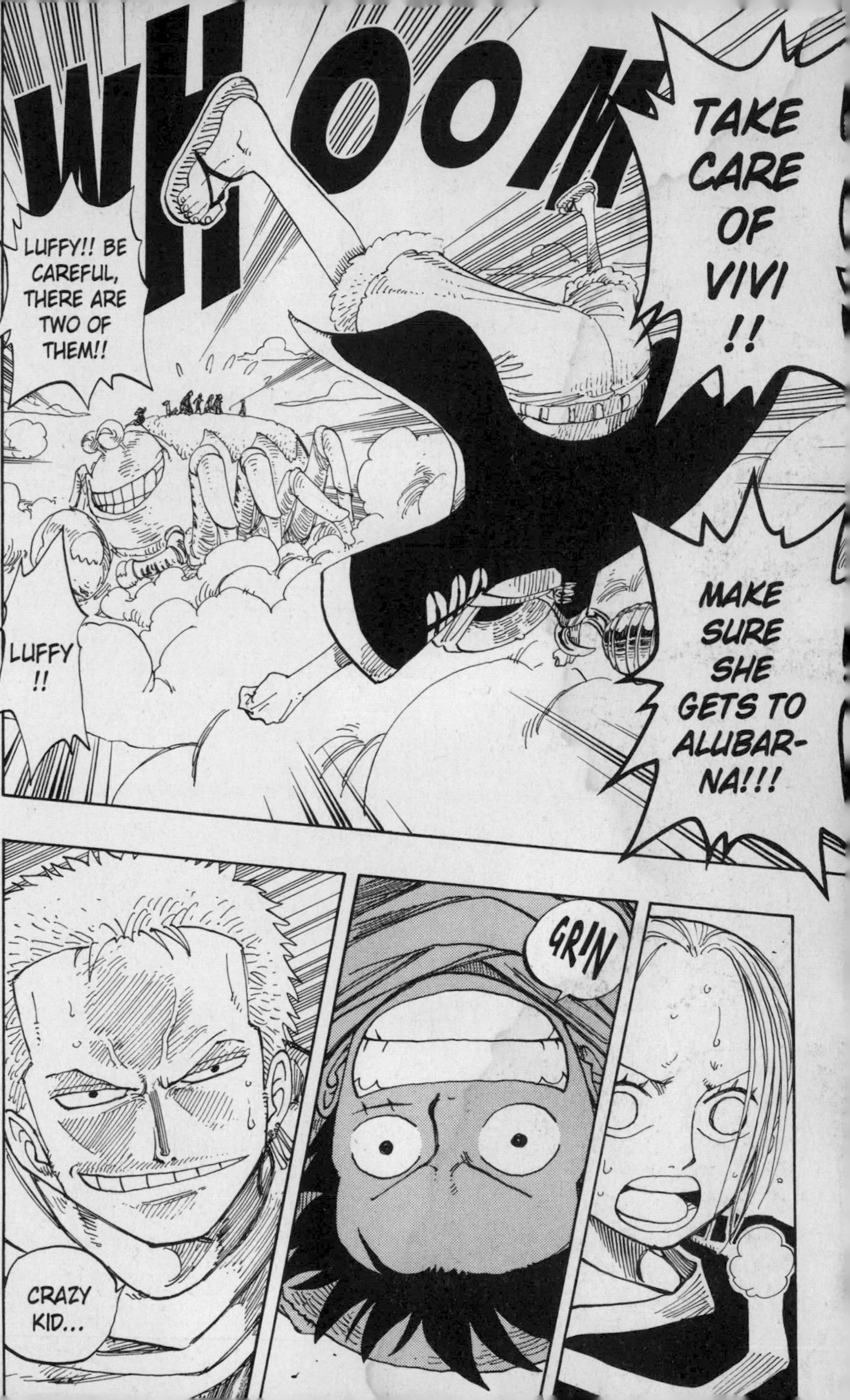
TAKE CARE OF VIVI !!
WHOOM
MAKE SURE SHE GETS TO ALUBAR-NA!!!
LUFFY!! BE CAREFUL, THERE ARE TWO OF THEM!!
LUFFY !!
GRIN
CRAZY KID...

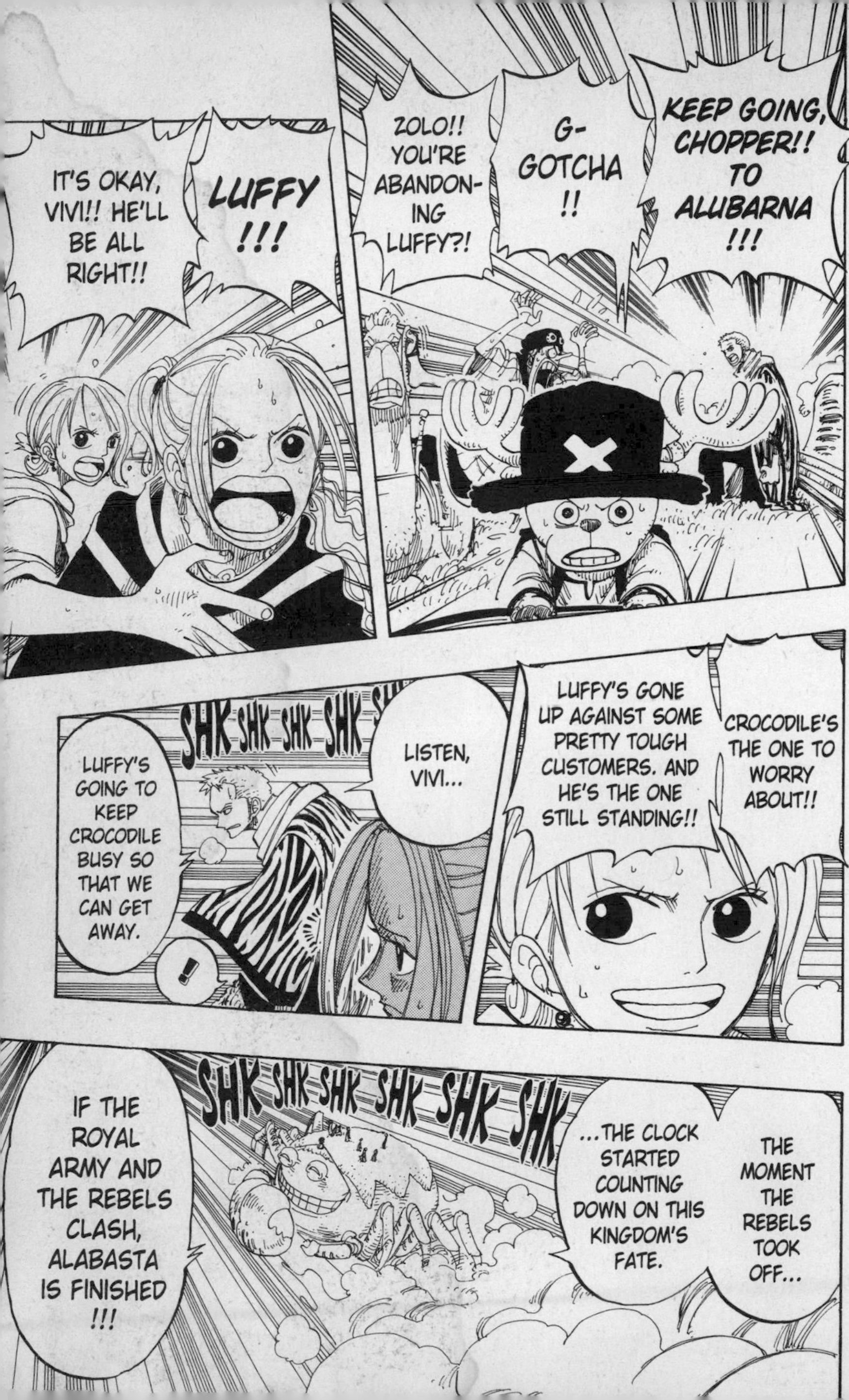
KEEP GOING, CHOPPER!! TO ALUBARNA!!!
G-GOTCHA!!
ZOLO!! YOU'RE ABANDONING LUFFY?!
LUFFY!!!
IT'S OKAY, VIVI!! HE'LL BE ALL RIGHT!!
CROCODILE'S THE ONE TO WORRY ABOUT!!
LUFFY'S GONE UP AGAINST SOME PRETTY TOUGH CUSTOMERS. AND HE'S THE ONE STILL STANDING!!
SHK SHK SHK SHK
LISTEN, VIVI...
LUFFY'S GOING TO KEEP CROCODILE BUSY SO THAT WE CAN GET AWAY.
!
THE MOMENT THE REBELS TOOK OFF...
...THE CLOCK STARTED COUNTING DOWN ON THIS KINGDOM'S FATE.
SHK SHK SHK SHK SHK SHK
IF THE ROYAL ARMY AND THE REBELS CLASH, ALABASTA IS FINISHED!!!

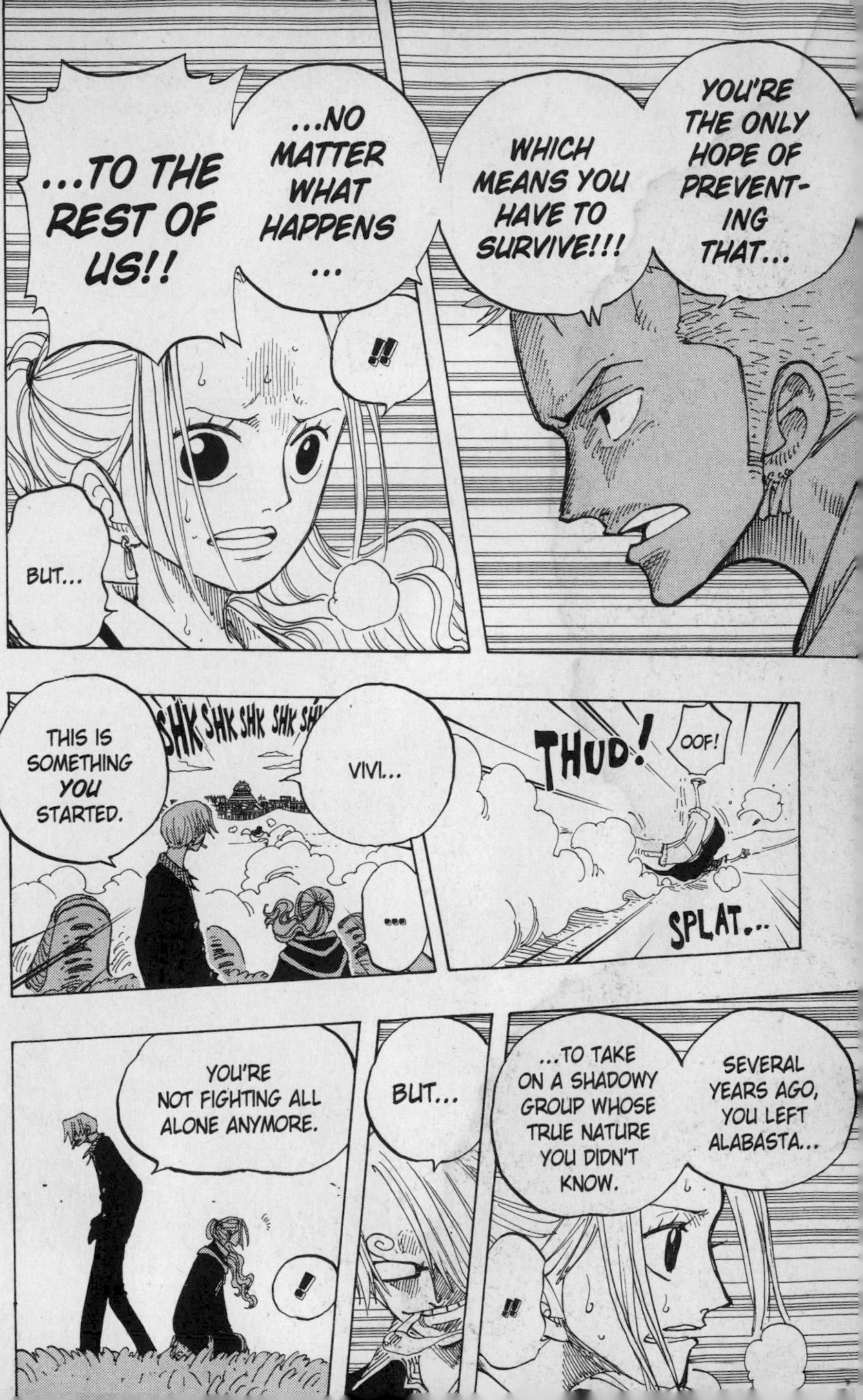

YOU'RE THE ONLY HOPE OF PREVENT-ING THAT...
WHICH MEANS YOU HAVE TO SURVIVE!!!
...NO MATTER WHAT HAPPENS...
...TO THE REST OF US!!
!!
BUT...
THUD!
OOF!
SPLAT...
VIVI...
SHK SHK SHK SHK SHK
THIS IS SOMETHING YOU STARTED.
...
SEVERAL YEARS AGO, YOU LEFT ALABASTA...
...TO TAKE ON A SHADOWY GROUP WHOSE TRUE NATURE YOU DIDN'T KNOW.
!!
BUT...
YOU'RE NOT FIGHTING ALL ALONE ANYMORE.
!

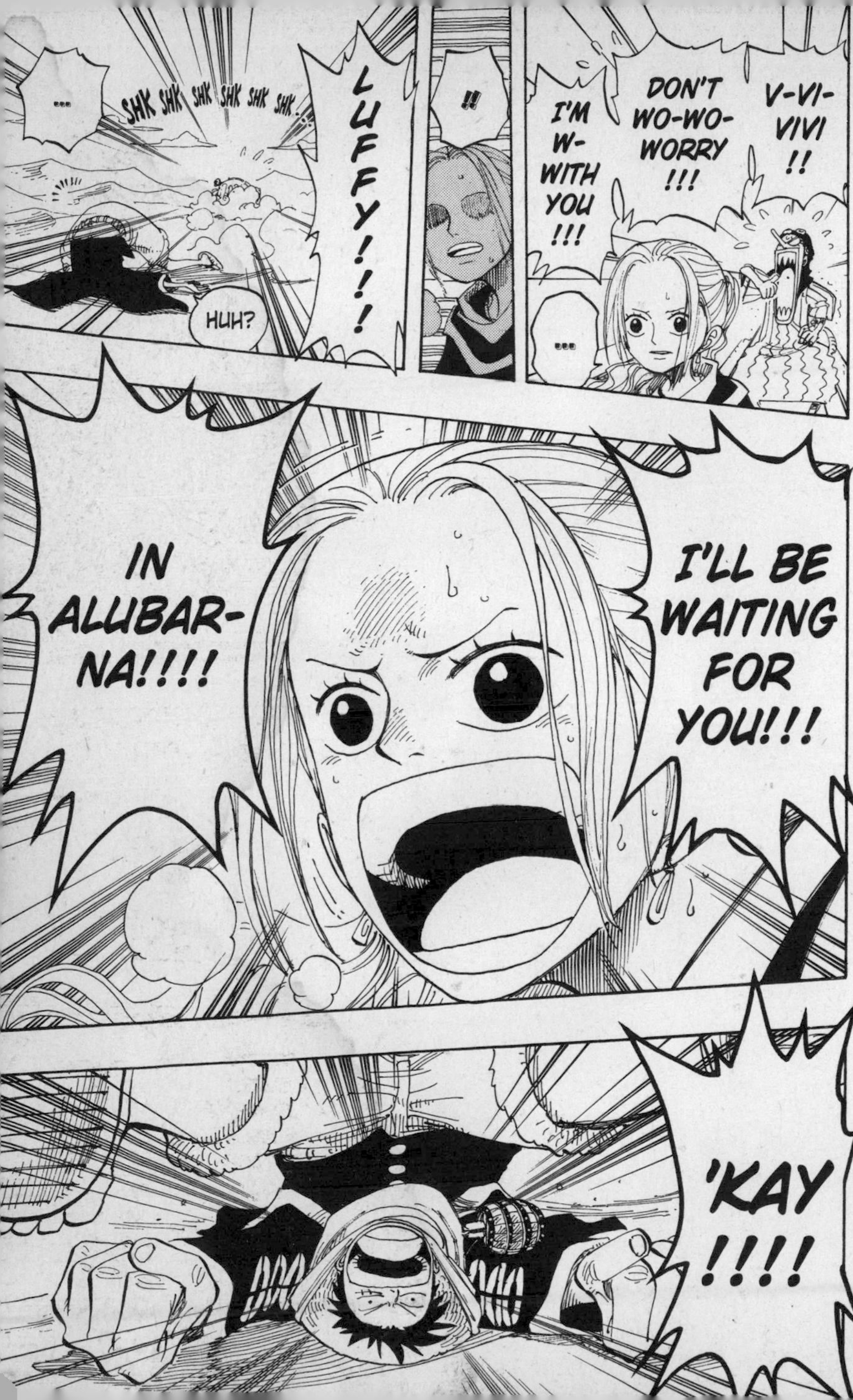
V-VI-VIVI!!
DON'T WO-WO-WORRY!!!
I'M W-WITH YOU!!!
...
!!
LUFFY!!!
SHK SHK SHK SHK SHK SHK
...
HUH?
I'LL BE WAITING FOR YOU!!!
IN ALUBARNA!!!!
'KAY!!!!

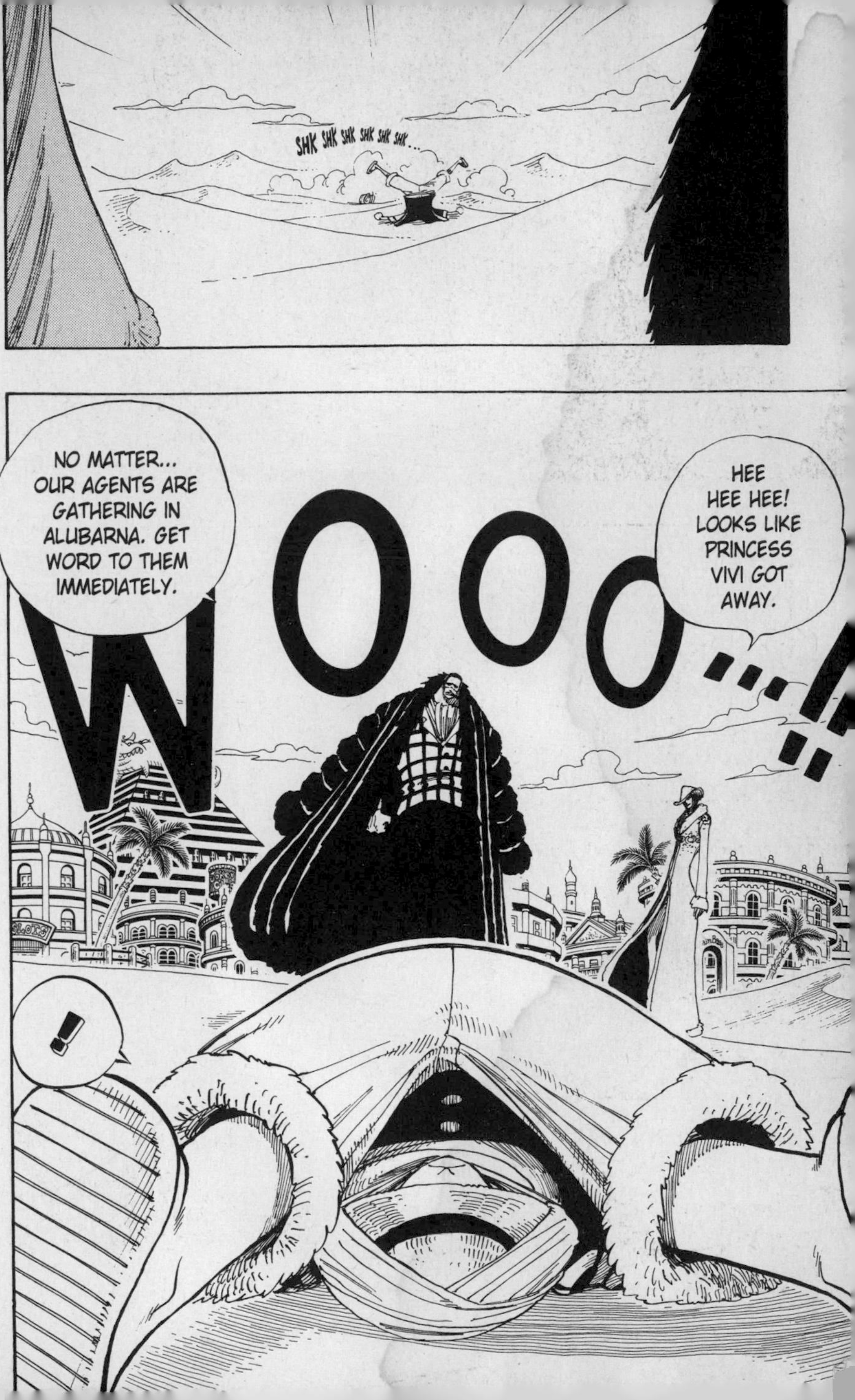
SHK SHK SHK SHK SHK SHK...
HEE HEE HEE! LOOKS LIKE PRINCESS VIVI GOT AWAY.
WOOO...!!
NO MATTER... OUR AGENTS ARE GATHERING IN ALUBARNA. GET WORD TO THEM IMMEDIATELY.
!

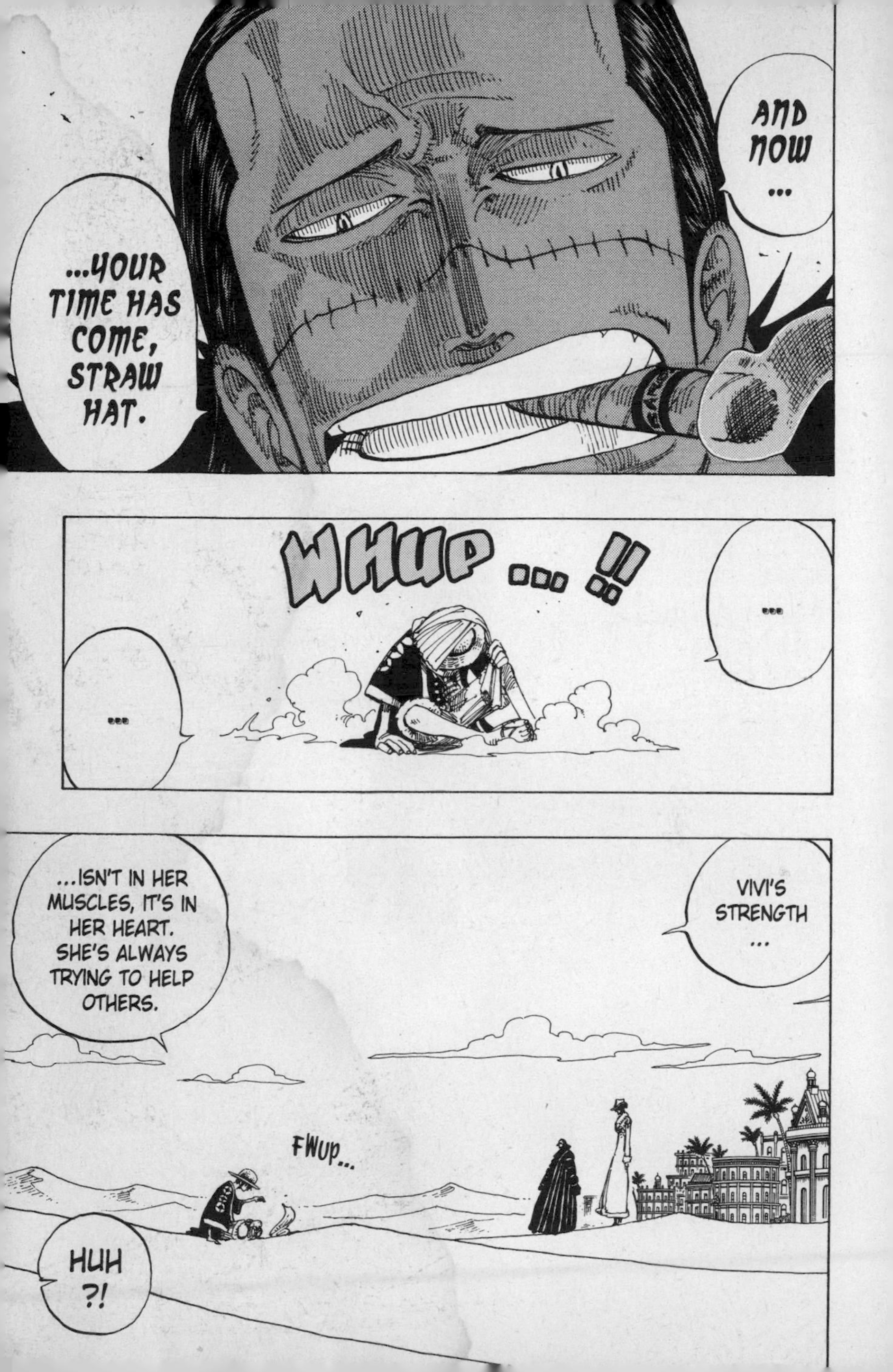
AND NOW ...
...YOUR TIME HAS COME, STRAW HAT.
WHUP ... !!
...
...
VIVI'S STRENGTH ...
...ISN'T IN HER MUSCLES, IT'S IN HER HEART. SHE'S ALWAYS TRYING TO HELP OTHERS.
FWUP...
HUH ?!

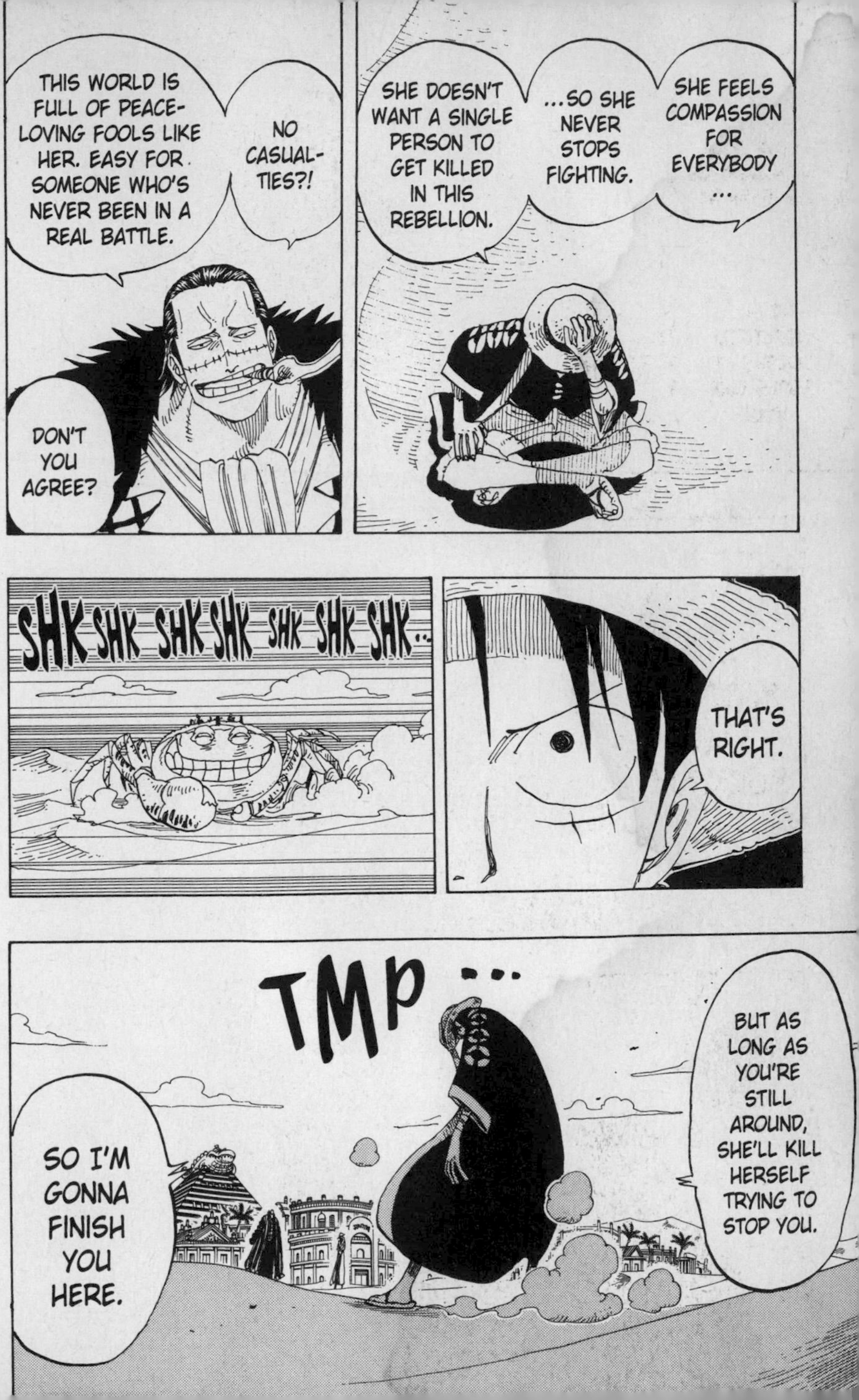
SHE FEELS COMPASSION FOR EVERYBODY ...
...SO SHE NEVER STOPS FIGHTING.
SHE DOESN'T WANT A SINGLE PERSON TO GET KILLED IN THIS REBELLION.
NO CASUAL-TIES?!
THIS WORLD IS FULL OF PEACE-LOVING FOOLS LIKE HER. EASY FOR SOMEONE WHO'S NEVER BEEN IN A REAL BATTLE.
DON'T YOU AGREE?
THAT'S RIGHT.
SHK SHK SHK SHK SHK SHK SHK...
BUT AS LONG AS YOU'RE STILL AROUND, SHE'LL KILL HERSELF TRYING TO STOP YOU.
TMP ...
SO I'M GONNA FINISH YOU HERE.

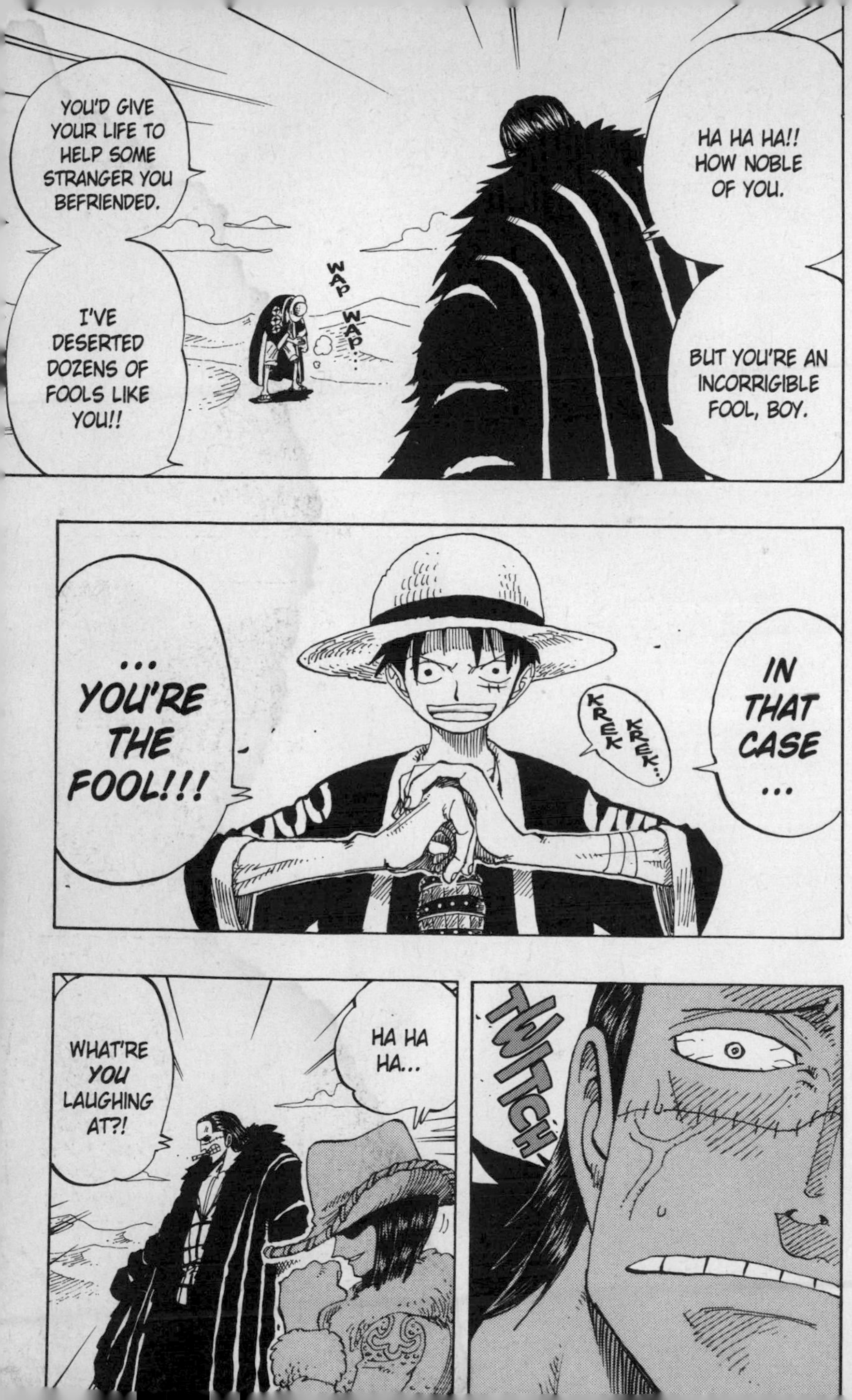
HA HA HA!! HOW NOBLE OF YOU.
BUT YOU'RE AN INCORRIGIBLE FOOL, BOY.
YOU'D GIVE YOUR LIFE TO HELP SOME STRANGER YOU BEFRIENDED.
I'VE DESERTED DOZENS OF FOOLS LIKE YOU!!
WAP WAP...
IN THAT CASE...
KREK KREK...
...YOU'RE THE FOOL!!!
TWITCH
HA HA HA...
WHAT'RE YOU LAUGHING AT?!

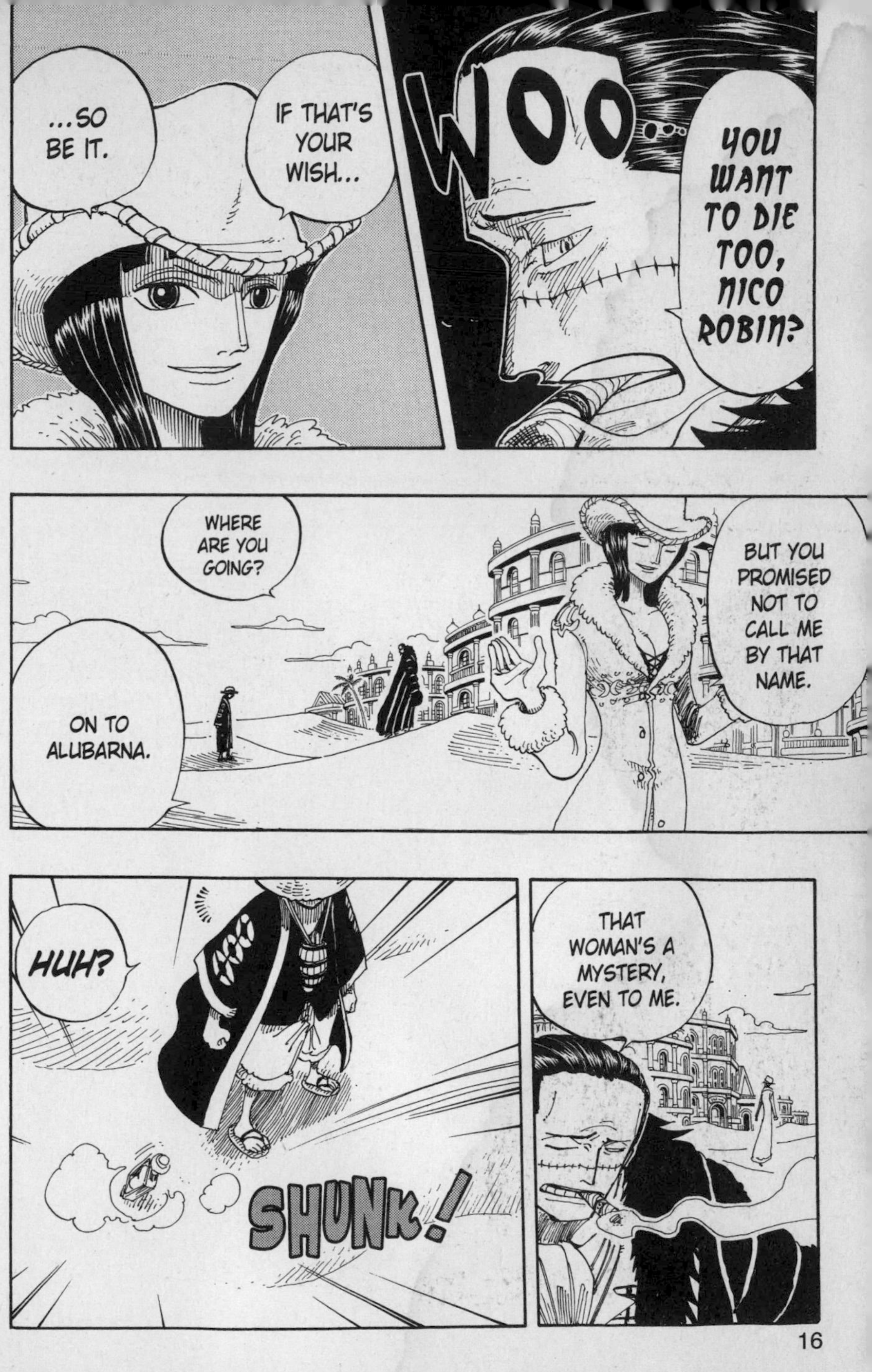
WOO
YOU WANT TO DIE TOO, NICO ROBIN?
IF THAT'S YOUR WISH...
...SO BE IT.
BUT YOU PROMISED NOT TO CALL ME BY THAT NAME.
WHERE ARE YOU GOING?
ON TO ALUBARNA.
THAT WOMAN'S A MYSTERY, EVEN TO ME.
HUH?
SHUNK!

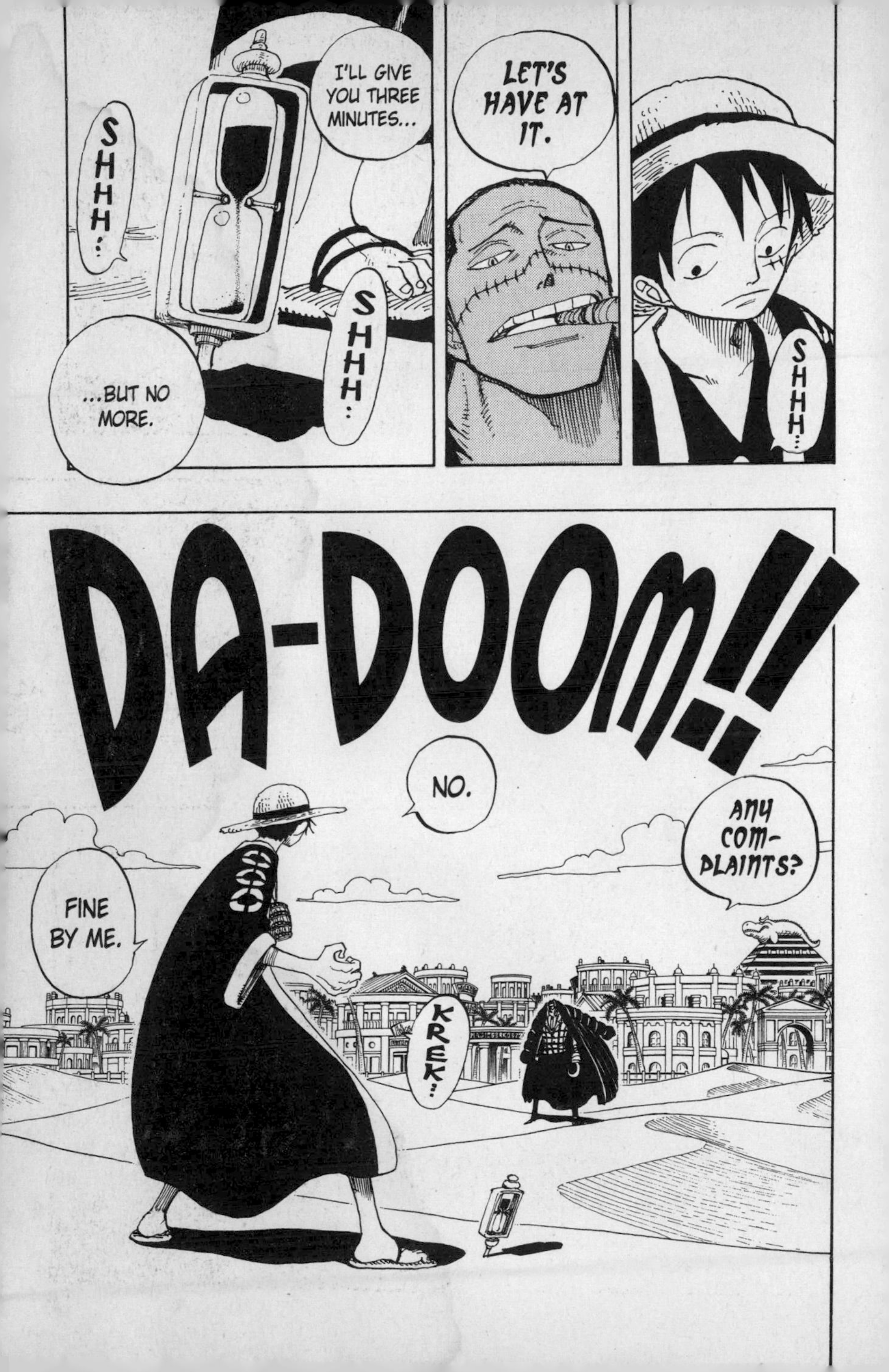
SHHH..
LET'S HAVE AT IT.
I'LL GIVE YOU THREE MINUTES...
SHHH..
SHHH..
...BUT NO MORE.
DA-DOOM!!
ANY COM-PLAINTS?
NO.
FINE BY ME.
KREK..

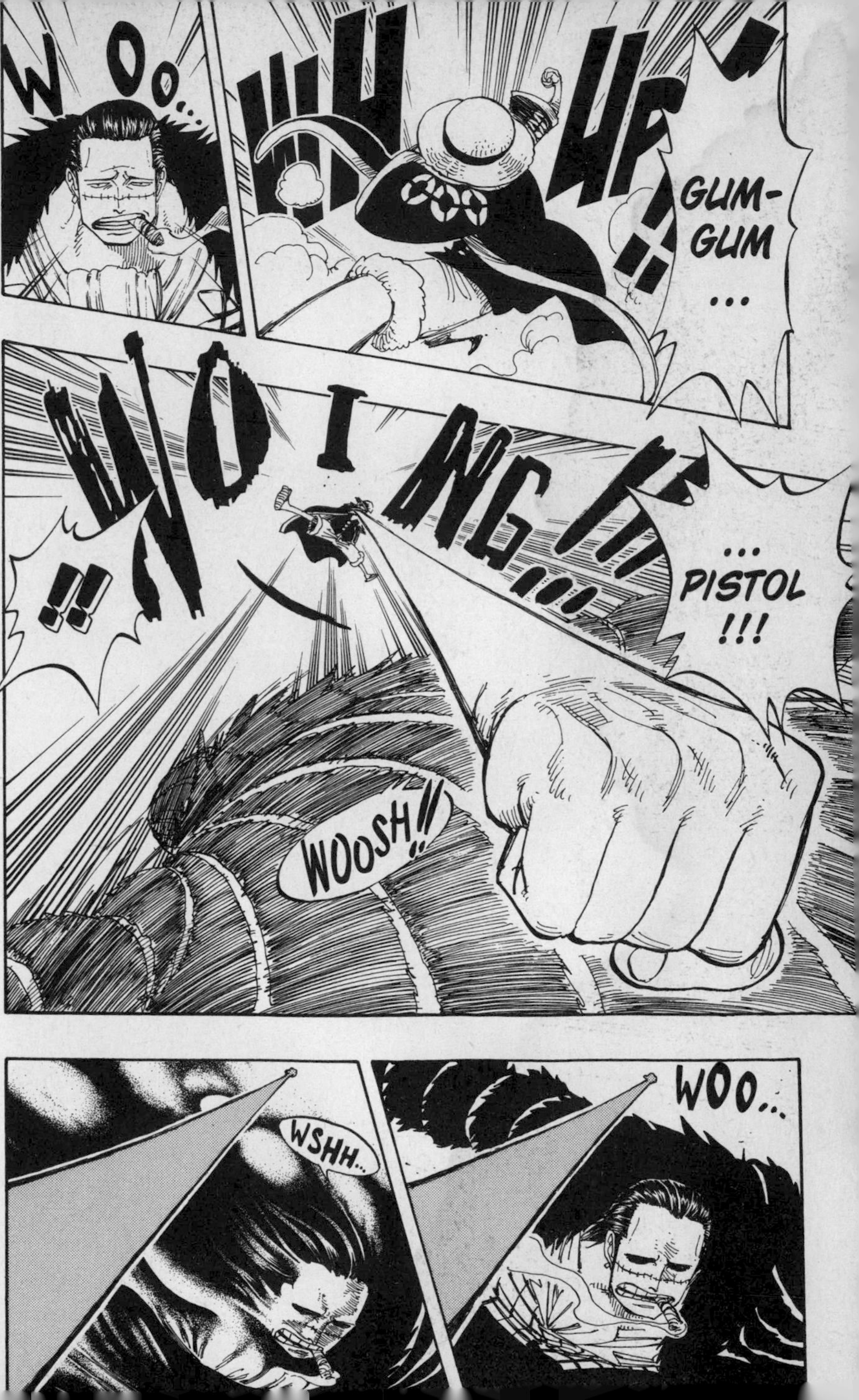
GUM-GUM ...
WHUP!!
WOO...
...PISTOL!!!
WOING!!
WOOSH!!
WOO...
WSHH...

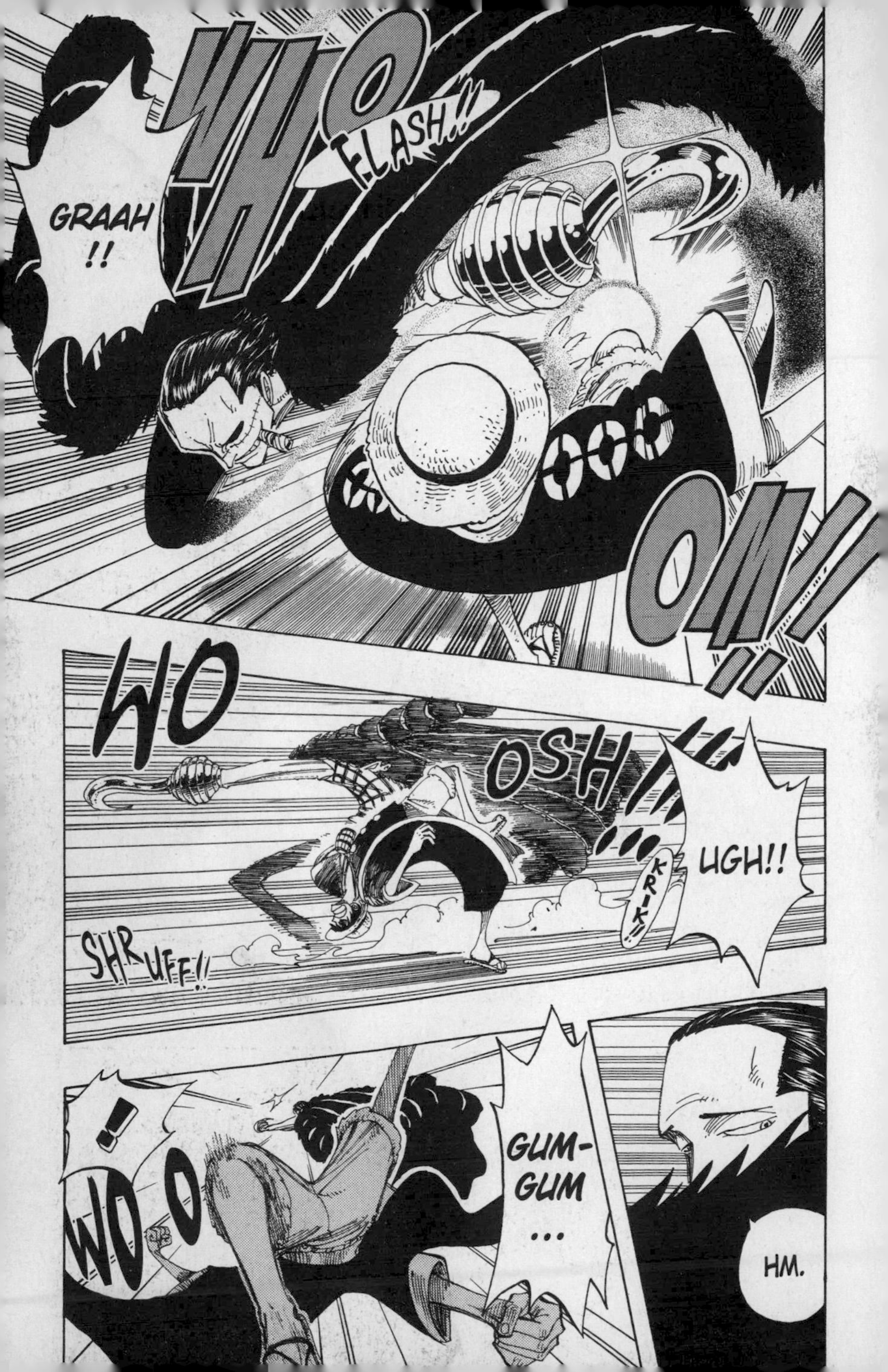
WHO
FLASH!!
GRAAH!!
OM!!
WO
OSH!!
UGH!!
KRIK!!
SHRUFF!!
HM.
GUM-GUM ...
!
WOO

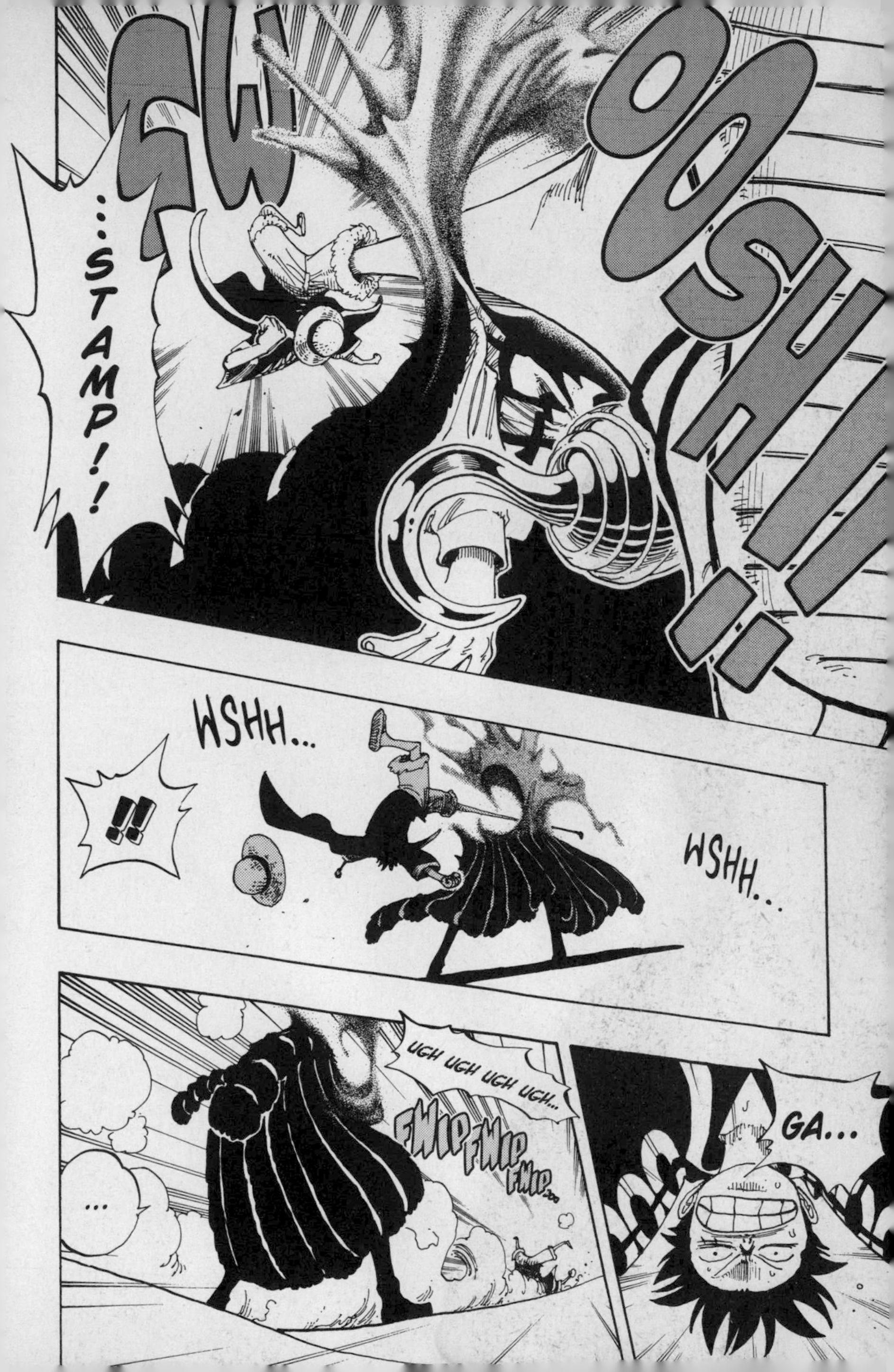
GWOOSH!!
...STAMP!!
WSHH...
WSHH...
!!
GA...
UGH UGH UGH UGH...
FWIP FWIP FWIP...
...

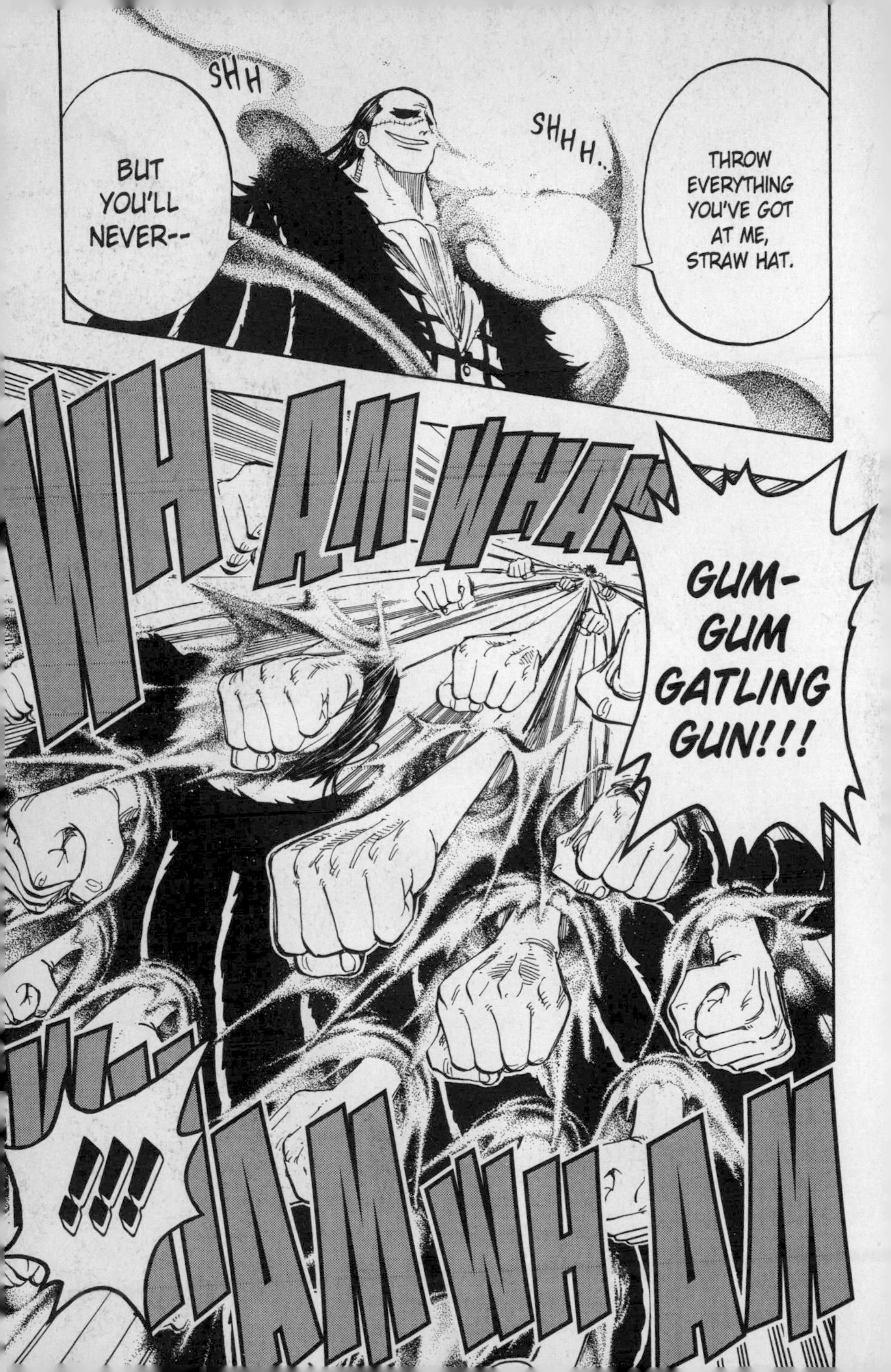
THROW EVERYTHING YOU'VE GOT AT ME, STRAW HAT.
SHHHH...
SHH
BUT YOU'LL NEVER--
GUM-GUM GATLING GUN!!!
WHAM WHAM
WHAM WHAM!!!

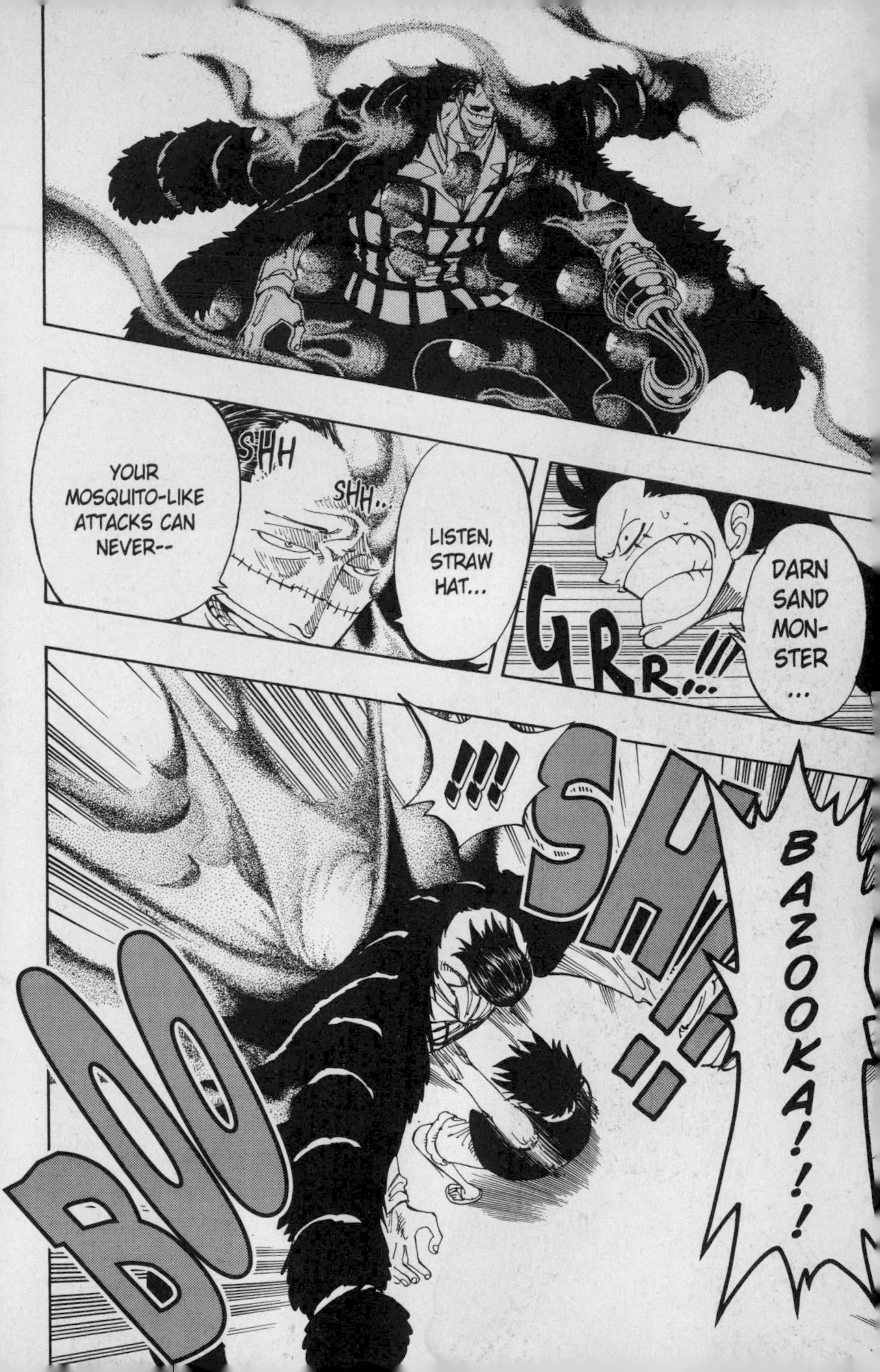
DARN SAND MON-STER...
GRR...!!
SHH
SHH...
LISTEN, STRAW HAT...
YOUR MOSQUITO-LIKE ATTACKS CAN NEVER--
!!!
BAZOOKA!!!
SH!!
BOO

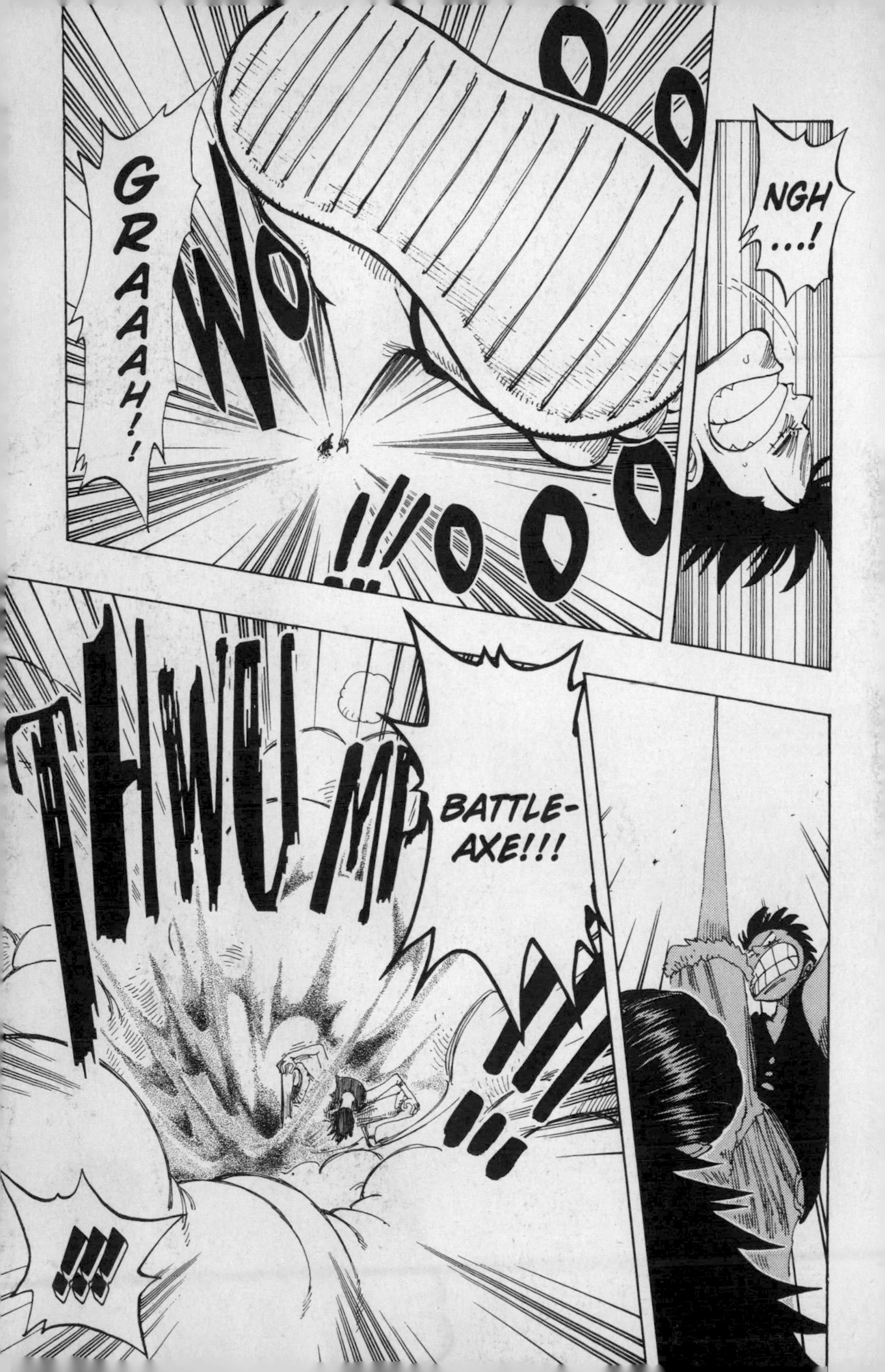
NGH ...!
GRAAAAH!!
WOOOOOO!!!
BATTLE-AXE!!!
THWUMP!!!
!!!

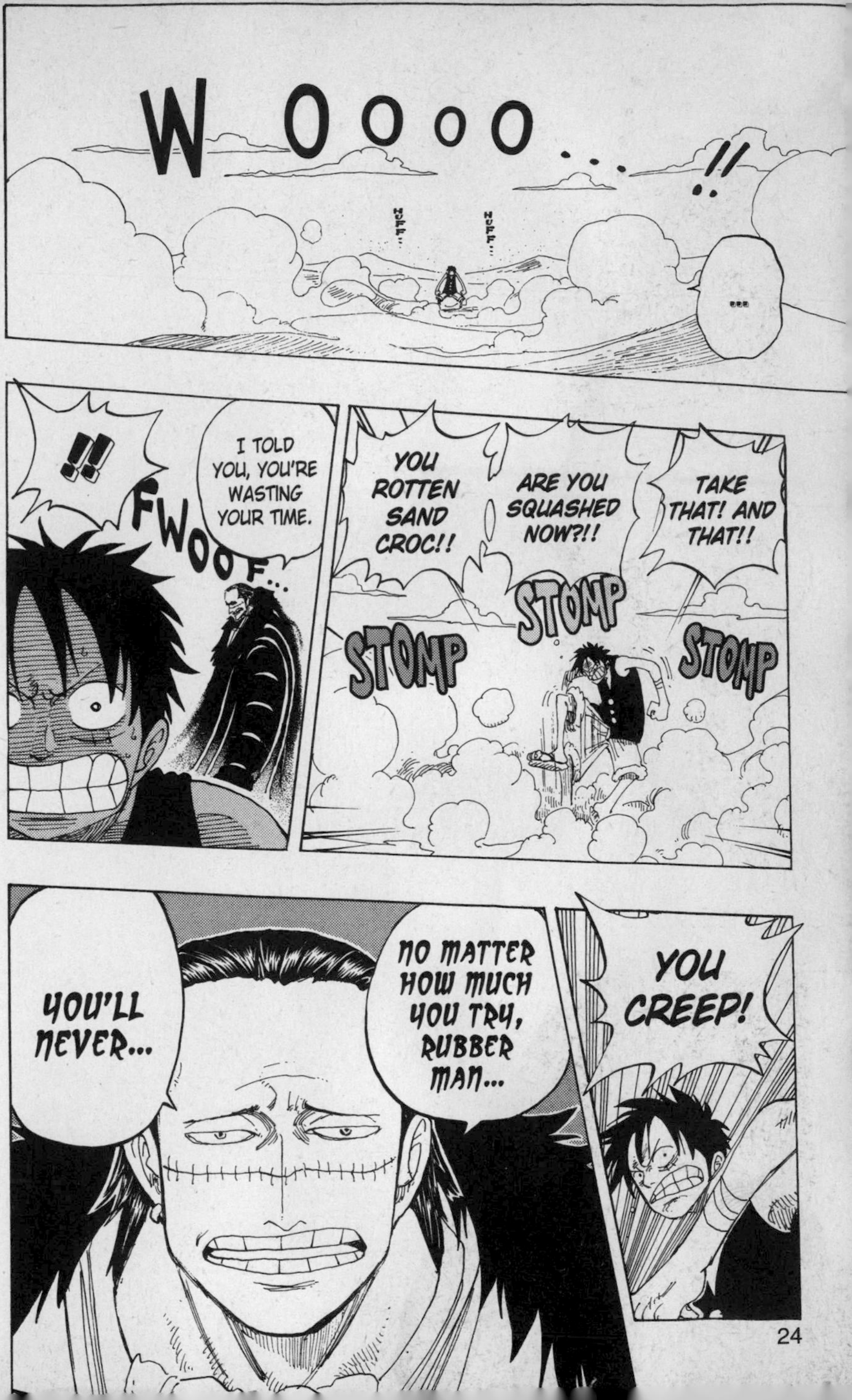
WOOOO...!!
...
HUFF... HUFF...
TAKE THAT! AND THAT!!
ARE YOU SQUASHED NOW?!!
YOU ROTTEN SAND CROC!!
STOMP
STOMP
STOMP
I TOLD YOU, YOU'RE WASTING YOUR TIME.
!!
FWOOF...
YOU CREEP!
NO MATTER HOW MUCH YOU TRY, RUBBER MAN...
YOU'LL NEVER...

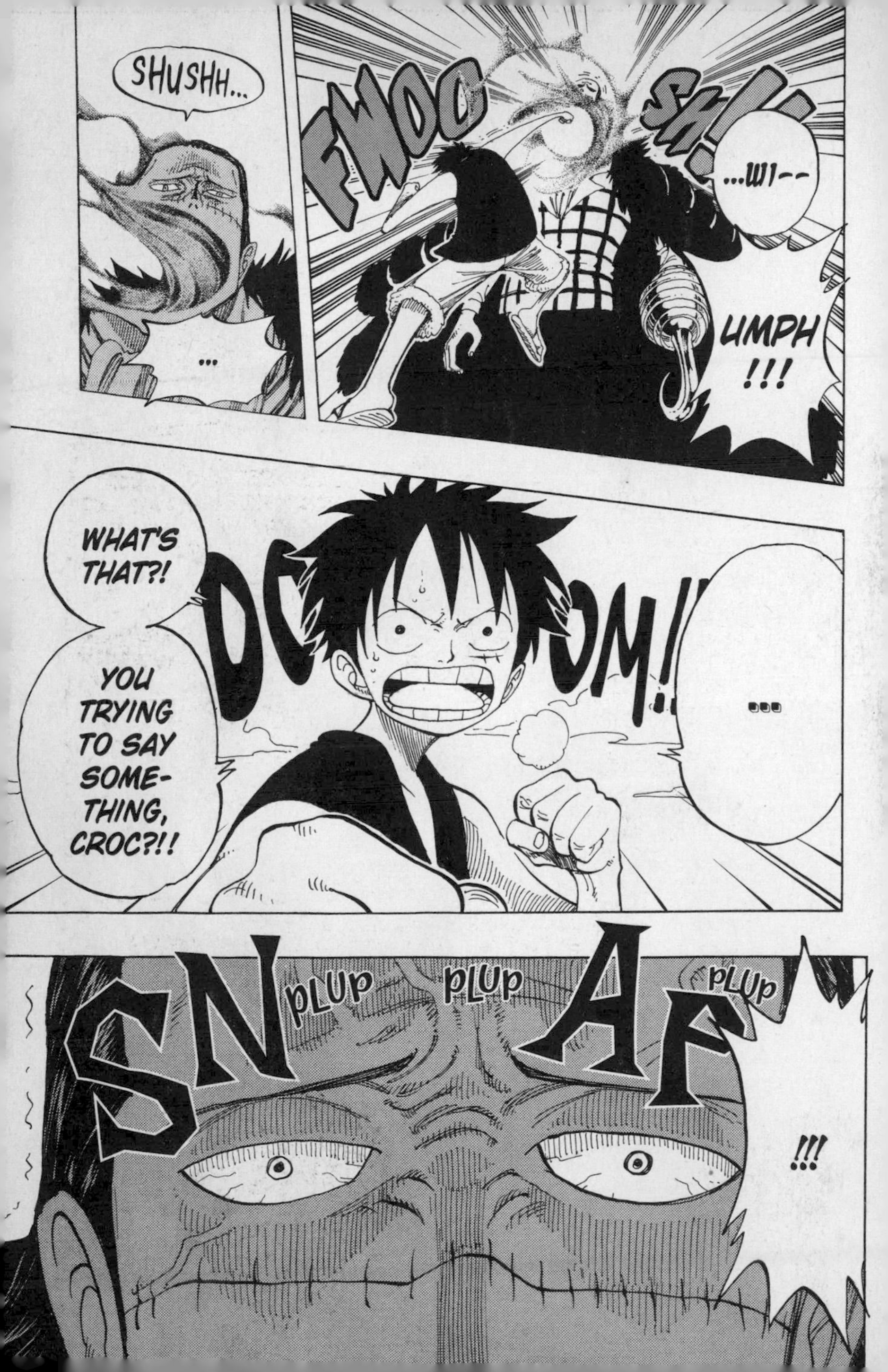
FWOOSH!!
...WI--
UMPH!!!
SHUSHH...
...
...
DOOM!!
WHAT'S THAT?!
YOU TRYING TO SAY SOME-THING, CROC?!!
SNAP!!!
plup
plup
plup

Question Corner

S B S

Reader: To all you good children reading the Question Corner, HOW ARE YOU?!

Good, you're very energetic. Today, a friend has come to visit. His name is Eiichiro. Welcome! (Applause) Thanks for coming! Okay, let's have little Eiichiro introduce this feature. Go ahead.

Oda: (Ahh, the day has finally come. Let's begin the Question Corner.) Uh...how are you, everybody? Okay, then...

Let's burst the S-pañola!
(I'm a failure.)

Q: 除了娜美外的船員、好像都一直案一樣的衣服吧？

A: Huh? Okay, I get it. This is a question from a *One Piece* reader in Taiwan. But since it's written in kanji characters, I think I can manage to make sense of it. It probably goes like this, "Except for Nami, why do all the crew members always wear the same clothes?" Well, there are a lot of reasons for that. First of all, they have several of the same outfit. And Nami doesn't give them much of a clothing allowance, either. Something like that.

Q: Oda Sensei, if Luffy, Zolo, Usopp, Nami and Sanji were animals, what would they be?

A: Luffy is a monkey. Zolo's...a shark. Usopp's an armadillo. Nami's a cat. And Sanji's a duck, I think. But the one I feel most confident about is Chopper.

He's a reindeer. (Ta-dah!)

Chapter 178:
GRAND LINE LEVEL

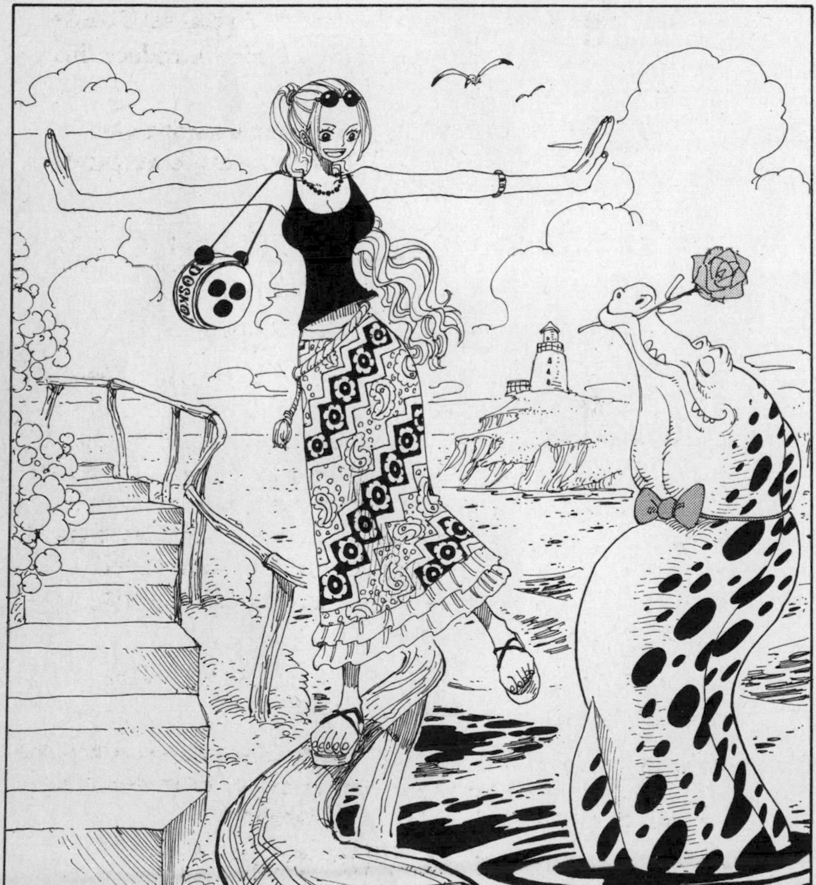
DOSKOI

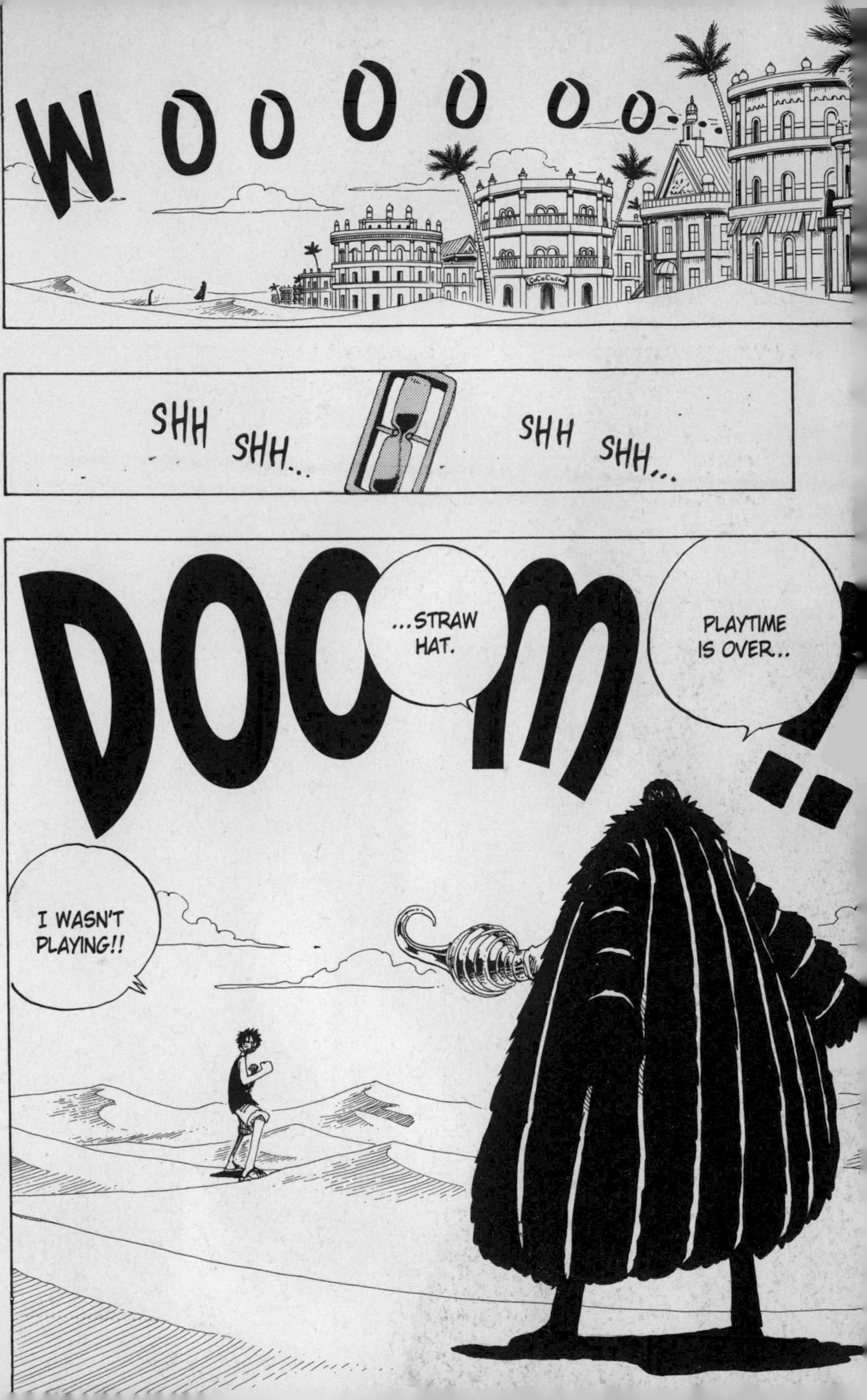
WOOOOOO
SHH SHH...
SHH SHH...
DOOM!!
PLAYTIME IS OVER..
...STRAW HAT.
I WASN'T PLAYING!!

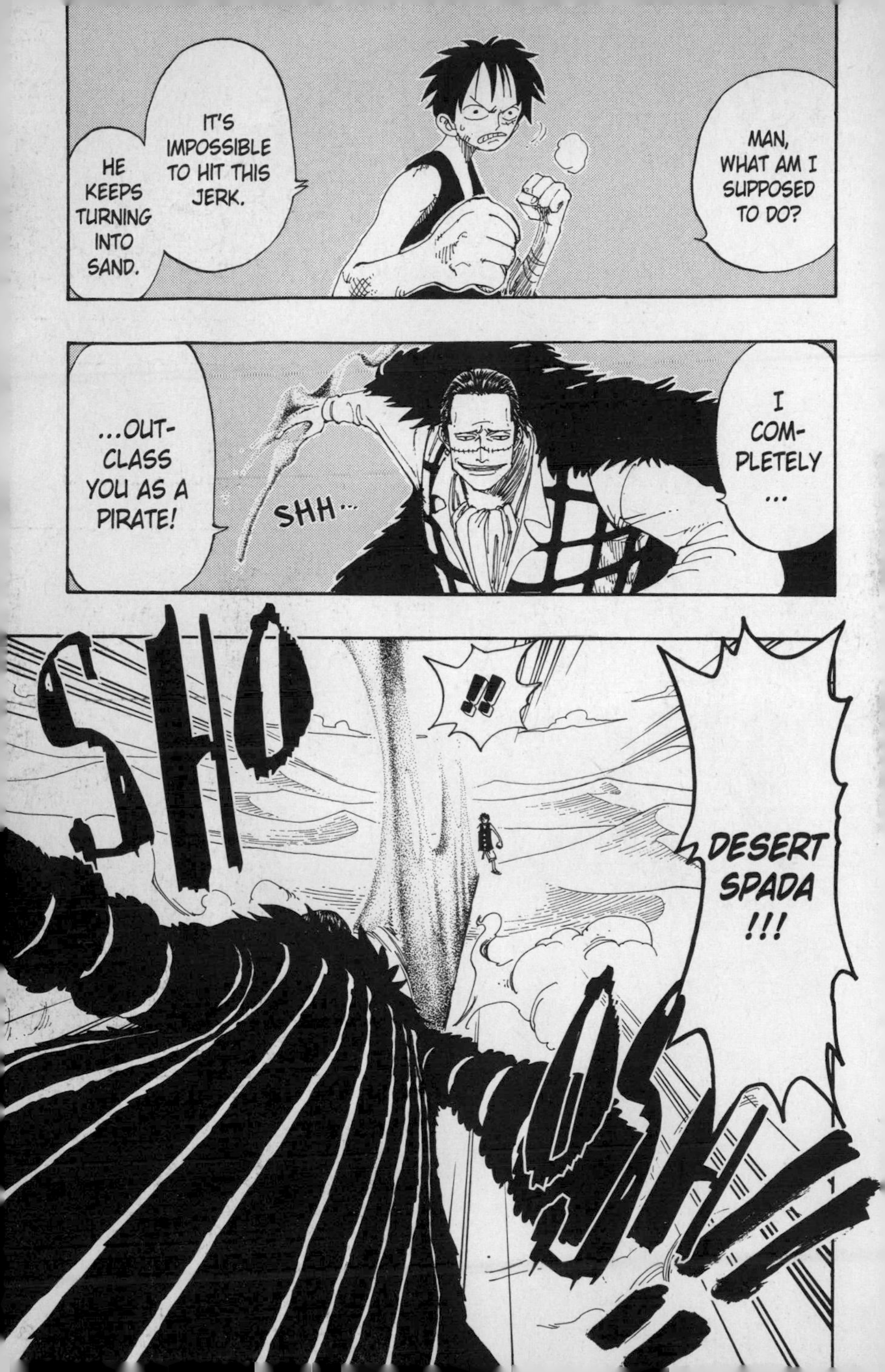
MAN, WHAT AM I SUPPOSED TO DO?
IT'S IMPOSSIBLE TO HIT THIS JERK.
HE KEEPS TURNING INTO SAND.
I COMPLETELY...
SHH...
...OUT-CLASS YOU AS A PIRATE!
DESERT SPADA!!!
!!
SHO

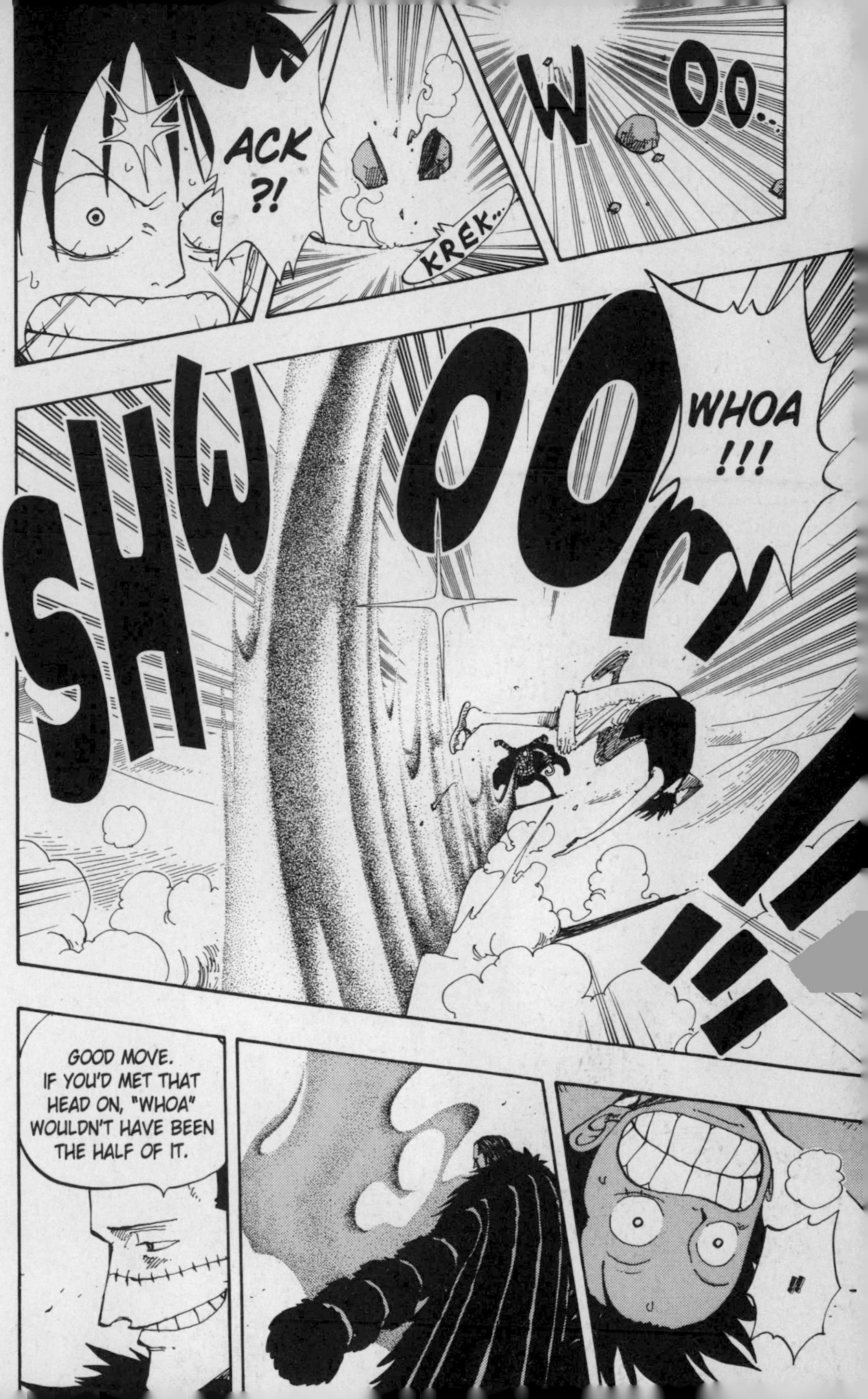
WOO...
KREK...
ACK ?!
WHOA !!!
SHWOOM!!!
!!
GOOD MOVE. IF YOU'D MET THAT HEAD ON, "WHOA" WOULDN'T HAVE BEEN THE HALF OF IT.

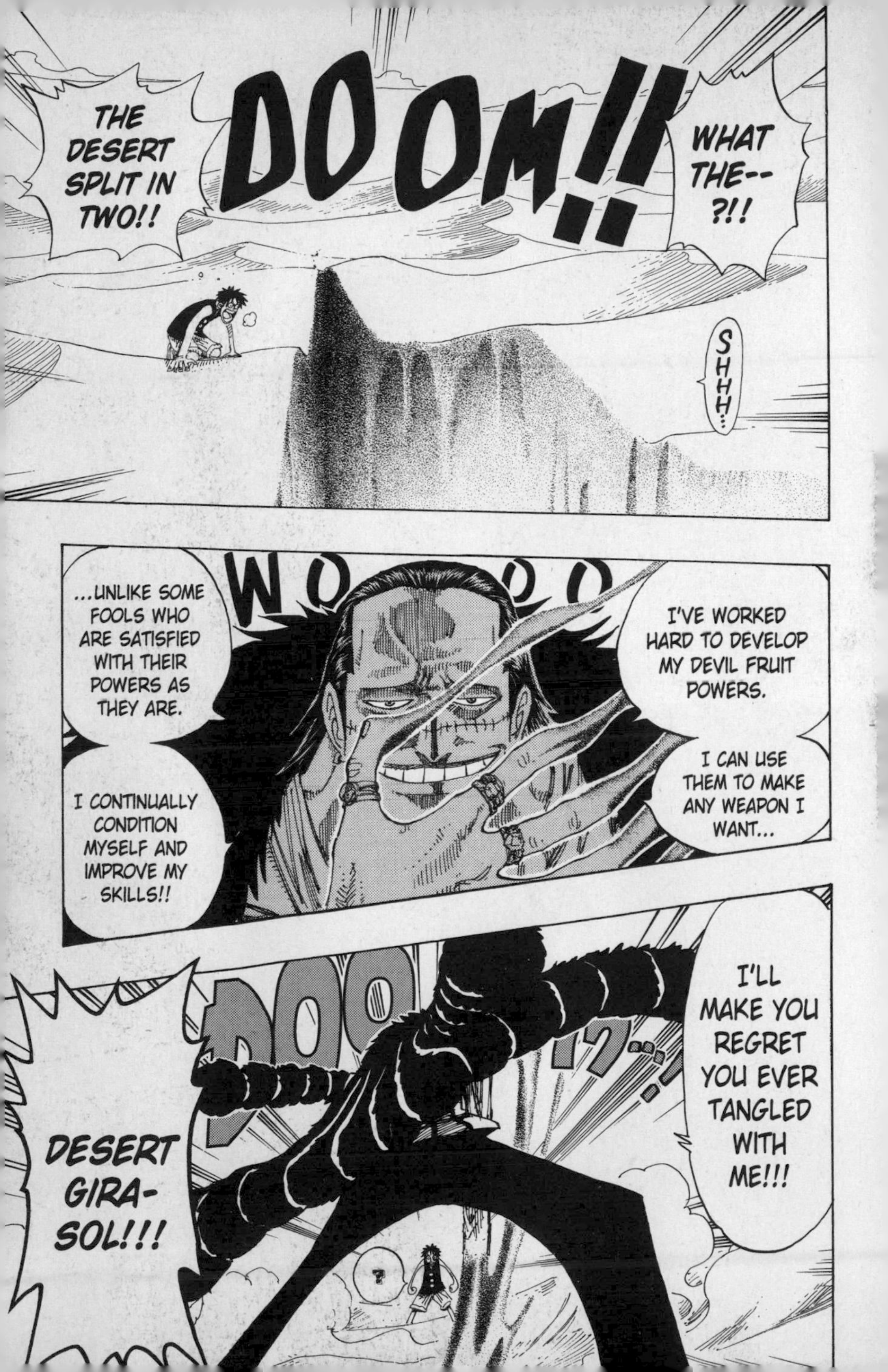
WHAT THE-- ?!!
DOOM!!
THE DESERT SPLIT IN TWO!!
SHHH...
I'VE WORKED HARD TO DEVELOP MY DEVIL FRUIT POWERS.
...UNLIKE SOME FOOLS WHO ARE SATISFIED WITH THEIR POWERS AS THEY ARE.
I CAN USE THEM TO MAKE ANY WEAPON I WANT...
I CONTINUALLY CONDITION MYSELF AND IMPROVE MY SKILLS!!
I'LL MAKE YOU REGRET YOU EVER TANGLED WITH ME!!!
DESERT GIRA-SOL!!!
?

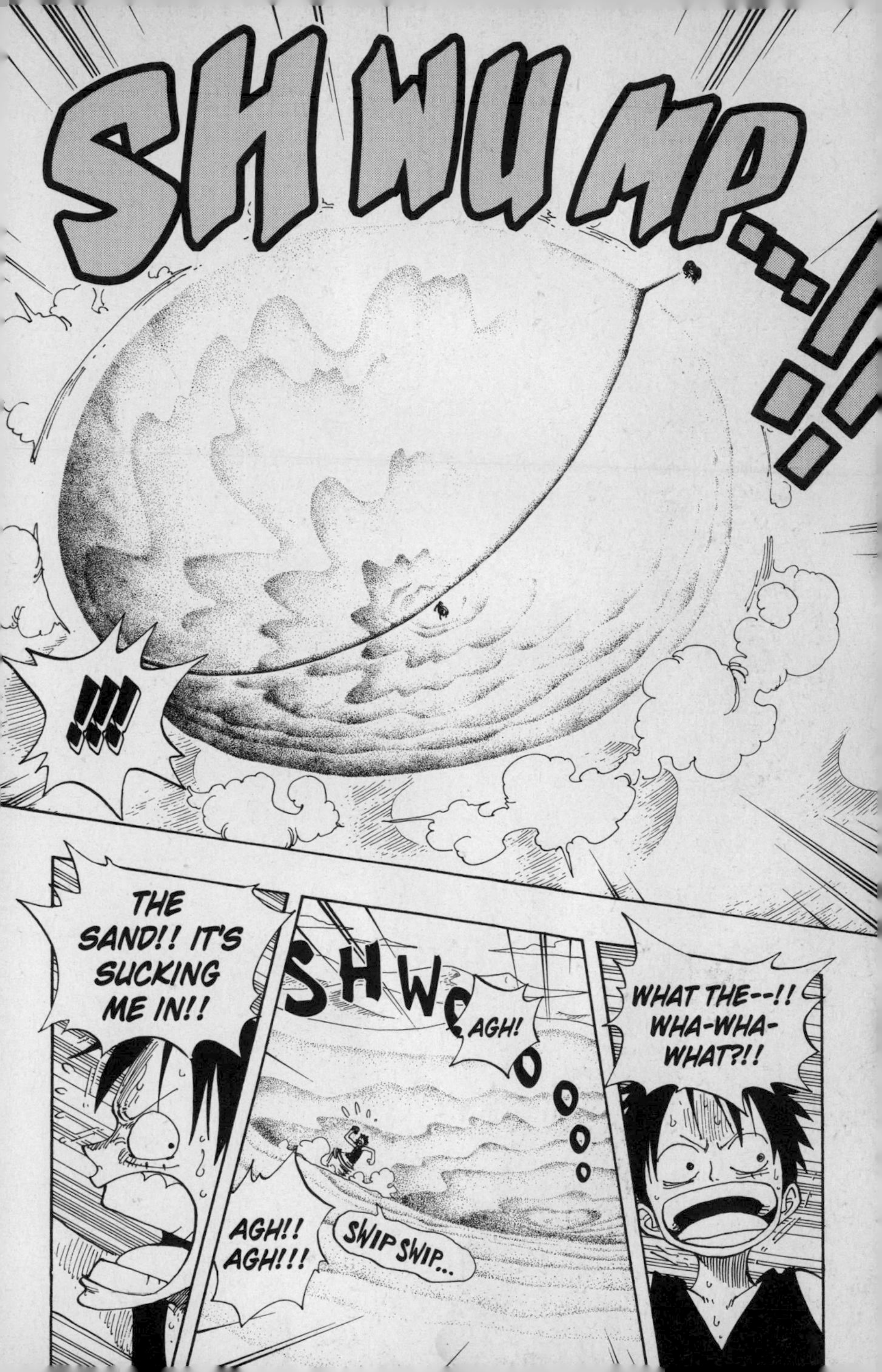
SHWUMP...!!
!!!
WHAT THE--!! WHA-WHA-WHAT?!!
AGH!
SHWOOOOOO
SWIP SWIP...
AGH!! AGH!!!
THE SAND!! IT'S SUCKING ME IN!!

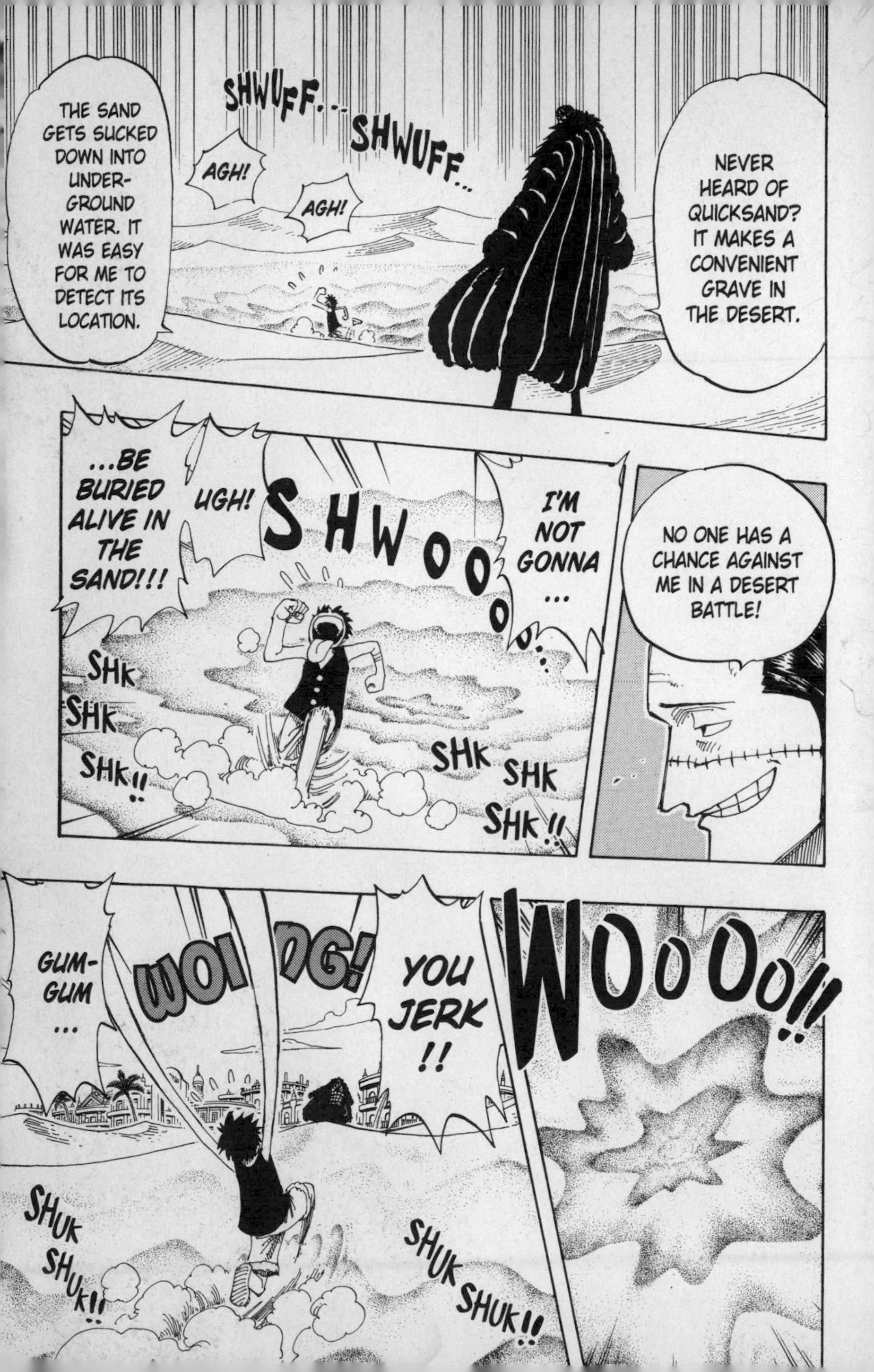
NEVER HEARD OF QUICKSAND? IT MAKES A CONVENIENT GRAVE IN THE DESERT.
SHWUFF... SHWUFF...
AGH!
AGH!
THE SAND GETS SUCKED DOWN INTO UNDER-GROUND WATER. IT WAS EASY FOR ME TO DETECT ITS LOCATION.
NO ONE HAS A CHANCE AGAINST ME IN A DESERT BATTLE!
I'M NOT GONNA ...
SHWOOOO...
UGH!
...BE BURIED ALIVE IN THE SAND!!!
SHK SHK SHK!!
SHK SHK SHK!!
WOOOOO!!
SHUK SHUK!!
YOU JERK !!
WOI DG!
GUM-GUM ...
SHUK SHUK!!

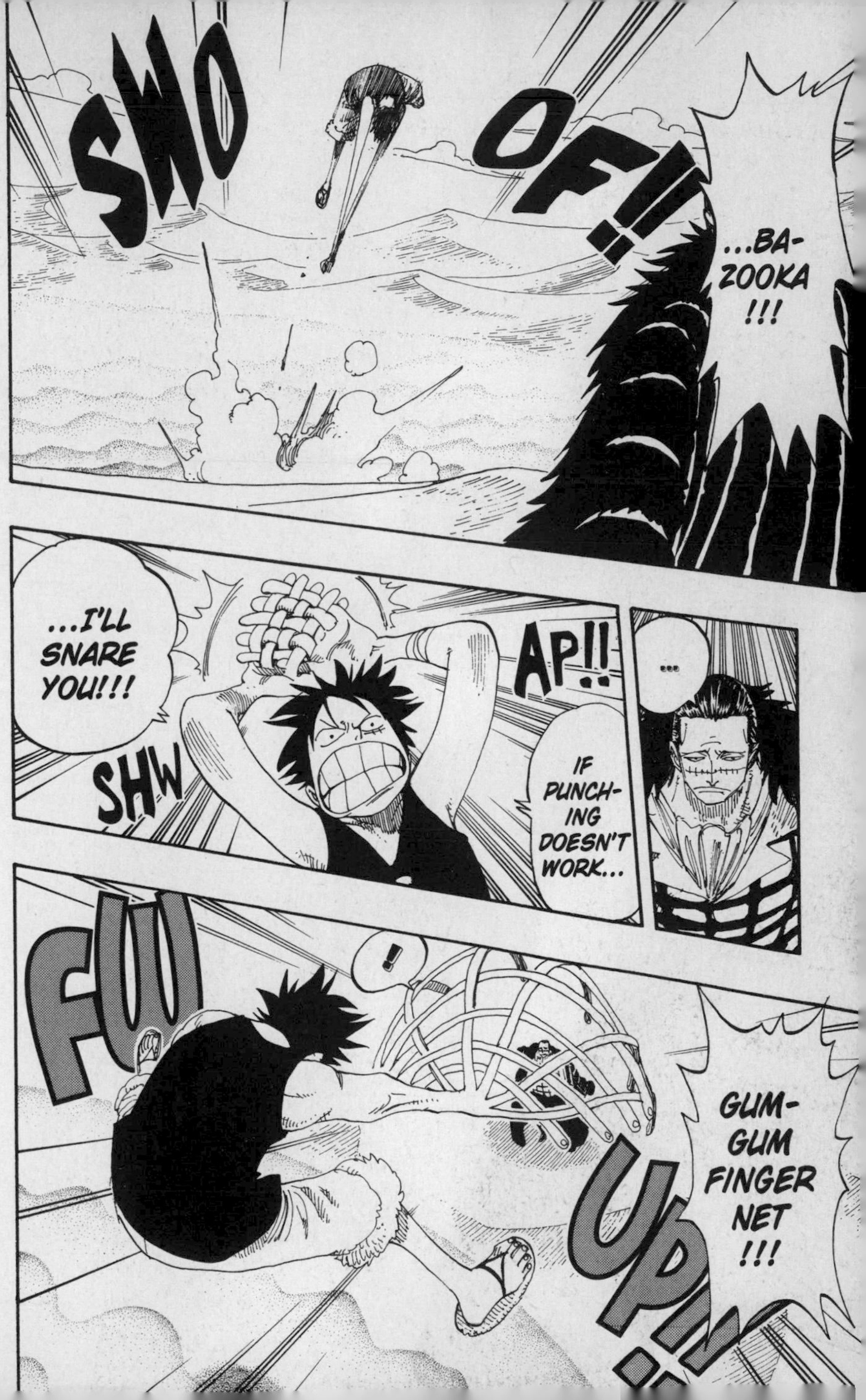
...BA-ZOOKA!!!
SHO
OF!!
...
IF PUNCH-ING DOESN'T WORK...
AP!!
...I'LL SNARE YOU!!!
SHW
GUM-GUM FINGER NET!!!
UP!!
!
FUU

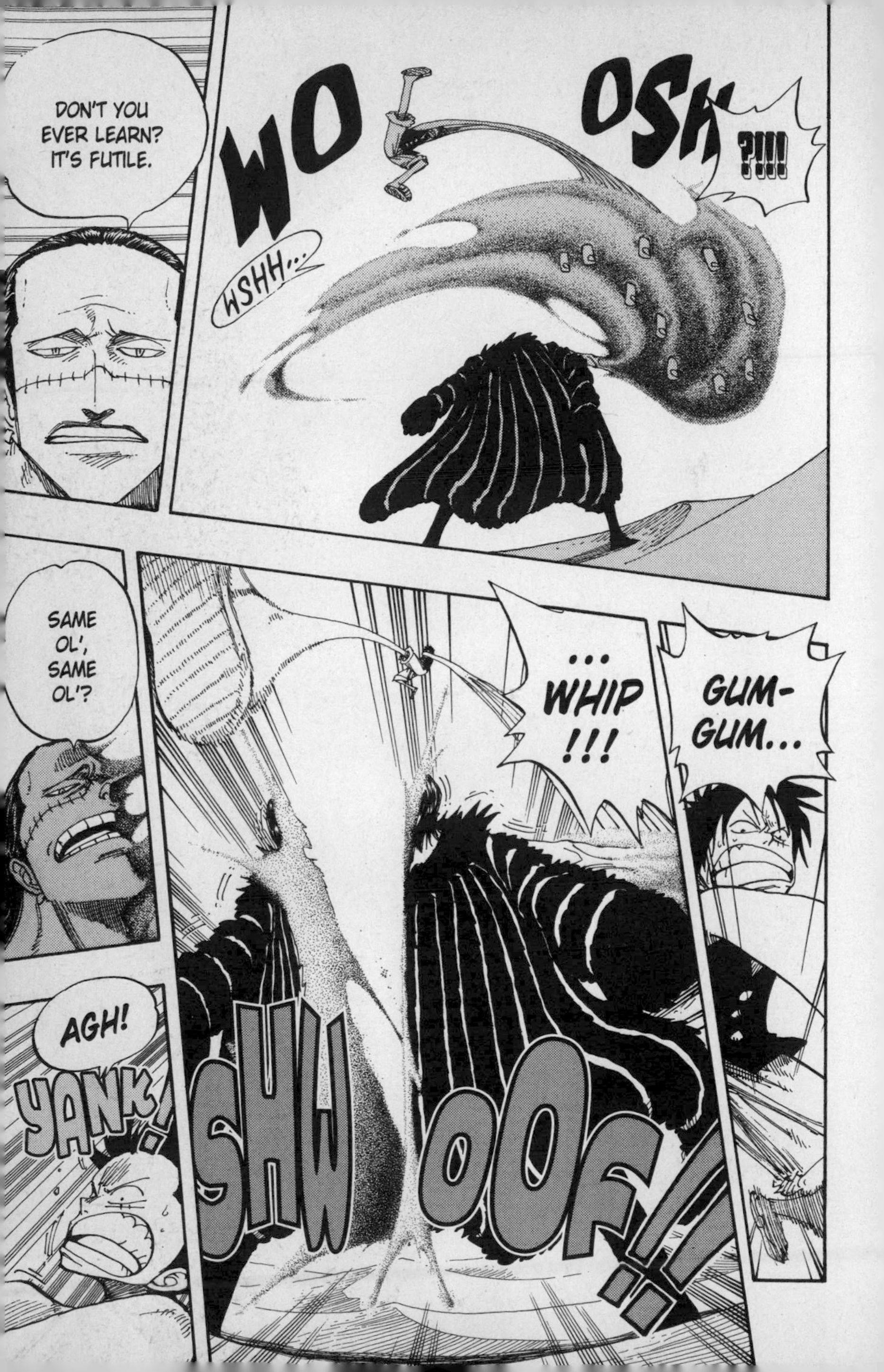
?!!!
WOOSH
WSHH...
DON'T YOU EVER LEARN? IT'S FUTILE.
GUM-GUM...
... WHIP !!!
SHWOOF!!
SAME OL', SAME OL'?
AGH!
YANK!

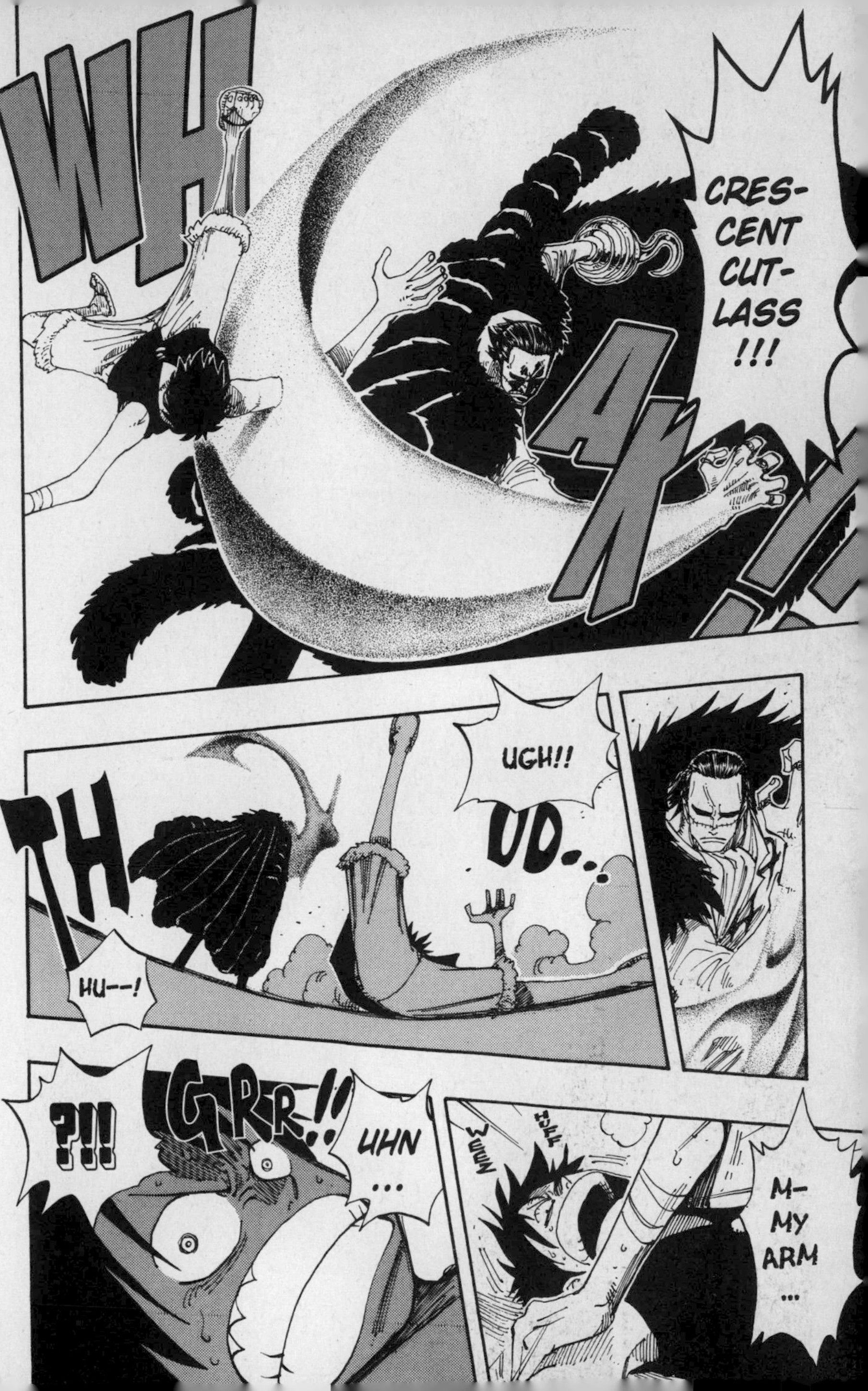
CRES-CENT CUT-LASS!!!
WH
AX
UGH!!
TH
UD...
HU--!
M-MY ARM...
HUFF
WEEZ
UHN...
GRR!!
?!!

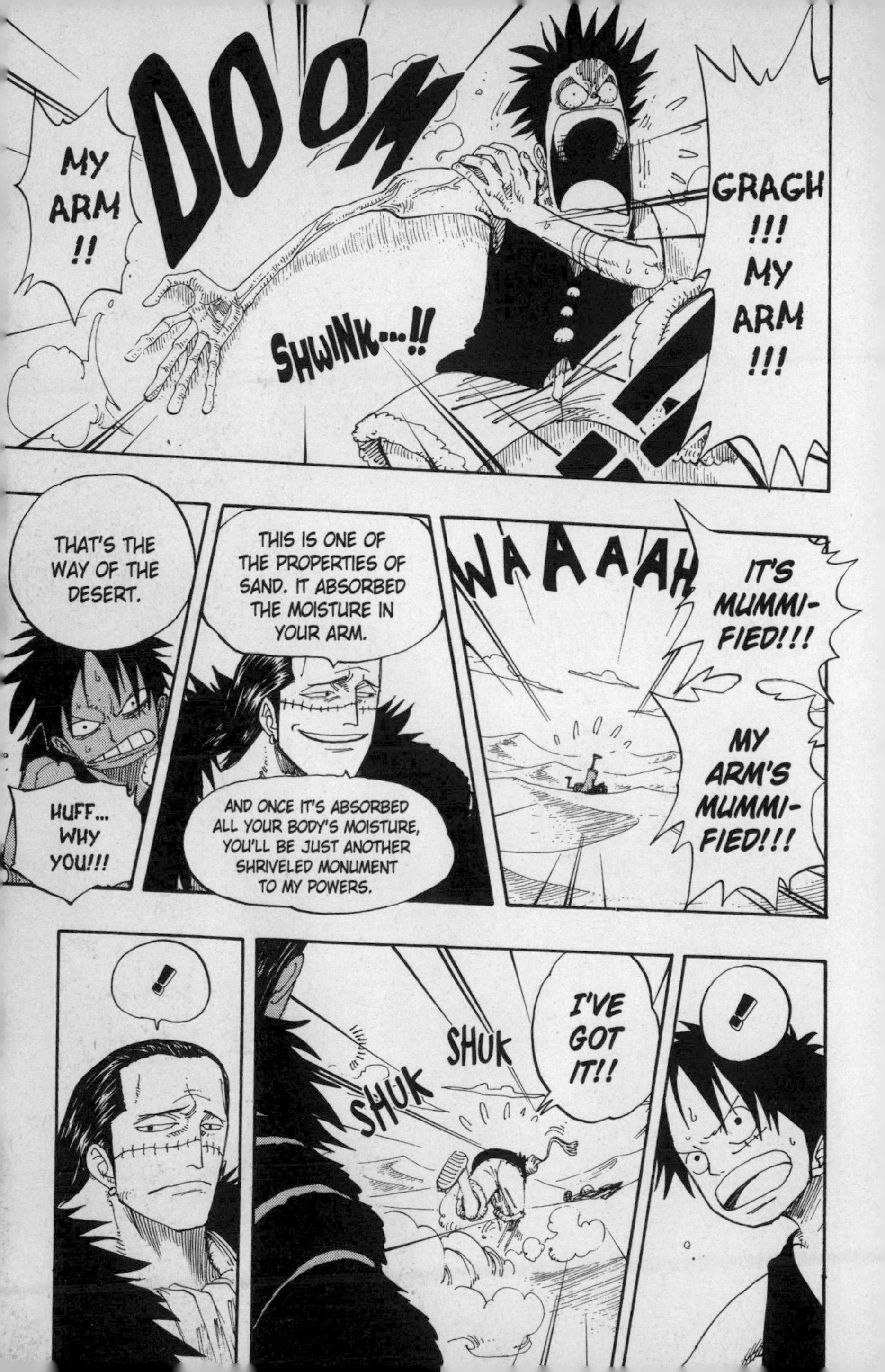
GRAGH!!! MY ARM!!!
DOOOM
SHWINK...!!
MY ARM!!
IT'S MUMMIFIED!!!
WAAAAH
MY ARM'S MUMMIFIED!!!
THIS IS ONE OF THE PROPERTIES OF SAND. IT ABSORBED THE MOISTURE IN YOUR ARM.
AND ONCE IT'S ABSORBED ALL YOUR BODY'S MOISTURE, YOU'LL BE JUST ANOTHER SHRIVELED MONUMENT TO MY POWERS.
THAT'S THE WAY OF THE DESERT.
HUFF... WHY YOU!!!
!
I'VE GOT IT!!
SHUK
SHUK
!

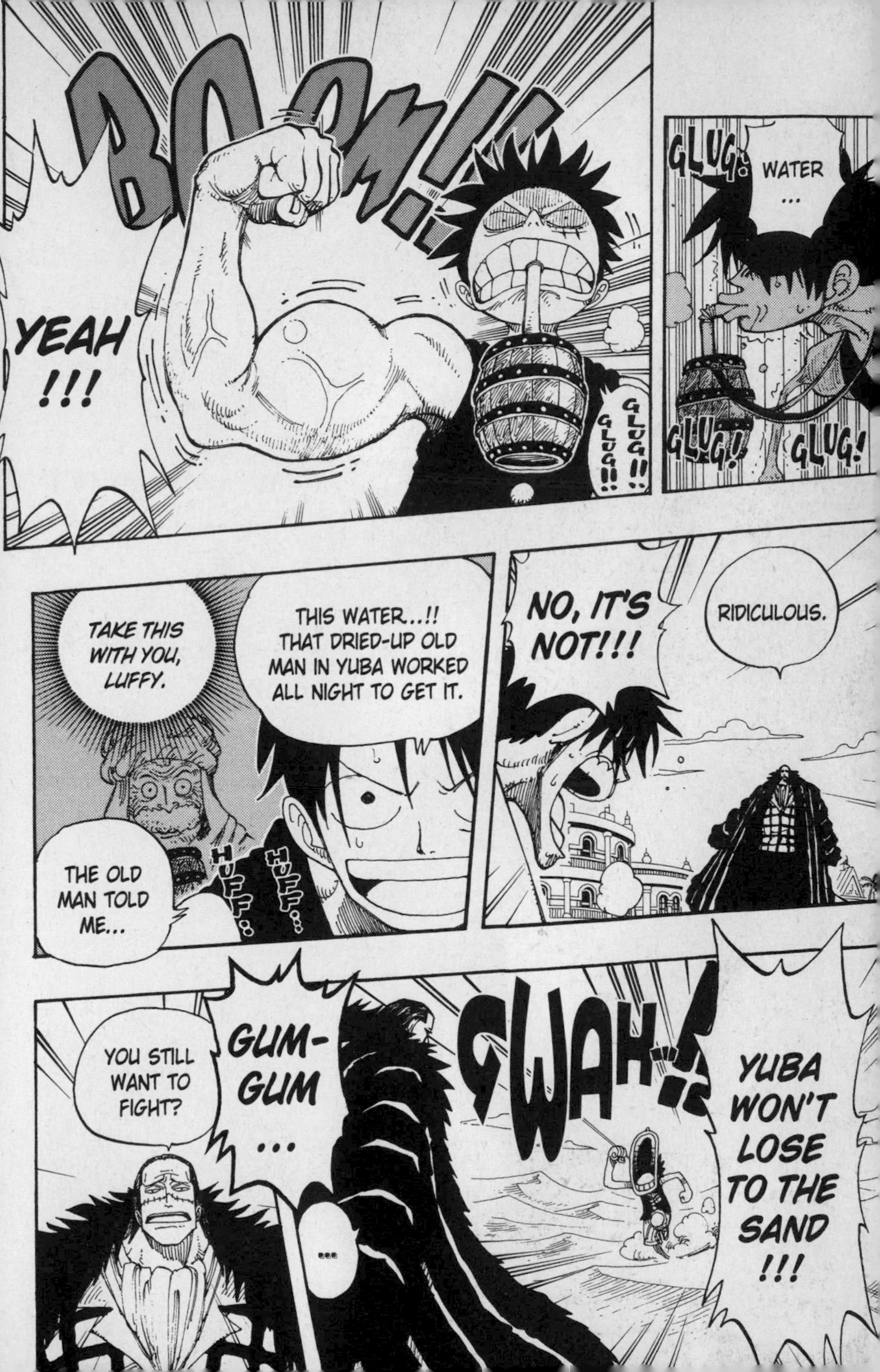
GLUG!
WATER ...
GLUG!
GLUG!
BOOM!!
GLUG!!
GLUG!!
YEAH !!!
RIDICULOUS.
NO, IT'S NOT!!!
THIS WATER...!! THAT DRIED-UP OLD MAN IN YUBA WORKED ALL NIGHT TO GET IT.
TAKE THIS WITH YOU, LUFFY.
HUFF..
HUFF..
THE OLD MAN TOLD ME...
YUBA WON'T LOSE TO THE SAND !!!
GWAH..!!
GUM-GUM ...
YOU STILL WANT TO FIGHT?
...

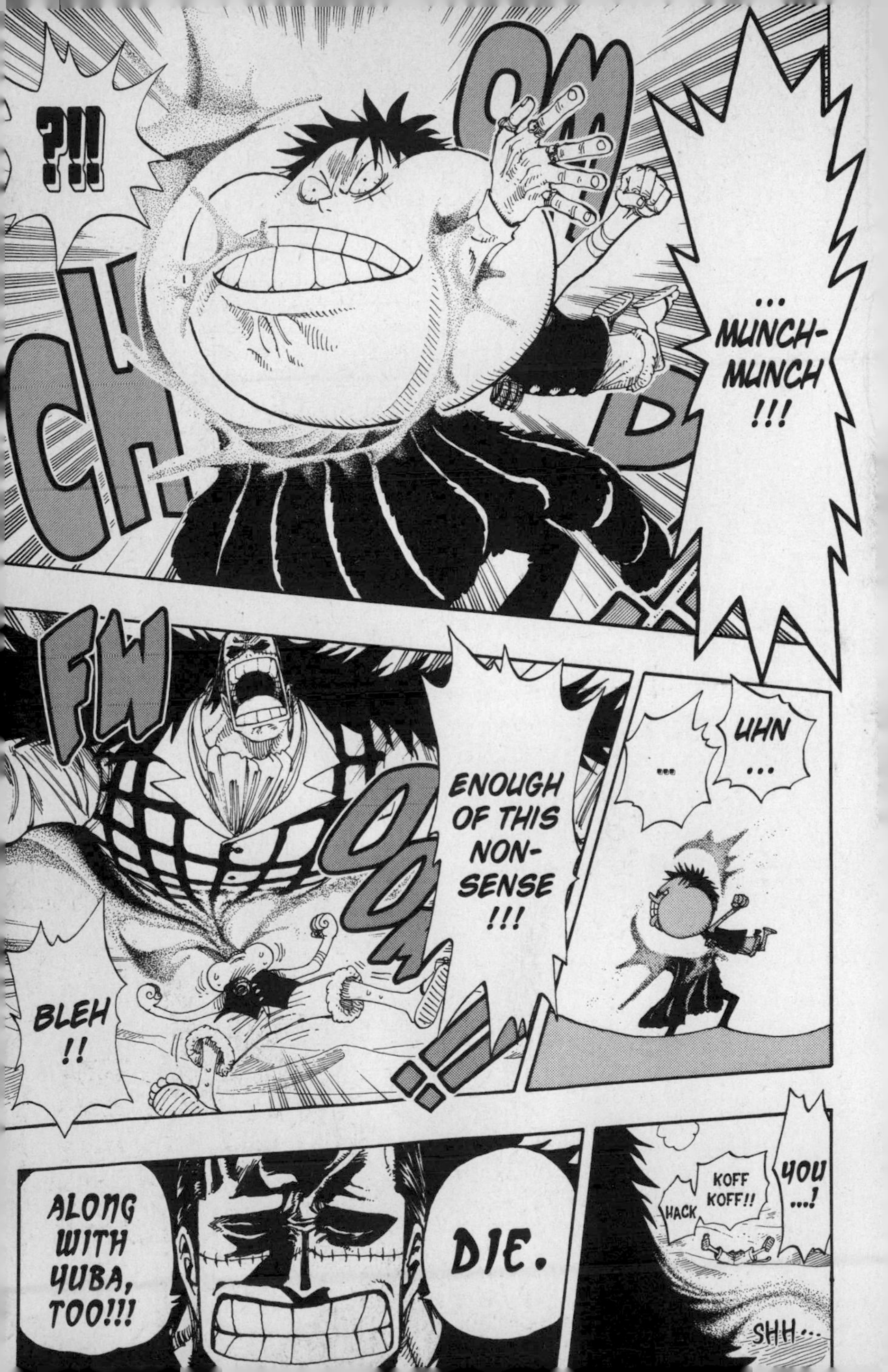
...MUNCH-MUNCH!!!
?!!
UHN...
...
ENOUGH OF THIS NON-SENSE!!!
FW
OOOM!!
BLEH!!
YOU...!
KOFF KOFF!!
HACK
SHH...
DIE.
ALONG WITH YUBA, TOO!!!

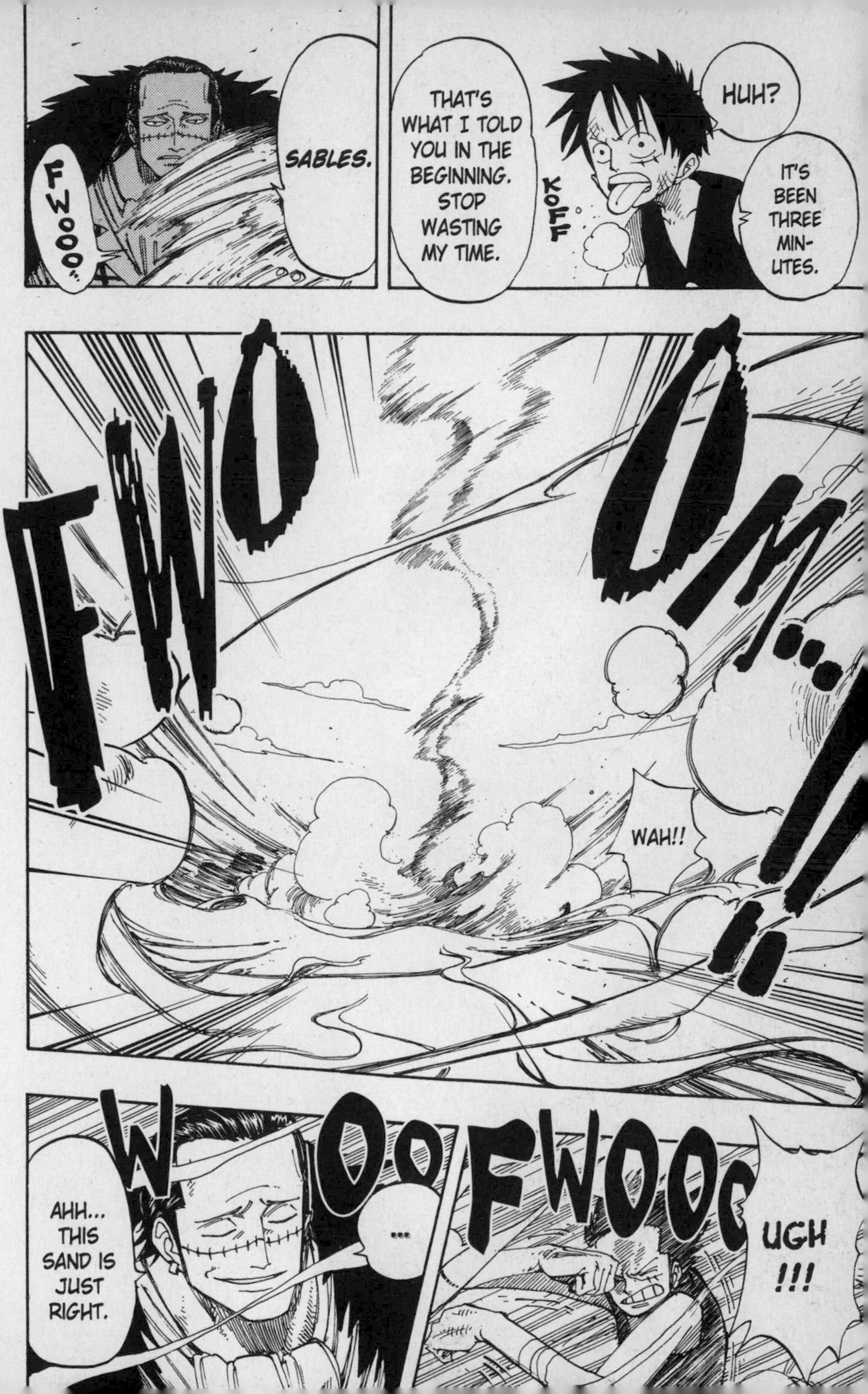
HUH?
IT'S BEEN THREE MIN-UTES.
KOFF
THAT'S WHAT I TOLD YOU IN THE BEGINNING. STOP WASTING MY TIME.
SABLES.
FWOOO...
FWOOOM...!!
WAH!!
UGH!!!
FWOOO
...
WOOO
AHH... THIS SAND IS JUST RIGHT.

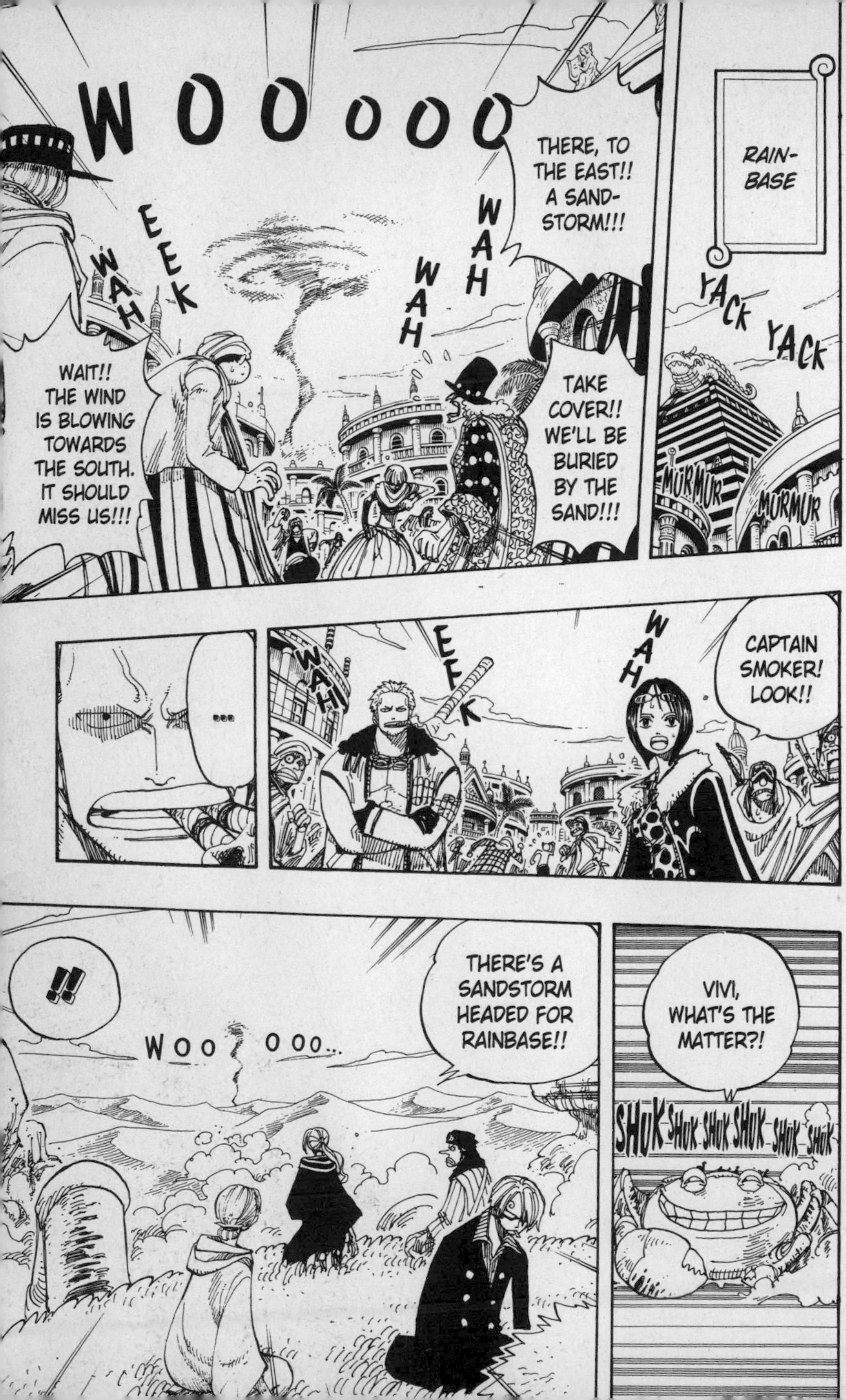
RAIN-BASE
YACK YACK
MURMUR
MURMUR
WOOOOOO
THERE, TO THE EAST!! A SANDSTORM!!!
WAH
WAH
TAKE COVER!! WE'LL BE BURIED BY THE SAND!!!
WAIT!! THE WIND IS BLOWING TOWARDS THE SOUTH. IT SHOULD MISS US!!!
EEEK
WAH
CAPTAIN SMOKER! LOOK!!
WAH
EEK
WAH
...
VIVI, WHAT'S THE MATTER?!
SHUK SHUK SHUK SHUK SHUK SHUK
THERE'S A SANDSTORM HEADED FOR RAINBASE!!
!!
WOO OOO...

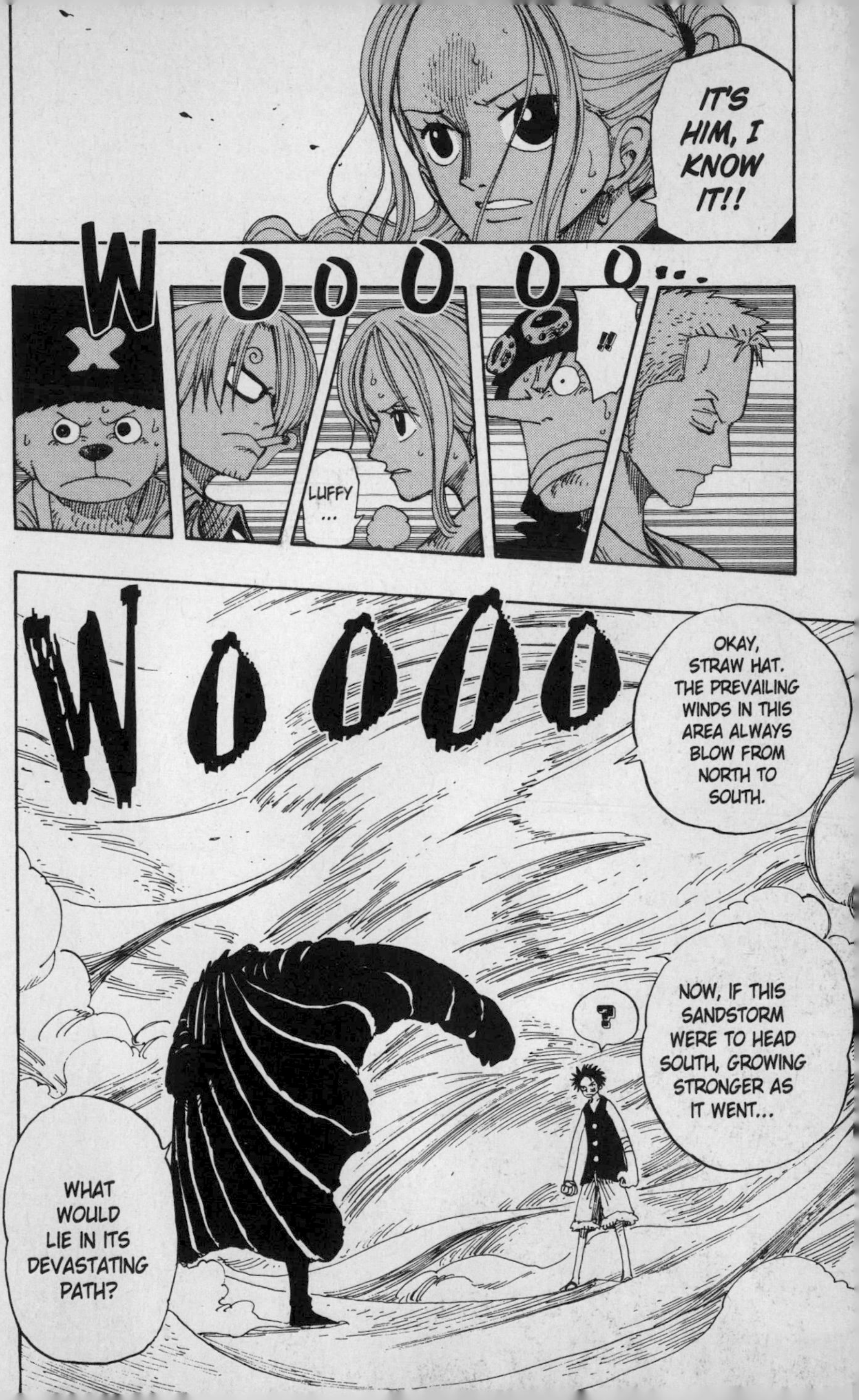
IT'S HIM, I KNOW IT!!
WOOOOO...
!!
LUFFY ...
OKAY, STRAW HAT. THE PREVAILING WINDS IN THIS AREA ALWAYS BLOW FROM NORTH TO SOUTH.
WOOOOO
?
NOW, IF THIS SANDSTORM WERE TO HEAD SOUTH, GROWING STRONGER AS IT WENT...
WHAT WOULD LIE IN ITS DEVASTATING PATH?

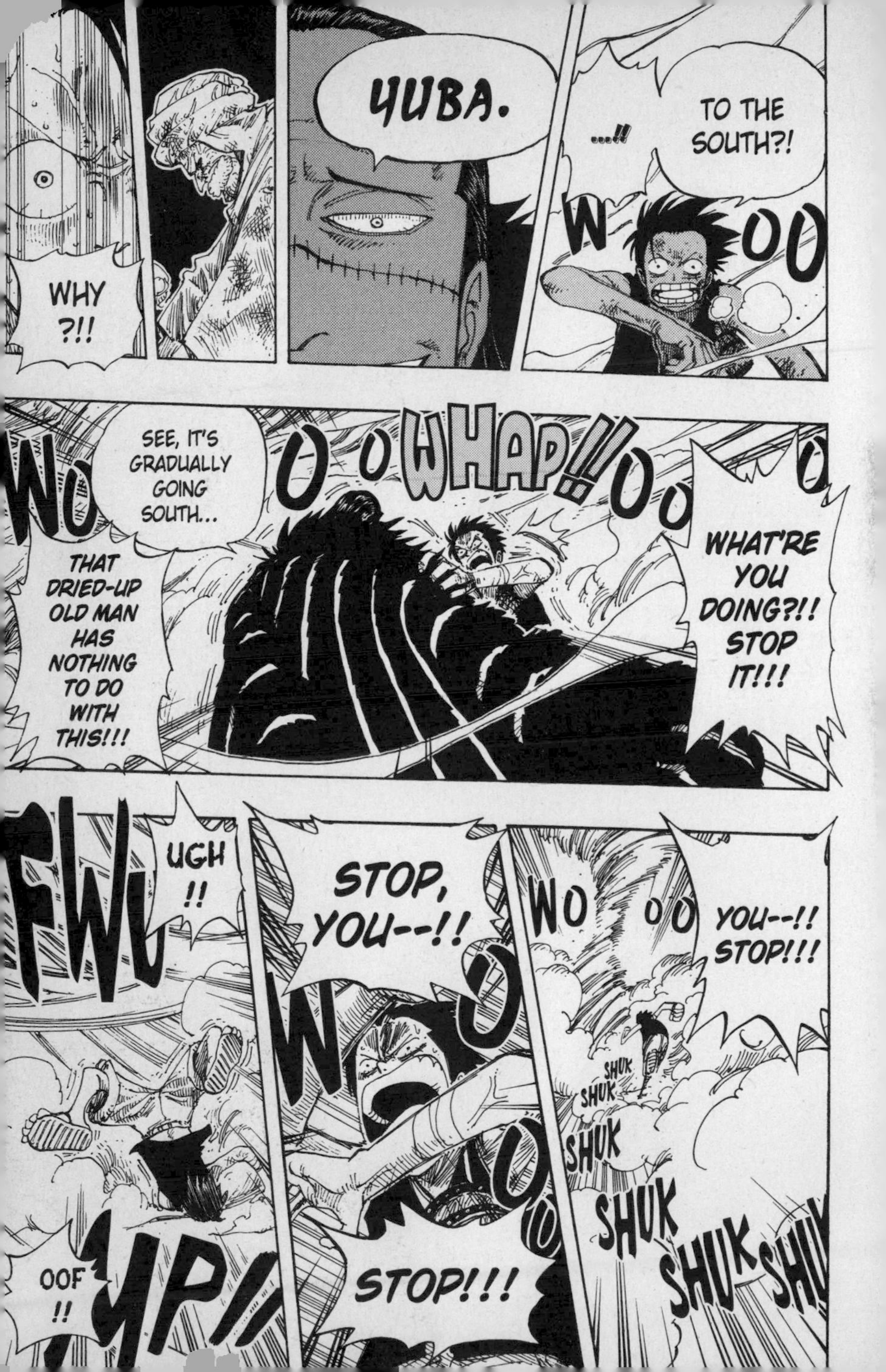

...!!
TO THE SOUTH?!
WOOO
YUBA.
WHY ?!!
WHAT'RE YOU DOING?!! STOP IT!!!
WOOO
WHAP!!
SEE, IT'S GRADUALLY GOING SOUTH...
THAT DRIED-UP OLD MAN HAS NOTHING TO DO WITH THIS!!!
WO
YOU--!! STOP!!!
WOOO
SHUK SHUK SHUK SHUK SHUK SHU
STOP, YOU--!!
WOOO
STOP!!!
UGH !!
FWU
MP!!
OOF !!

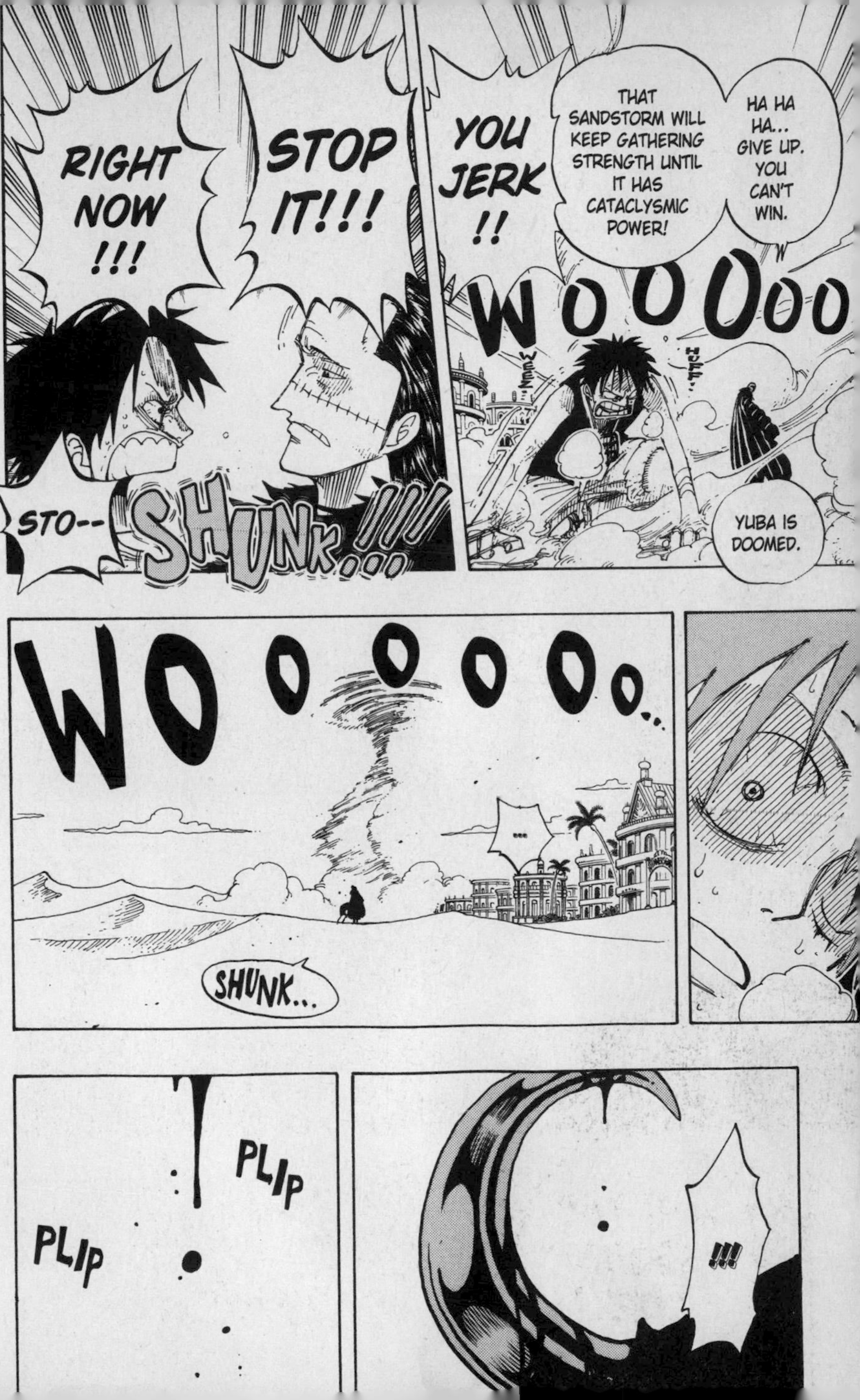
HA HA HA... GIVE UP. YOU CAN'T WIN.
THAT SANDSTORM WILL KEEP GATHERING STRENGTH UNTIL IT HAS CATACLYSMIC POWER!
YOU JERK !!
WOOOOOO
HUFF
WEEZ
YUBA IS DOOMED.
STOP IT!!!
RIGHT NOW !!!
STO--
SHUNK!!!...
WOOOOOO...
...
SHUNK...
!!!
PLIP
PLIP

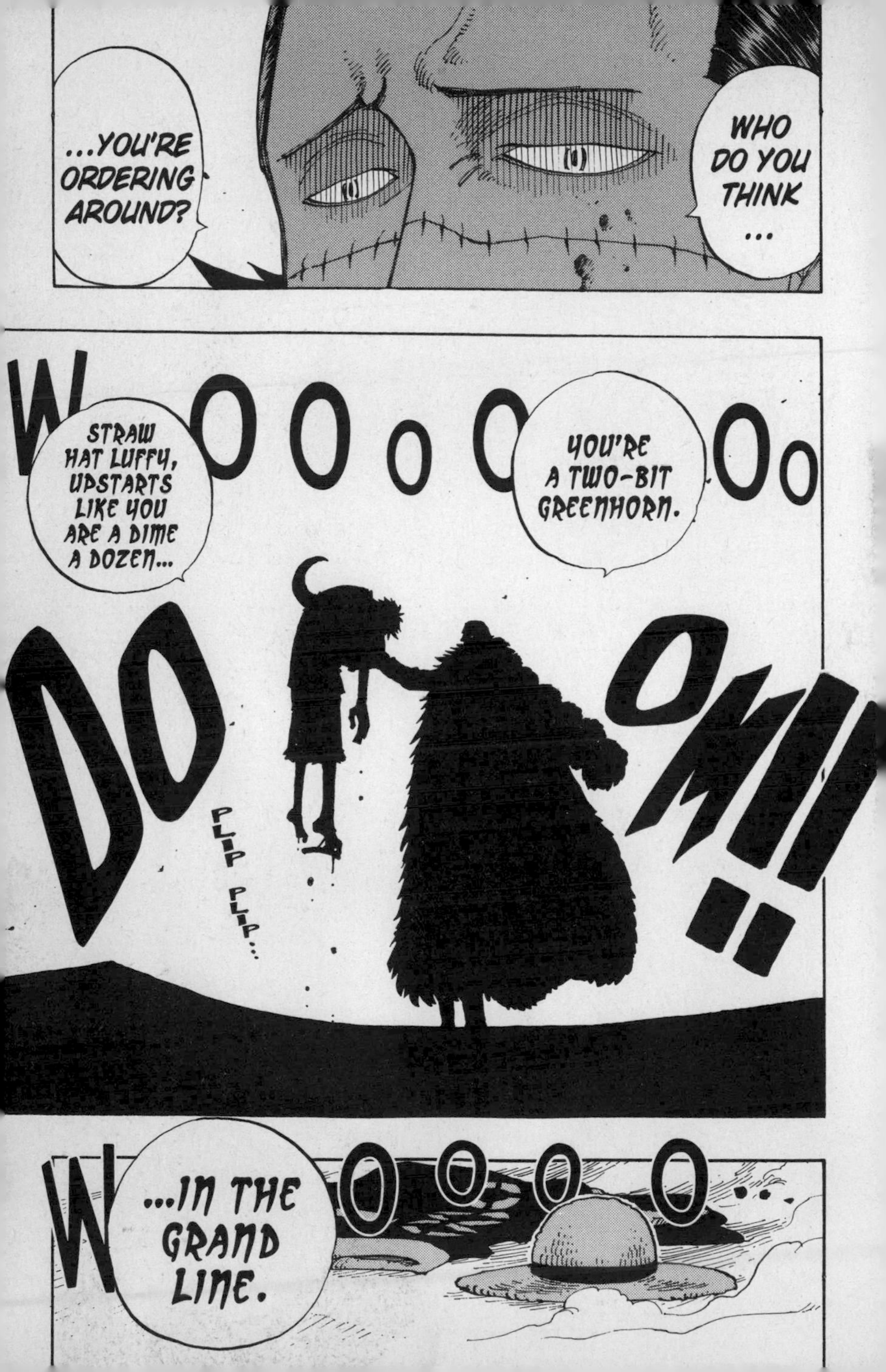
WHO DO YOU THINK ...
...YOU'RE ORDERING AROUND?
WOOOoOOOo
YOU'RE A TWO-BIT GREENHORN.
STRAW HAT LUFFY, UPSTARTS LIKE YOU ARE A DIME A DOZEN...
DOON!!
PLIP PLIP PLIP...
WOOOOO
...IN THE GRAND LINE.

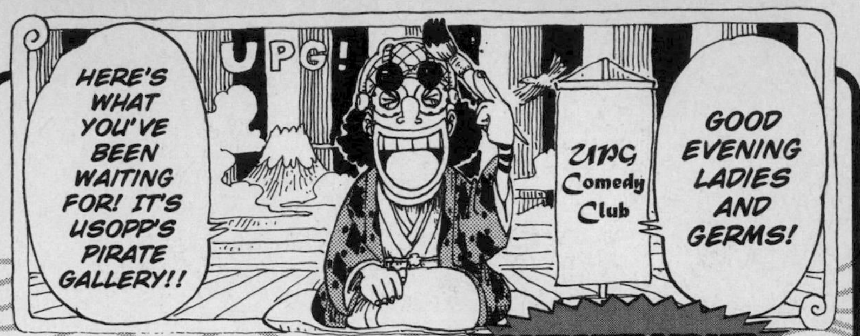
GOOD EVENING LADIES AND GERMS!
UPG Comedy Club
UPG!
HERE'S WHAT YOU'VE BEEN WAITING FOR! IT'S USOPP'S PIRATE GALLERY!!

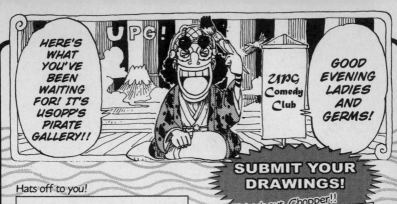

SUBMIT YOUR DRAWINGS!

Oh no! Watch out, Chopper!!

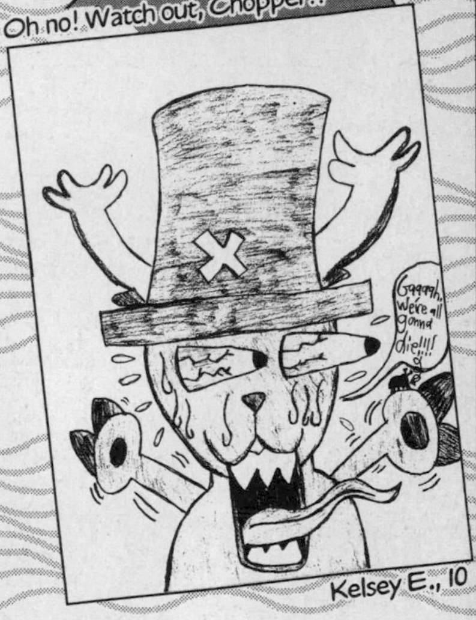
Gaaaah, We're all gonna die!!!

Kelsey E., 10

Hats off to you!

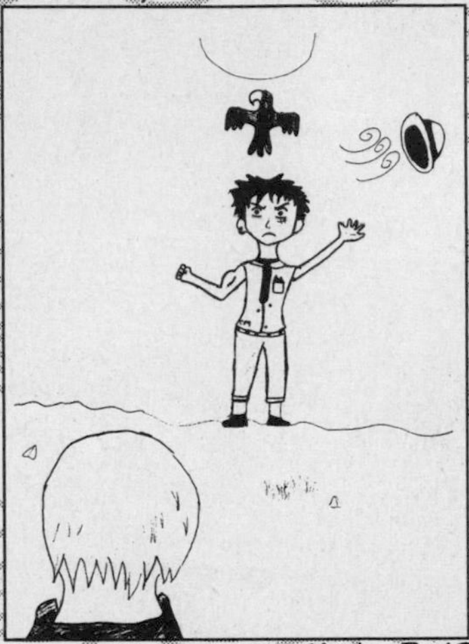

Marlon B., 15

Food thieves beware!

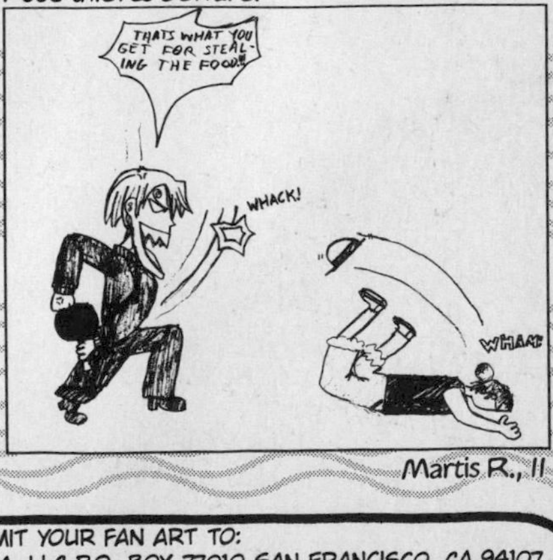
THATS WHAT YOU GET FOR STEAL-ING THE FOOD!!
WHACK!
WHAM

Martis R., 11

Hello ladies! ♥

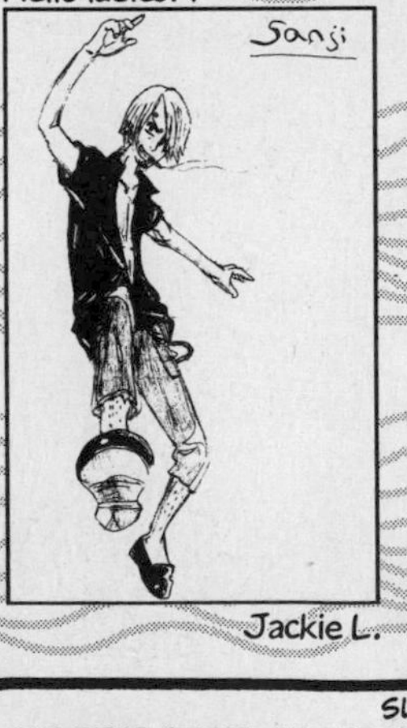
Sanji

Jackie L.

SUBMIT YOUR FAN ART TO:
ONE PIECE EDITOR C/O VIZ MEDIA, LLC P.O. BOX 77010 SAN FRANCISCO, CA 94107
*REMEMBER TO INCLUDE YOUR NAME, AGE AND PARENT RELEASE FORM!!

USOPP'S COMMENTS WERE TRANSMITTED THROUGH THE U.S. SHONEN JUMP TEAM -EDITOR

Chapter 179: SHOWDOWN AT ALUBARNA

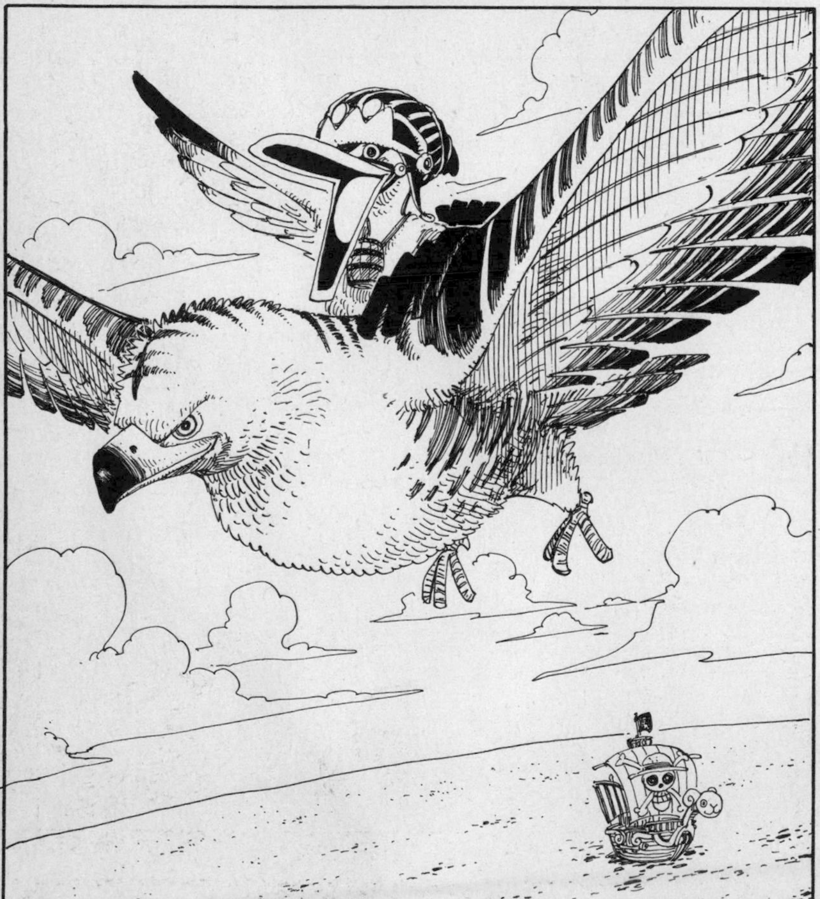

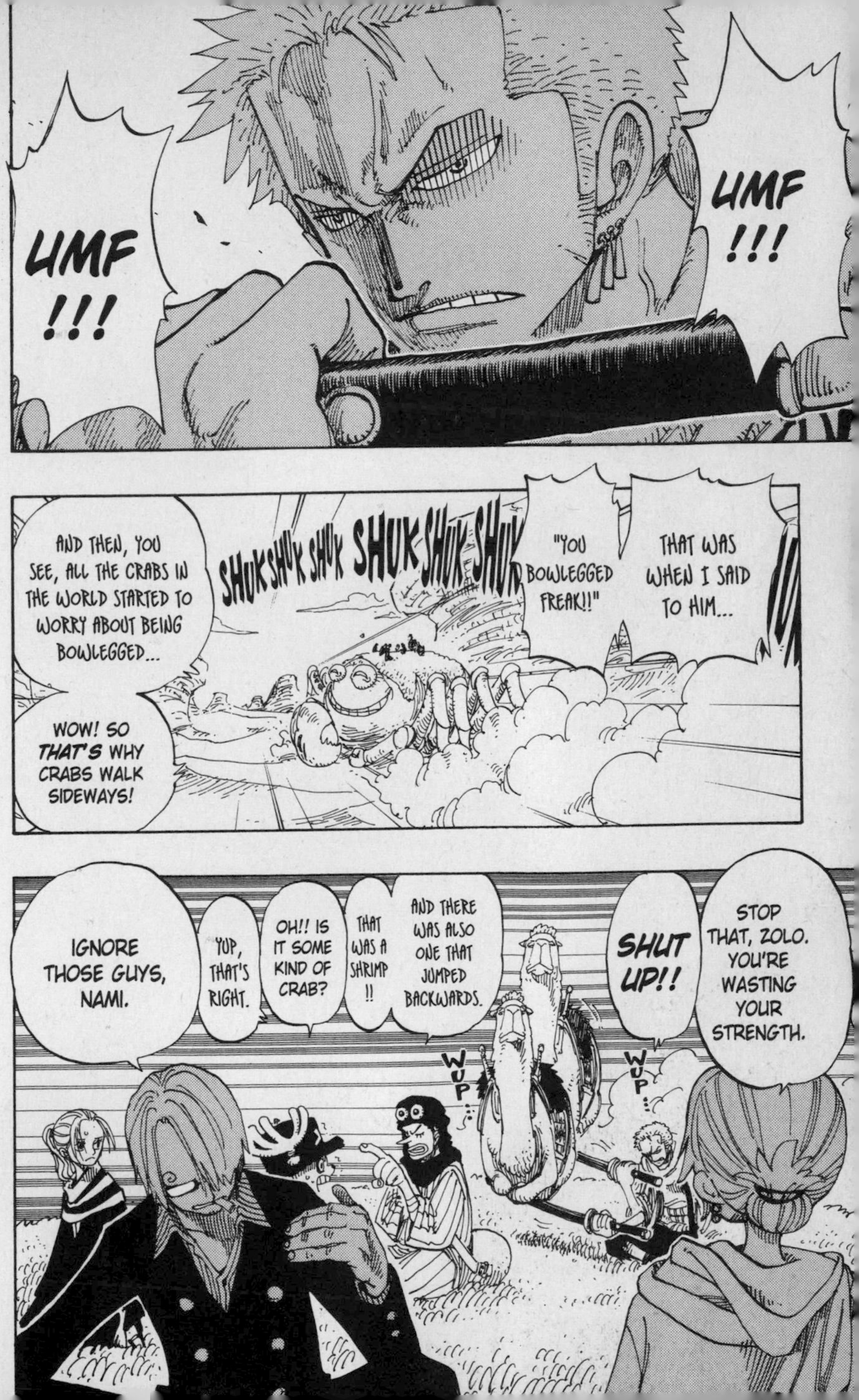
UMF !!!
UMF !!!
THAT WAS WHEN I SAID TO HIM...
"YOU BOWLEGGED FREAK!!"
SHUK SHUK SHUK SHUK SHUK SHUK
AND THEN, YOU SEE, ALL THE CRABS IN THE WORLD STARTED TO WORRY ABOUT BEING BOWLEGGED...
WOW! SO *THAT'S* WHY CRABS WALK SIDEWAYS!
STOP THAT, ZOLO. YOU'RE WASTING YOUR STRENGTH.
SHUT UP!!
WUP...
WUP...
AND THERE WAS ALSO ONE THAT JUMPED BACKWARDS.
THAT WAS A SHRIMP !!
OH!! IS IT SOME KIND OF CRAB?
YUP, THAT'S RIGHT.
IGNORE THOSE GUYS, NAMI.

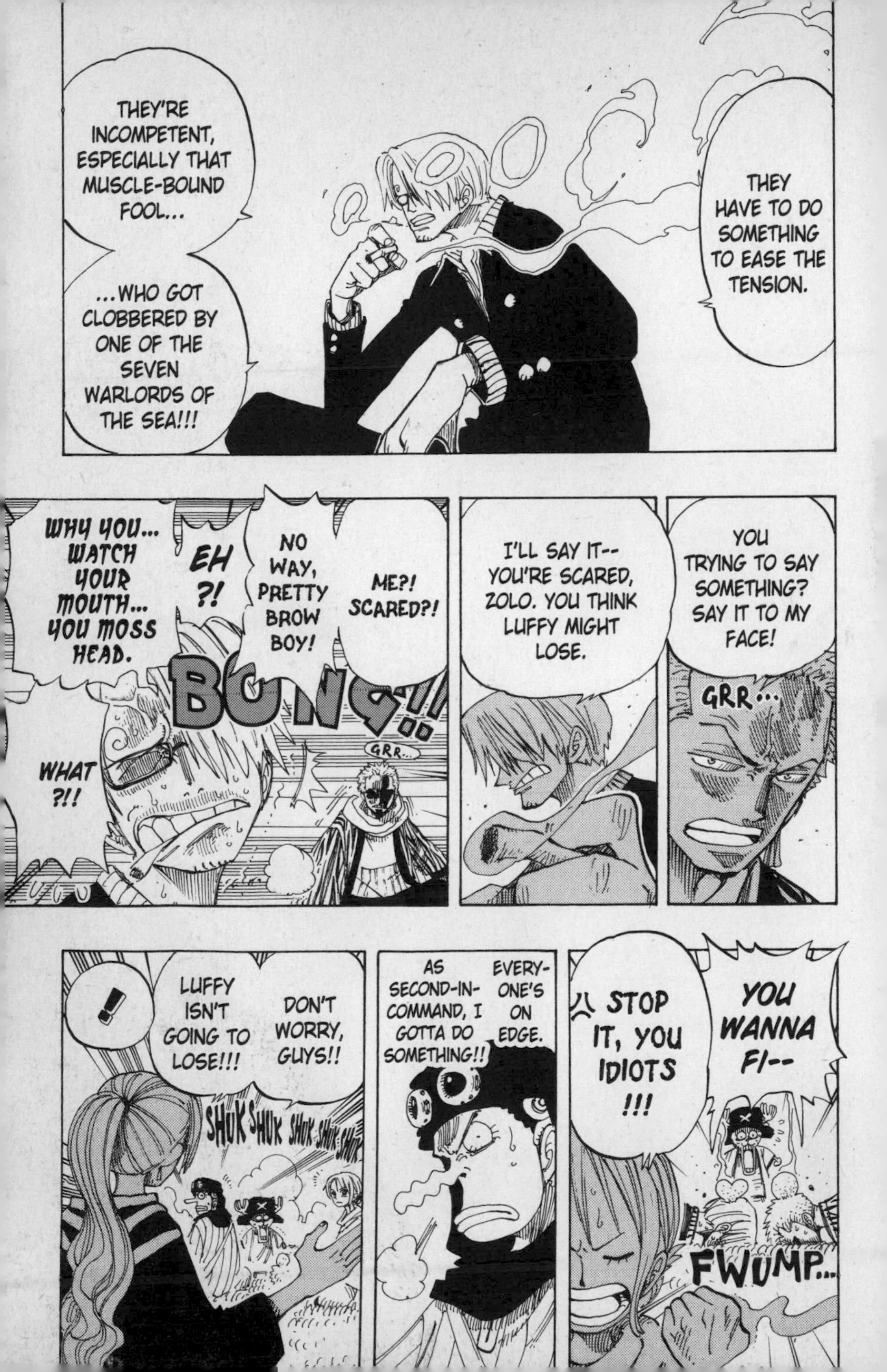
THEY HAVE TO DO SOMETHING TO EASE THE TENSION.
THEY'RE INCOMPETENT, ESPECIALLY THAT MUSCLE-BOUND FOOL...
...WHO GOT CLOBBERED BY ONE OF THE SEVEN WARLORDS OF THE SEA!!!
YOU TRYING TO SAY SOMETHING? SAY IT TO MY FACE!
GRR...
I'LL SAY IT-- YOU'RE SCARED, ZOLO. YOU THINK LUFFY MIGHT LOSE.
ME?! SCARED?!
NO WAY, PRETTY BROW BOY!
EH ?!
WHY YOU... WATCH YOUR MOUTH... YOU MOSS HEAD.
BONG!!
GRR...
WHAT ?!!
YOU WANNA FI--
STOP IT, YOU IDIOTS !!!
FWUMP...
EVERY-ONE'S ON EDGE.
AS SECOND-IN-COMMAND, I GOTTA DO SOMETHING!!
!
DON'T WORRY, GUYS!!
LUFFY ISN'T GOING TO LOSE!!!
SHUK SHUK SHUK SHUK SHUK

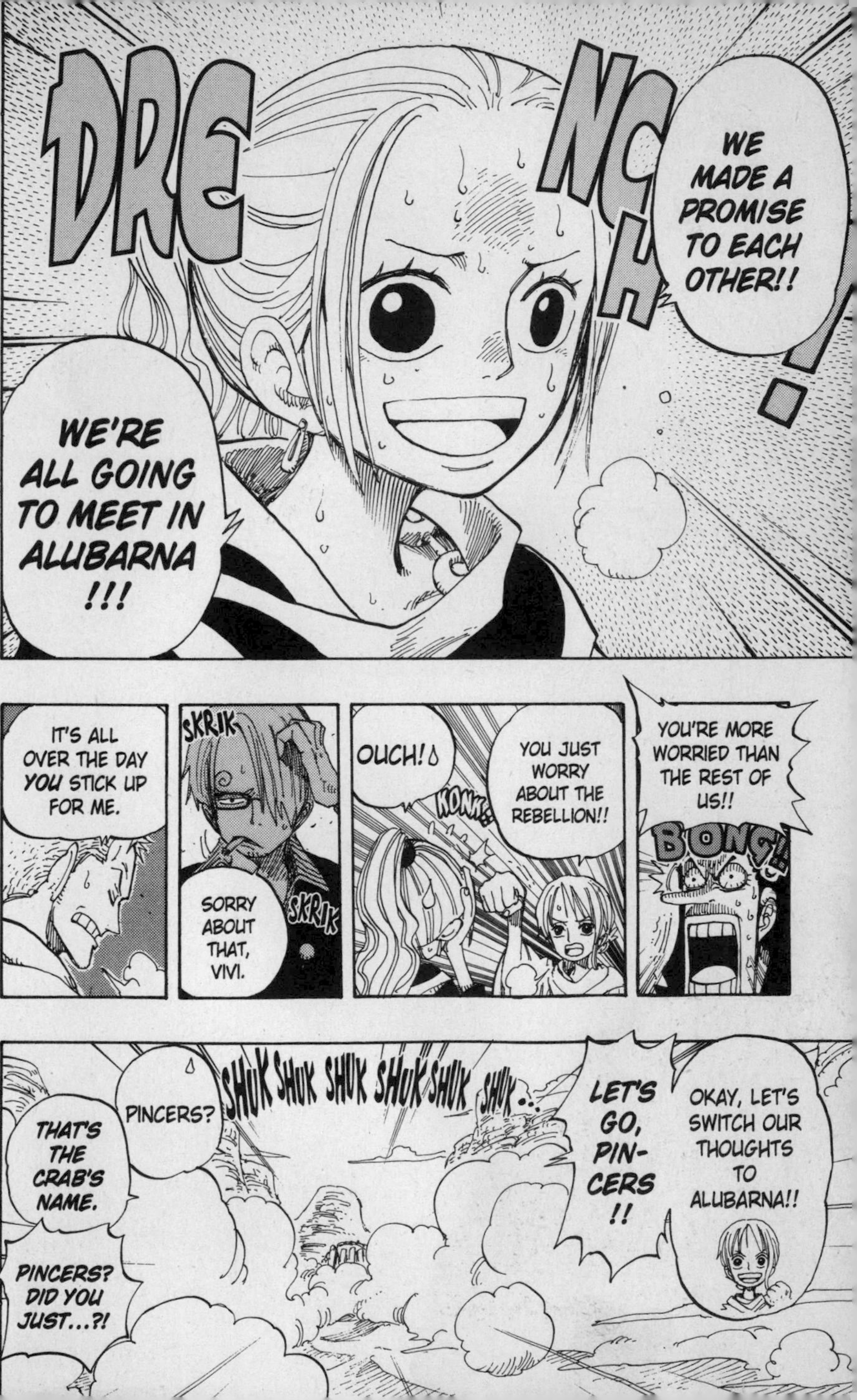
WE MADE A PROMISE TO EACH OTHER!!
WE'RE ALL GOING TO MEET IN ALUBARNA!!!
YOU'RE MORE WORRIED THAN THE REST OF US!!
BONG!!
YOU JUST WORRY ABOUT THE REBELLION!!
OUCH!
KONK
SKRIK
SORRY ABOUT THAT, VIVI.
SKRIK
IT'S ALL OVER THE DAY YOU STICK UP FOR ME.
OKAY, LET'S SWITCH OUR THOUGHTS TO ALUBARNA!!
LET'S GO, PIN-CERS!!
SHUK SHUK SHUK SHUK SHUK SHUK
PINCERS?
THAT'S THE CRAB'S NAME.
PINCERS? DID YOU JUST...?!

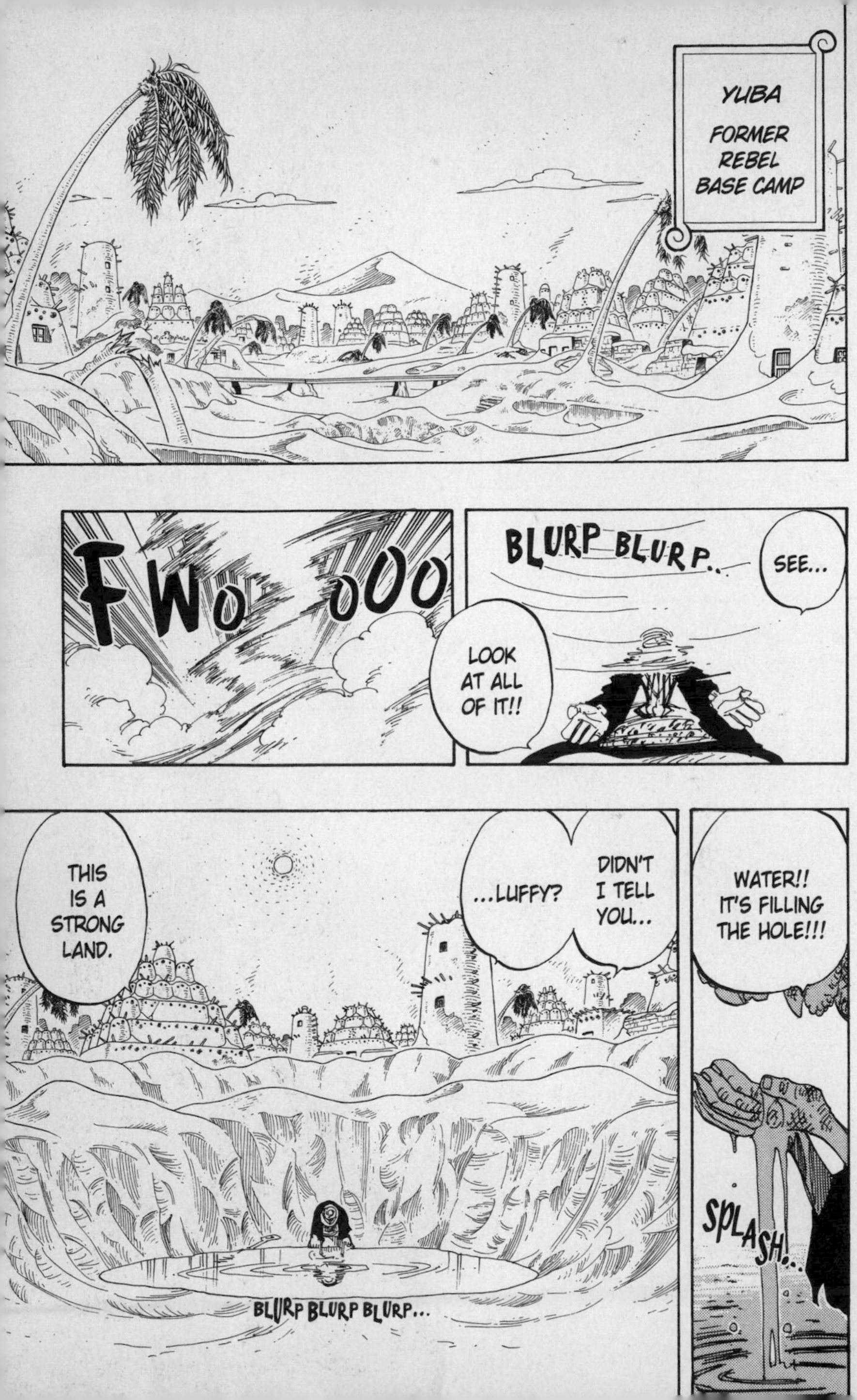
YUBA
FORMER REBEL BASE CAMP
SEE...
BLURP BLURP...
LOOK AT ALL OF IT!!
FWOOOO
WATER!! IT'S FILLING THE HOLE!!!
SPLASH!..
DIDN'T I TELL YOU...
...LUFFY?
THIS IS A STRONG LAND.
BLURP BLURP BLURP...

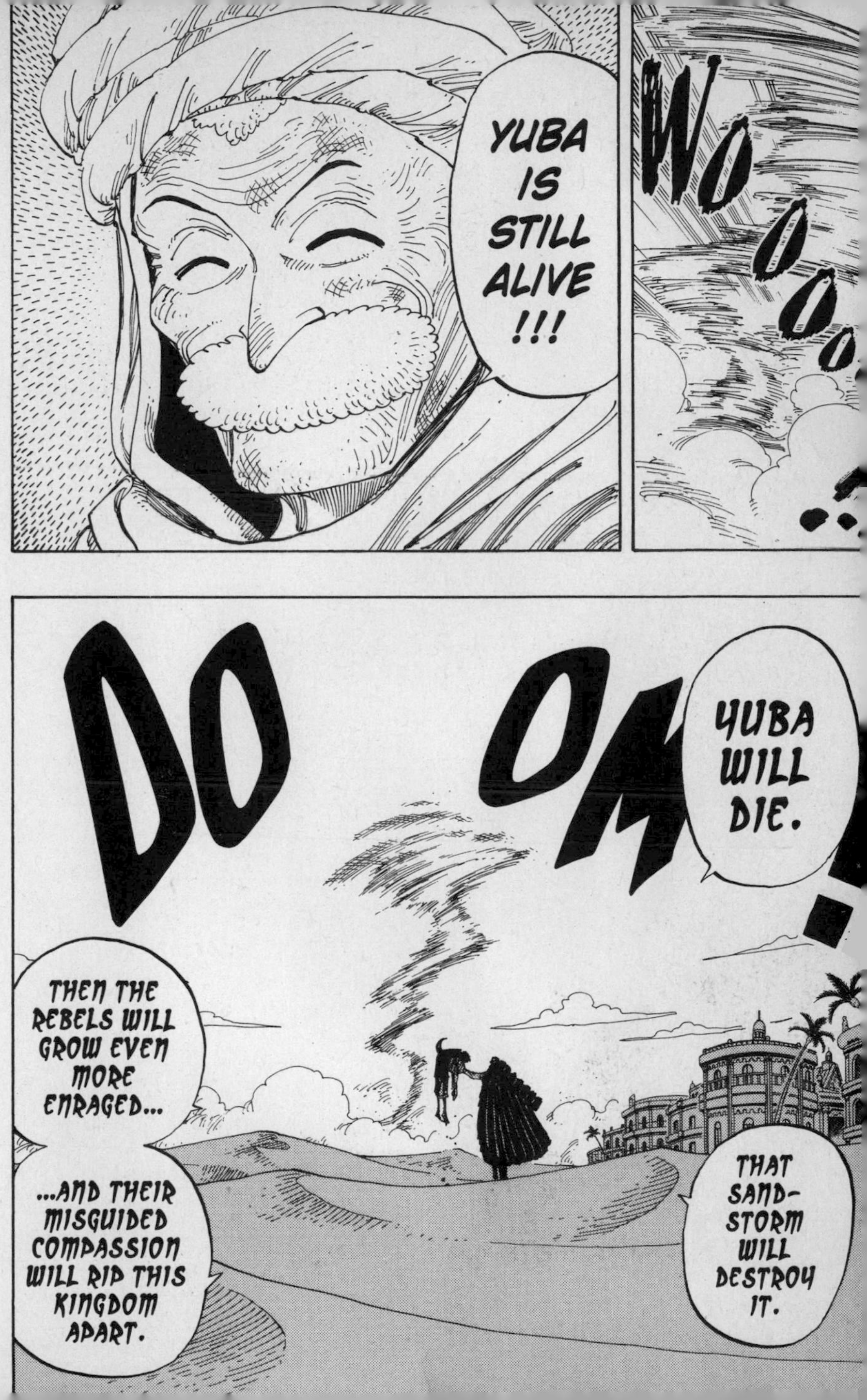

WOOOOO..
YUBA IS STILL ALIVE!!!
DOOM!!
YUBA WILL DIE.
THAT SAND-STORM WILL DESTROY IT.
THEN THE REBELS WILL GROW EVEN MORE ENRAGED...
...AND THEIR MISGUIDED COMPASSION WILL RIP THIS KINGDOM APART.

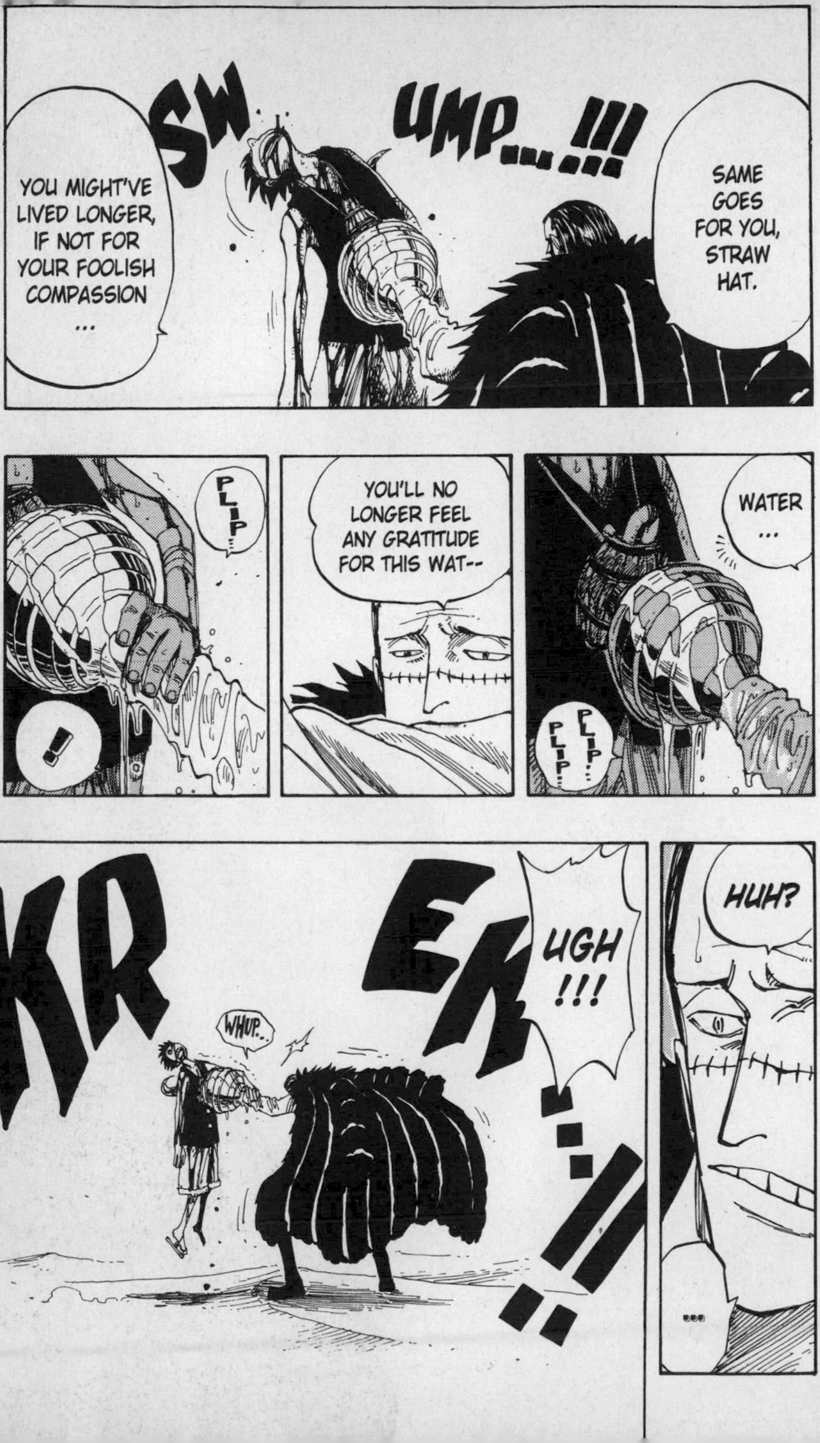
SAME GOES FOR YOU, STRAW HAT.
SWUMP...!!!
YOU MIGHT'VE LIVED LONGER, IF NOT FOR YOUR FOOLISH COMPASSION ...
WATER ...
PLIP... PLIP...
YOU'LL NO LONGER FEEL ANY GRATITUDE FOR THIS WAT--
PLIP...
!
HUH?
...
UGH !!!
KREK...!!
WHUP...

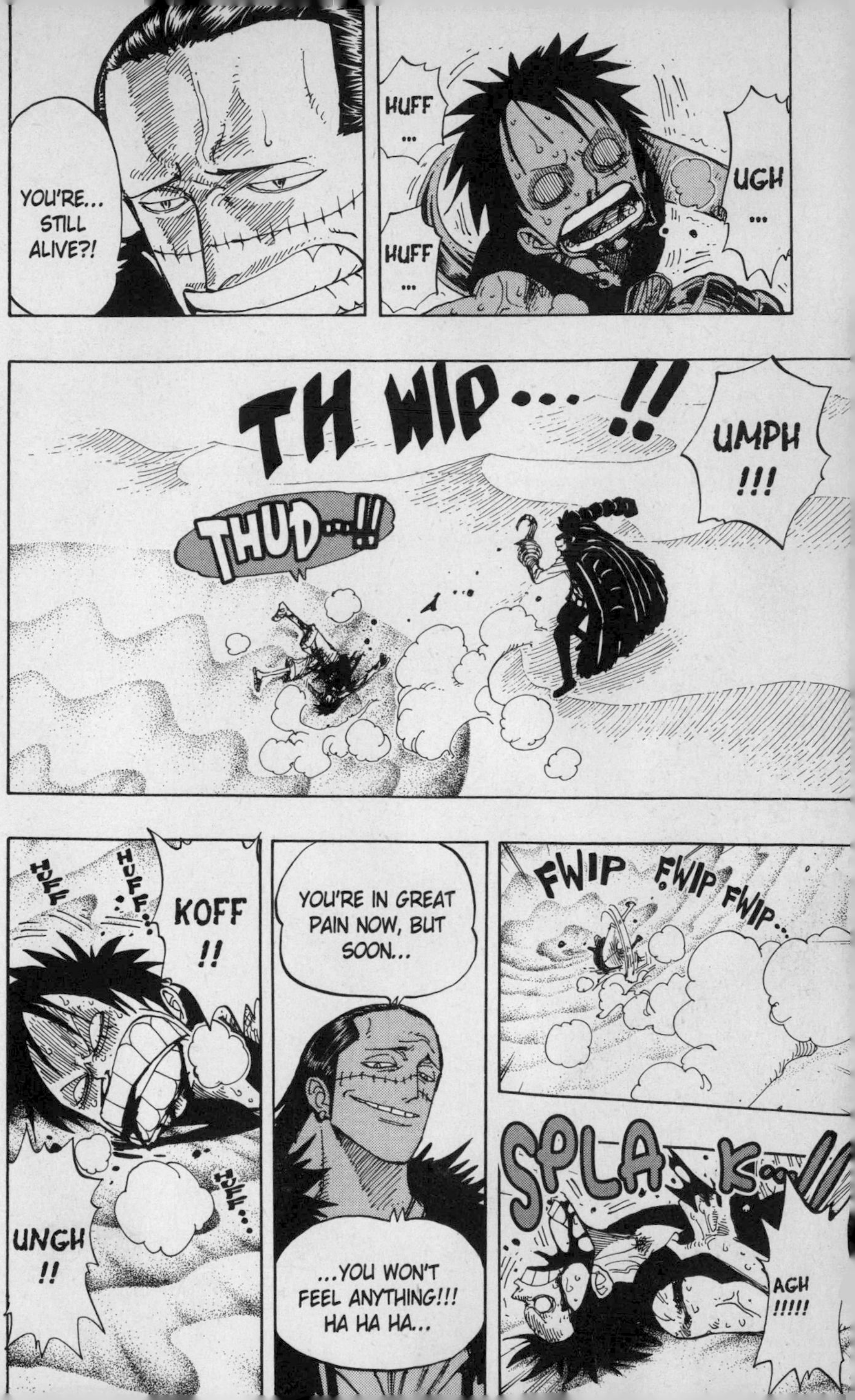
UGH ...
HUFF ...
HUFF ...
YOU'RE... STILL ALIVE?!
UMPH !!!
TH WIP...!!
THUD...!!
FWIP FWIP FWIP FWIP...
SPLA K...!!
AGH !!!!!
YOU'RE IN GREAT PAIN NOW, BUT SOON...
...YOU WON'T FEEL ANYTHING!!! HA HA HA...
KOFF !!
HUFF
HUFF...
HUFF...
UNGH !!

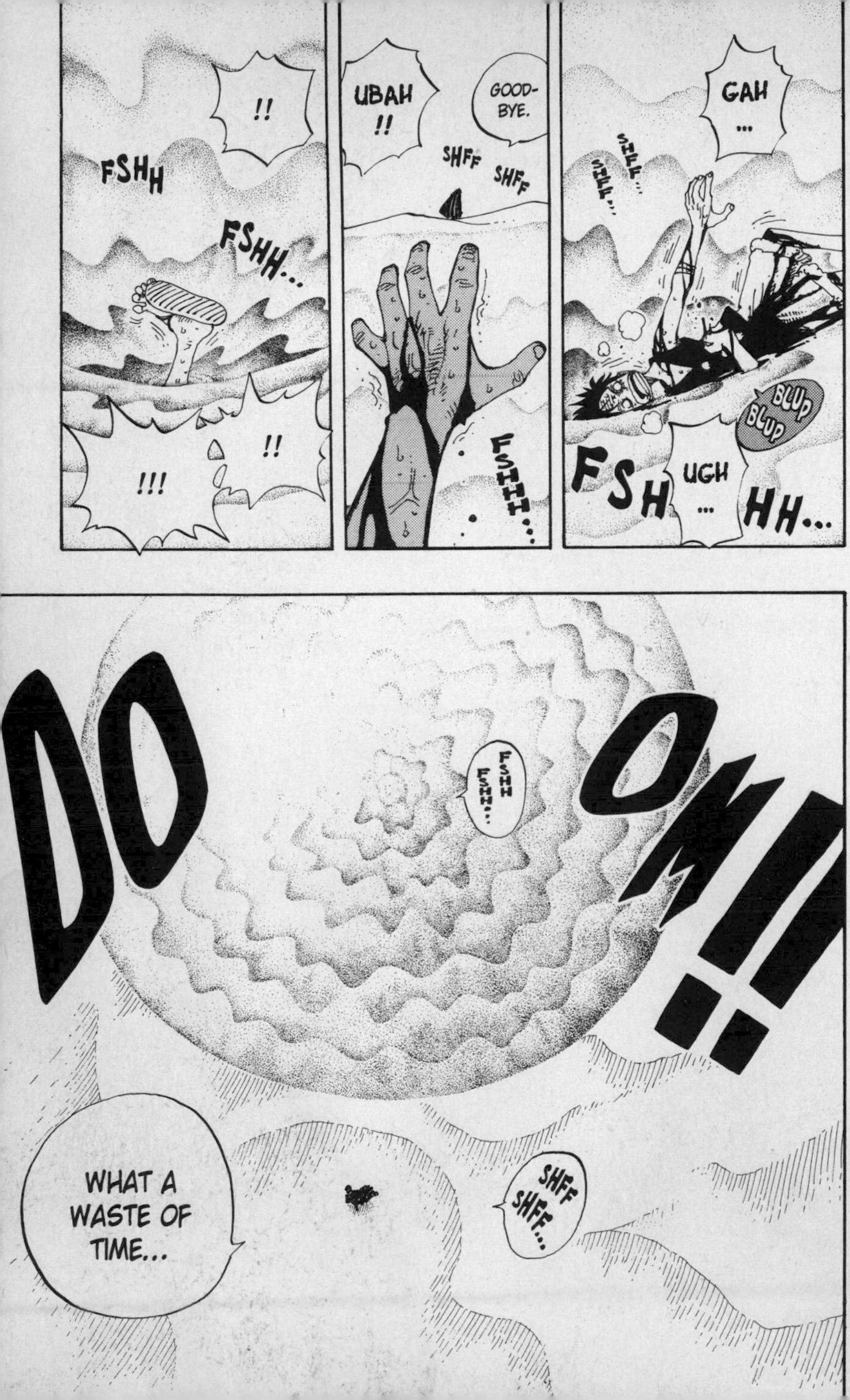
GAH...
SHFF...
SHFF...
BLUP
BLUP
FSH
UGH...
HH...
GOOD-BYE.
UBAH!!
SHFF
SHFF
FSHHH...
!!
FSHH
FSHH...
!!
!!!
DOOM!!
FSHH
FSHH...
WHAT A WASTE OF TIME...
SHFF
SHFF...

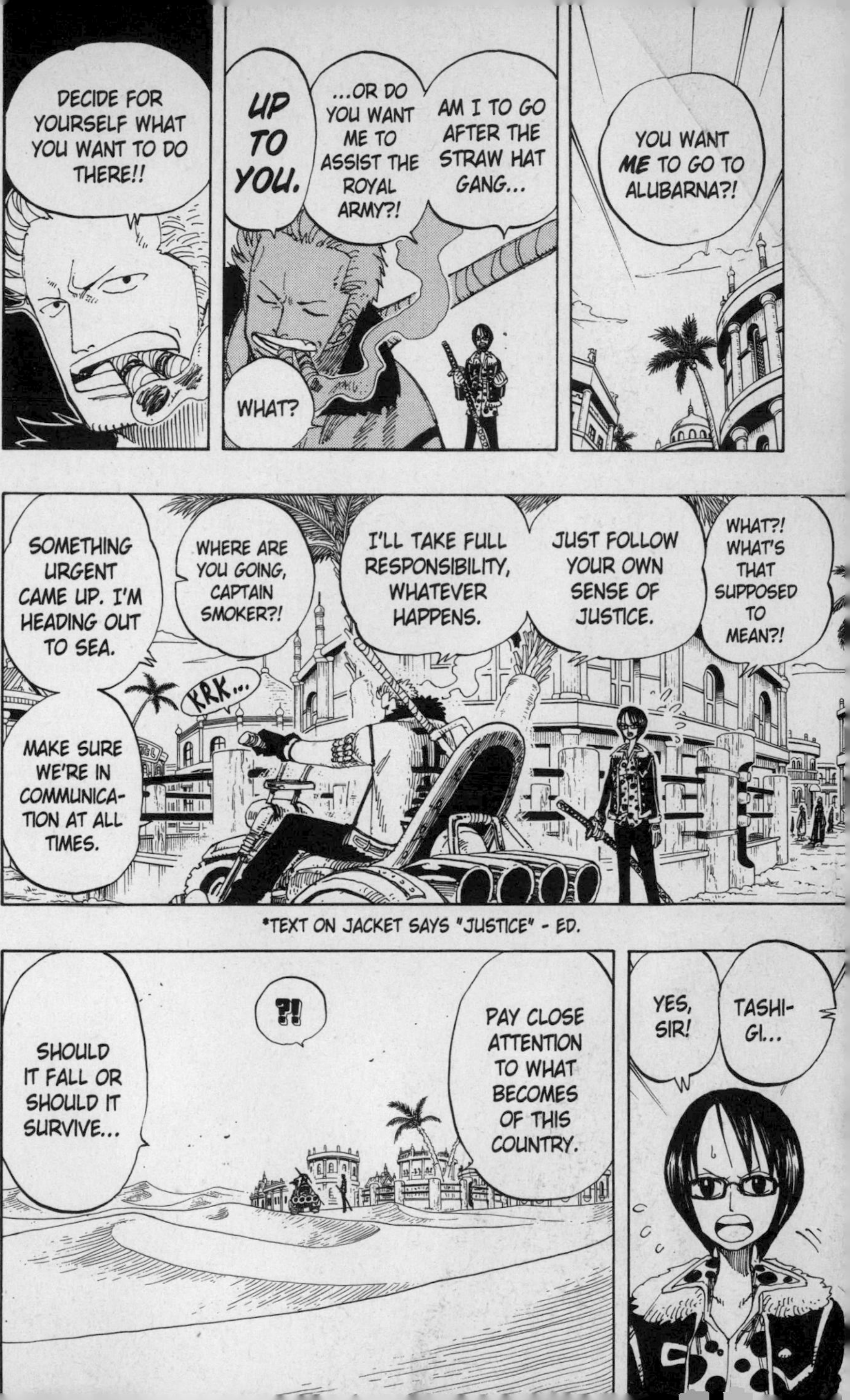
YOU WANT ME TO GO TO ALUBARNA?!
AM I TO GO AFTER THE STRAW HAT GANG...
...OR DO YOU WANT ME TO ASSIST THE ROYAL ARMY?!
UP TO YOU.
WHAT?
DECIDE FOR YOURSELF WHAT YOU WANT TO DO THERE!!
WHAT?! WHAT'S THAT SUPPOSED TO MEAN?!
JUST FOLLOW YOUR OWN SENSE OF JUSTICE.
I'LL TAKE FULL RESPONSIBILITY, WHATEVER HAPPENS.
WHERE ARE YOU GOING, CAPTAIN SMOKER?!
SOMETHING URGENT CAME UP. I'M HEADING OUT TO SEA.
KRK...
MAKE SURE WE'RE IN COMMUNICATION AT ALL TIMES.
TASHI-GI...
YES, SIR!
PAY CLOSE ATTENTION TO WHAT BECOMES OF THIS COUNTRY.
?!
SHOULD IT FALL OR SHOULD IT SURVIVE...

*TEXT ON JACKET SAYS "JUSTICE" - ED.

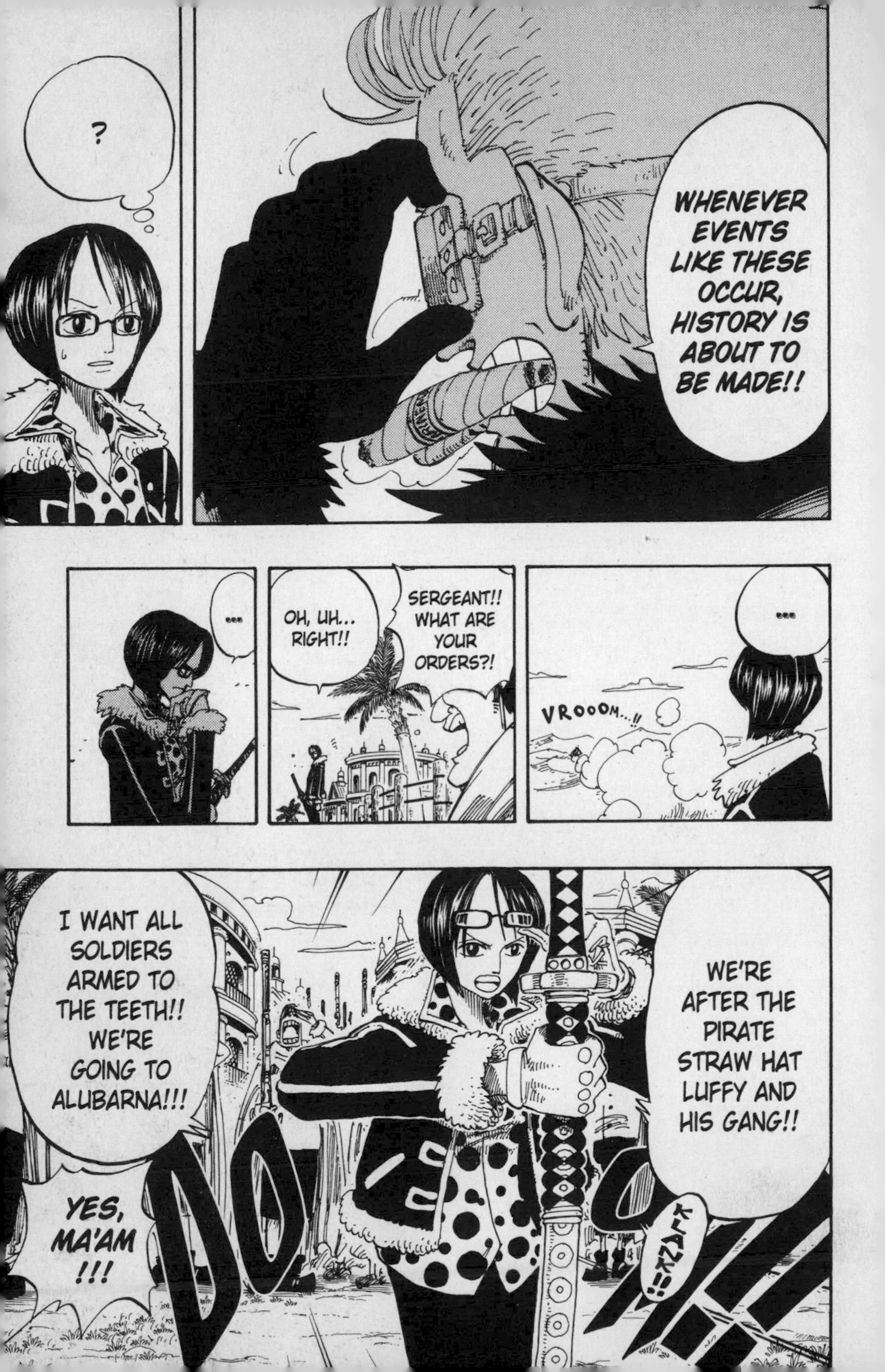
WHENEVER EVENTS LIKE THESE OCCUR, HISTORY IS ABOUT TO BE MADE!!
?
...
VROOOM...!!
SERGEANT!! WHAT ARE YOUR ORDERS?!
OH, UH... RIGHT!!
...
WE'RE AFTER THE PIRATE STRAW HAT LUFFY AND HIS GANG!!
I WANT ALL SOLDIERS ARMED TO THE TEETH!! WE'RE GOING TO ALUBARNA!!!
KLANK!!
YES, MA'AM!!!

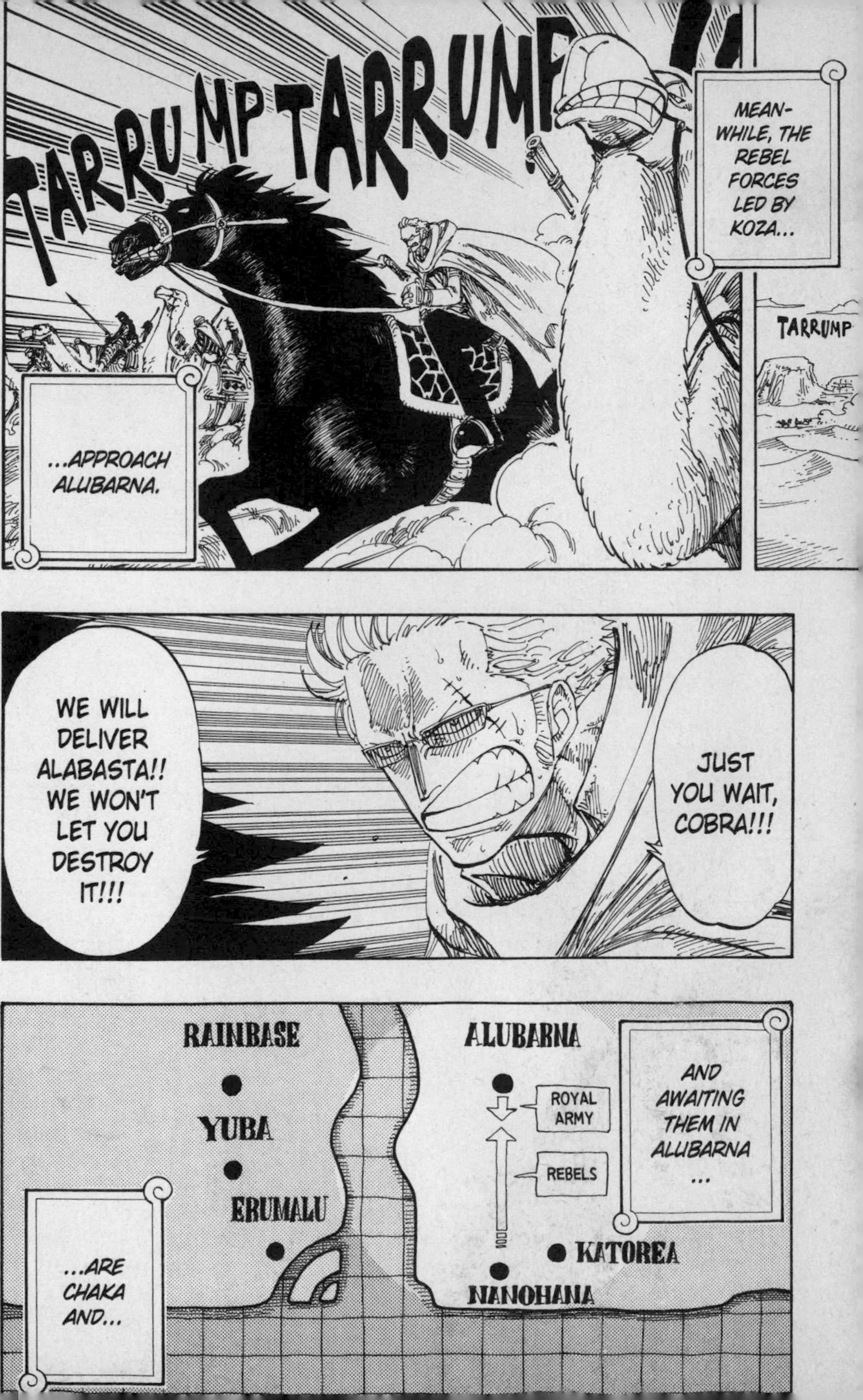
TARRUMP
MEAN-WHILE, THE REBEL FORCES LED BY KOZA...
TARRUMP TARRUMP TARRUMP
...APPROACH ALUBARNA.
JUST YOU WAIT, COBRA!!!
WE WILL DELIVER ALABASTA!! WE WON'T LET YOU DESTROY IT!!!
AND AWAITING THEM IN ALUBARNA ...
ALUBARNA
ROYAL ARMY
REBELS
KATOREA
NANOHANA
RAINBASE
YUBA
ERUMALU
...ARE CHAKA AND...

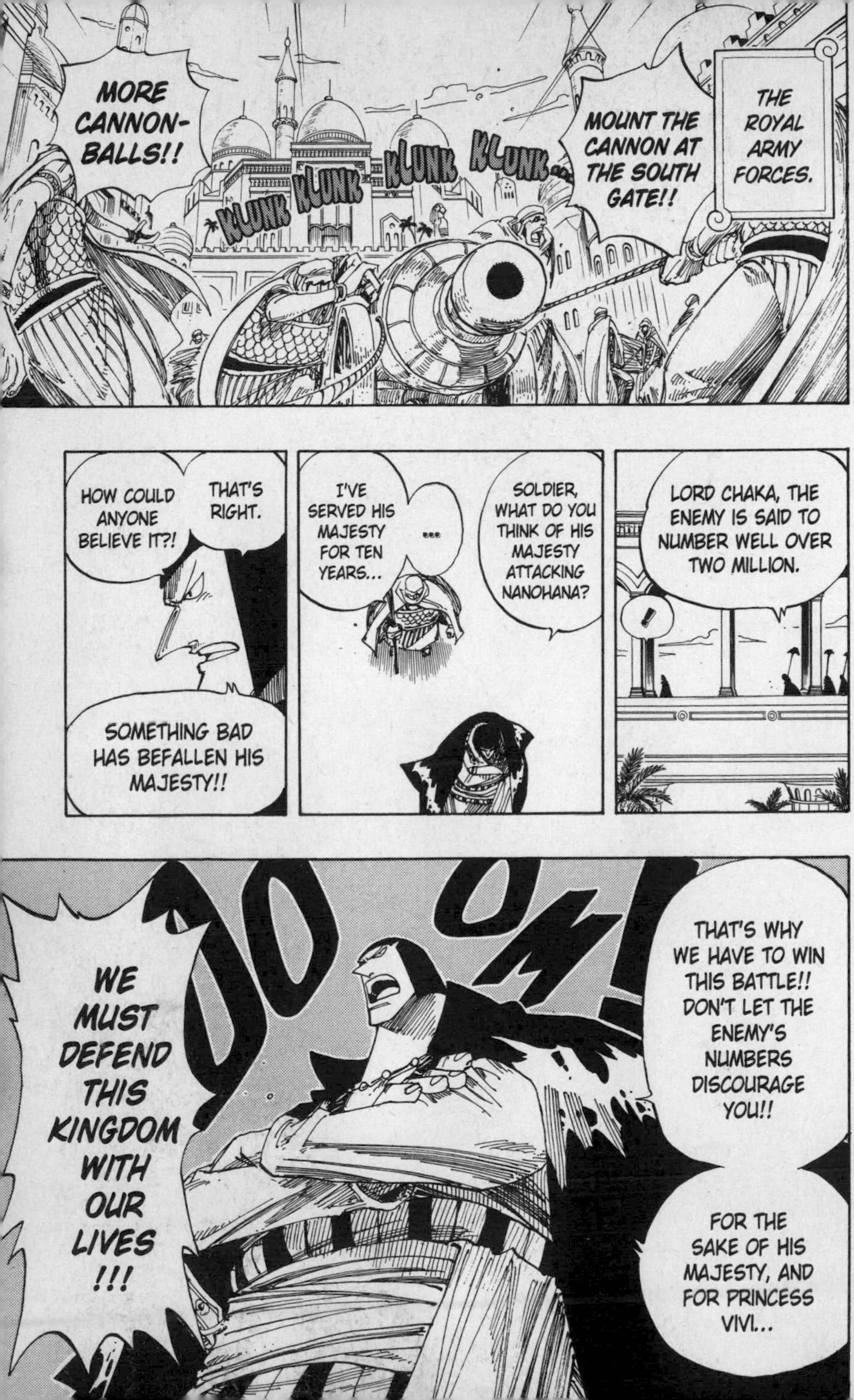
THE ROYAL ARMY FORCES.
MOUNT THE CANNON AT THE SOUTH GATE!!
KLUNK KLUNK KLUNK KLUNK...
MORE CANNON-BALLS!!
LORD CHAKA, THE ENEMY IS SAID TO NUMBER WELL OVER TWO MILLION.
!
SOLDIER, WHAT DO YOU THINK OF HIS MAJESTY ATTACKING NANOHANA?
I'VE SERVED HIS MAJESTY FOR TEN YEARS...
...
THAT'S RIGHT.
HOW COULD ANYONE BELIEVE IT?!
SOMETHING BAD HAS BEFALLEN HIS MAJESTY!!
THAT'S WHY WE HAVE TO WIN THIS BATTLE!! DON'T LET THE ENEMY'S NUMBERS DISCOURAGE YOU!!
FOR THE SAKE OF HIS MAJESTY, AND FOR PRINCESS VIVI...
DOOM!
WE MUST DEFEND THIS KINGDOM WITH OUR LIVES!!!

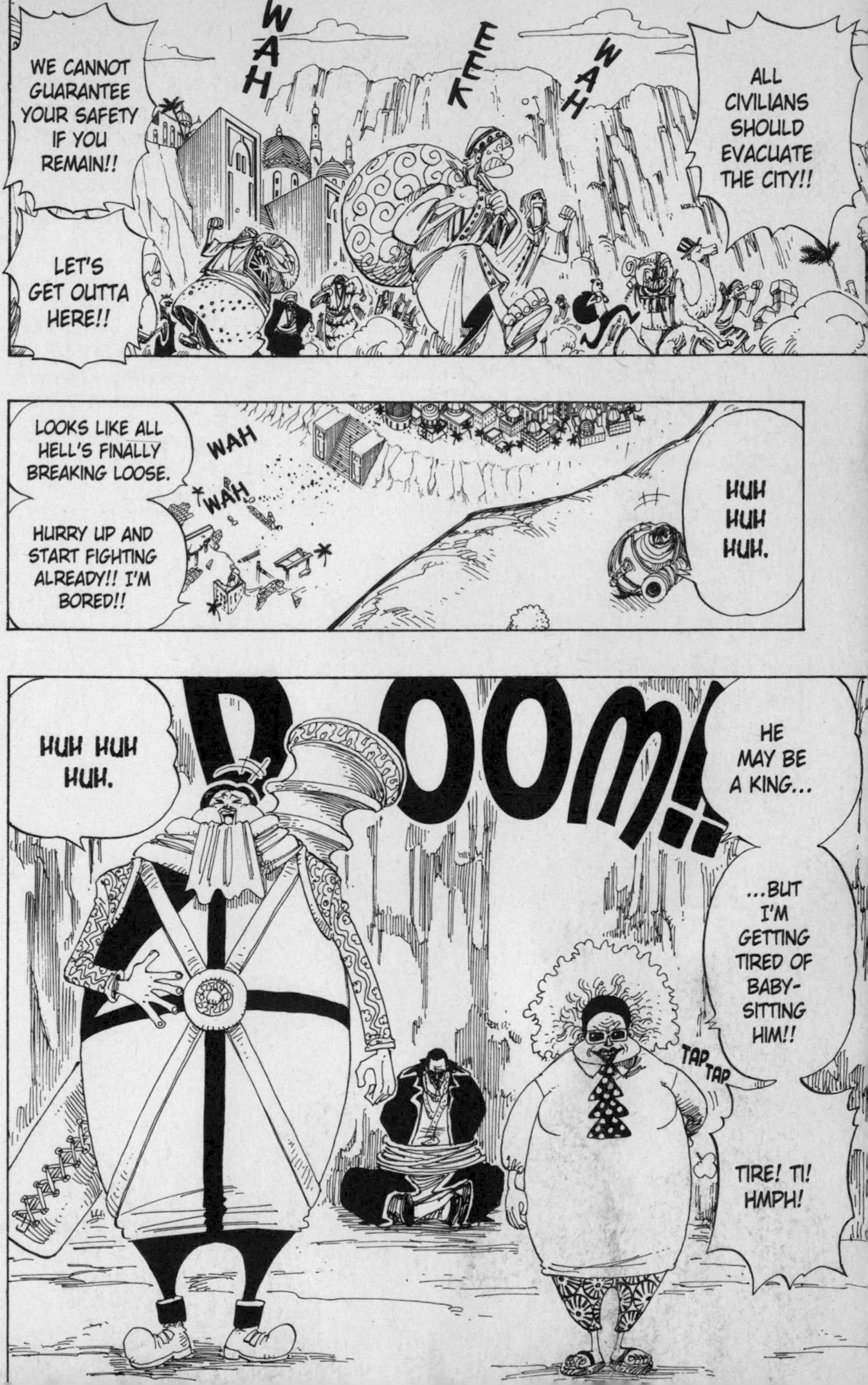
ALL CIVILIANS SHOULD EVACUATE THE CITY!!
WAH
EEK
WAH
WE CANNOT GUARANTEE YOUR SAFETY IF YOU REMAIN!!
LET'S GET OUTTA HERE!!
HUH HUH HUH.
LOOKS LIKE ALL HELL'S FINALLY BREAKING LOOSE.
WAH
WAH
HURRY UP AND START FIGHTING ALREADY!! I'M BORED!!
HE MAY BE A KING...
...BUT I'M GETTING TIRED OF BABY-SITTING HIM!!
TAP TAP
TIRE! TI! HMPH!
BOOM!!
HUH HUH HUH.

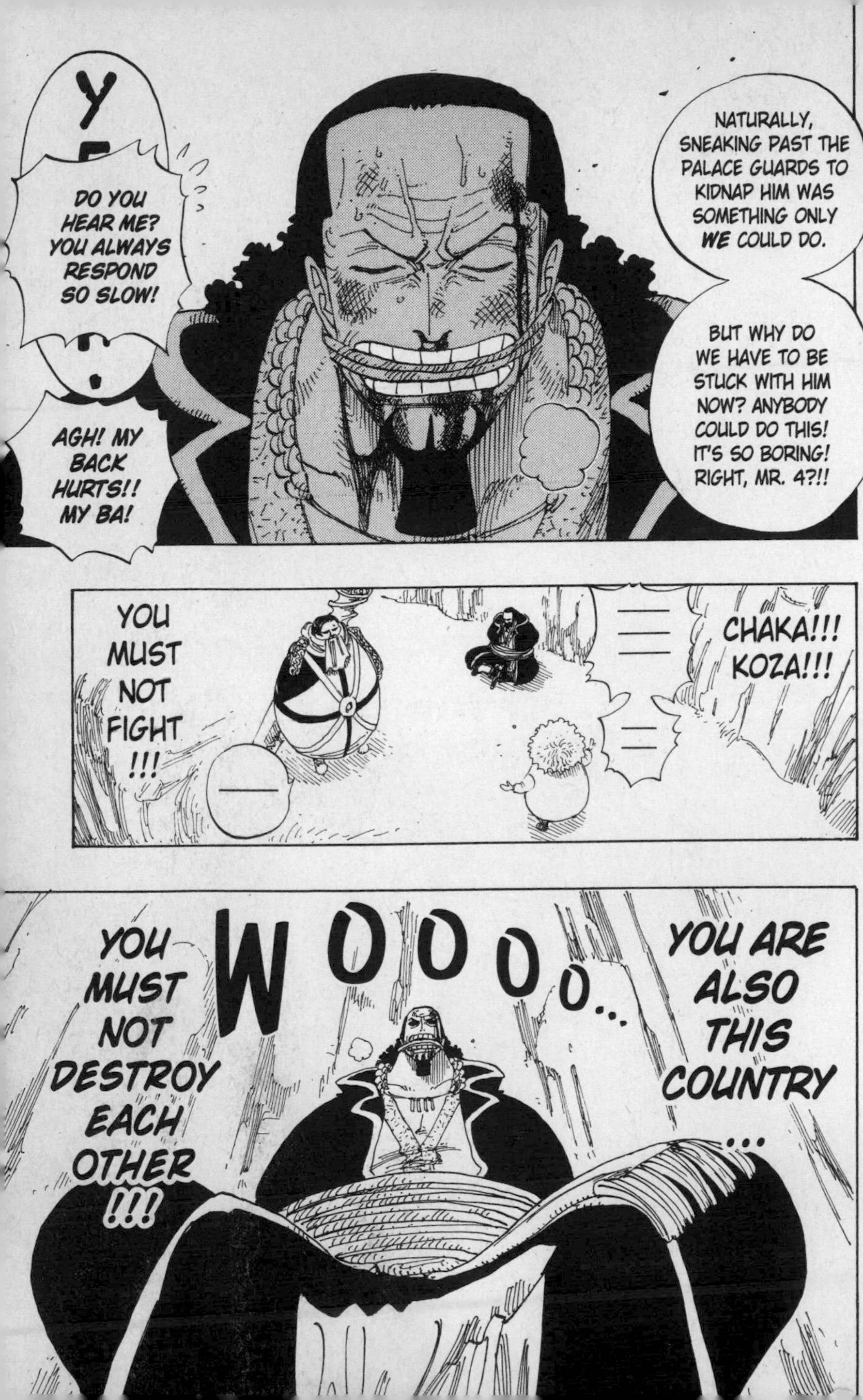
NATURALLY, SNEAKING PAST THE PALACE GUARDS TO KIDNAP HIM WAS SOMETHING ONLY WE COULD DO.
BUT WHY DO WE HAVE TO BE STUCK WITH HIM NOW? ANYBODY COULD DO THIS! IT'S SO BORING! RIGHT, MR. 4?!!
DO YOU HEAR ME? YOU ALWAYS RESPOND SO SLOW!
AGH! MY BACK HURTS!! MY BA!
CHAKA!!! KOZA!!!
YOU MUST NOT FIGHT!!!
YOU ARE ALSO THIS COUNTRY...
WOOOOO...
YOU MUST NOT DESTROY EACH OTHER!!!

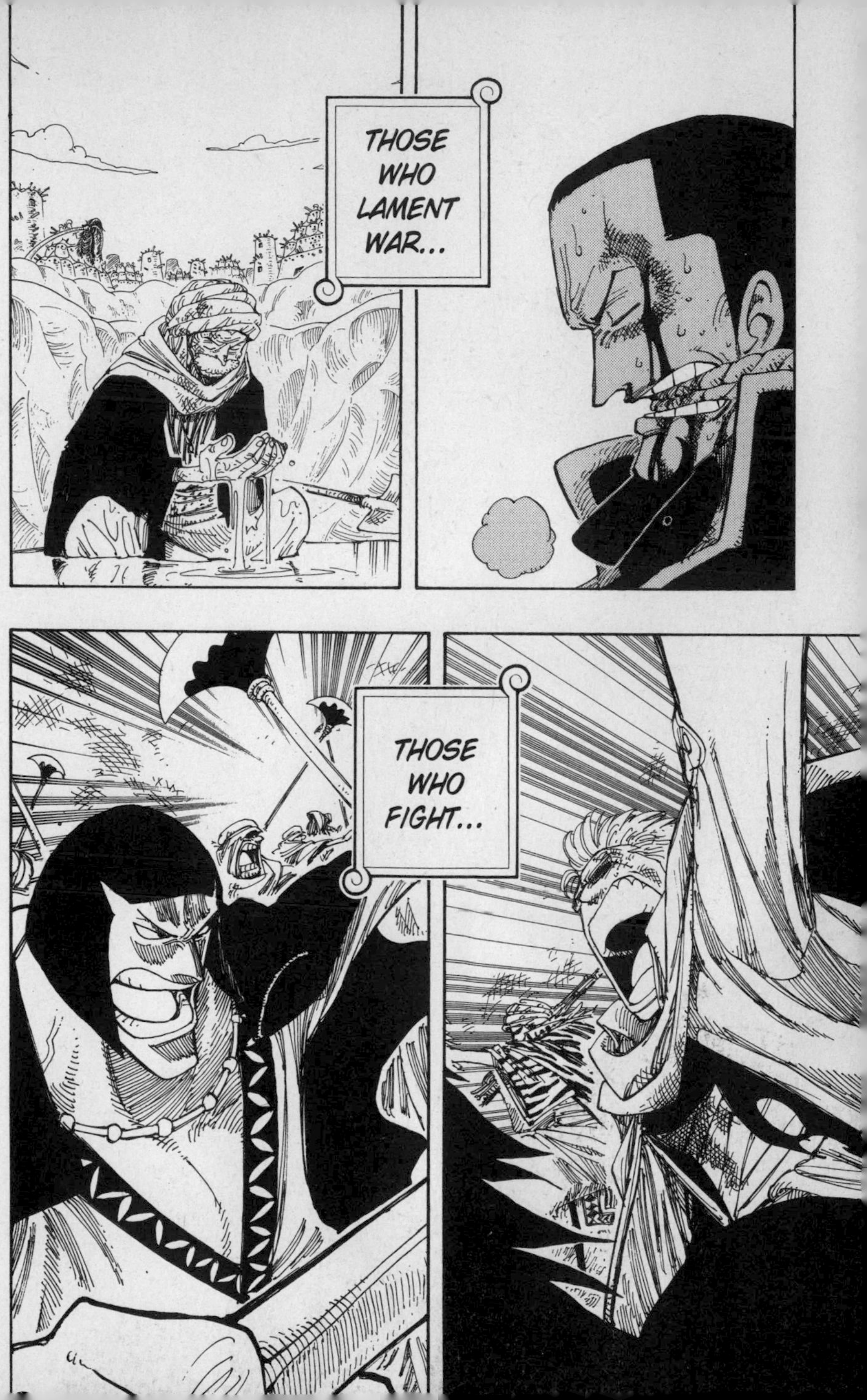
THOSE WHO LAMENT WAR...
THOSE WHO FIGHT...

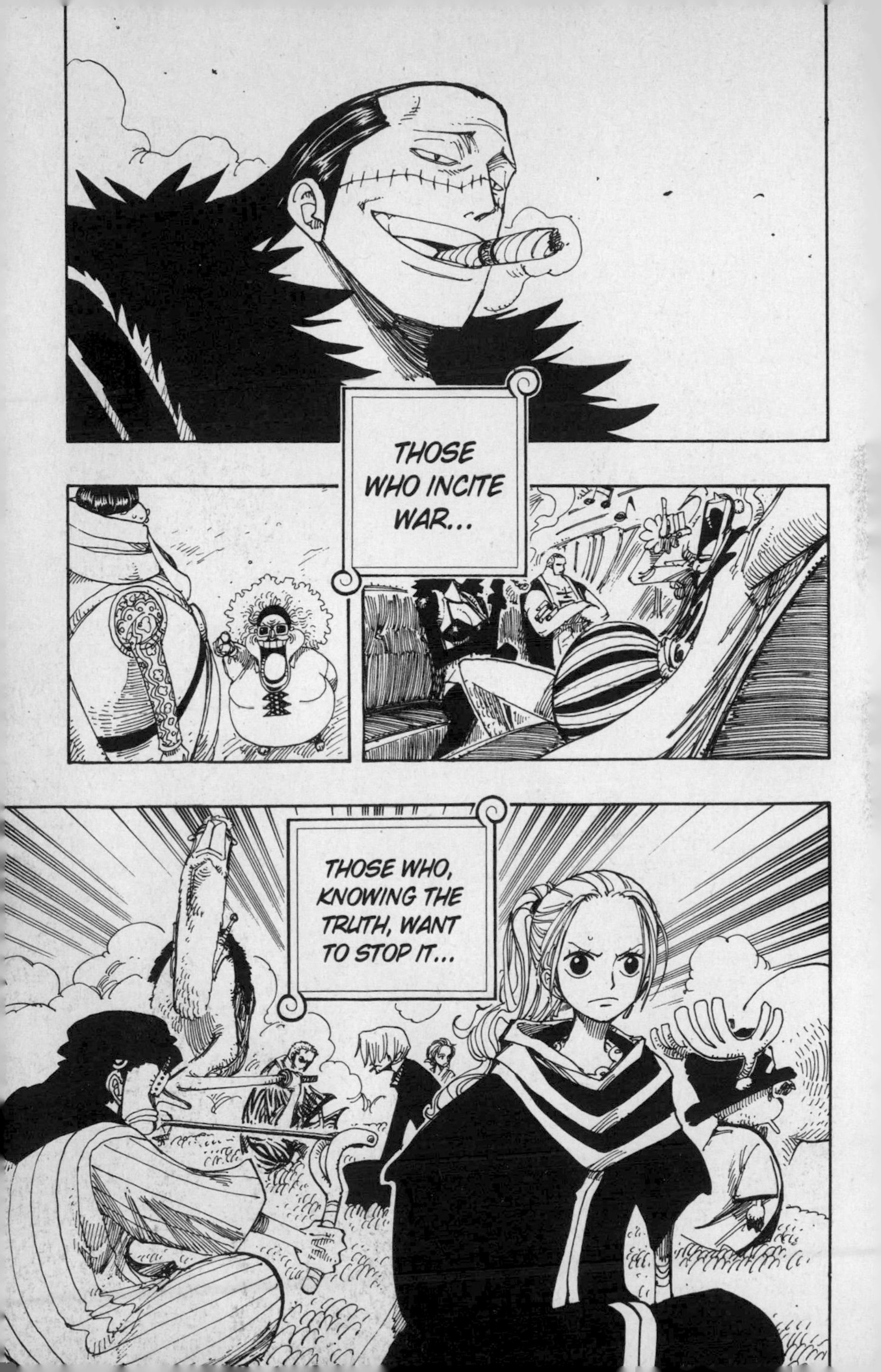
THOSE WHO INCITE WAR...
THOSE WHO, KNOWING THE TRUTH, WANT TO STOP IT...

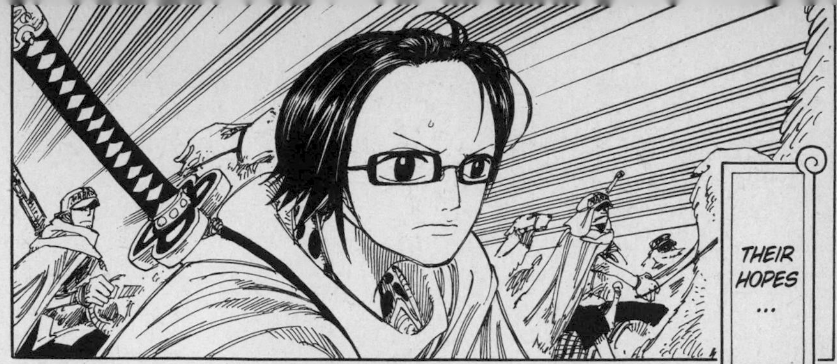
THEIR HOPES ...

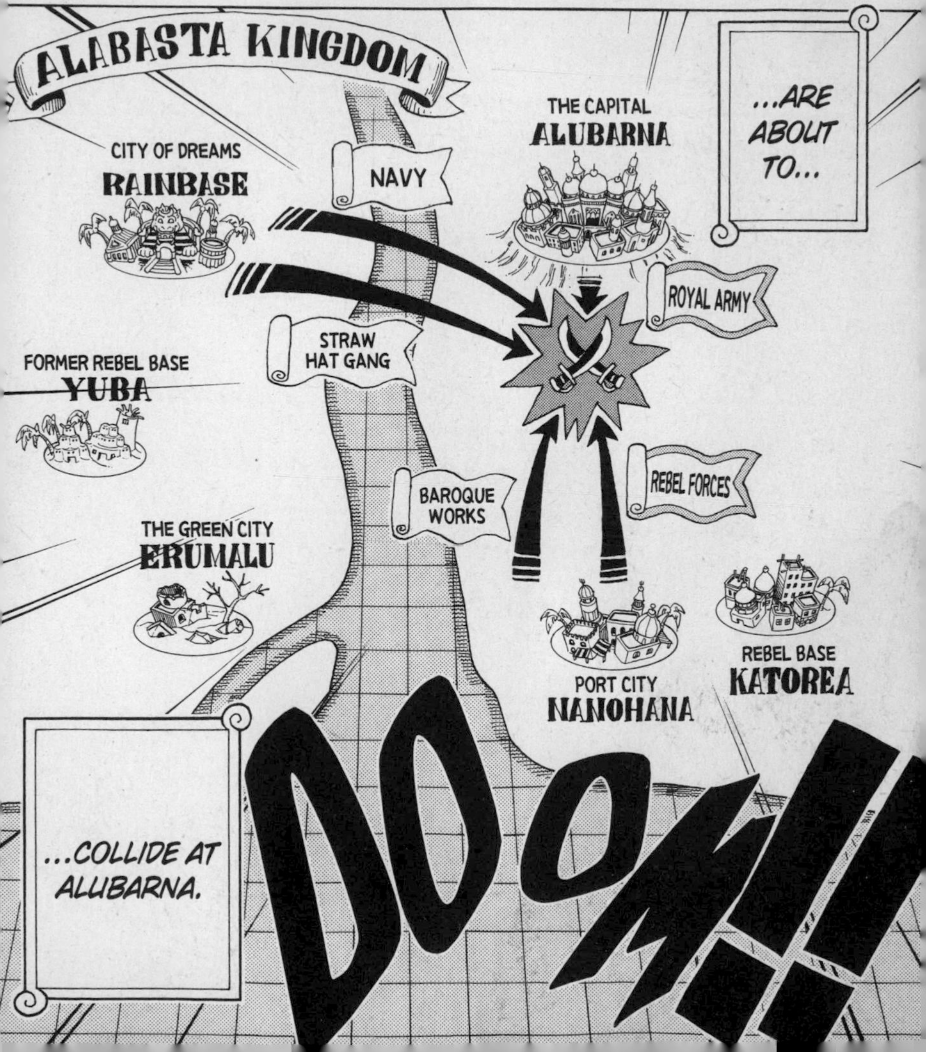
...ARE ABOUT TO...
ALABASTA KINGDOM
THE CAPITAL
ALUBARNA
ROYAL ARMY
NAVY
CITY OF DREAMS
RAINBASE
STRAW HAT GANG
FORMER REBEL BASE
YUBA
REBEL FORCES
BAROQUE WORKS
THE GREEN CITY
ERUMALU
REBEL BASE
KATOREA
PORT CITY
NANOHANA
DOOM!!
...COLLIDE AT ALUBARNA.

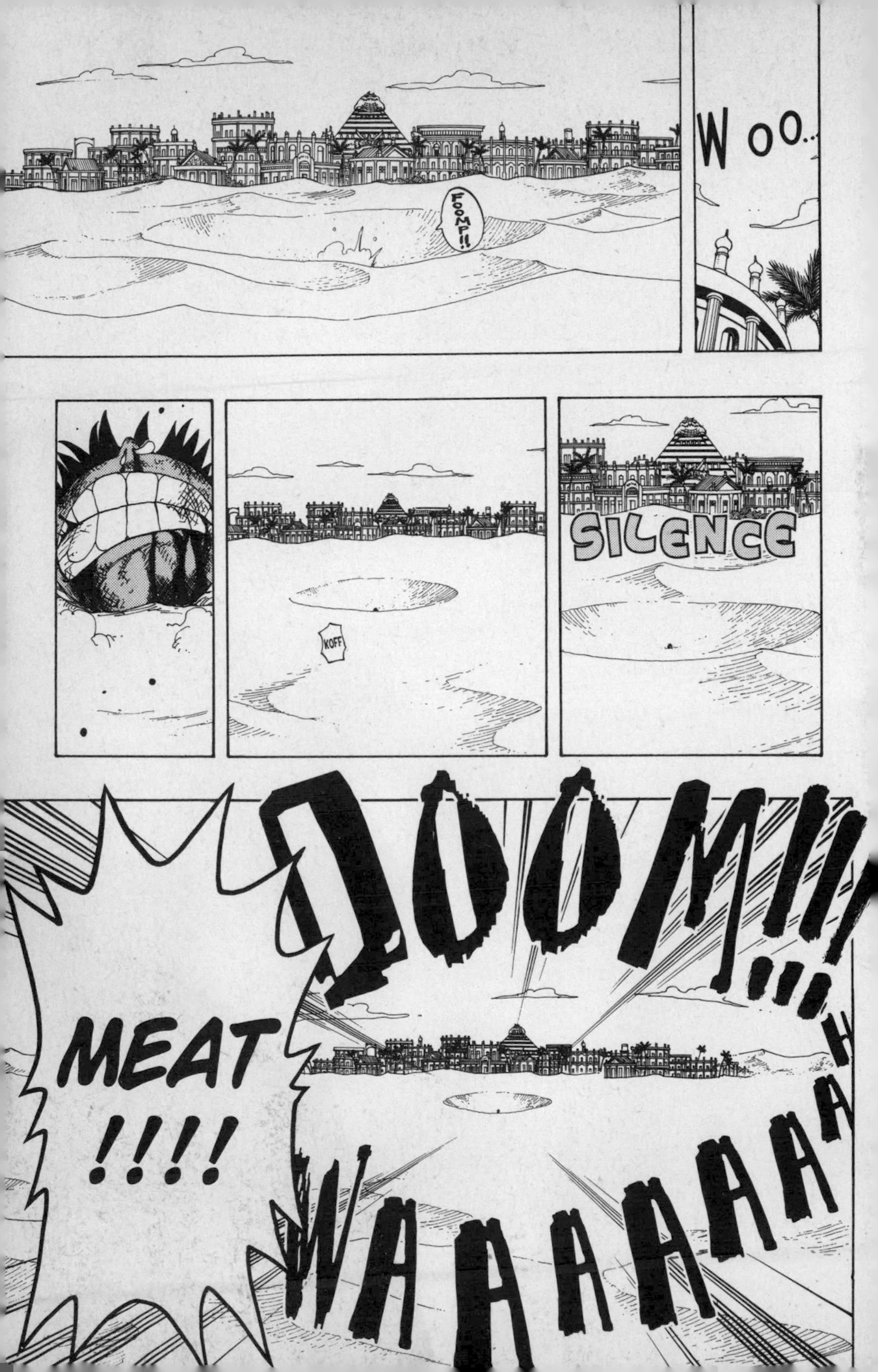
WOO...
FOOMP!!
SILENCE
KOFF
DOOM!!!
MEAT!!!!
WAAAAAAAH

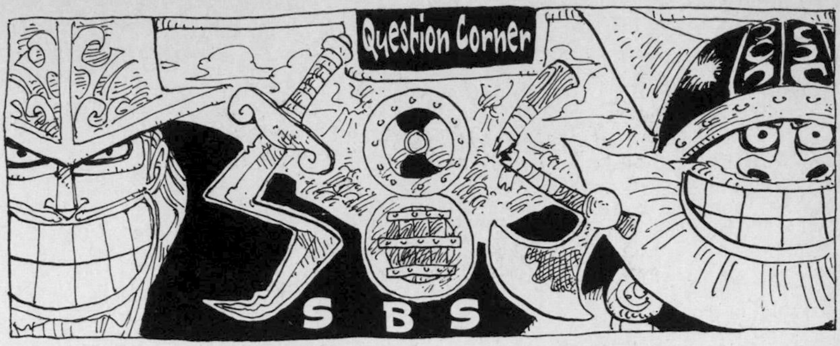
Question Corner
SBS

Q: Doesn't Buggy bleed when he comes apart?

A: D-Don't say such c-creepy things! It'd be horrible if he sprayed blood every time!

Q: I have a secret I'd like to tell Master Oda (in a regular letter). Please (x 10) tell me your home address. See you. Wa ha ha ha ha ha ha ha!

A: Okay. Let's see, my zip code is 202-- Hey, if I told you that, everyone'll be ding dong ditch'ing my house.

Q: Can you tell me what Tashigi's age, height, and weight is? ♡

A: Tashigi, you say? Tashigi is 21. She's quite mature. She's on the tall side at 5' 7". As for her weight, she's a lady, so let's not go there.

Q: Here's a question for you, Mr. Oda! When Ace ate the Flame-Flame Fruit did he:
1. Gain the power to turn his body into flames?
2. Gain the power to make flames shoot out of his body?
Which is it?

A: The answer is 1. But his most deadly move--the Fire Fist--makes his fiery knuckles expand by increasing the temperature, so it's also like 2.

Q: The Question Corner has begun. (Past tense)

A: Ha ha ha! That can't be... Oh!! It has begun!! (Duh!)

Chapter 180:
ALABASTA ANIMAL LAND

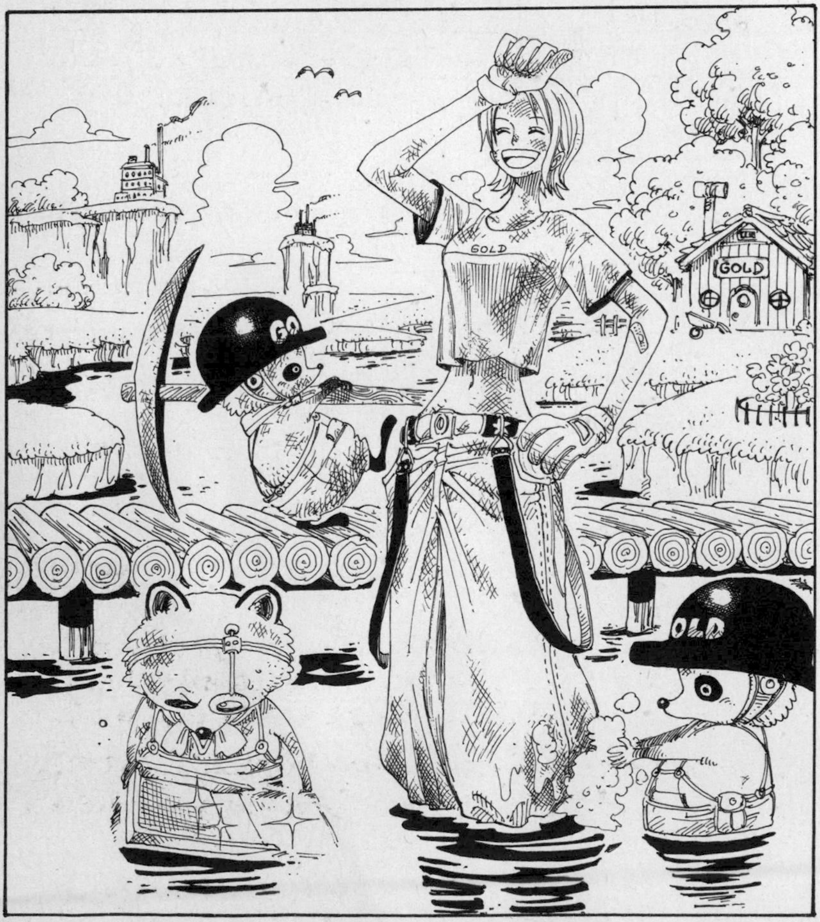
GOLD
GOLD

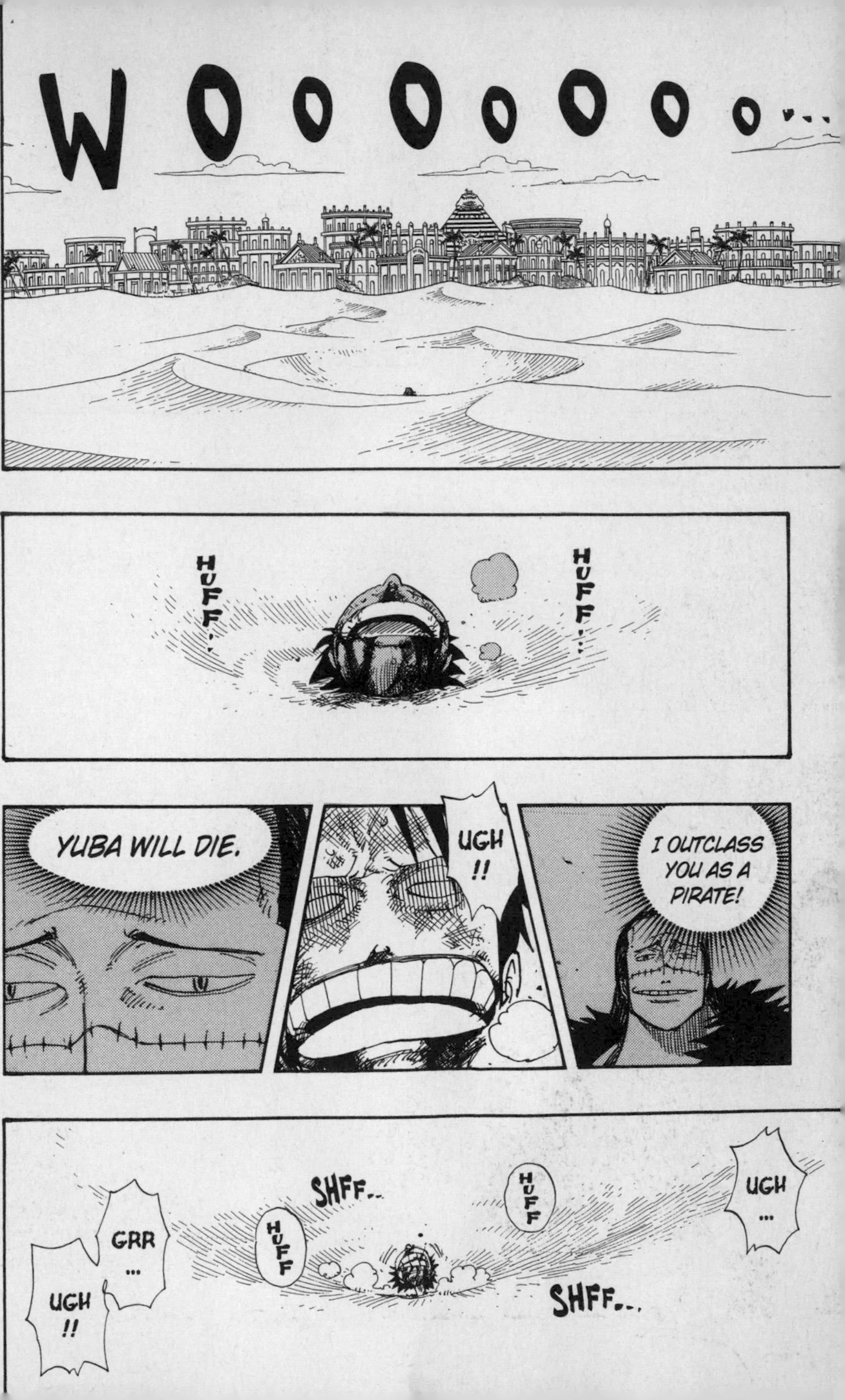
WOOOOOOO...
HUFF...
HUFF...
I OUTCLASS YOU AS A PIRATE!
UGH !!
YUBA WILL DIE.
UGH ...
HUFF
SHFF...
HUFF
GRR ...
SHFF...
UGH !!

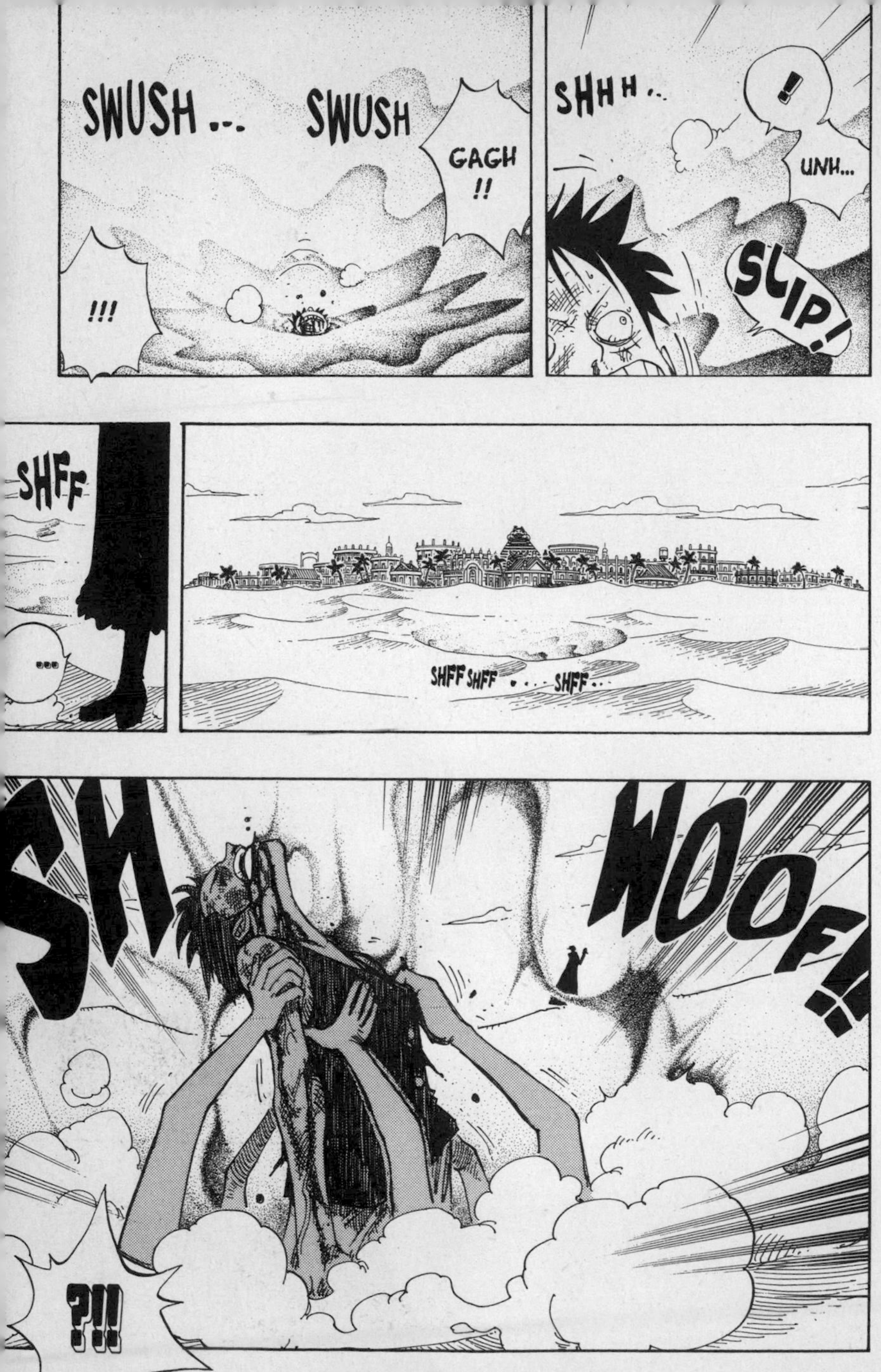
!
SHHH..
UNH...
SLIP!
SWUSH... SWUSH
GAGH!!
!!!
SHFF SHFF.... SHFF...
SHFF
...
SHWOOF!!
?!!

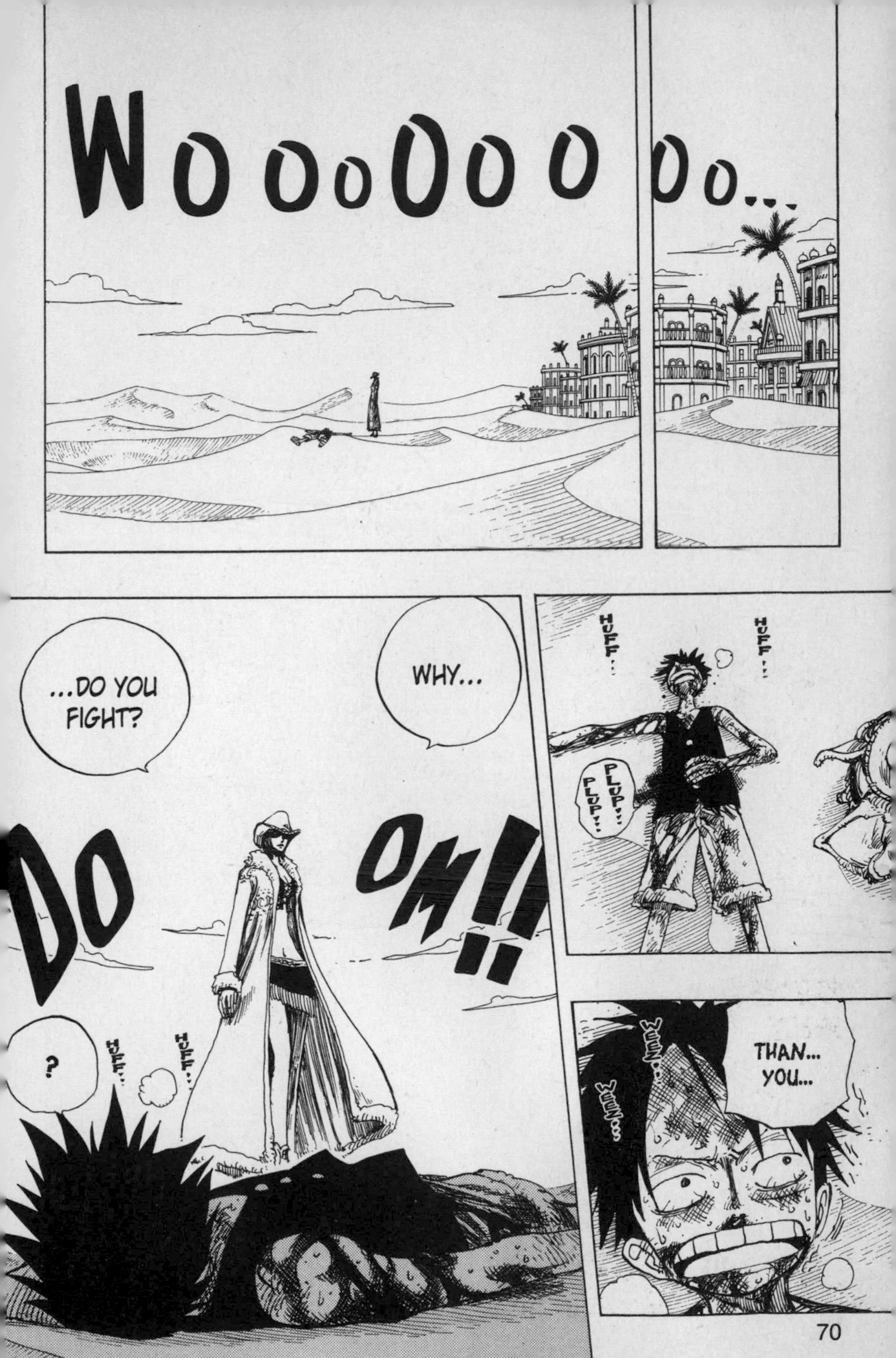
WOooOOOO Oo...
HUFF...
HUFF...
PLUP... PLUP...
WEEZ...
WEEZ...
THAN... YOU...
WHY...
...DO YOU FIGHT?
DOOM!!
?
HUFF...
HUFF...

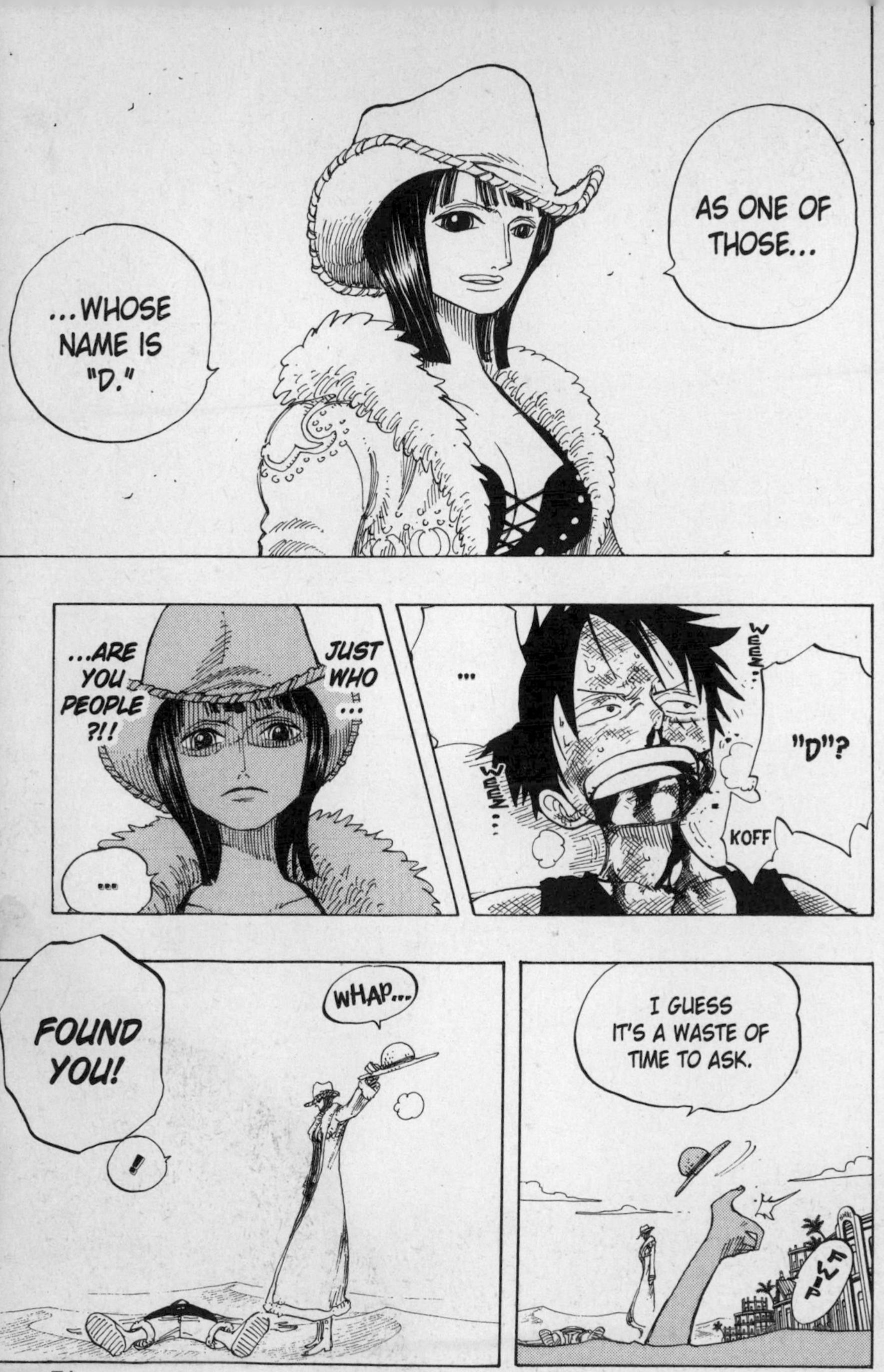
AS ONE OF THOSE...
...WHOSE NAME IS "D."
WEEZ...
"D"?
KOFF
WEEZ...
...
JUST WHO ...
...ARE YOU PEOPLE ?!!
...
I GUESS IT'S A WASTE OF TIME TO ASK.
WHAP...
FOUND YOU!
!

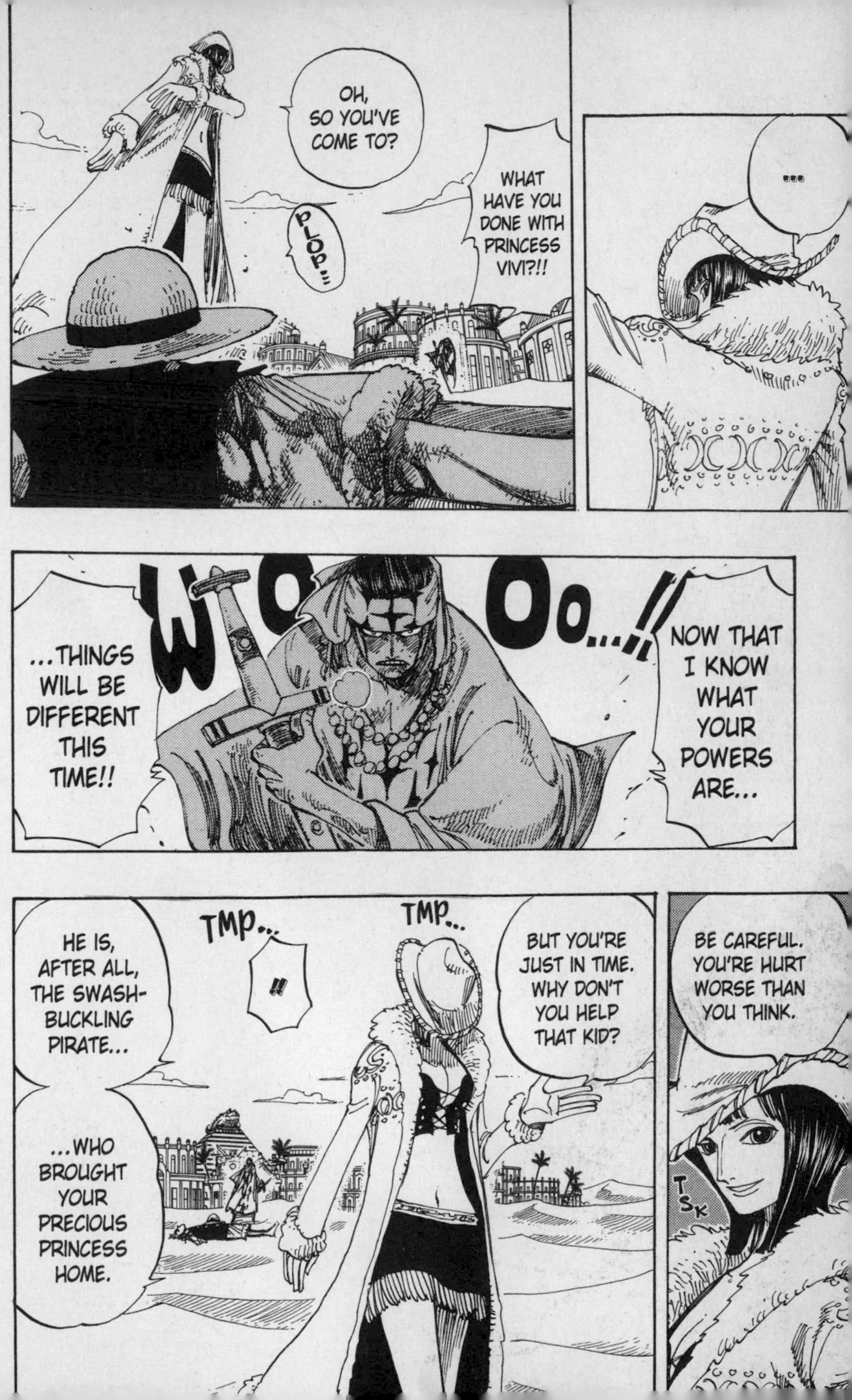
...
OH, SO YOU'VE COME TO?
WHAT HAVE YOU DONE WITH PRINCESS VIVI?!!
PLOP...
NOW THAT I KNOW WHAT YOUR POWERS ARE...
WOOOo...!!
...THINGS WILL BE DIFFERENT THIS TIME!!
BE CAREFUL. YOU'RE HURT WORSE THAN YOU THINK.
TSK
BUT YOU'RE JUST IN TIME. WHY DON'T YOU HELP THAT KID?
TMP...
TMP...
!!
HE IS, AFTER ALL, THE SWASH-BUCKLING PIRATE...
...WHO BROUGHT YOUR PRECIOUS PRINCESS HOME.

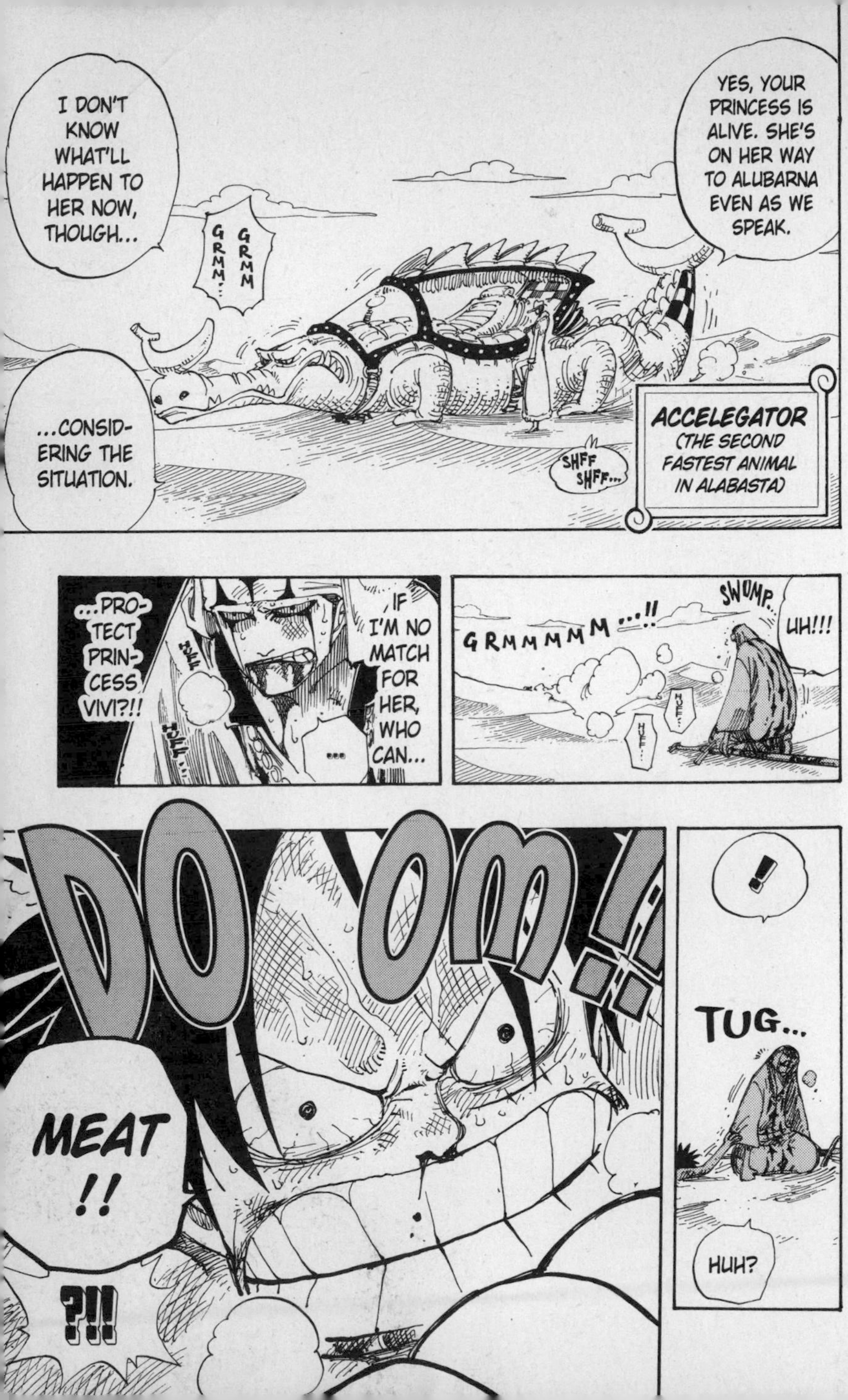
YES, YOUR PRINCESS IS ALIVE. SHE'S ON HER WAY TO ALUBARNA EVEN AS WE SPEAK.
ACCELEGATOR (THE SECOND FASTEST ANIMAL IN ALABASTA)
GRMM GRMM...
I DON'T KNOW WHAT'LL HAPPEN TO HER NOW, THOUGH...
SHFF SHFF...
...CONSID-ERING THE SITUATION.
SWOMP...
UH!!!
GRMMMMM...!!
HUFF...
HUFF...
IF I'M NO MATCH FOR HER, WHO CAN...
...PRO-TECT PRIN-CESS VIVI?!!
HUFF
HUFF...
...
!
TUG...
HUH?
DOOM!!
MEAT !!
?!!

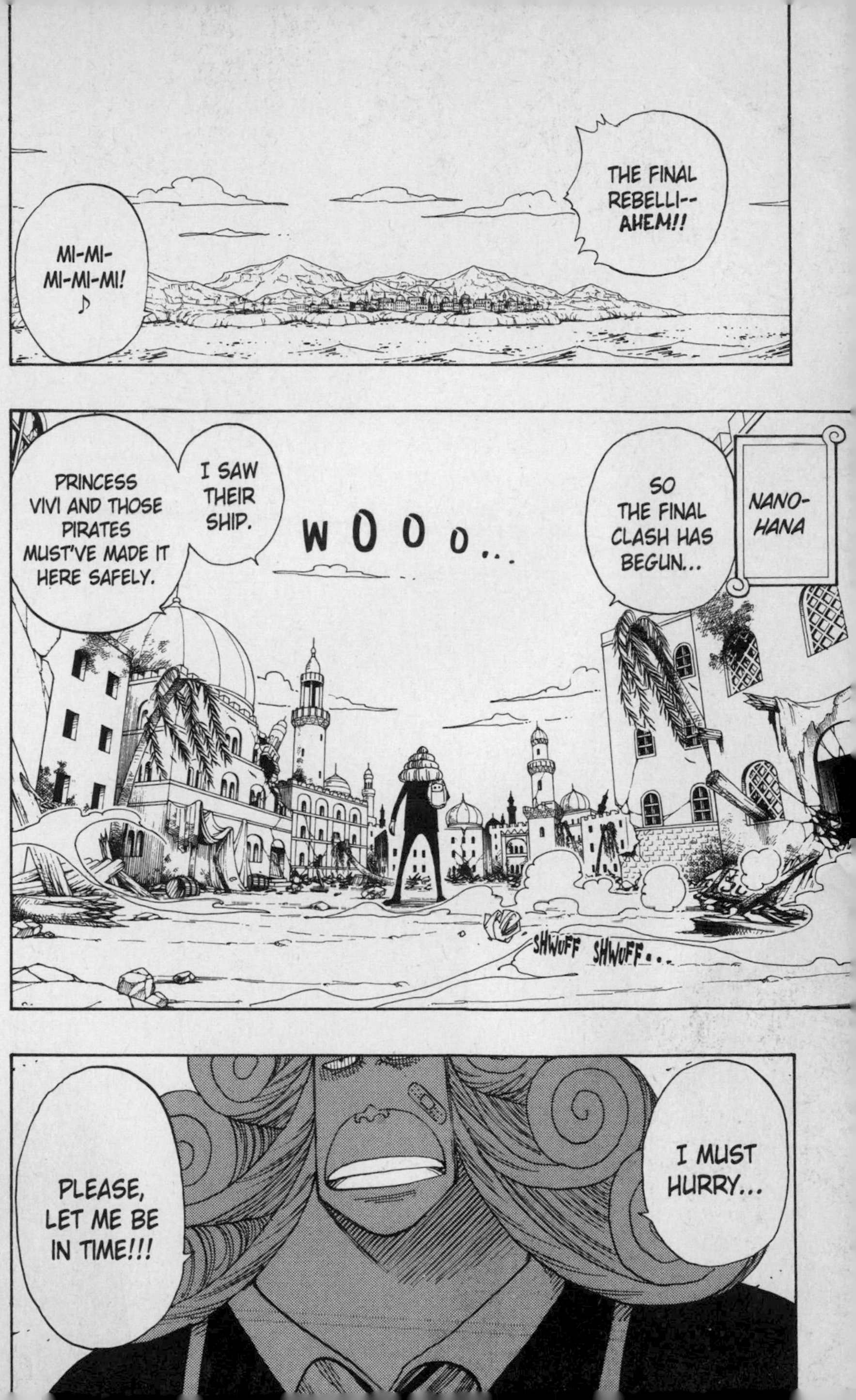
THE FINAL REBELLI-- AHEM!!
MI-MI-MI-MI-MI! ♪
NANO-HANA
SO THE FINAL CLASH HAS BEGUN...
WOOO...
I SAW THEIR SHIP.
PRINCESS VIVI AND THOSE PIRATES MUST'VE MADE IT HERE SAFELY.
SHWUFF SHWUFF...
I MUST HURRY...
PLEASE, LET ME BE IN TIME!!!

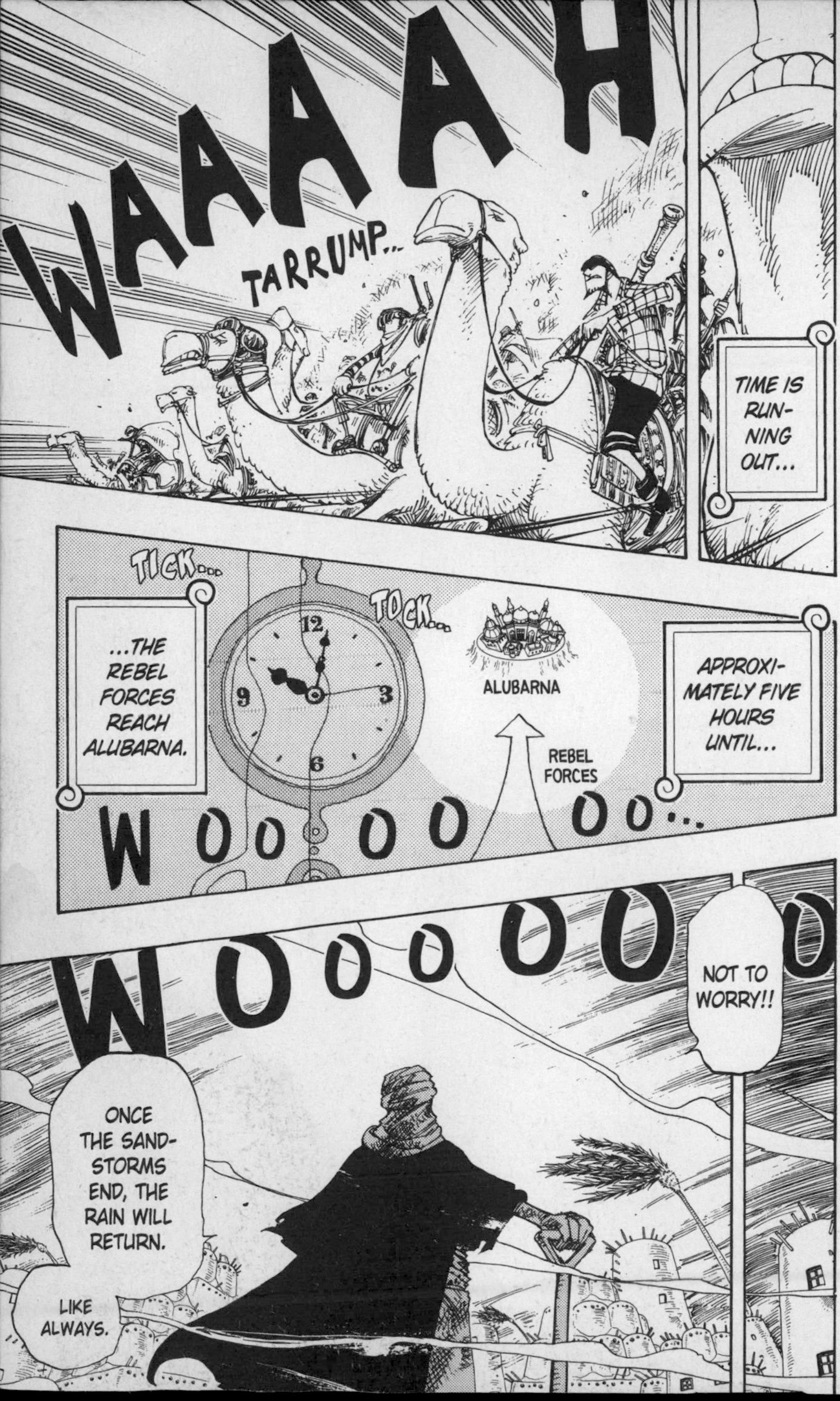
TIME IS RUN-NING OUT...
WAAAAH
TARRUMP...
APPROXI-MATELY FIVE HOURS UNTIL...
TOCK...
ALUBARNA
REBEL FORCES
TICK...
...THE REBEL FORCES REACH ALUBARNA.
WOOOO OO...
WOOOOOOO
NOT TO WORRY!!
ONCE THE SAND-STORMS END, THE RAIN WILL RETURN.
LIKE ALWAYS.

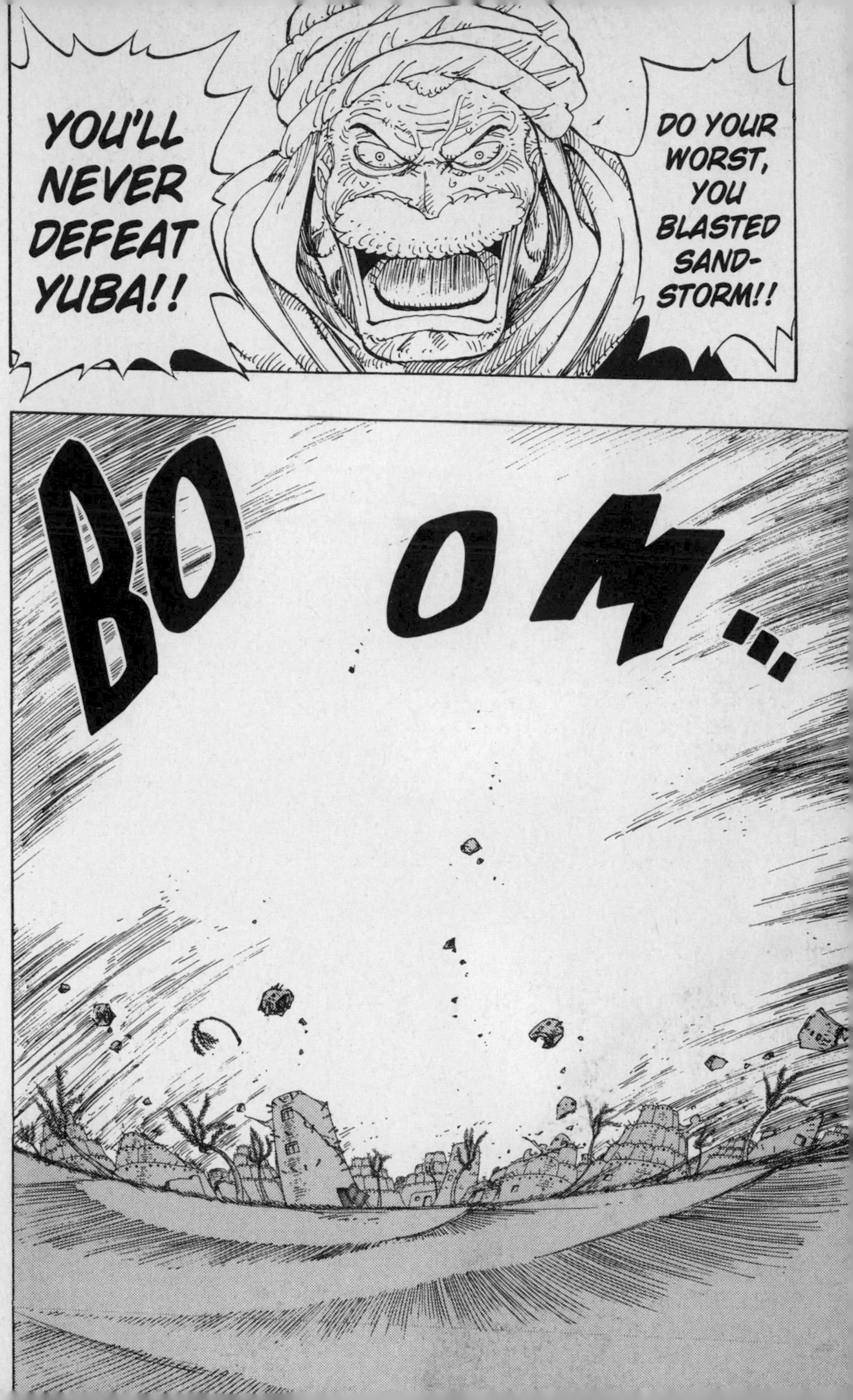
DO YOUR WORST, YOU BLASTED SAND-STORM!!
YOU'LL NEVER DEFEAT YUBA!!
BOOM...

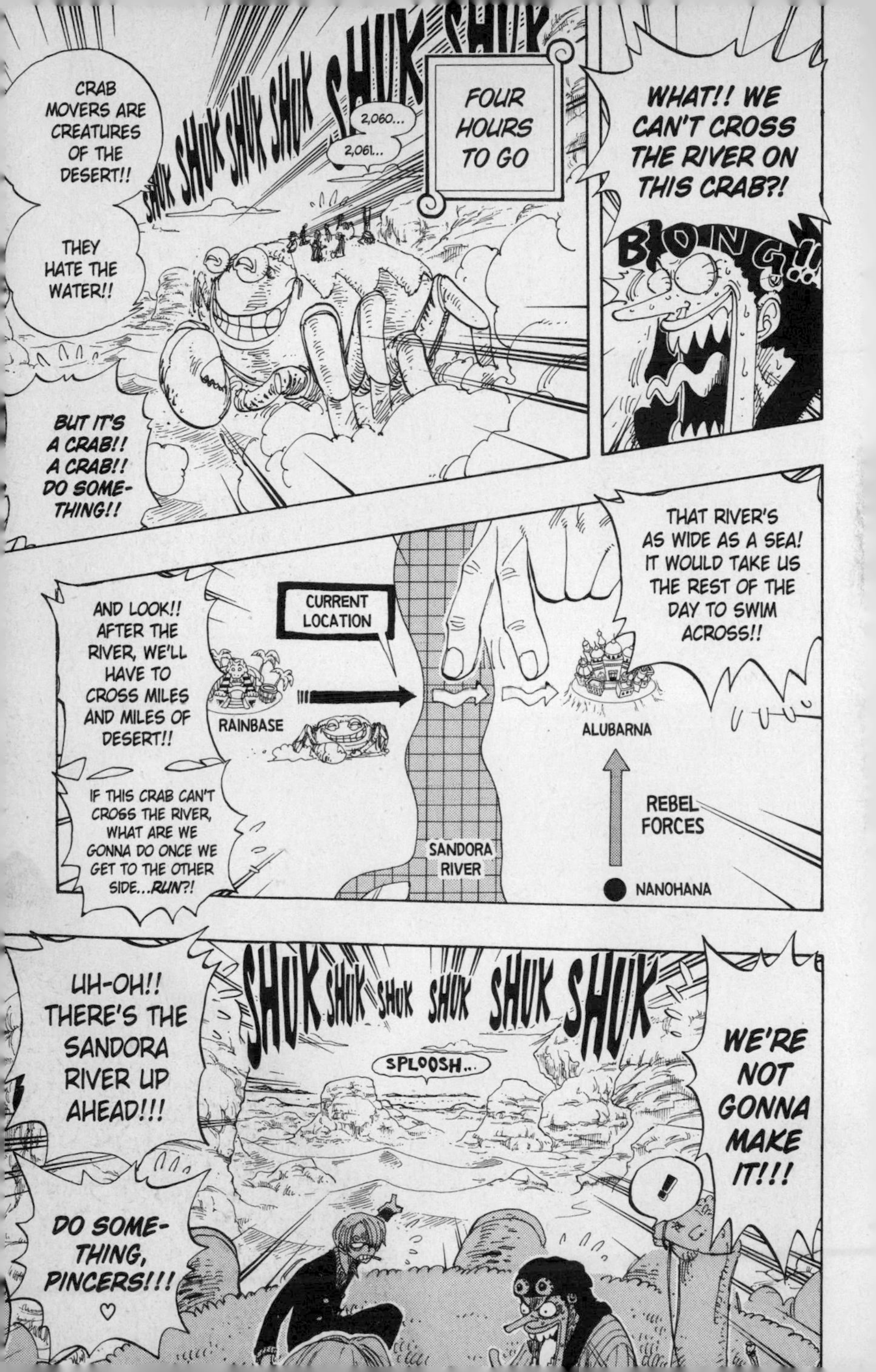
WHAT!! WE CAN'T CROSS THE RIVER ON THIS CRAB?!
BONG!!
FOUR HOURS TO GO
SHUK SHUK SHUK SHUK SHUK SHUK
2,060...
2,061...
CRAB MOVERS ARE CREATURES OF THE DESERT!!
THEY HATE THE WATER!!
BUT IT'S A CRAB!! A CRAB!! DO SOME-THING!!
THAT RIVER'S AS WIDE AS A SEA! IT WOULD TAKE US THE REST OF THE DAY TO SWIM ACROSS!!
ALUBARNA
REBEL FORCES
NANOHANA
SANDORA RIVER
CURRENT LOCATION
RAINBASE
AND LOOK!! AFTER THE RIVER, WE'LL HAVE TO CROSS MILES AND MILES OF DESERT!!
IF THIS CRAB CAN'T CROSS THE RIVER, WHAT ARE WE GONNA DO ONCE WE GET TO THE OTHER SIDE...RUN?!
WE'RE NOT GONNA MAKE IT!!!
SHUK SHUK SHUK SHUK SHUK SHUK
SPLOOSH..
!
UH-OH!! THERE'S THE SANDORA RIVER UP AHEAD!!!
DO SOME-THING, PINCERS!!! ♡

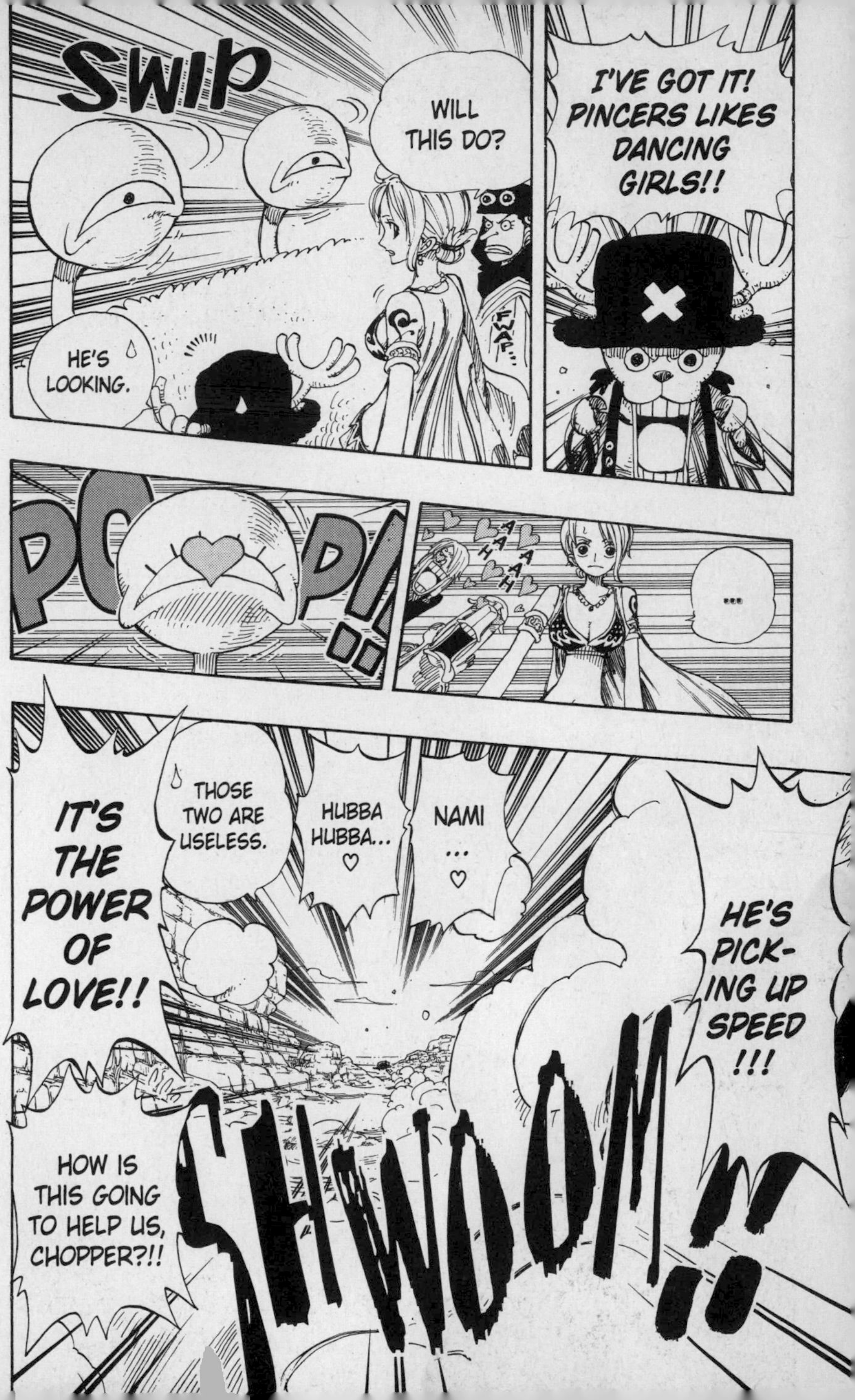
I'VE GOT IT! PINCERS LIKES DANCING GIRLS!!
WILL THIS DO?
SWIP
FWAP...
HE'S LOOKING.
...
POP!!
HE'S PICK-ING UP SPEED!!!
NAMI... ♡
HUBBA HUBBA... ♡
THOSE TWO ARE USELESS.
IT'S THE POWER OF LOVE!!
SHWOOM!!
HOW IS THIS GOING TO HELP US, CHOPPER?!!

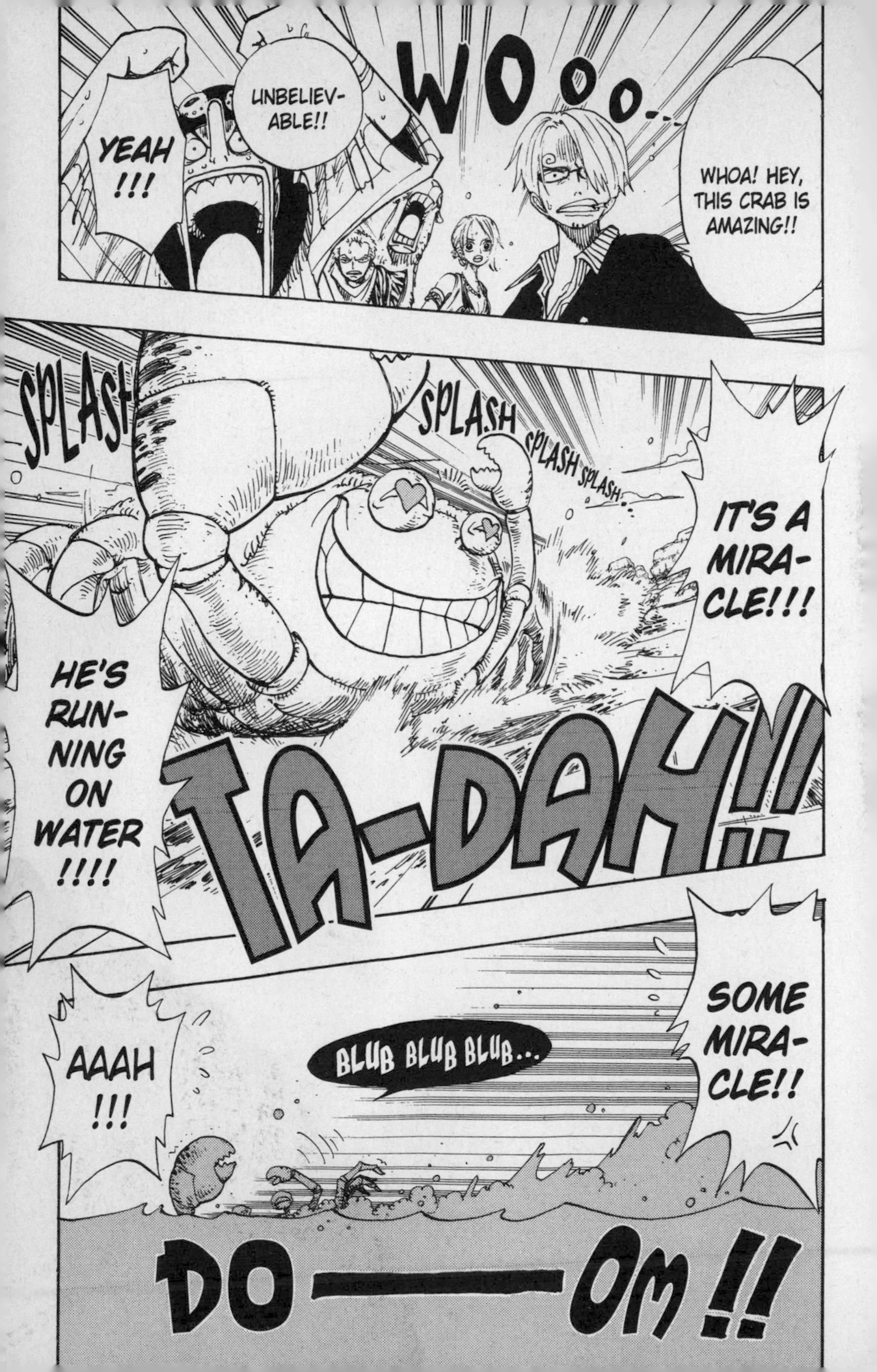
WHOA! HEY, THIS CRAB IS AMAZING!!
WOOO...
UNBELIEV-ABLE!!
YEAH!!!
IT'S A MIRA-CLE!!!
SPLASH SPLASH SPLASH
SPLASH
SPLASH
TA-DAH!!
HE'S RUN-NING ON WATER!!!!
SOME MIRA-CLE!!
BLUB BLUB BLUB...
AAAH!!!
DO——OM!!

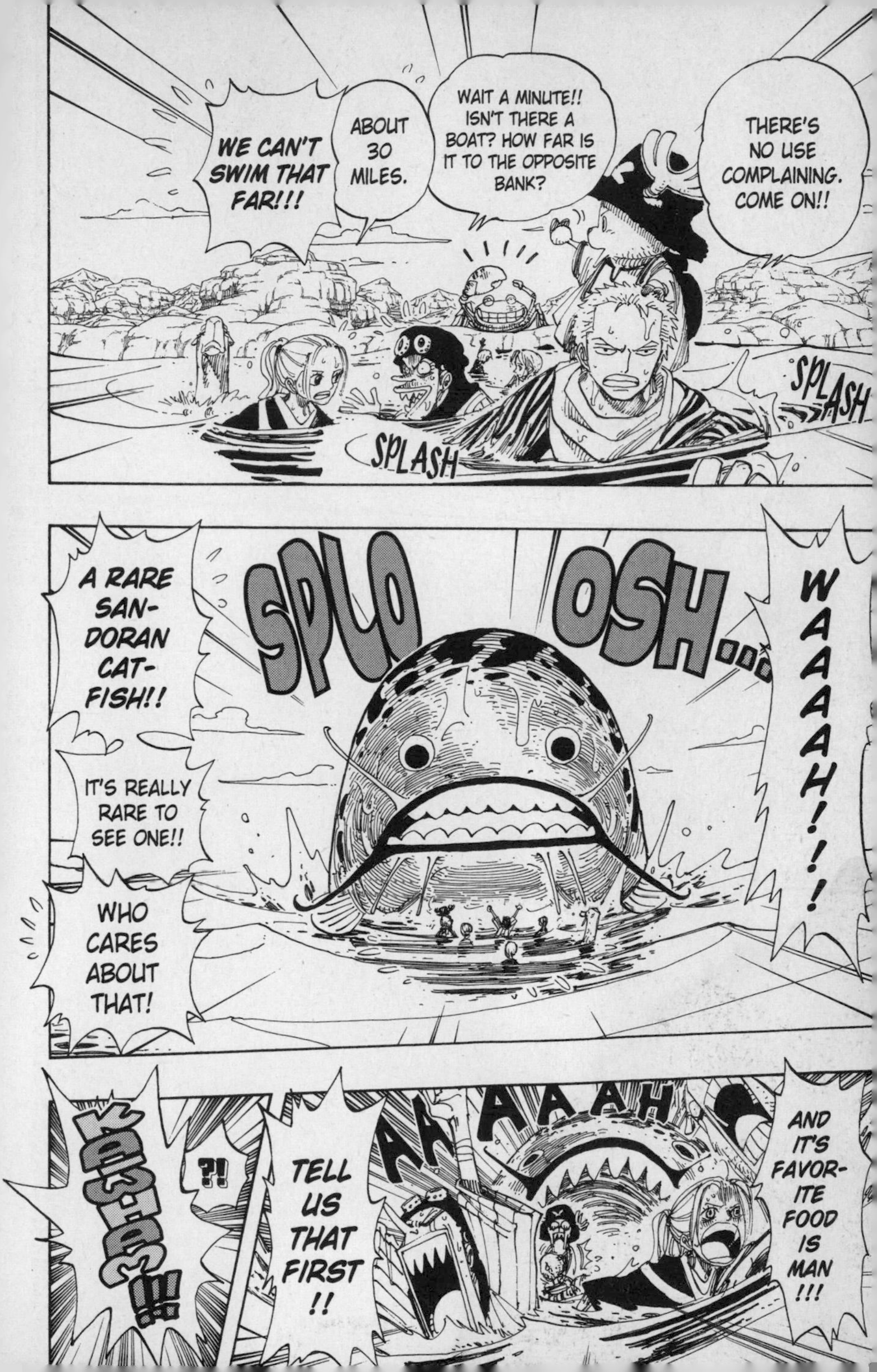
THERE'S NO USE COMPLAINING. COME ON!!
WAIT A MINUTE!! ISN'T THERE A BOAT? HOW FAR IS IT TO THE OPPOSITE BANK?
ABOUT 30 MILES.
WE CAN'T SWIM THAT FAR!!!
SPLASH
SPLASH
WAAAAAH!!!
SPLO OSH...
A RARE SAN-DORAN CAT-FISH!!
IT'S REALLY RARE TO SEE ONE!!
WHO CARES ABOUT THAT!
AND IT'S FAVORITE-ITE FOOD IS MAN!!!
AAAAAH
TELL US THAT FIRST!!
?!

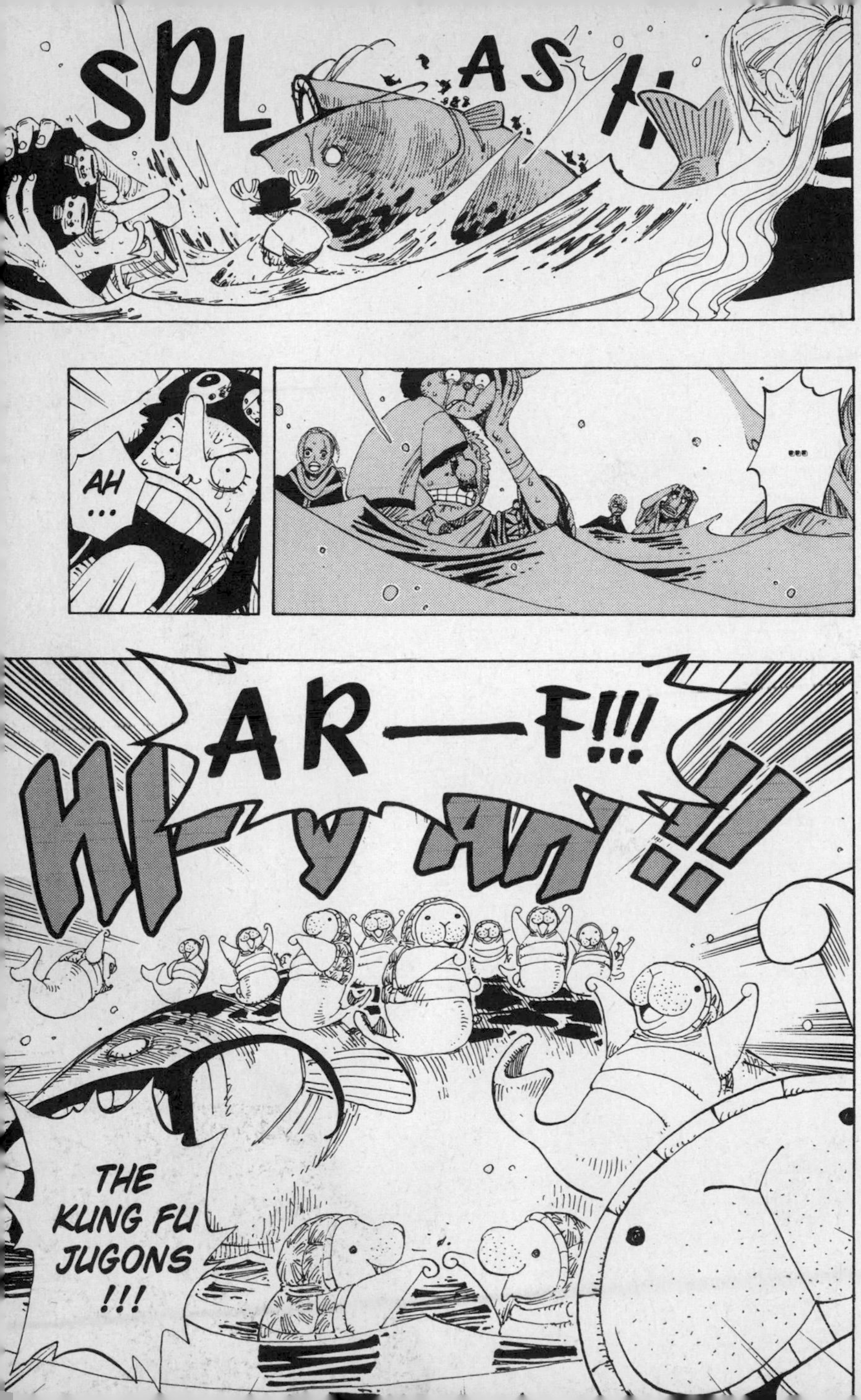
SPLASH
...
AH ...
AR——F!!!
HI-YAH!!
THE KUNG FU JUGONS !!!

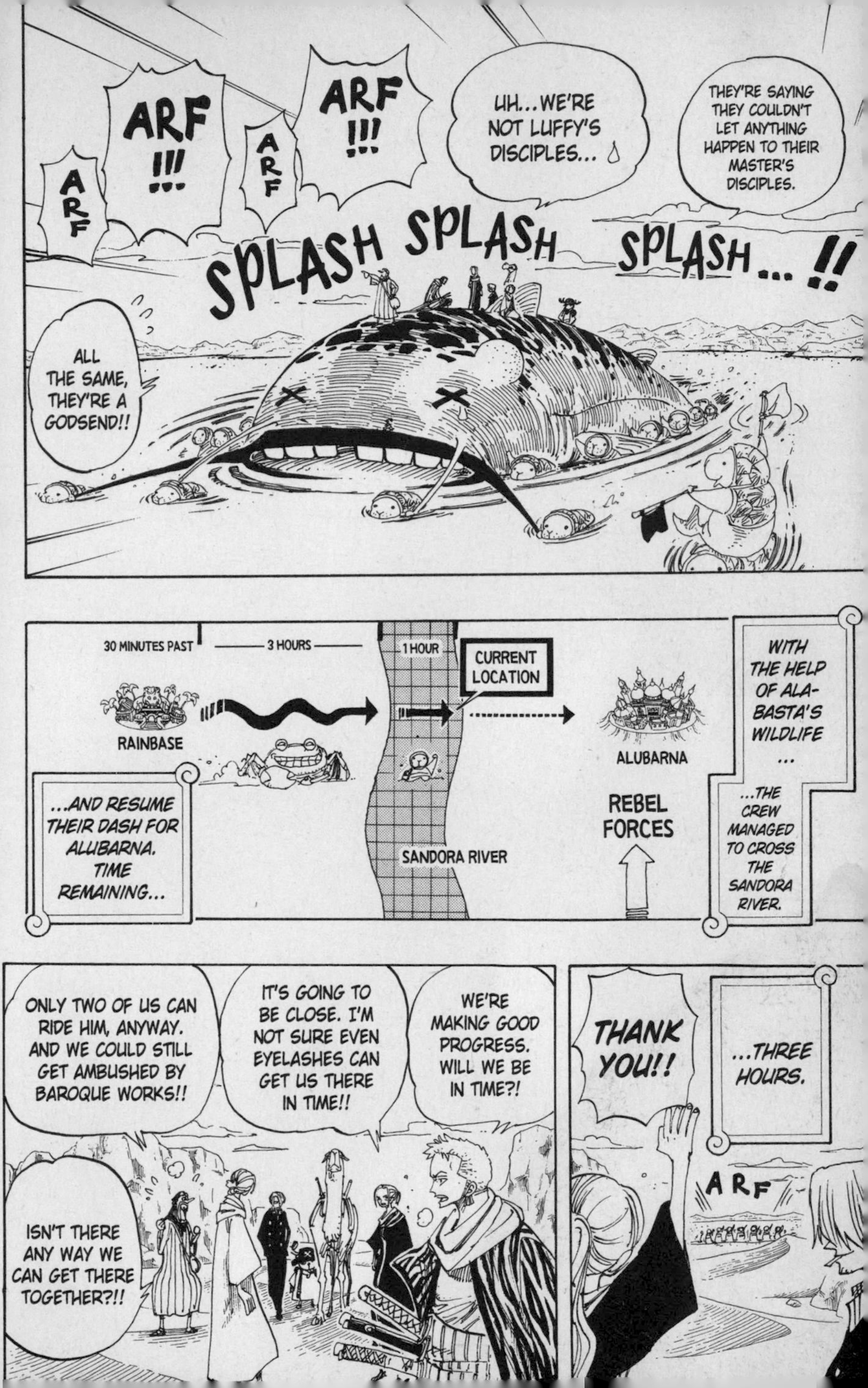
THEY'RE SAYING THEY COULDN'T LET ANYTHING HAPPEN TO THEIR MASTER'S DISCIPLES.
UH...WE'RE NOT LUFFY'S DISCIPLES...
ARF !!!
ARF
ARF !!!
ARF
SPLASH SPLASH SPLASH...!!
ALL THE SAME, THEY'RE A GODSEND!!
WITH THE HELP OF ALABASTA'S WILDLIFE...
...THE CREW MANAGED TO CROSS THE SANDORA RIVER.
CURRENT LOCATION
ALUBARNA
REBEL FORCES
SANDORA RIVER
1 HOUR
3 HOURS
30 MINUTES PAST
RAINBASE
...AND RESUME THEIR DASH FOR ALUBARNA. TIME REMAINING...
...THREE HOURS.
ARF
THANK YOU!!
WE'RE MAKING GOOD PROGRESS. WILL WE BE IN TIME?!
IT'S GOING TO BE CLOSE. I'M NOT SURE EVEN EYELASHES CAN GET US THERE IN TIME!!
ONLY TWO OF US CAN RIDE HIM, ANYWAY. AND WE COULD STILL GET AMBUSHED BY BAROQUE WORKS!!
ISN'T THERE ANY WAY WE CAN GET THERE TOGETHER?!!

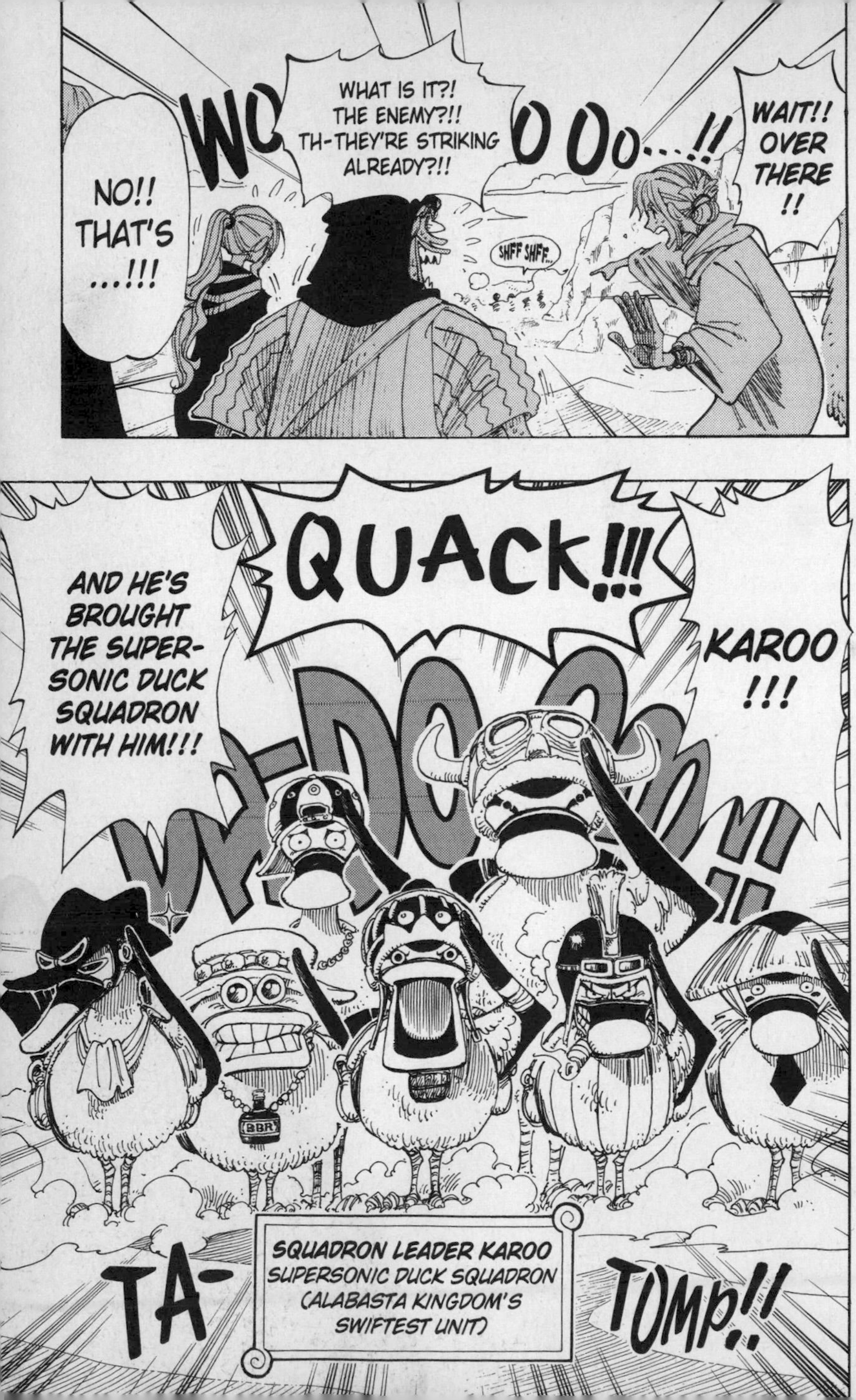
WAIT!! OVER THERE !!
WHAT IS IT?! THE ENEMY?!! TH-THEY'RE STRIKING ALREADY?!!
WOOOOo...!!
SHFF SHFF...
NO!! THAT'S ...!!!
KAROO !!!
QUACK!!!
AND HE'S BROUGHT THE SUPER-SONIC DUCK SQUADRON WITH HIM!!!
BBR
SQUADRON LEADER KAROO
SUPERSONIC DUCK SQUADRON
(ALABASTA KINGDOM'S
SWIFTEST UNIT)
TA-
TOMP!!

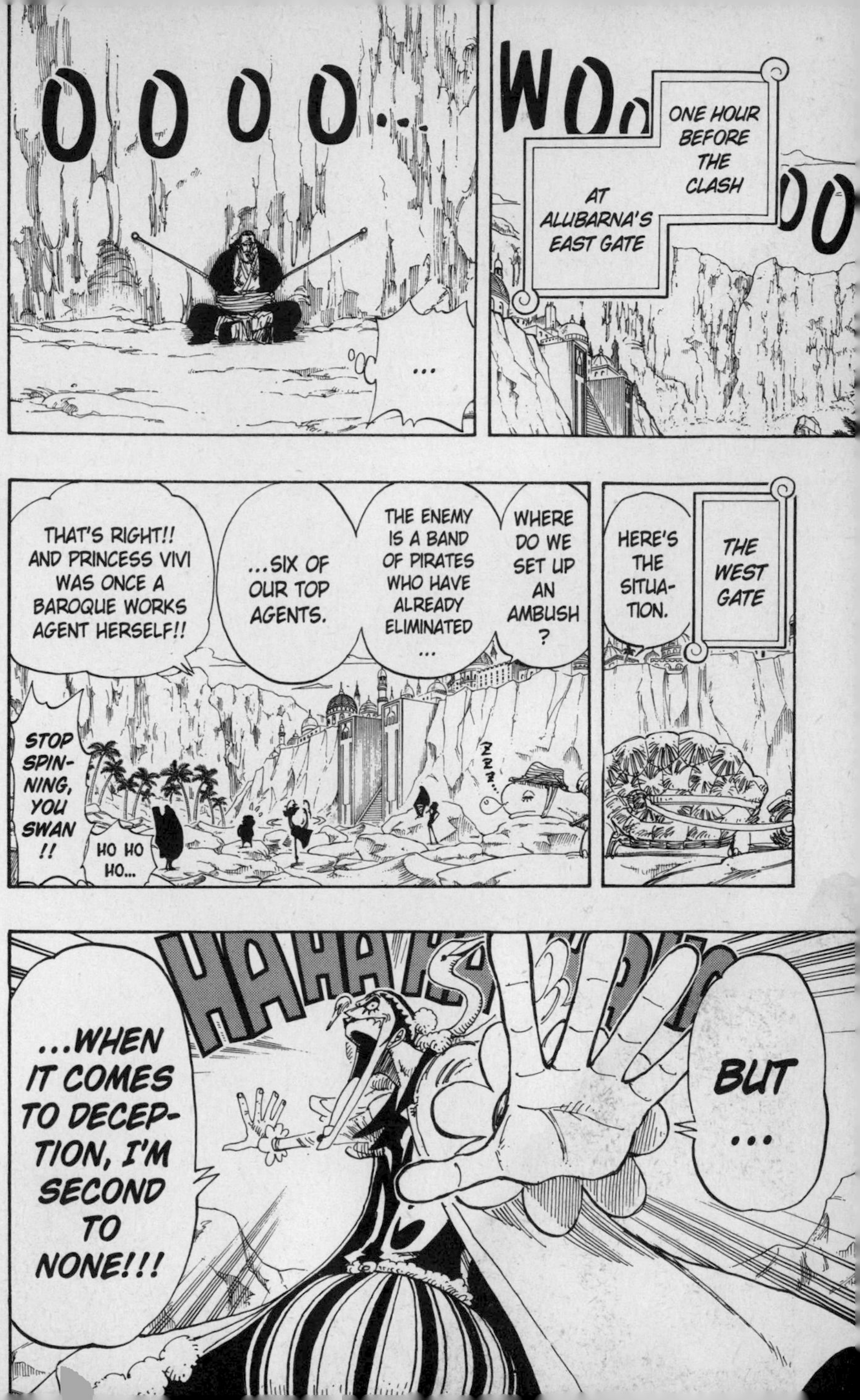
WOO
OO
ONE HOUR BEFORE THE CLASH
AT ALUBARNA'S EAST GATE
OOOO...
...
THE WEST GATE
HERE'S THE SITUATION.
WHERE DO WE SET UP AN AMBUSH?
THE ENEMY IS A BAND OF PIRATES WHO HAVE ALREADY ELIMINATED...
...SIX OF OUR TOP AGENTS.
THAT'S RIGHT!! AND PRINCESS VIVI WAS ONCE A BAROQUE WORKS AGENT HERSELF!!
STOP SPINNING, YOU SWAN!!
HO HO HO...
HAHA
BUT...
...WHEN IT COMES TO DECEPTION, I'M SECOND TO NONE!!!

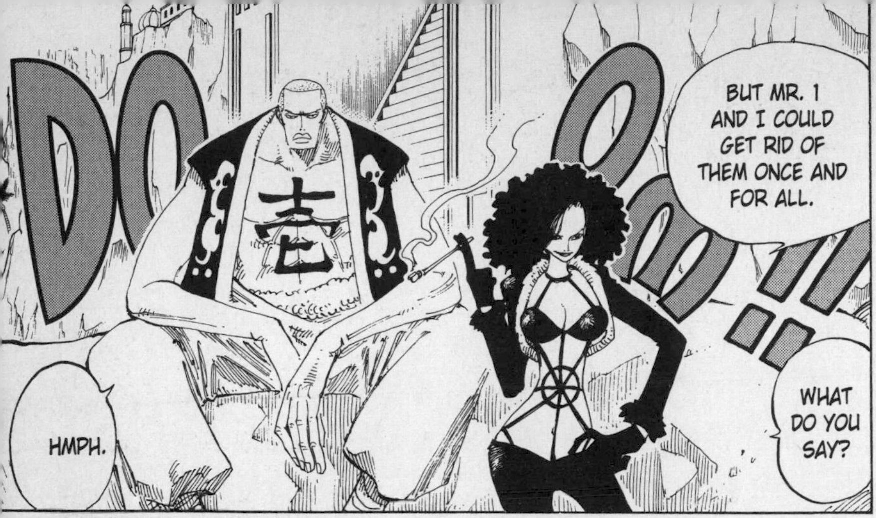
BUT MR. 1 AND I COULD GET RID OF THEM ONCE AND FOR ALL.
WHAT DO YOU SAY?
HMPH.

*TEXT ON CHEST SAYS "ONE" - ED.

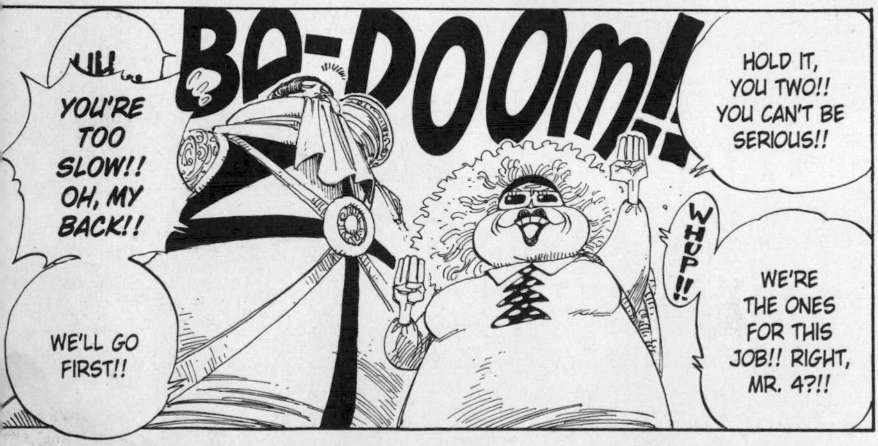
HOLD IT, YOU TWO!! YOU CAN'T BE SERIOUS!!
BE-DOOM!!
WHUP!!
WE'RE THE ONES FOR THIS JOB!! RIGHT, MR. 4?!!
UH...
YOU'RE TOO SLOW!! OH, MY BACK!!
WE'LL GO FIRST!!

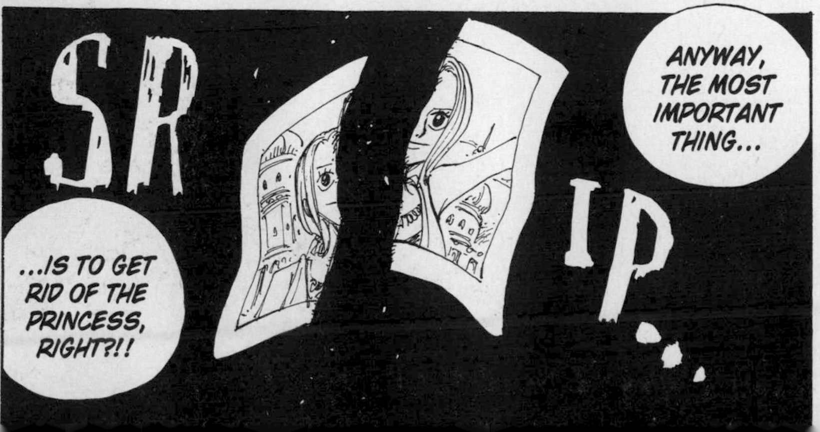
ANYWAY, THE MOST IMPORTANT THING...
SRIP
...IS TO GET RID OF THE PRINCESS, RIGHT?!!

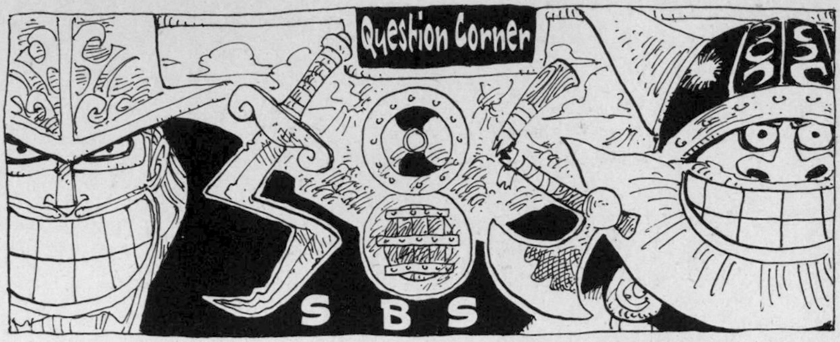
Question Corner
SBS

Q: A friend said to me, "You're a girl! Why are you reading *Shonen Jump*!!" So I said, "Why shouldn't a girl read *Shonen Jump*? Is it against the law? I was a boy in my previous life!!!" (Probably.)

A: I see. So you had an argument over that, did you, "Ms. West"? Well, don't you worry! It's okay!! You see, *Shonen Jump* is a boy's magazine whose readership is 30 percent girls. It's true. Three out of every ten *Jump* readers are girls. And it's a similar percentage for *One Piece* readers. So think of it as having about 1.2 million comrades (according to my rough calculations) throughout Japan. As long as they understand a boy's fiery spirit, boys, girls, old guys and old ladies are all welcome, darn it!!

Q: Oda Sensei! There was a music question on my final exam the other day! As I worked through the questions, Bach's name suddenly appeared. Bach was a baroque composer. Could it be that Igaram, who looks like Bach, and the baroque school inspired Baroque Works?!! That's it, isn't it?

A:

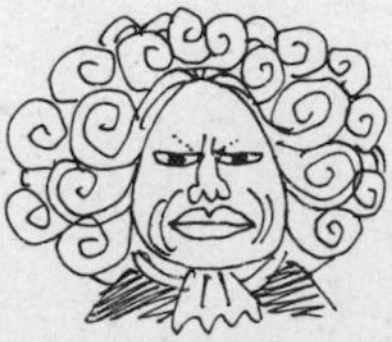

Bach
(rough sketch)

That's right. But this is extremely difficult to explain. Baroque is a style of art, literature and music that became popular in Europe during about the 17th century. This is just my own interpretation, but the baroque style was unnecessarily ostentatious and excessively ornamental. That's why Baroque Works is made up of such flamboyant characters.

Chapter 181: SUPERSONIC DUCK QUIZ

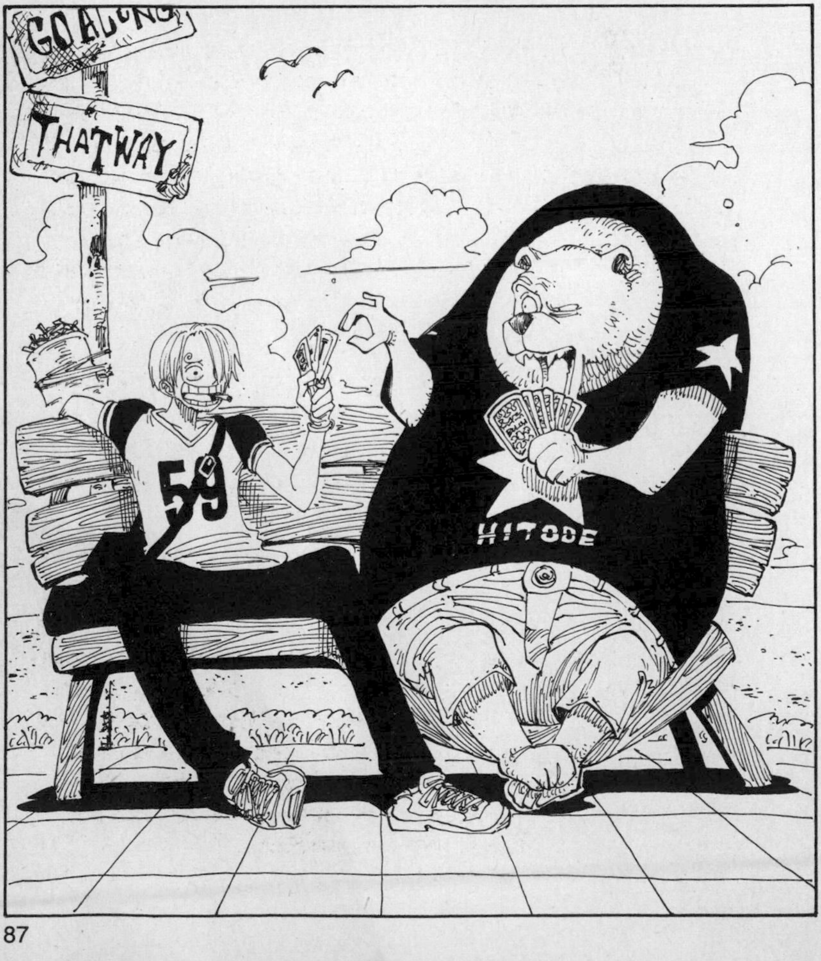
GO ALONG
THAT WAY
59
HITODE

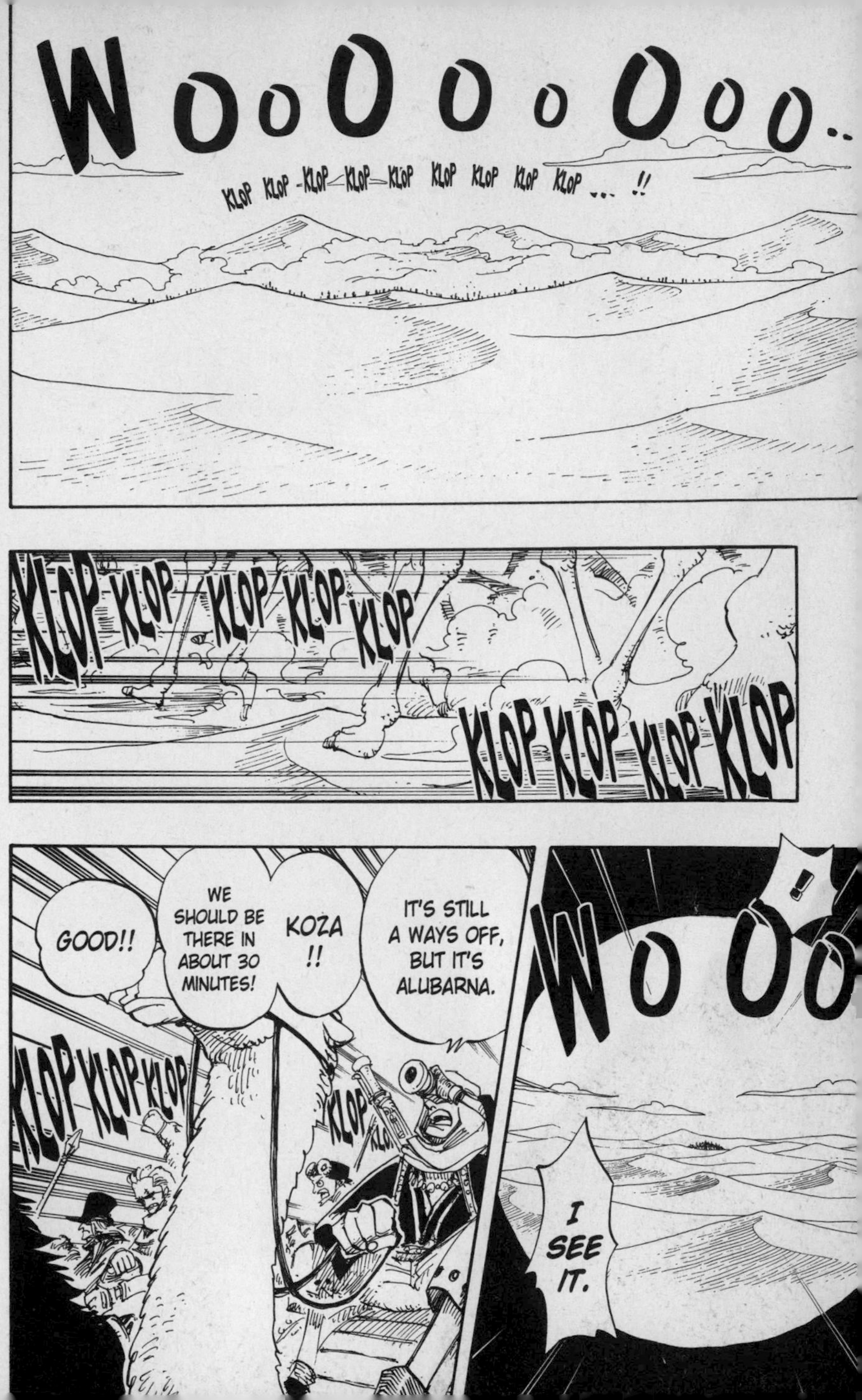
WOOOOOOOOO..
KLOP KLOP KLOP KLOP KLOP KLOP KLOP KLOP KLOP ... !!
KLOP KLOP KLOP KLOP KLOP
KLOP KLOP KLOP KLOP
WO OO
!
I SEE IT.
IT'S STILL A WAYS OFF, BUT IT'S ALUBARNA.
KOZA !!
WE SHOULD BE THERE IN ABOUT 30 MINUTES!
GOOD!!
KLOP KLOP KLOP
KLOP

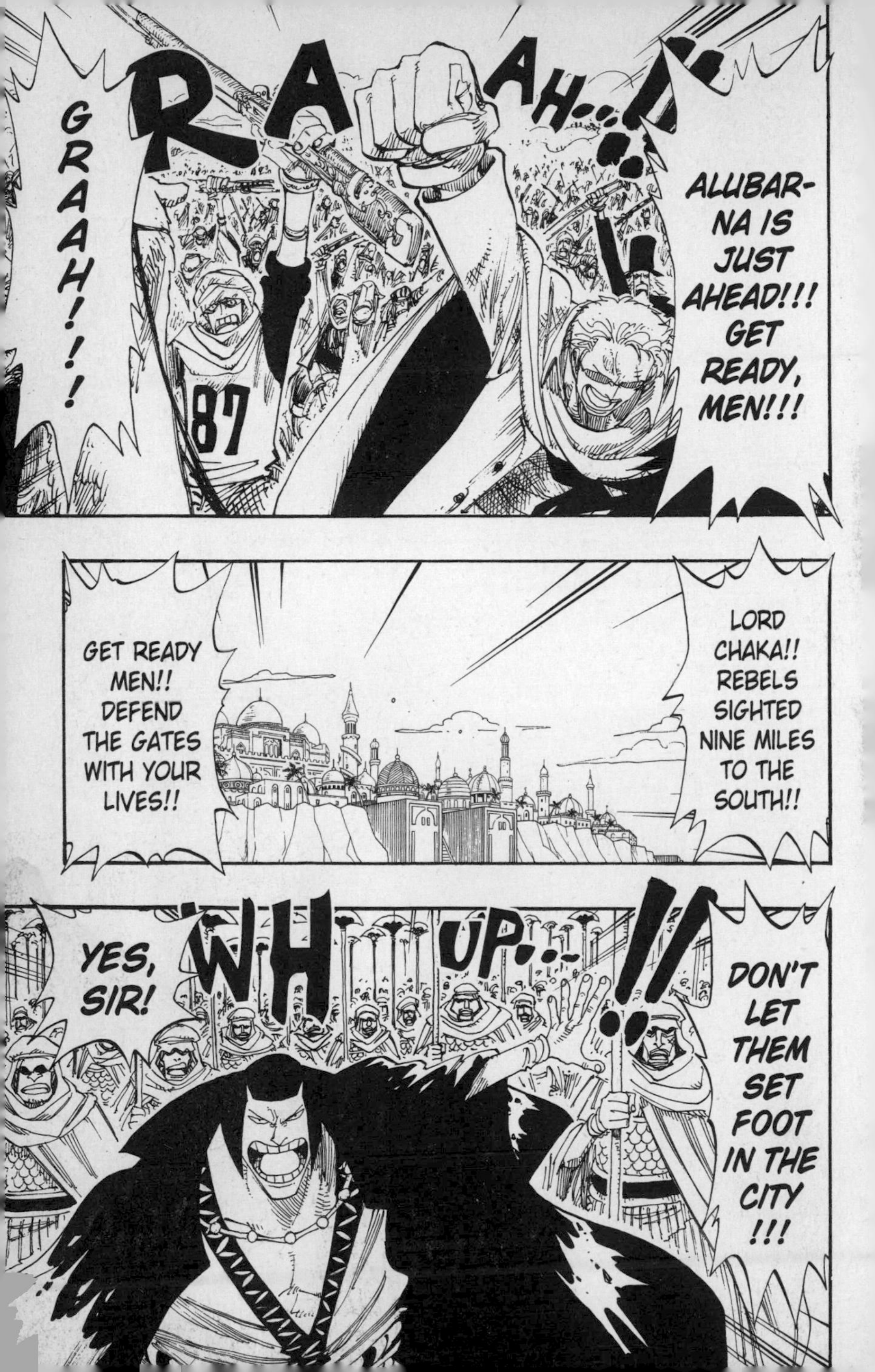
ALUBARNA IS JUST AHEAD!!! GET READY, MEN!!!
RAAH...!!
GRAAH!!!
87
LORD CHAKA!! REBELS SIGHTED NINE MILES TO THE SOUTH!!
GET READY MEN!! DEFEND THE GATES WITH YOUR LIVES!!
DON'T LET THEM SET FOOT IN THE CITY!!!
WHUP...!!
YES, SIR!

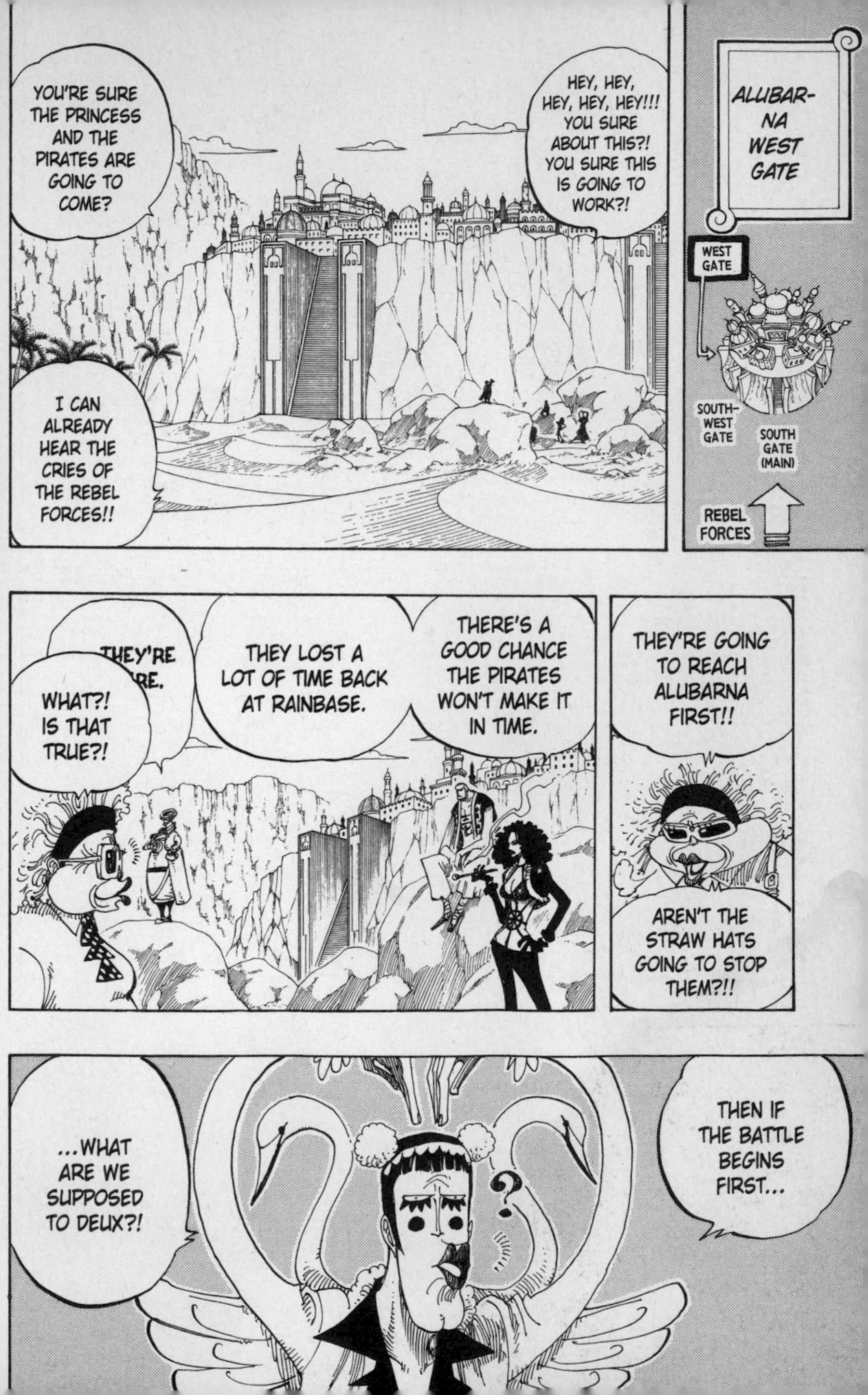
ALUBARNA WEST GATE
WEST GATE
SOUTH-WEST GATE
SOUTH GATE (MAIN)
REBEL FORCES
HEY, HEY, HEY, HEY, HEY!!! YOU SURE ABOUT THIS?! YOU SURE THIS IS GOING TO WORK?!
YOU'RE SURE THE PRINCESS AND THE PIRATES ARE GOING TO COME?
I CAN ALREADY HEAR THE CRIES OF THE REBEL FORCES!!
THEY'RE GOING TO REACH ALUBARNA FIRST!!
AREN'T THE STRAW HATS GOING TO STOP THEM?!!
THERE'S A GOOD CHANCE THE PIRATES WON'T MAKE IT IN TIME.
THEY LOST A LOT OF TIME BACK AT RAINBASE.
THEY'RE
WHAT?! IS THAT TRUE?!
THEN IF THE BATTLE BEGINS FIRST...
...WHAT ARE WE SUPPOSED TO DEUX?!

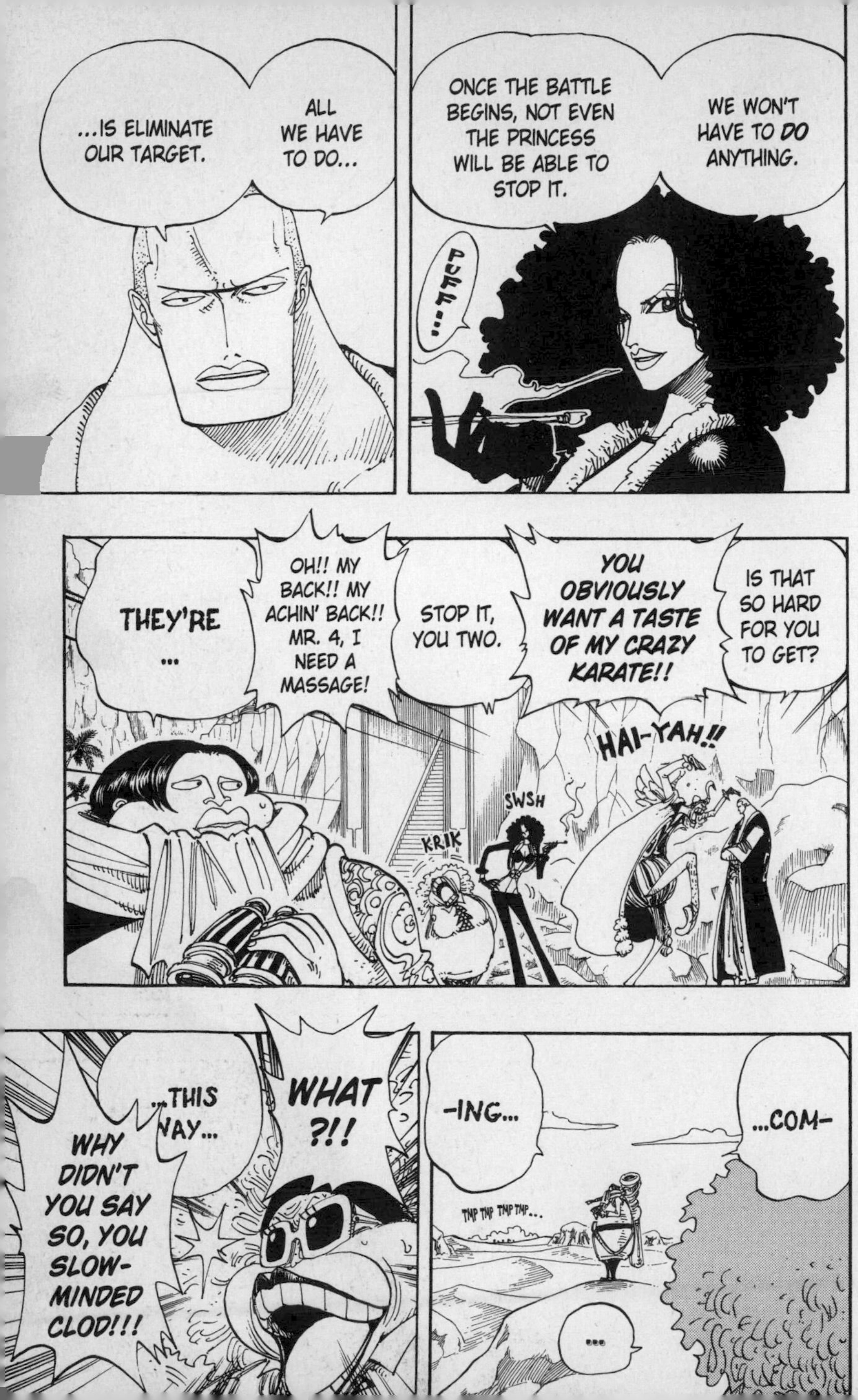
WE WON'T HAVE TO DO ANYTHING.
ONCE THE BATTLE BEGINS, NOT EVEN THE PRINCESS WILL BE ABLE TO STOP IT.
PUFF...
ALL WE HAVE TO DO...
...IS ELIMINATE OUR TARGET.
IS THAT SO HARD FOR YOU TO GET?
YOU OBVIOUSLY WANT A TASTE OF MY CRAZY KARATE!!
STOP IT, YOU TWO.
OH!! MY BACK!! MY ACHIN' BACK!! MR. 4, I NEED A MASSAGE!
THEY'RE ...
HAI-YAH!!
SWSH
KRIK
...COM-
-ING...
TMP TMP TMP TMP...
...
WHAT ?!!
...THIS WAY...
WHY DIDN'T YOU SAY SO, YOU SLOW-MINDED CLOD!!!

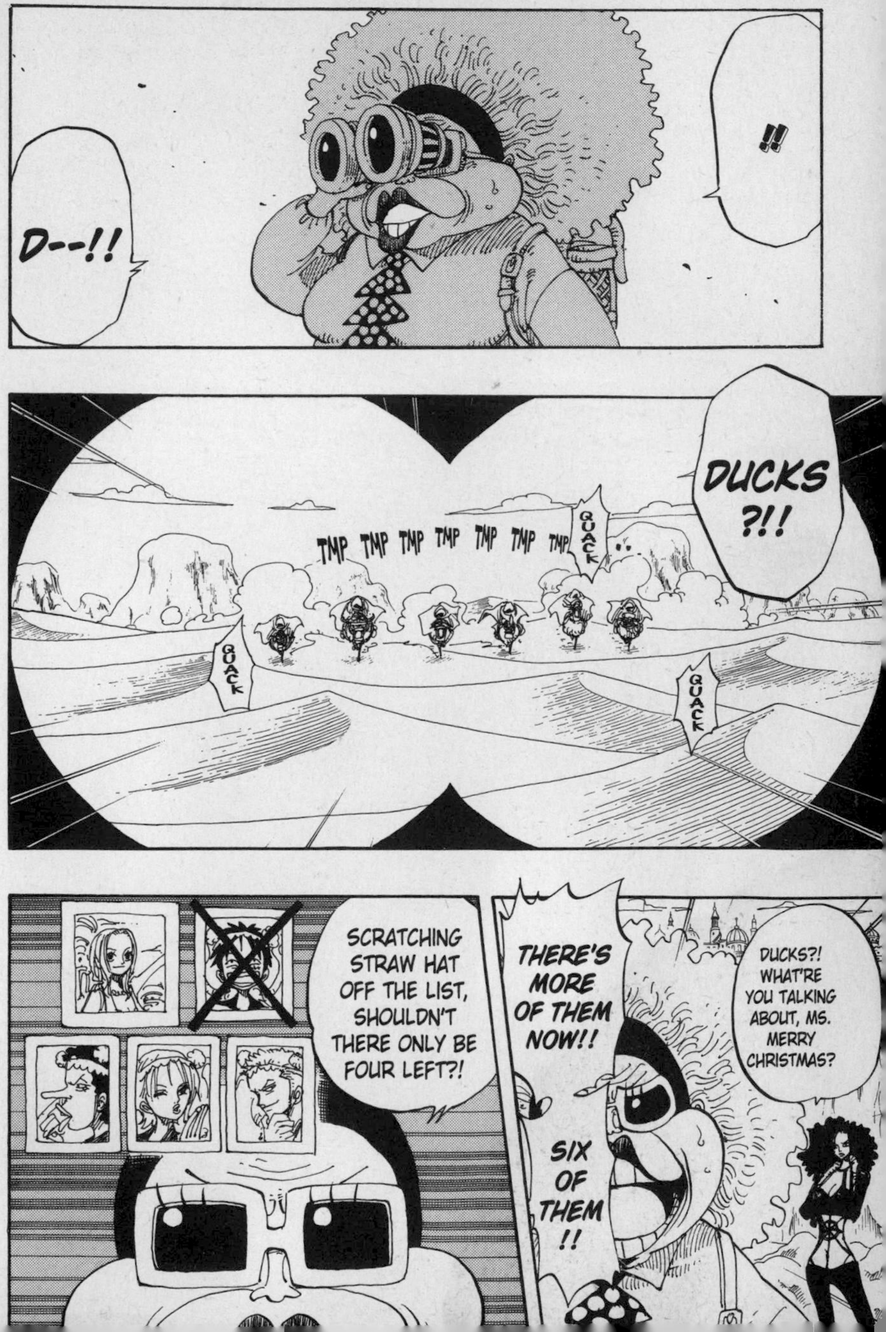
!!
D--!!
DUCKS ?!!
QUACK
TMP TMP TMP TMP TMP TMP TMP
QUACK
QUACK
DUCKS?! WHAT'RE YOU TALKING ABOUT, MS. MERRY CHRISTMAS?
THERE'S MORE OF THEM NOW!!
SIX OF THEM !!
SCRATCHING STRAW HAT OFF THE LIST, SHOULDN'T THERE ONLY BE FOUR LEFT?!

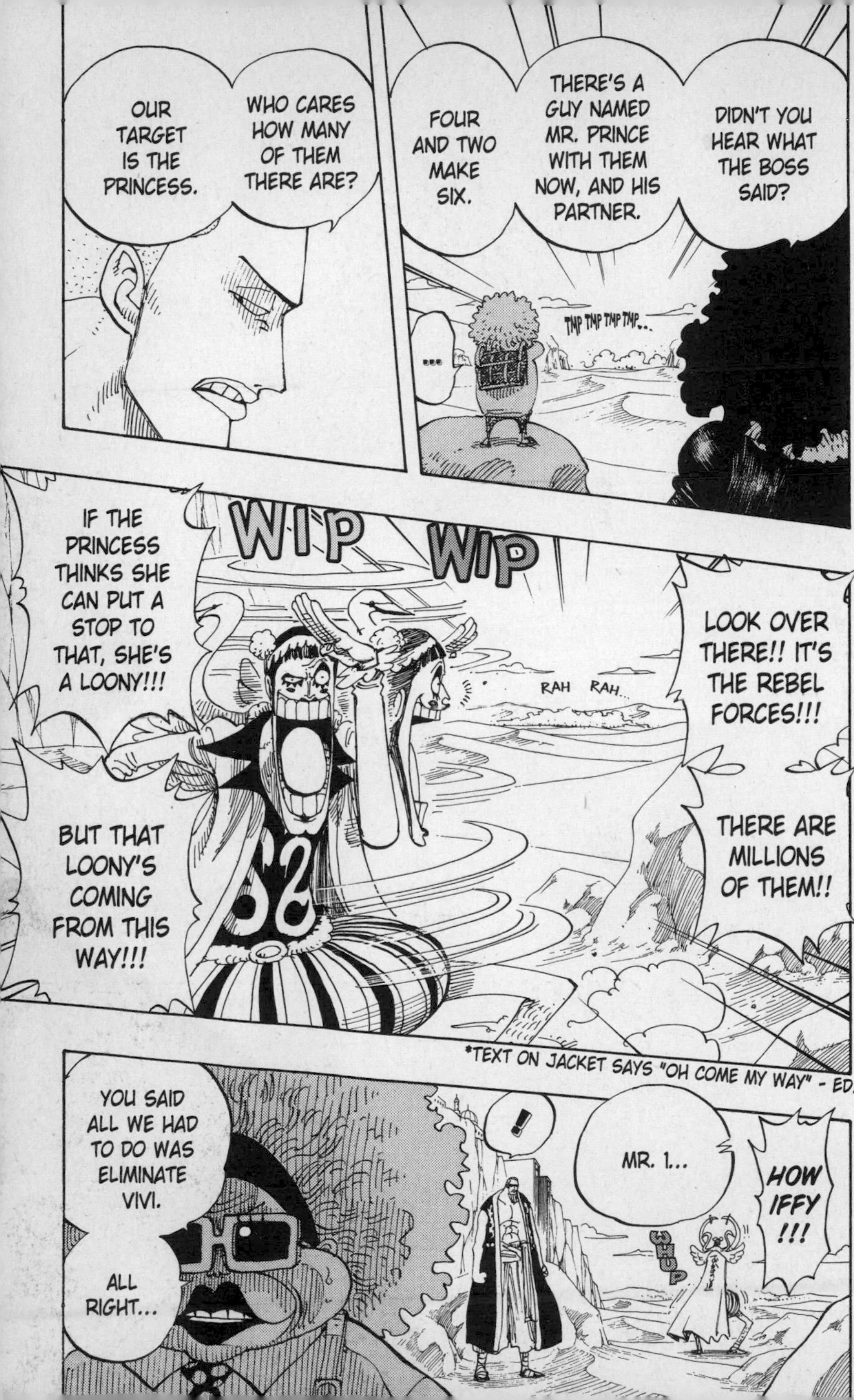
DIDN'T YOU HEAR WHAT THE BOSS SAID?
THERE'S A GUY NAMED MR. PRINCE WITH THEM NOW, AND HIS PARTNER.
FOUR AND TWO MAKE SIX.
TMP TMP TMP TMP...
...
WHO CARES HOW MANY OF THEM THERE ARE?
OUR TARGET IS THE PRINCESS.
LOOK OVER THERE!! IT'S THE REBEL FORCES!!!
THERE ARE MILLIONS OF THEM!!
RAH RAH...
WIP WIP
IF THE PRINCESS THINKS SHE CAN PUT A STOP TO THAT, SHE'S A LOONY!!!
BUT THAT LOONY'S COMING FROM THIS WAY!!!
HOW IFFY!!!
MR. 1...
!
YOU SAID ALL WE HAD TO DO WAS ELIMINATE VIVI.
ALL RIGHT...
*TEXT ON JACKET SAYS "OH COME MY WAY" - ED.

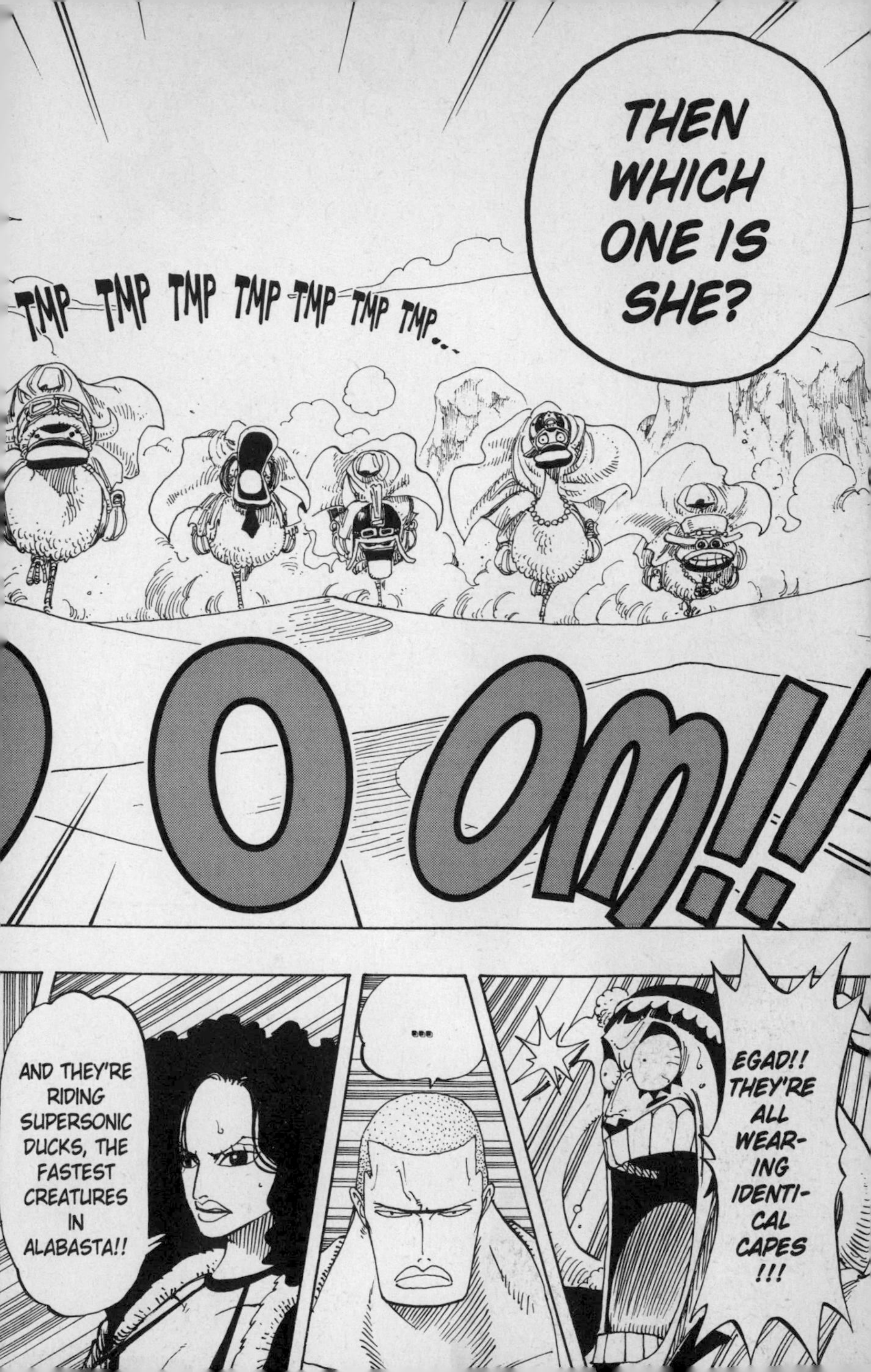
THEN WHICH ONE IS SHE?
TMP TMP TMP TMP TMP TMP TMP...
OOM!!
EGAD!! THEY'RE ALL WEAR-ING IDENTI-CAL CAPES!!!
...
AND THEY'RE RIDING SUPERSONIC DUCKS, THE FASTEST CREATURES IN ALABASTA!!

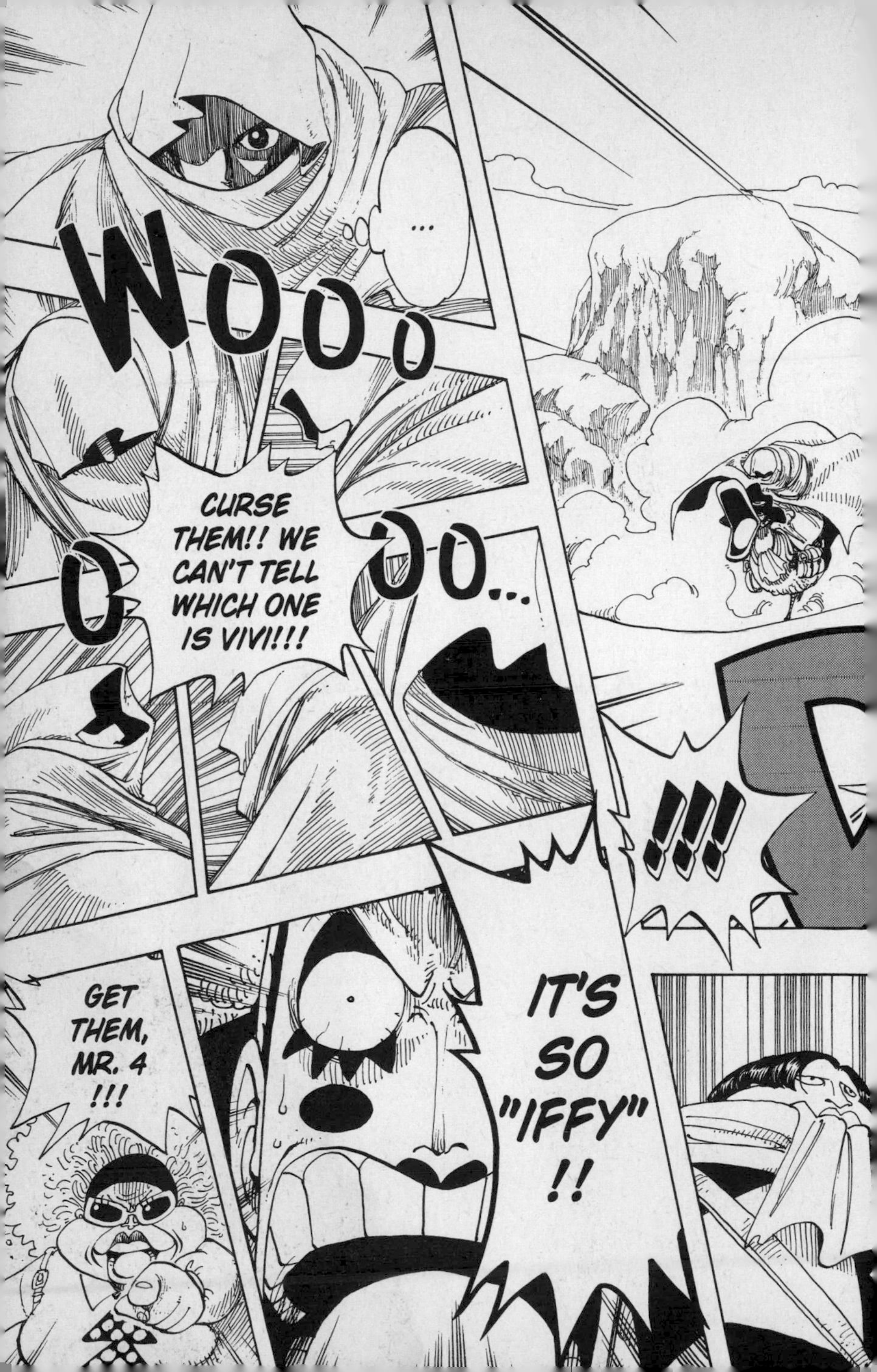
...
WOOOO
OOO...
CURSE THEM!! WE CAN'T TELL WHICH ONE IS VIVI!!!
!!!
IT'S SO "IFFY" !!
GET THEM, MR. 4 !!!

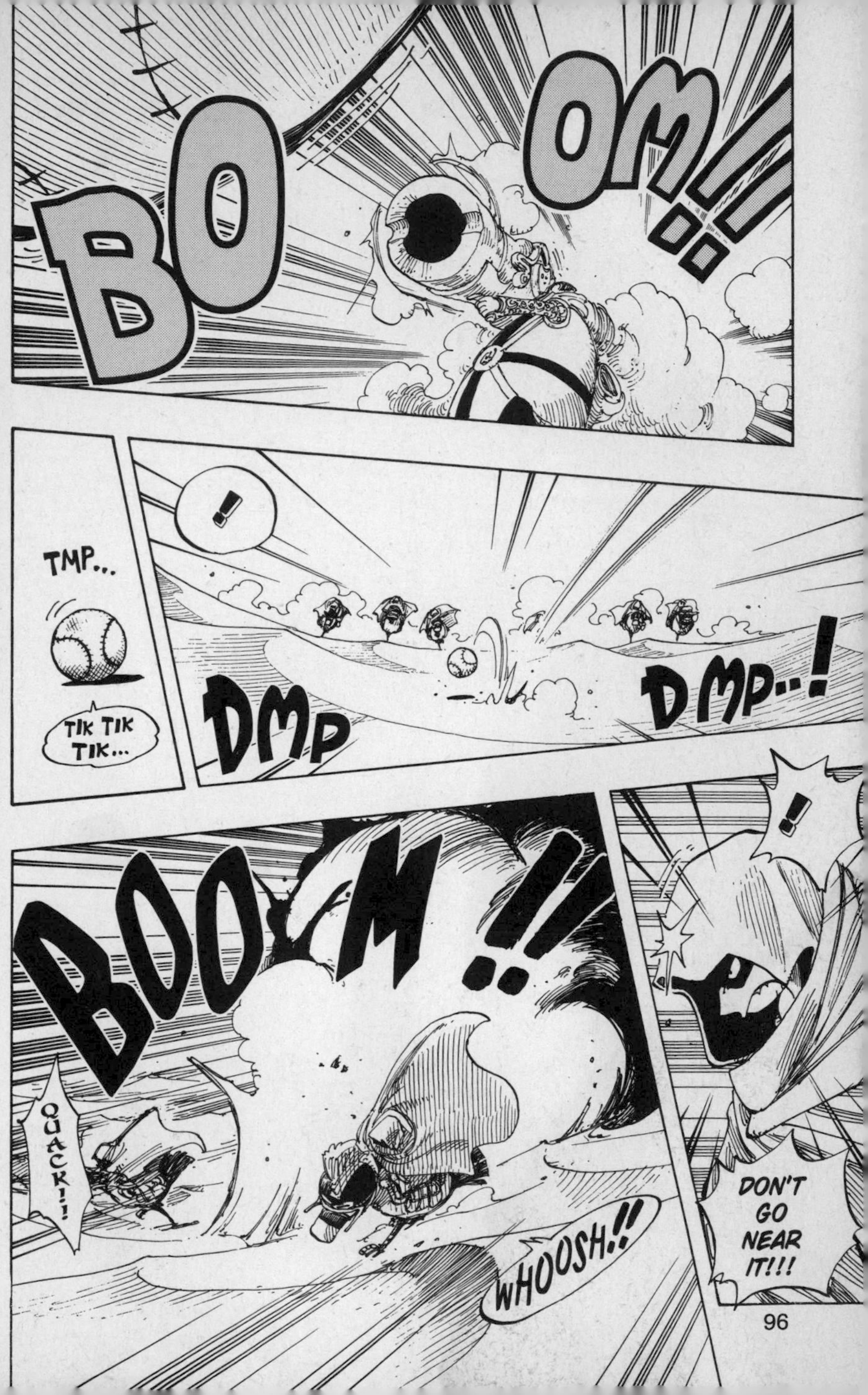
BOOOM!!
!
DMP..!
DMP
TMP...
TIK TIK TIK...
!
DON'T GO NEAR IT!!!
BOOM!!
WHOOSH!!
QUACK!!

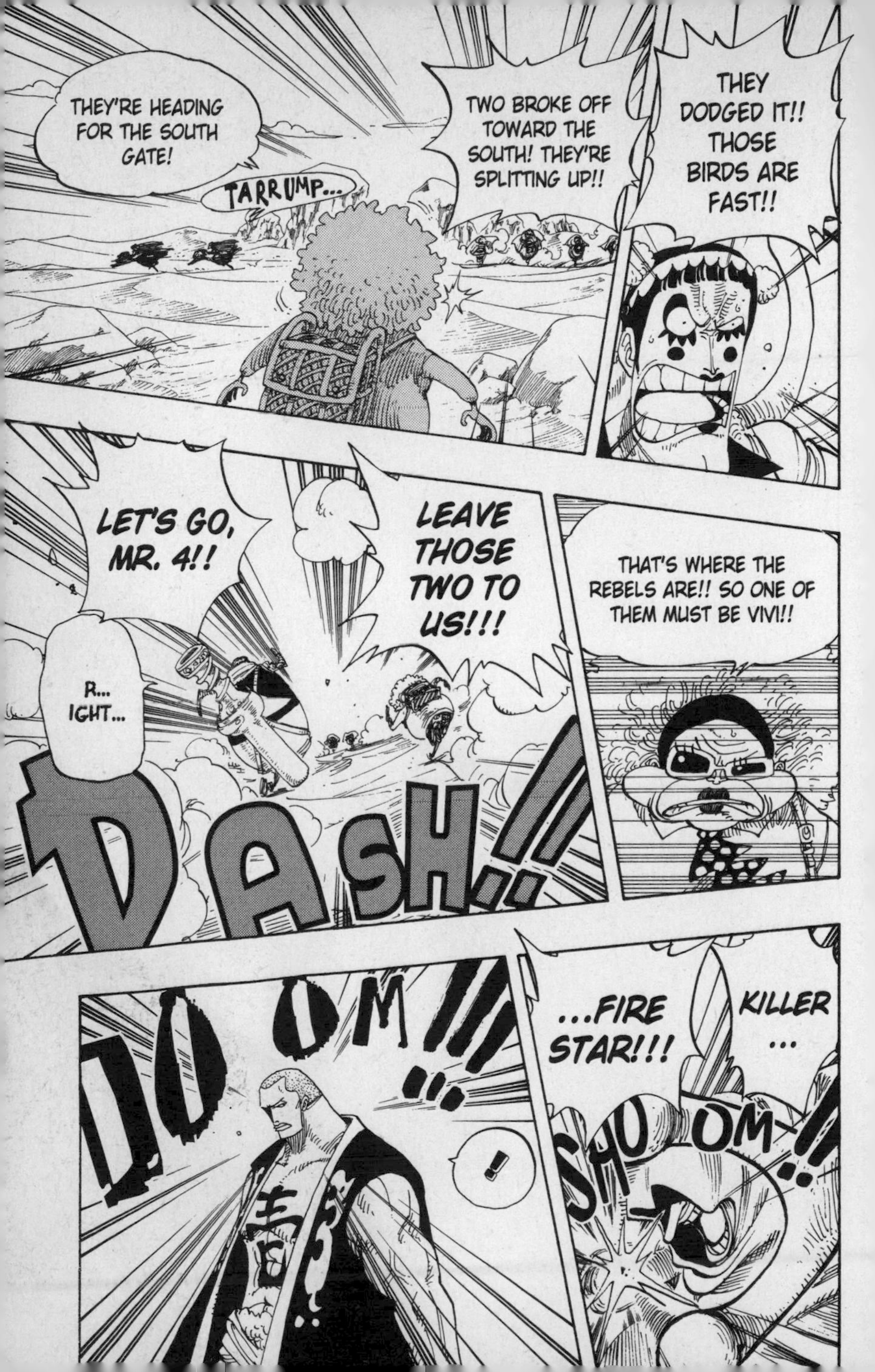
THEY DODGED IT!! THOSE BIRDS ARE FAST!!
TWO BROKE OFF TOWARD THE SOUTH! THEY'RE SPLITTING UP!!
THEY'RE HEADING FOR THE SOUTH GATE!
TARRUMP...
THAT'S WHERE THE REBELS ARE!! SO ONE OF THEM MUST BE VIVI!!
LEAVE THOSE TWO TO US!!!
LET'S GO, MR. 4!!
R... IGHT...
DASH..!!
KILLER ...
...FIRE STAR!!!
SHOOM!!
!
DOOM!!..

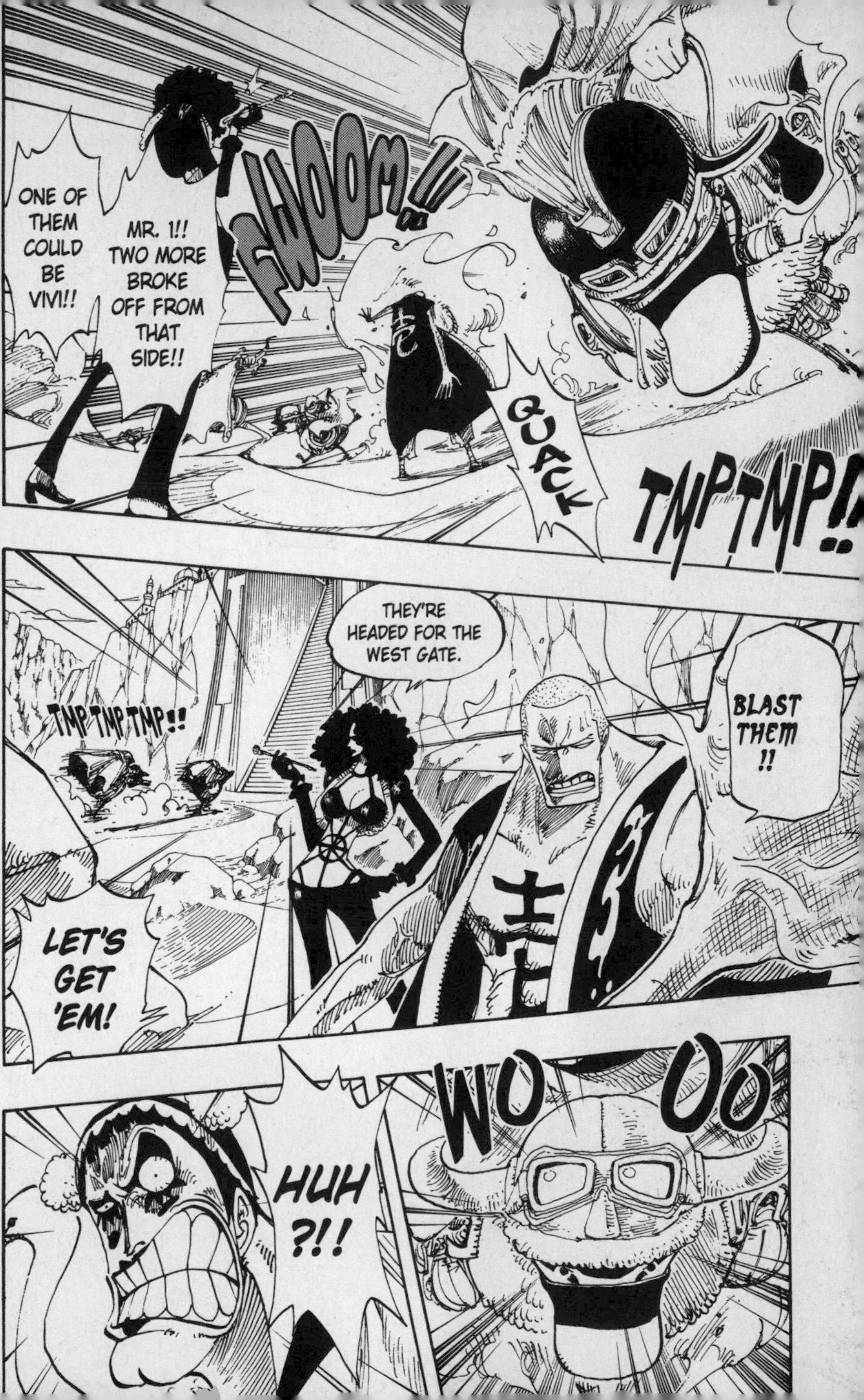
TMPTMP!!
QUACK
FWOOM!!
MR. 1!! TWO MORE BROKE OFF FROM THAT SIDE!!
ONE OF THEM COULD BE VIVI!!
BLAST THEM!!
THEY'RE HEADED FOR THE WEST GATE.
TMP TMP TMP!!
LET'S GET 'EM!
WOOO
HUH?!!

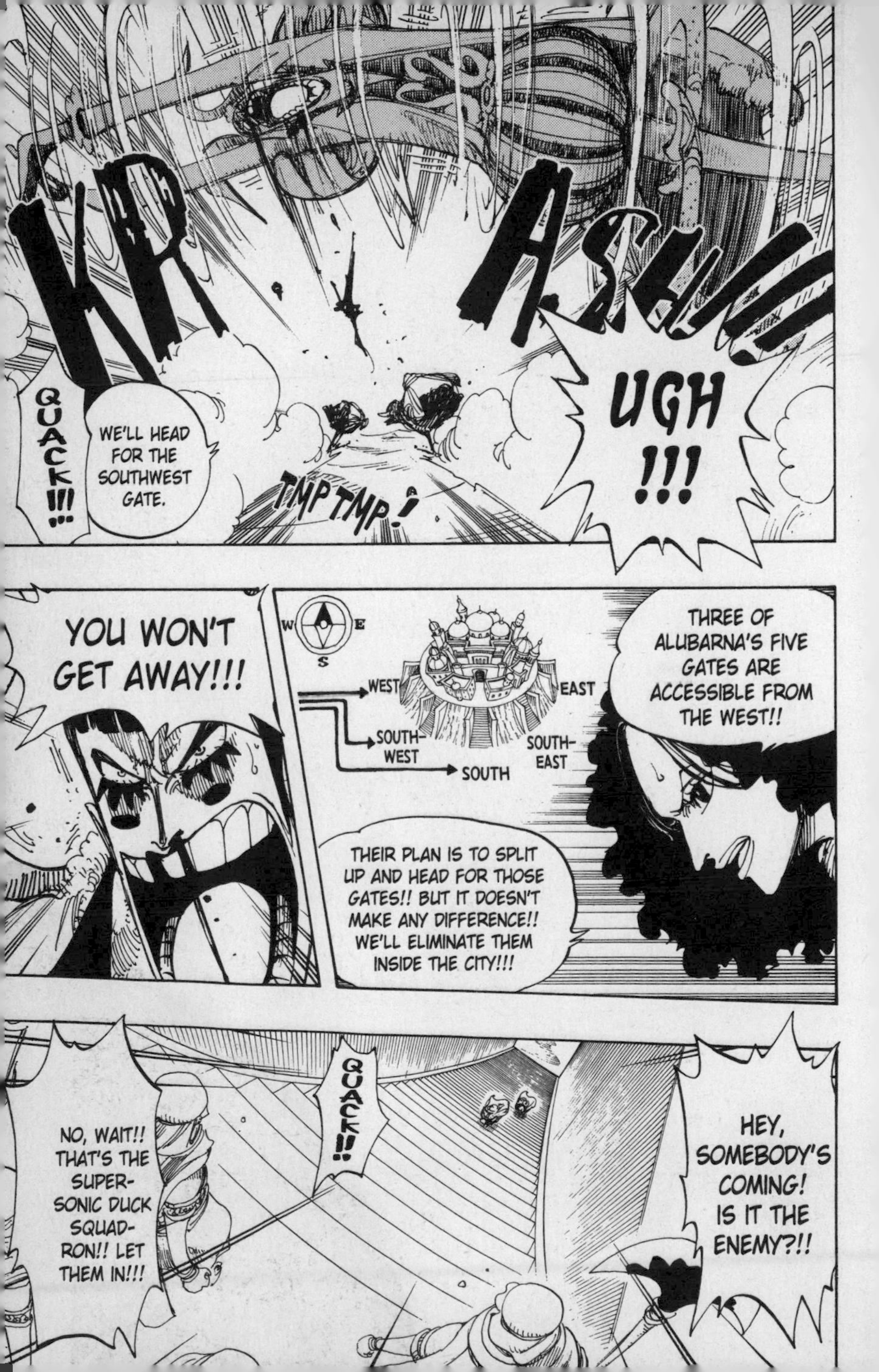
KR
ASH
UGH !!!
TMP TMP
WE'LL HEAD FOR THE SOUTHWEST GATE.
QUACK!!!
THREE OF ALUBARNA'S FIVE GATES ARE ACCESSIBLE FROM THE WEST!!
W
E
S
WEST
EAST
SOUTH-WEST
SOUTH-EAST
SOUTH
THEIR PLAN IS TO SPLIT UP AND HEAD FOR THOSE GATES!! BUT IT DOESN'T MAKE ANY DIFFERENCE!! WE'LL ELIMINATE THEM INSIDE THE CITY!!!
YOU WON'T GET AWAY!!!
HEY, SOMEBODY'S COMING! IS IT THE ENEMY?!!
QUACK!!
NO, WAIT!! THAT'S THE SUPER-SONIC DUCK SQUAD-RON!! LET THEM IN!!!

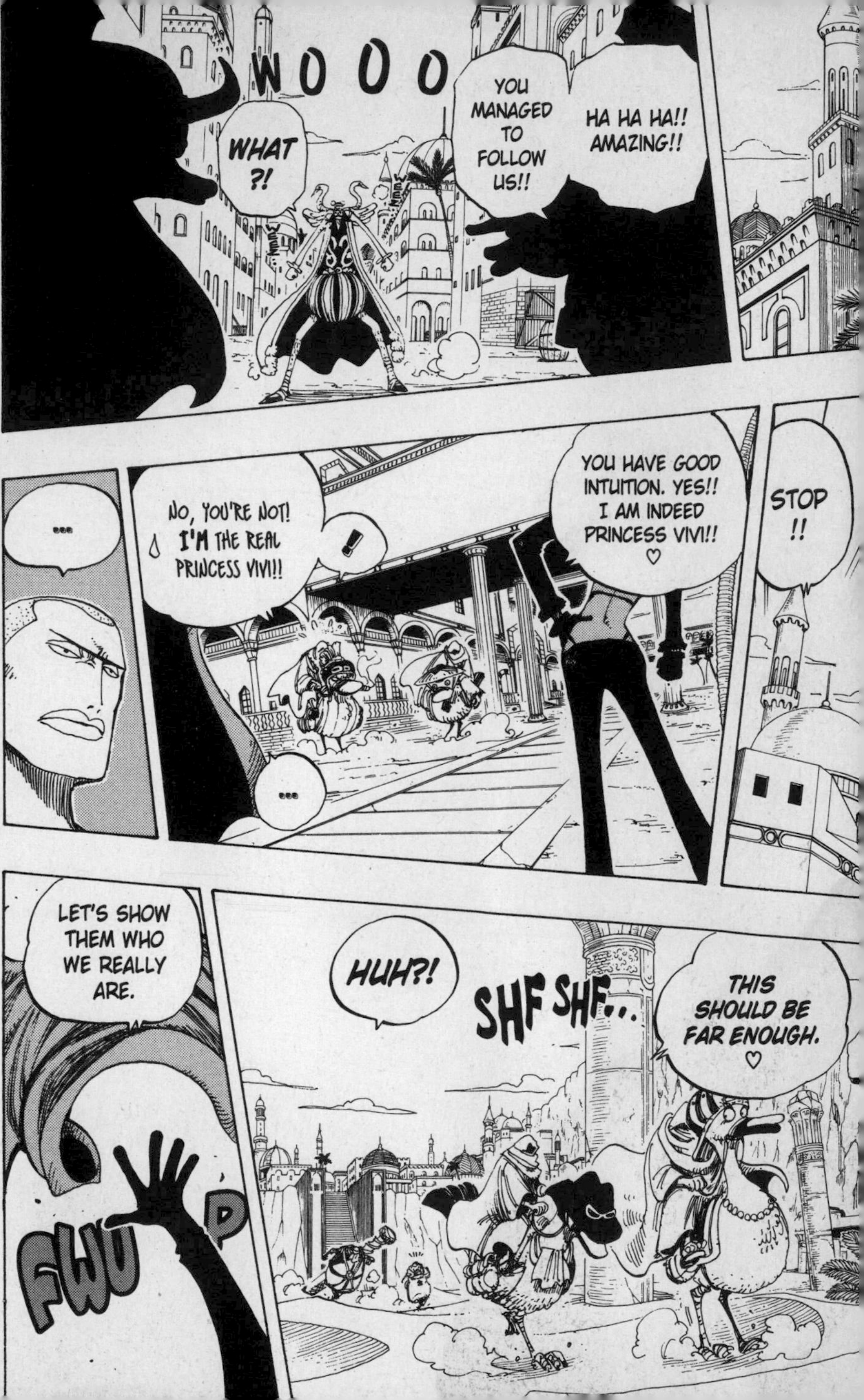
HA HA HA!! AMAZING!!
YOU MANAGED TO FOLLOW US!!
WOOO
WHAT?!
STOP!!
YOU HAVE GOOD INTUITION. YES!! I AM INDEED PRINCESS VIVI!! ♡
!
NO, YOU'RE NOT! I'M THE REAL PRINCESS VIVI!!
...
...
THIS SHOULD BE FAR ENOUGH. ♡
SHF SHF...
HUH?!
LET'S SHOW THEM WHO WE REALLY ARE.
FWUP

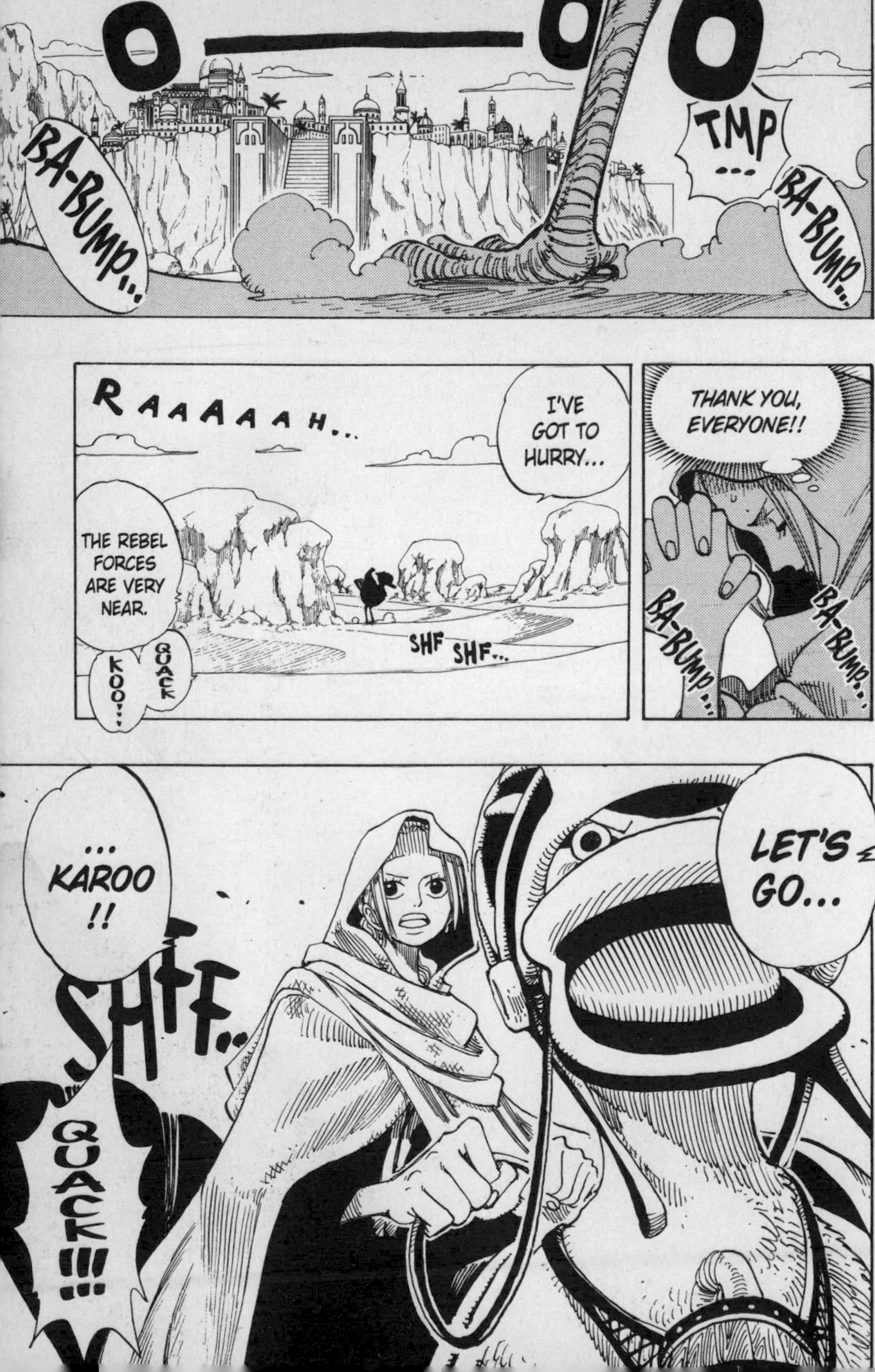
O———OO
TMP...
BA-BUMP...
BA-BUMP...
THANK YOU, EVERYONE!!
BA-BUMP...
BA-BUMP...
I'VE GOT TO HURRY...
RAAAAAH...
THE REBEL FORCES ARE VERY NEAR.
SHF SHF...
QUACK
KOO!...
LET'S GO...
... KAROO !!
SHF...
QUACK!!!

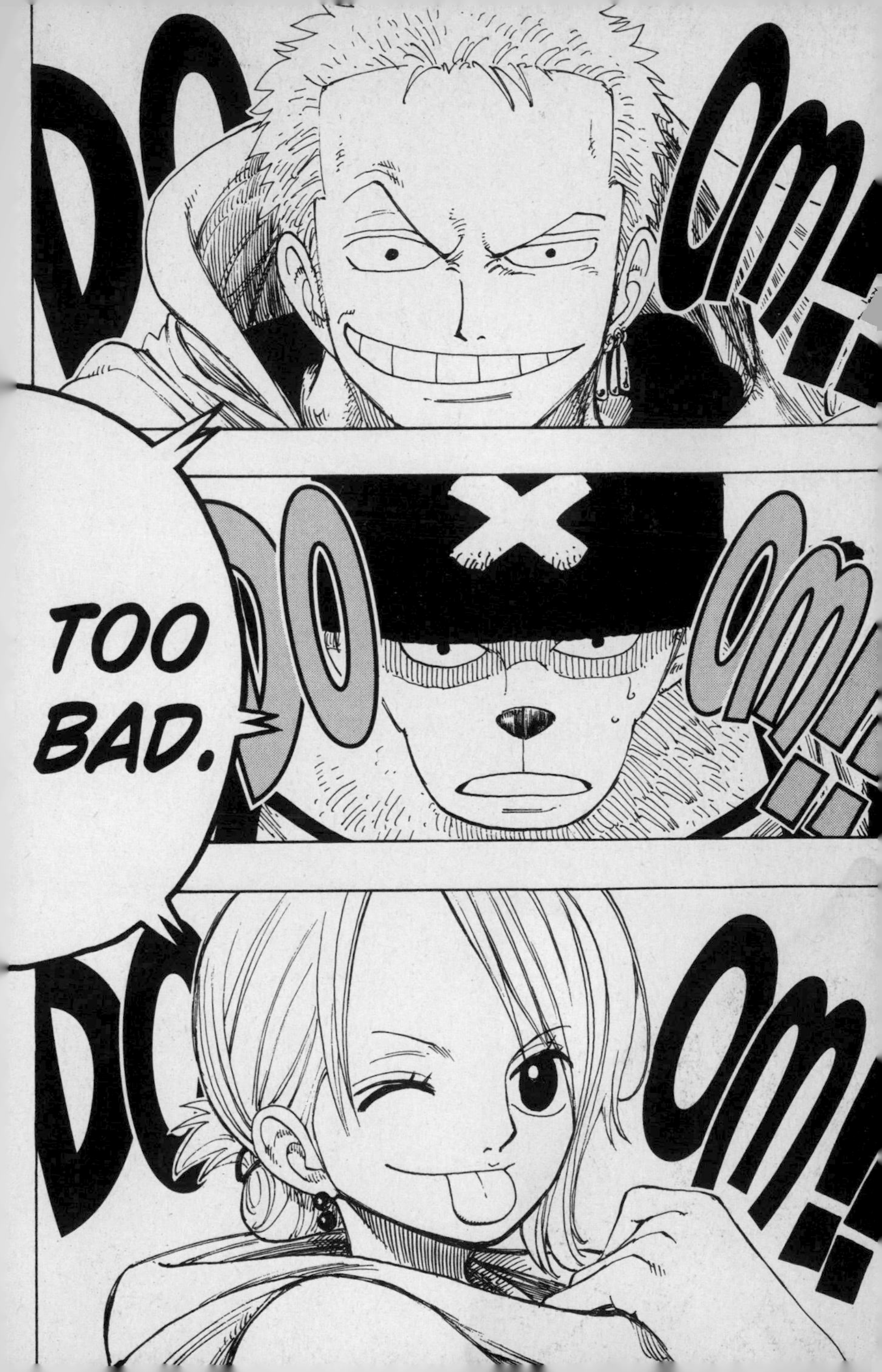
DOOM!!
DOOM!!
TOO BAD.
DOOM!!

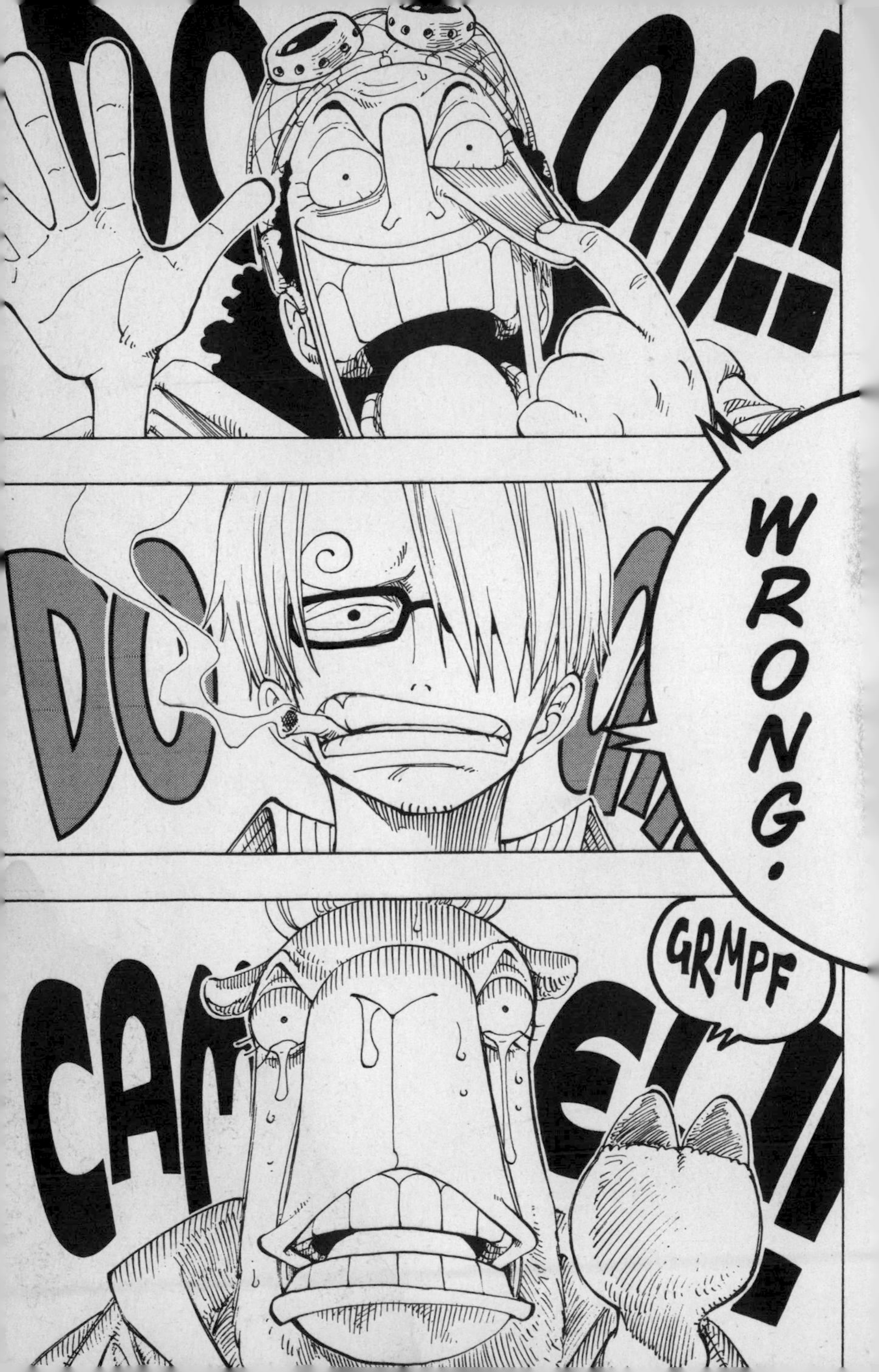
WRONG.
GRMPF

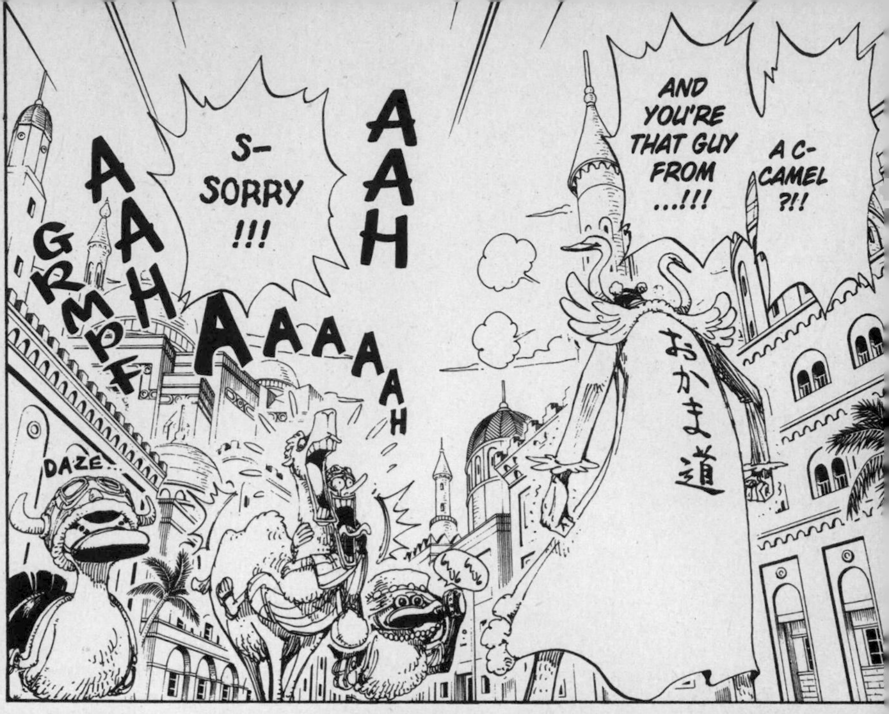
A C-CAMEL ?!!
AND YOU'RE THAT GUY FROM ...!!!
おかま道
AAH
S-SORRY !!!
AAHH
AAAAAAH
GRMPF
DAZE...

*TEXT ON JACKET SAYS "ONE" - ED.

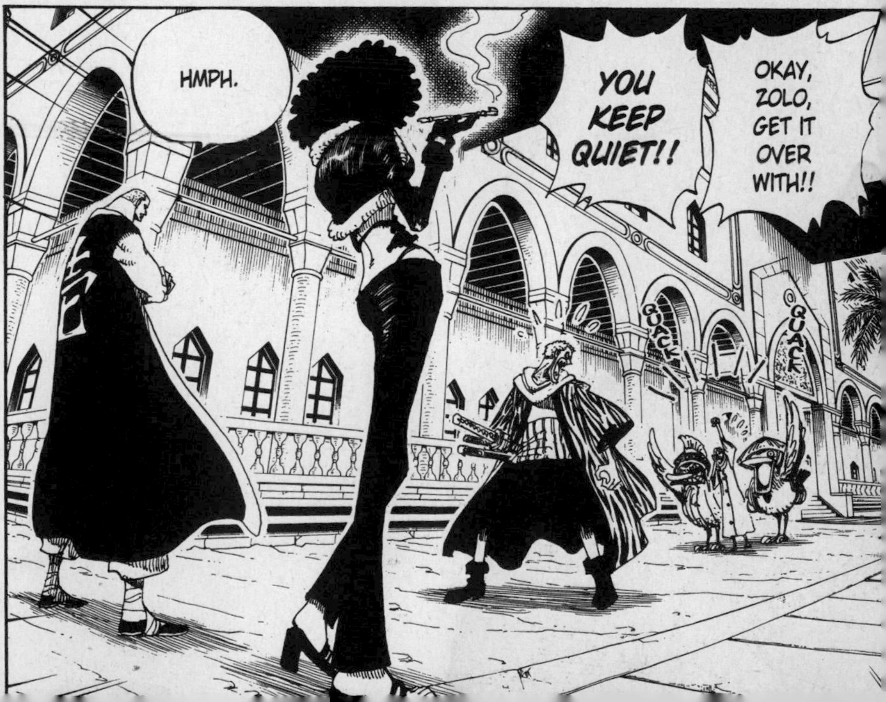
OKAY, ZOLO, GET IT OVER WITH!!
YOU KEEP QUIET!!
HMPH.
QUACK
QUACK

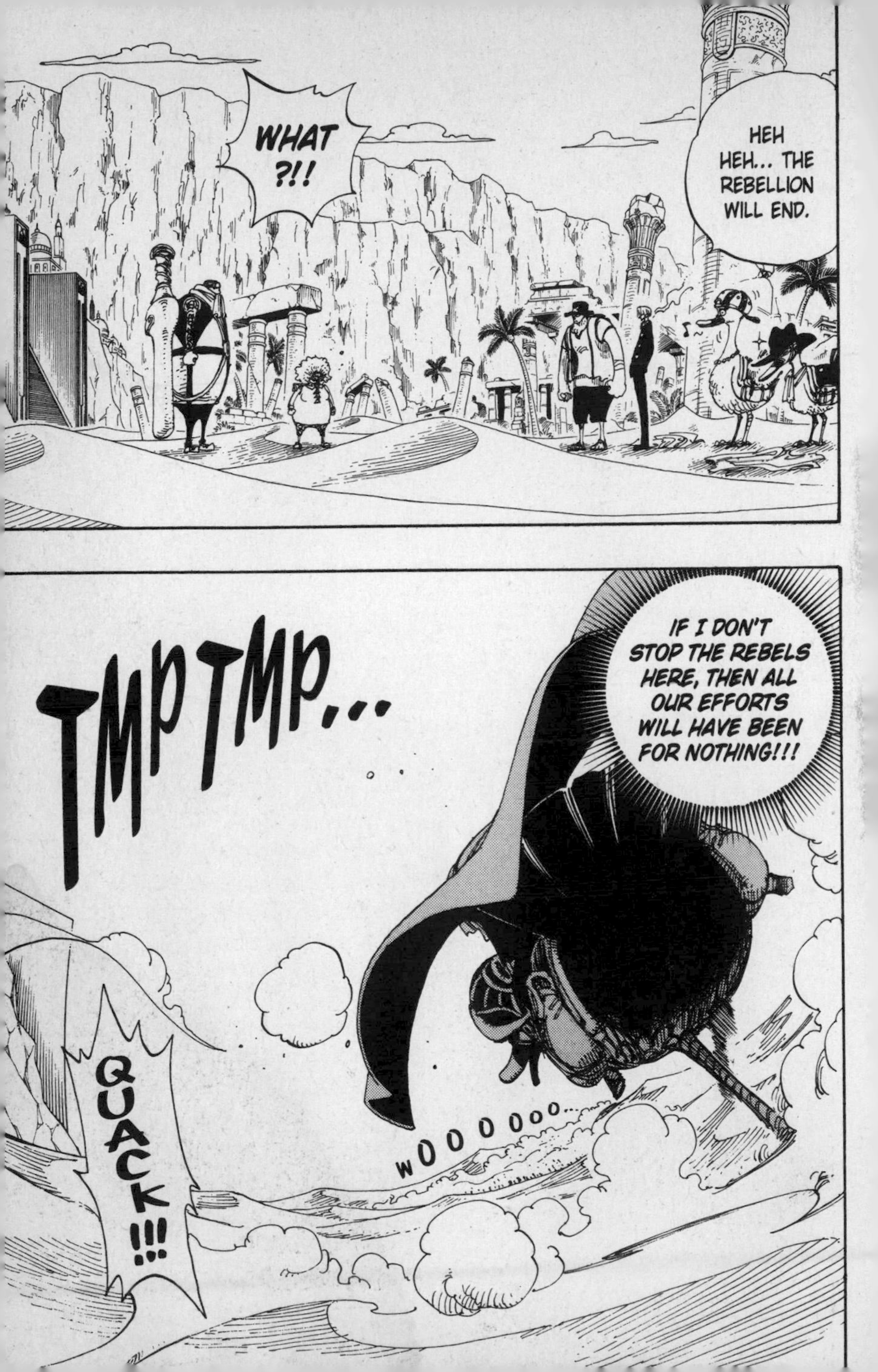
HEH HEH... THE REBELLION WILL END.
WHAT ?!!
IF I DON'T STOP THE REBELS HERE, THEN ALL OUR EFFORTS WILL HAVE BEEN FOR NOTHING!!!
TMP TMP...
WOOOOOO...
QUACK!!!

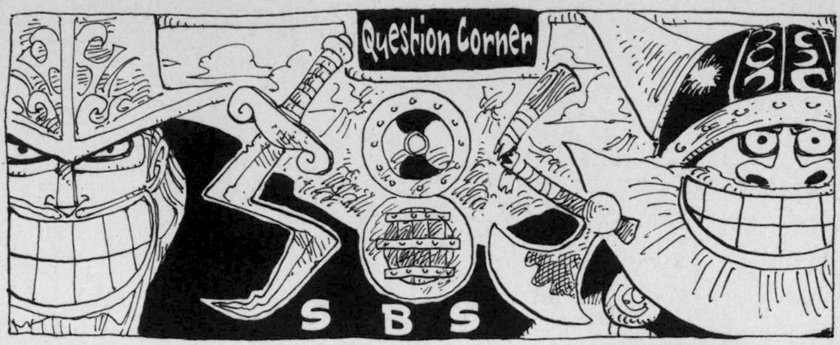
Question Corner
SBS

Q: I have a favor to ask. I picked up a White Walky (a.k.a. Wooly Hippo) on the street. Can you care for it at your place, Oda Sensei?
--New York Cocoa

A: I don't want it.

Q: This question comes from a 28-year-old male in Tokyo (occupation: manga editor) who wants to know the names of each of the members of the Supersonic Duck Squadron. Oda Sensei, you really hit a soft spot with me. They're so cute!! Anyway, I realize it might be a bother, but give it your best shot. I'm counting on you.

A: Hey! Hey! Now hold on just a minute, you. You're Asada, a.k.a. Daasa, that *Jump* editor with a weakness for cute things who was formerly assigned to *One Piece,* aren't you?! You thought you could fool me, didn't you? You pretended to be a fan and sent in a work-related question! This is a sacred place for our readers! Well, okay. And thanks for helping me for four and a half years. Okay, I'll answer your question, since I received it from other people as well. Starting with the bottom row, from left to right, they are: Cowboy, Bourbon Jr., Karoo, Centaur, and Hikoichi. The top two are Stomp and Ivan X. That's it. I had given them all names, but I thought that revealing them would just confuse people, so that's why I hadn't.

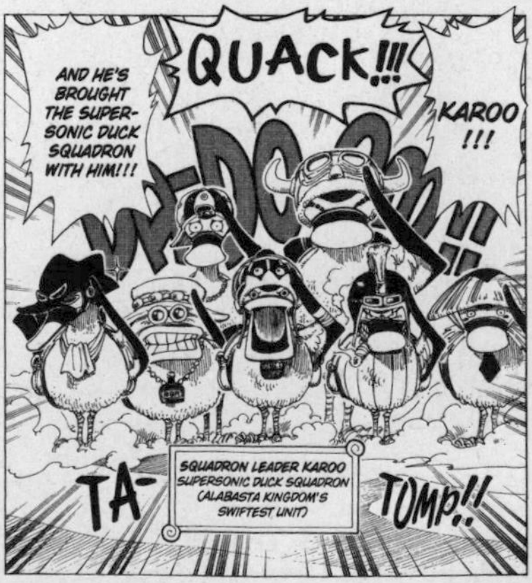
KAROO !!!
QUACK!!!
AND HE'S BROUGHT THE SUPERSONIC DUCK SQUADRON WITH HIM!!!
SQUADRON LEADER KAROO SUPERSONIC DUCK SQUADRON (ALABASTA KINGDOM'S SWIFTEST UNIT)
TA-
TOMP!!

Chapter 182: ROAR

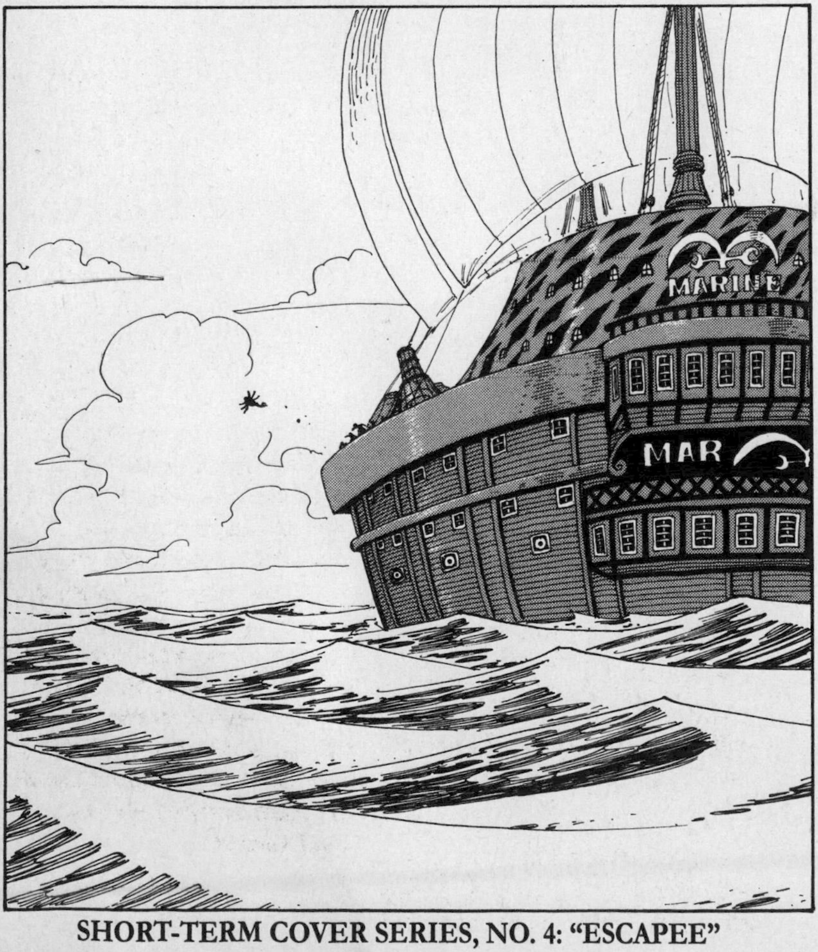
MARINE
MAR

SHORT-TERM COVER SERIES, NO. 4: "ESCAPEE"

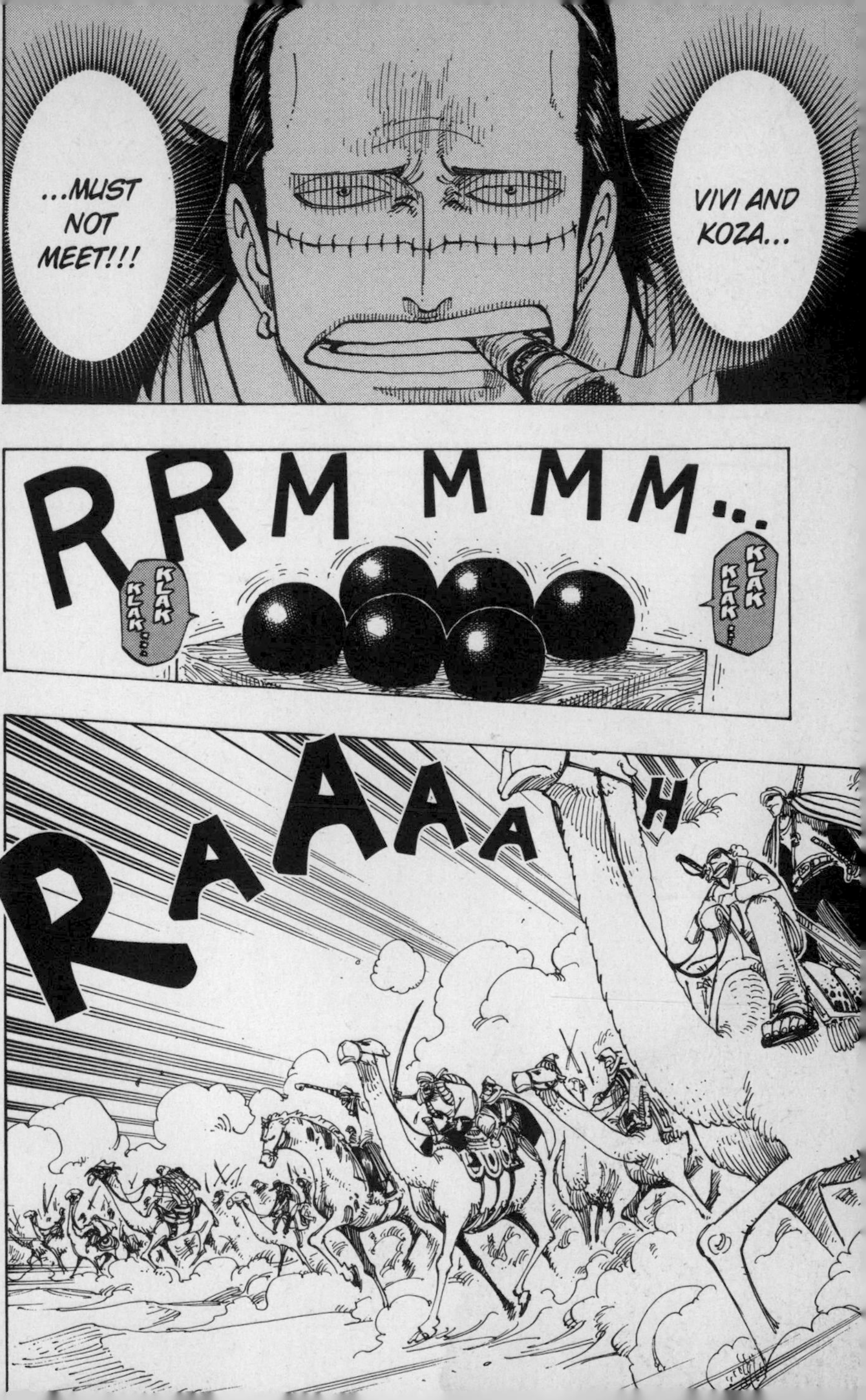
VIVI AND KOZA...
...MUST NOT MEET!!!
RRMMMMM...
KLAK KLAK...
KLAK KLAK...
RAAAAH

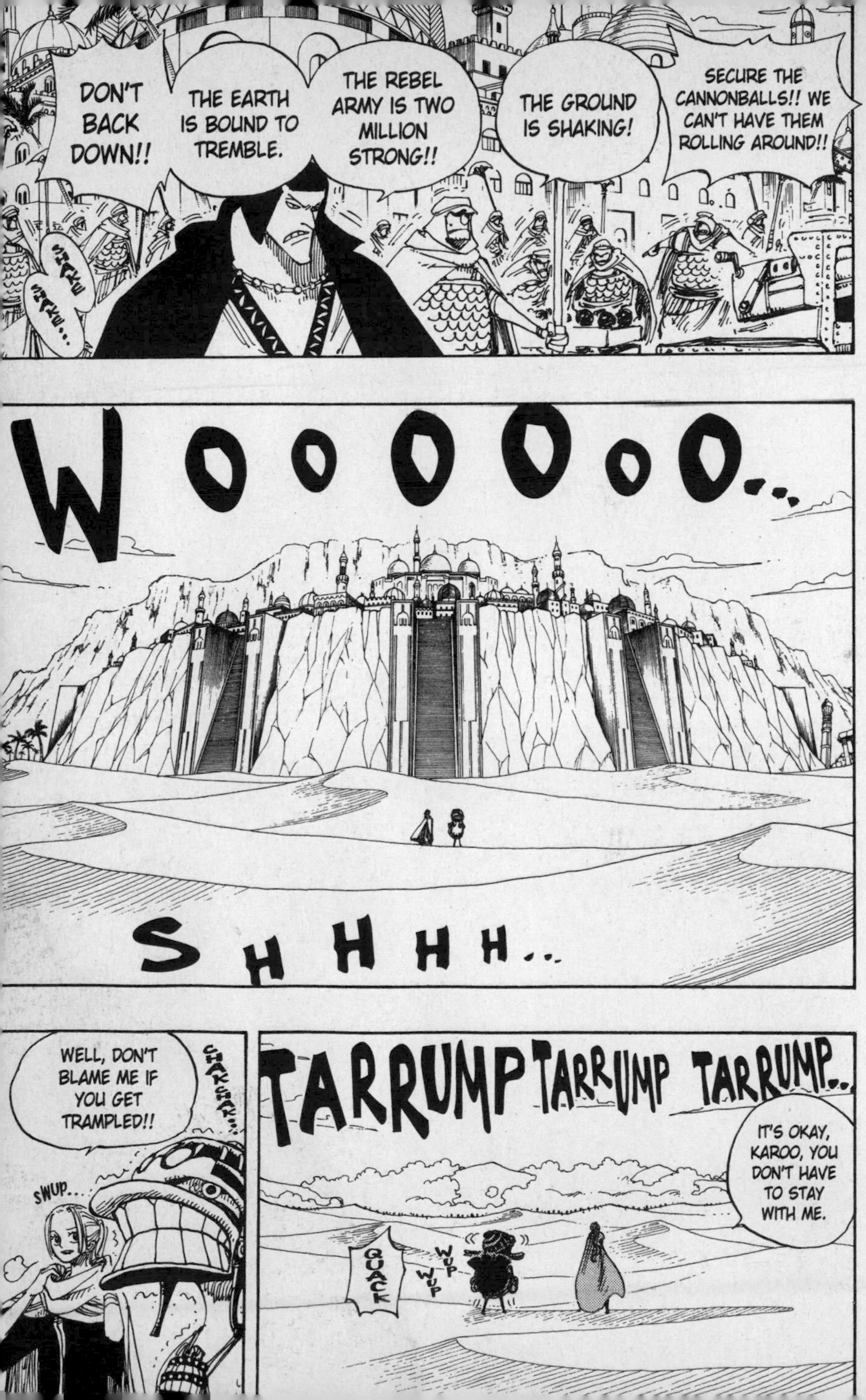
SECURE THE CANNONBALLS!! WE CAN'T HAVE THEM ROLLING AROUND!!
THE GROUND IS SHAKING!
THE REBEL ARMY IS TWO MILLION STRONG!!
THE EARTH IS BOUND TO TREMBLE.
DON'T BACK DOWN!!
SHAKE
SHAKE...
WOOOOOO...
SHHHH...
TARRUMP TARRUMP TARRUMP...
IT'S OKAY, KAROO, YOU DON'T HAVE TO STAY WITH ME.
WUP
WUP
QUACK
WELL, DON'T BLAME ME IF YOU GET TRAMPLED!!
CHAK CHAK...
SWUP...

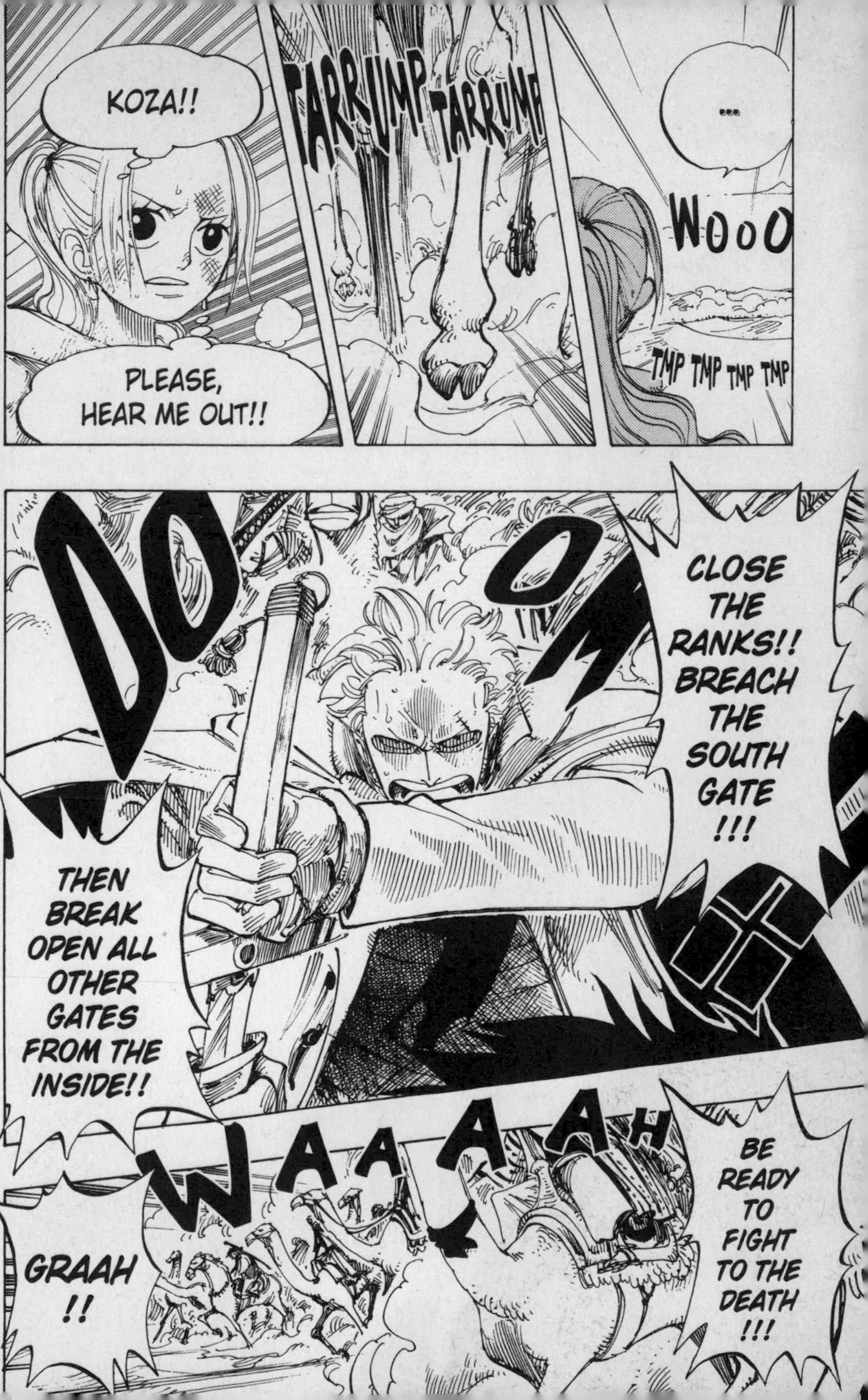
...
WOOOO
TMP TMP TMP TMP
TARRUMP TARRUMP
KOZA!!
PLEASE, HEAR ME OUT!!
CLOSE THE RANKS!! BREACH THE SOUTH GATE!!!
THEN BREAK OPEN ALL OTHER GATES FROM THE INSIDE!!
WAAAAH
BE READY TO FIGHT TO THE DEATH!!!
GRAAH!!

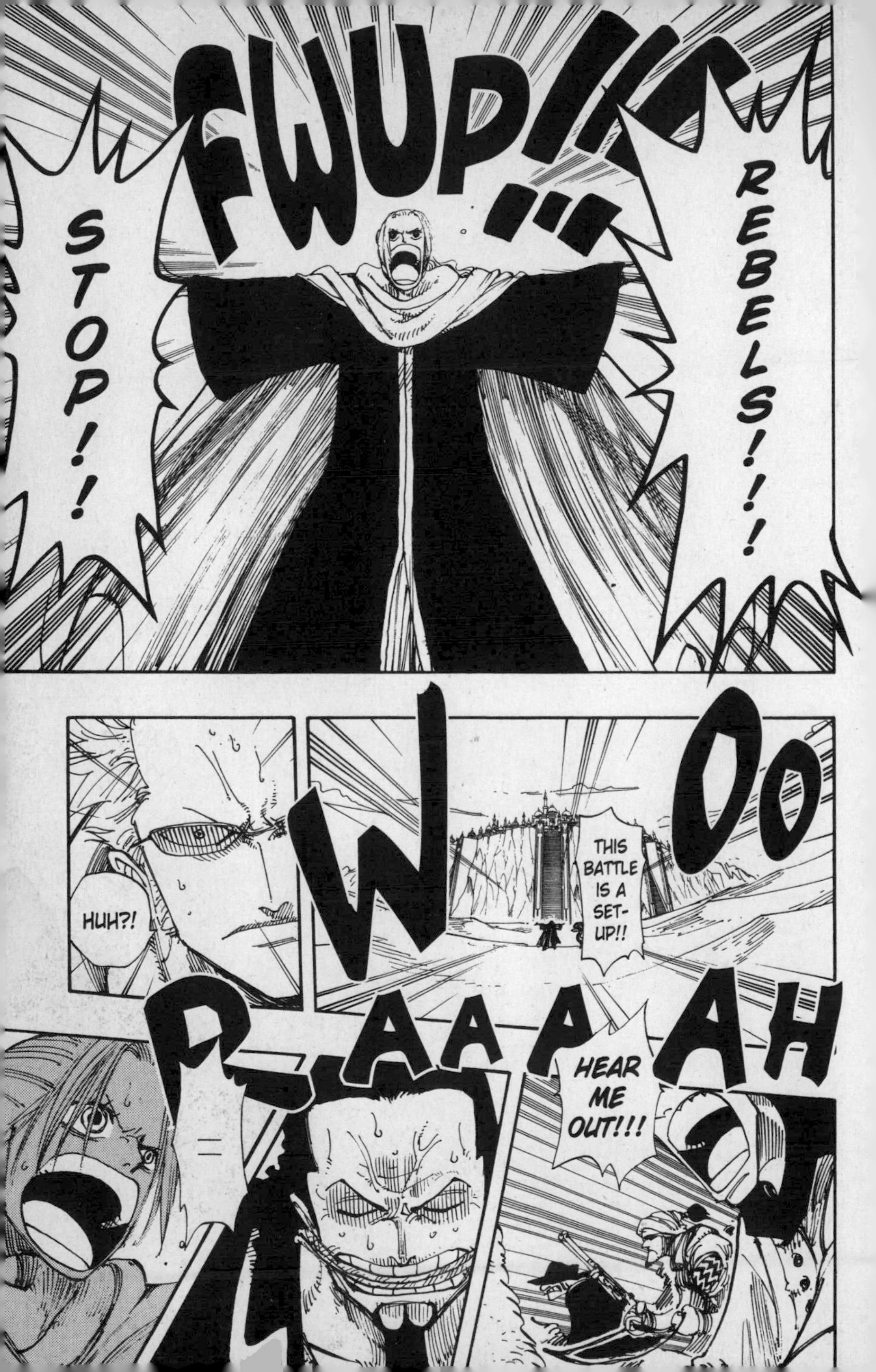
FWUP!!!
REBELS!!!
STOP!!
WOO
THIS BATTLE IS A SET-UP!!
HUH?!
RAAAAH
HEAR ME OUT!!!

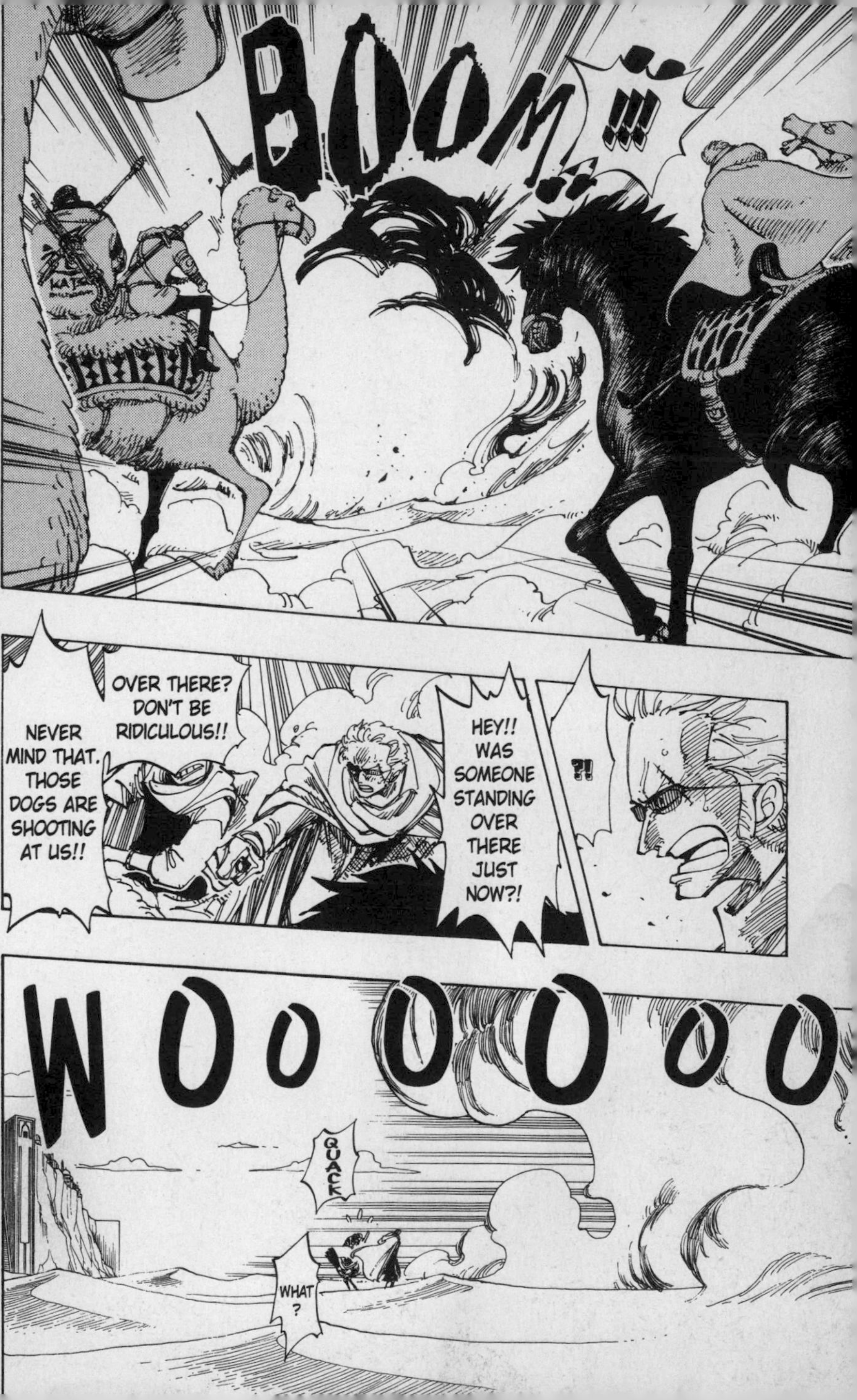
BOOM!!!
?!
HEY!! WAS SOMEONE STANDING OVER THERE JUST NOW?!
OVER THERE? DON'T BE RIDICULOUS!!
NEVER MIND THAT. THOSE DOGS ARE SHOOTING AT US!!
WOOOOOOO
QUACK
WHAT?

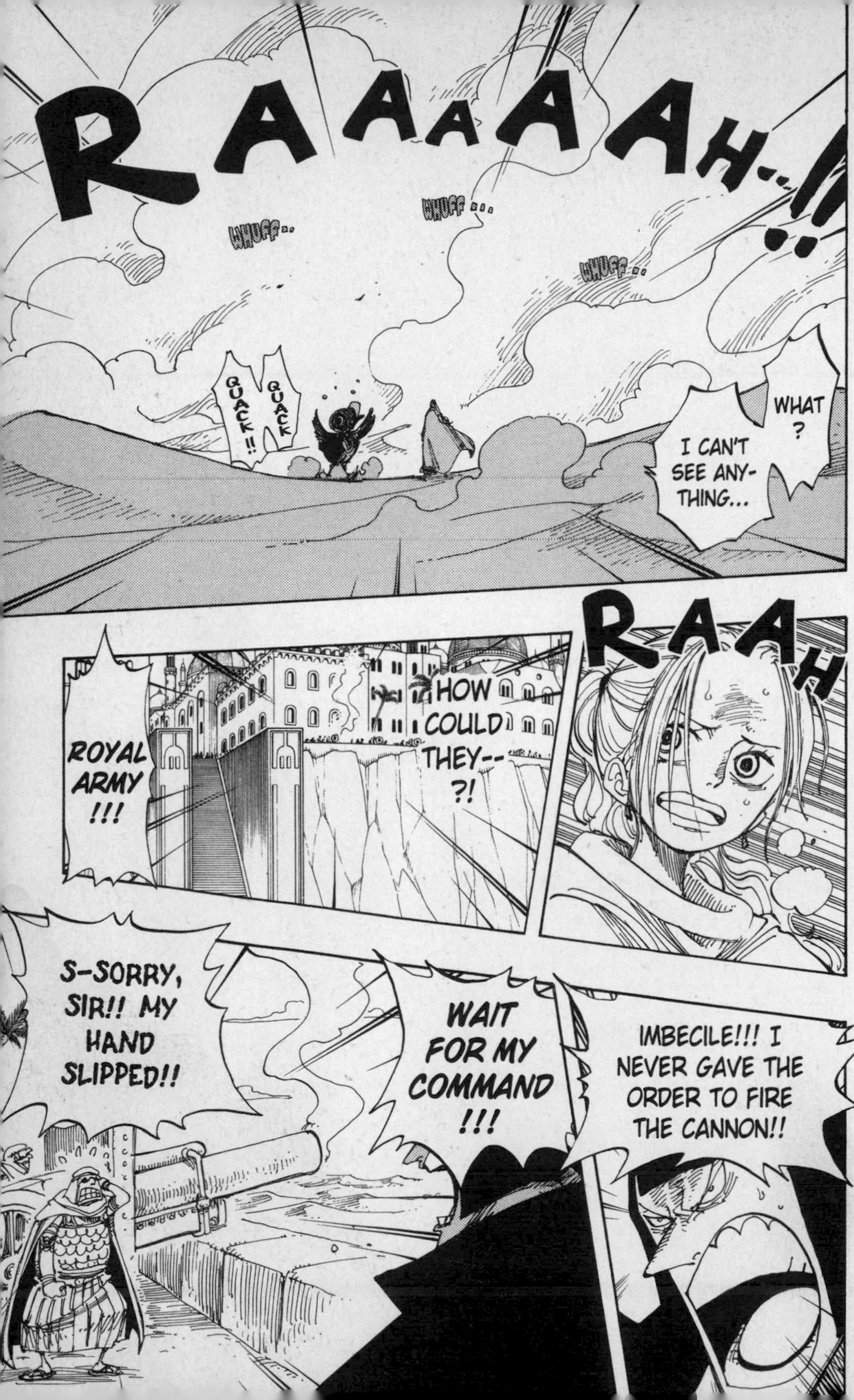
RAAAAAH--!!
WHUFF..
WHUFF...
WHUFF..
WHAT?
I CAN'T SEE ANYTHING...
QUACK
QUACK!!
RAAH
HOW COULD THEY--?!
ROYAL ARMY!!!
IMBECILE!!! I NEVER GAVE THE ORDER TO FIRE THE CANNON!!
WAIT FOR MY COMMAND!!!
S-SORRY, SIR!! MY HAND SLIPPED!!

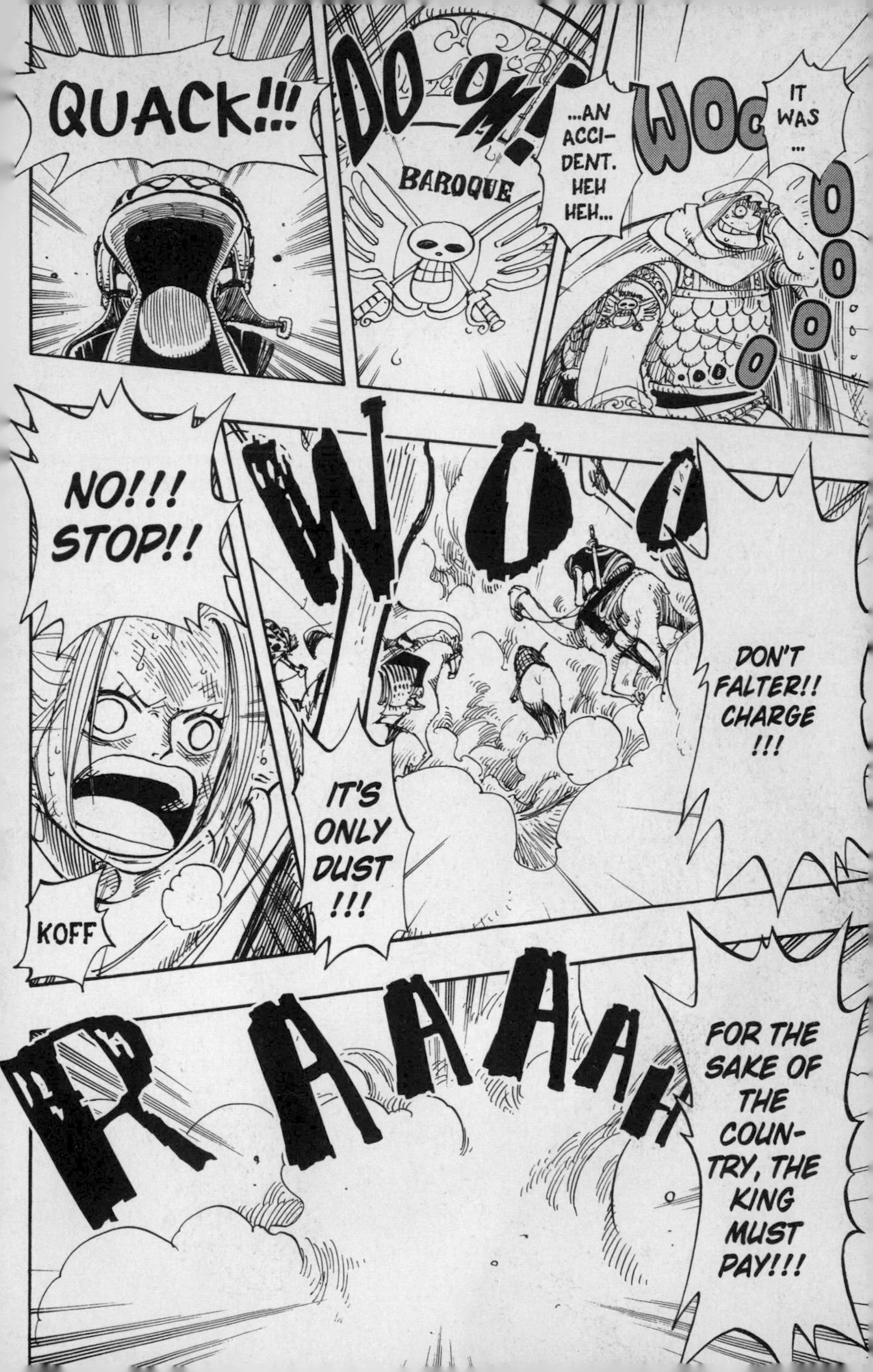
WOOOOOOO
IT WAS ...
...AN ACCIDENT. HEH HEH...
DOOM!
BAROQUE
QUACK!!!
WOOO
DON'T FALTER!! CHARGE!!!
IT'S ONLY DUST!!!
NO!!! STOP!!
KOFF
FOR THE SAKE OF THE COUNTRY, THE KING MUST PAY!!!
RAAAAH

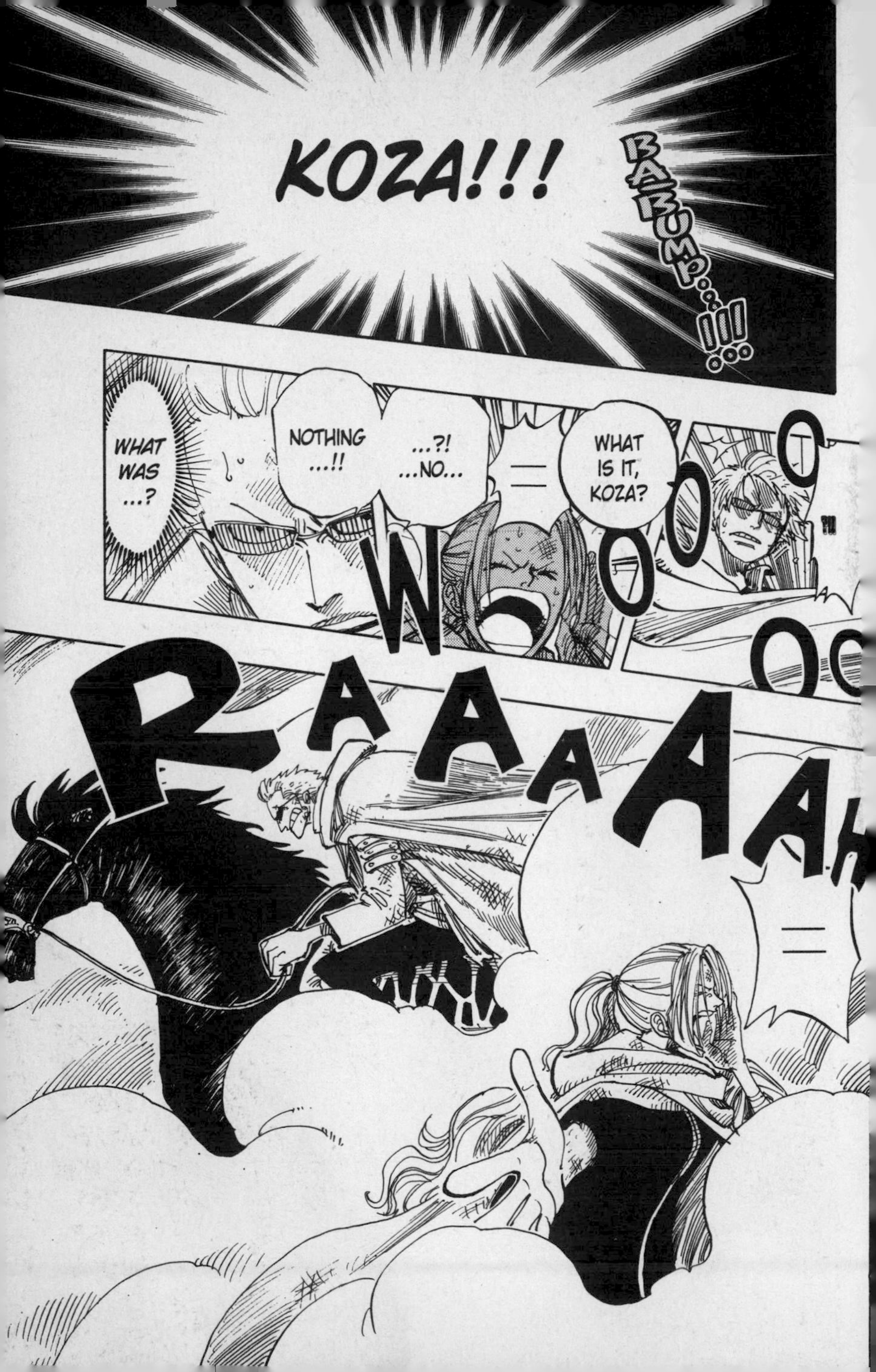
BA-BUMP...!!!
KOZA!!!
WHAT IS IT, KOZA?
...?! ...NO...
NOTHING ...!!
WHAT WAS ...?
WOOOOO
RAAAAAH

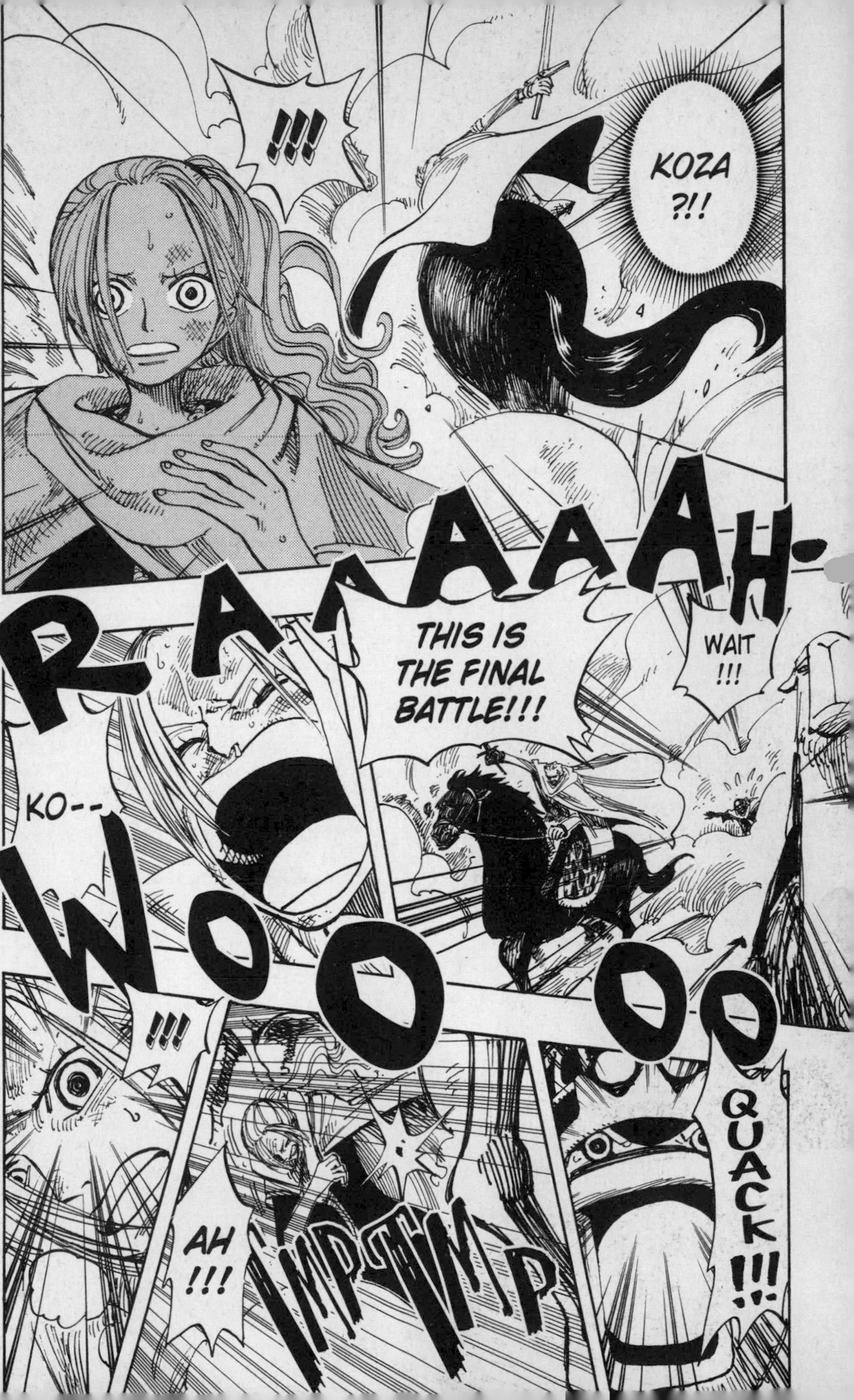
KOZA ?!!
!!!
RAAAAH-
WAIT !!!
THIS IS THE FINAL BATTLE!!!
KO--
WOOOOO
QUACK !!!
AH !!!
!!!

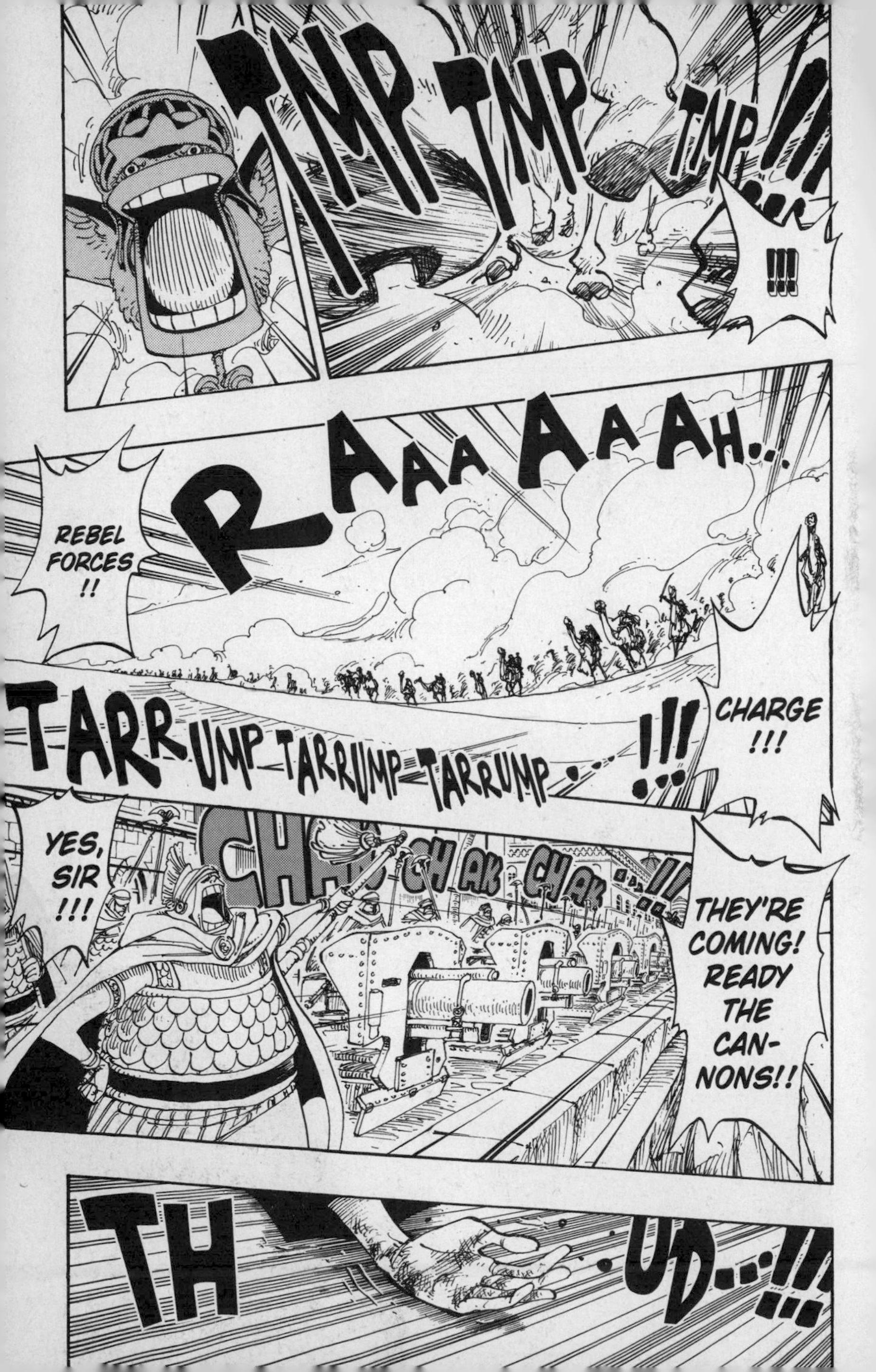
TMP TMP TMP!!
...!!!
RAAAAAAH...
REBEL FORCES !!
CHARGE !!!
TARRUMP TARRUMP TARRUMP...!!!
THEY'RE COMING! READY THE CAN-NONS!!
CHAK CHAK CHAK CHAK...!!
YES, SIR !!!
THUD...!!!

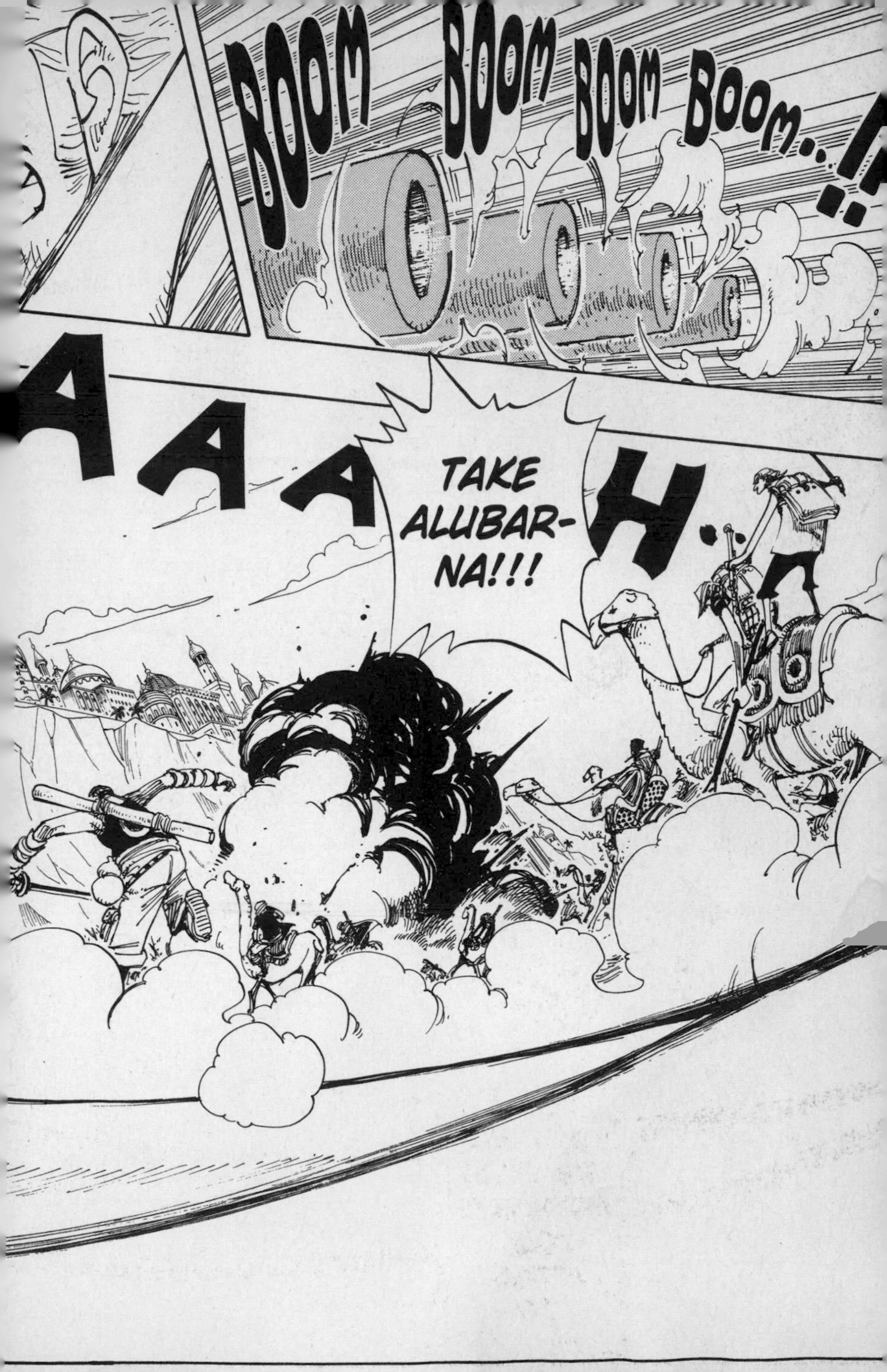
BOOM BOOM BOOM BOOM..!!
AAAAH
TAKE ALUBAR-NA!!!

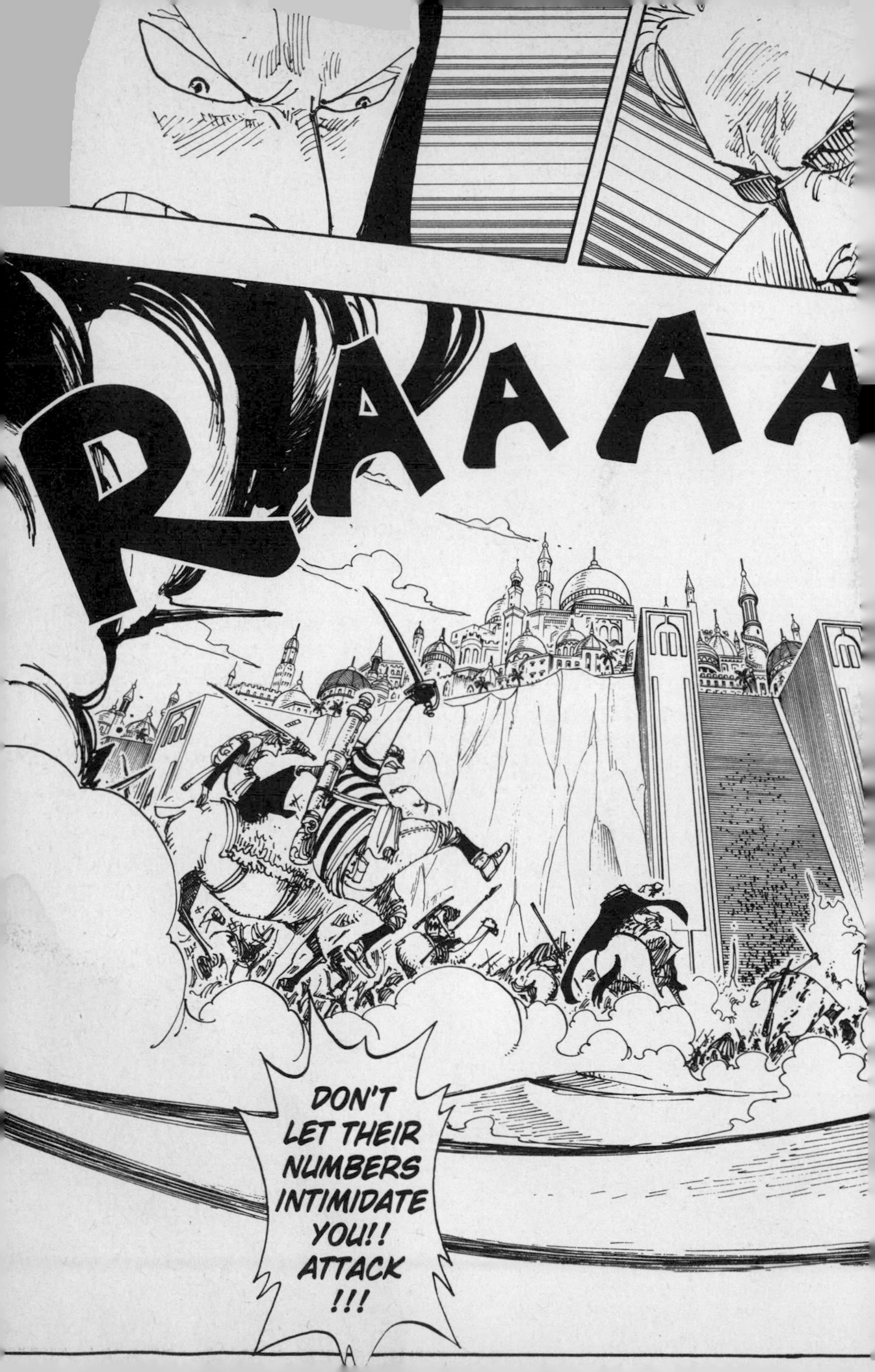
RAAAA
DON'T LET THEIR NUMBERS INTIMIDATE YOU!! ATTACK !!!

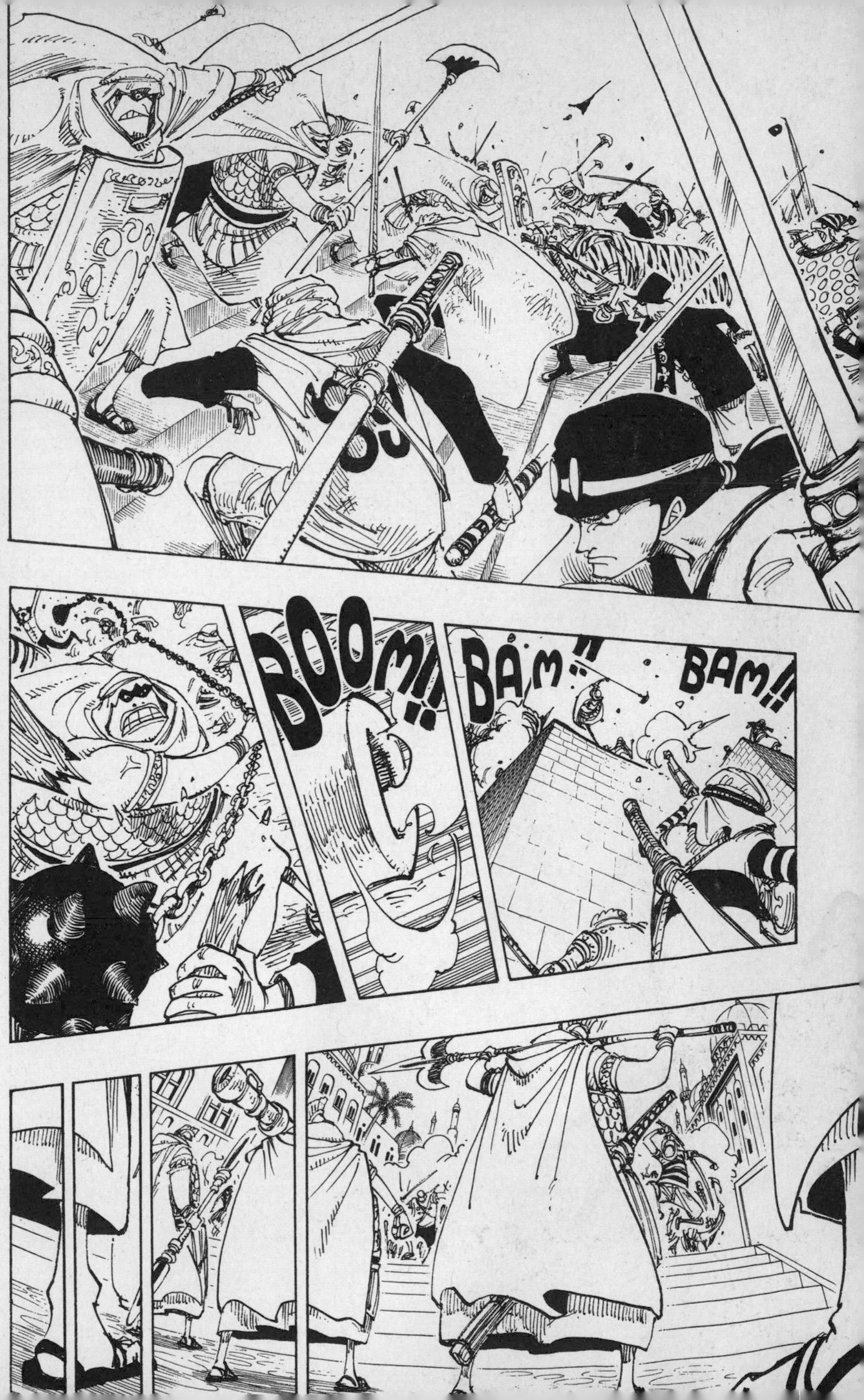
BAM!!
BAM!!
BOOM!!

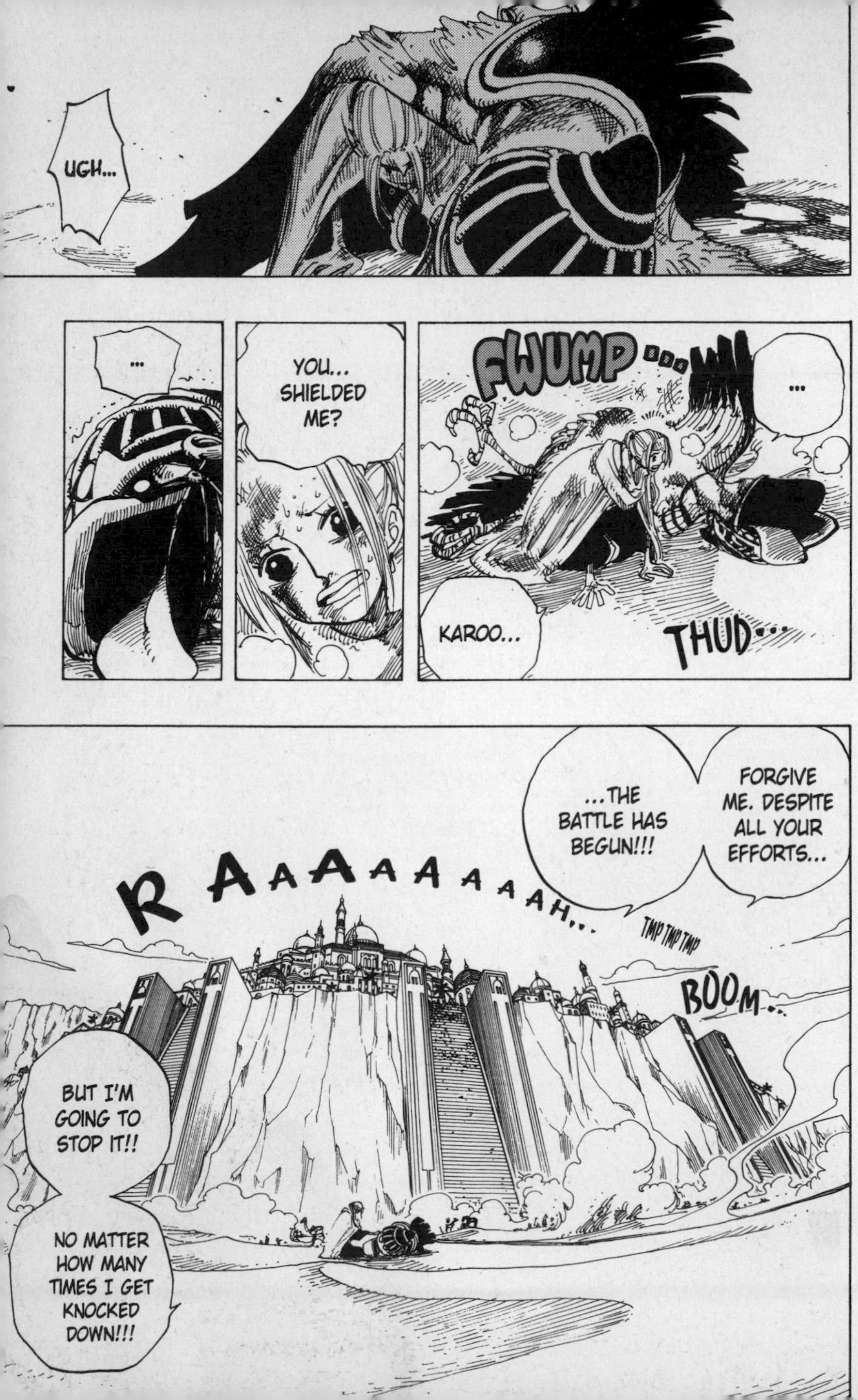
UGH...
...
FWUMP...
KAROO...
THUD...
YOU... SHIELDED ME?
...
FORGIVE ME. DESPITE ALL YOUR EFFORTS...
...THE BATTLE HAS BEGUN!!!
RAAAAAAAAAH...
TMP TMP TMP
BOOM...
BUT I'M GOING TO STOP IT!!
NO MATTER HOW MANY TIMES I GET KNOCKED DOWN!!!

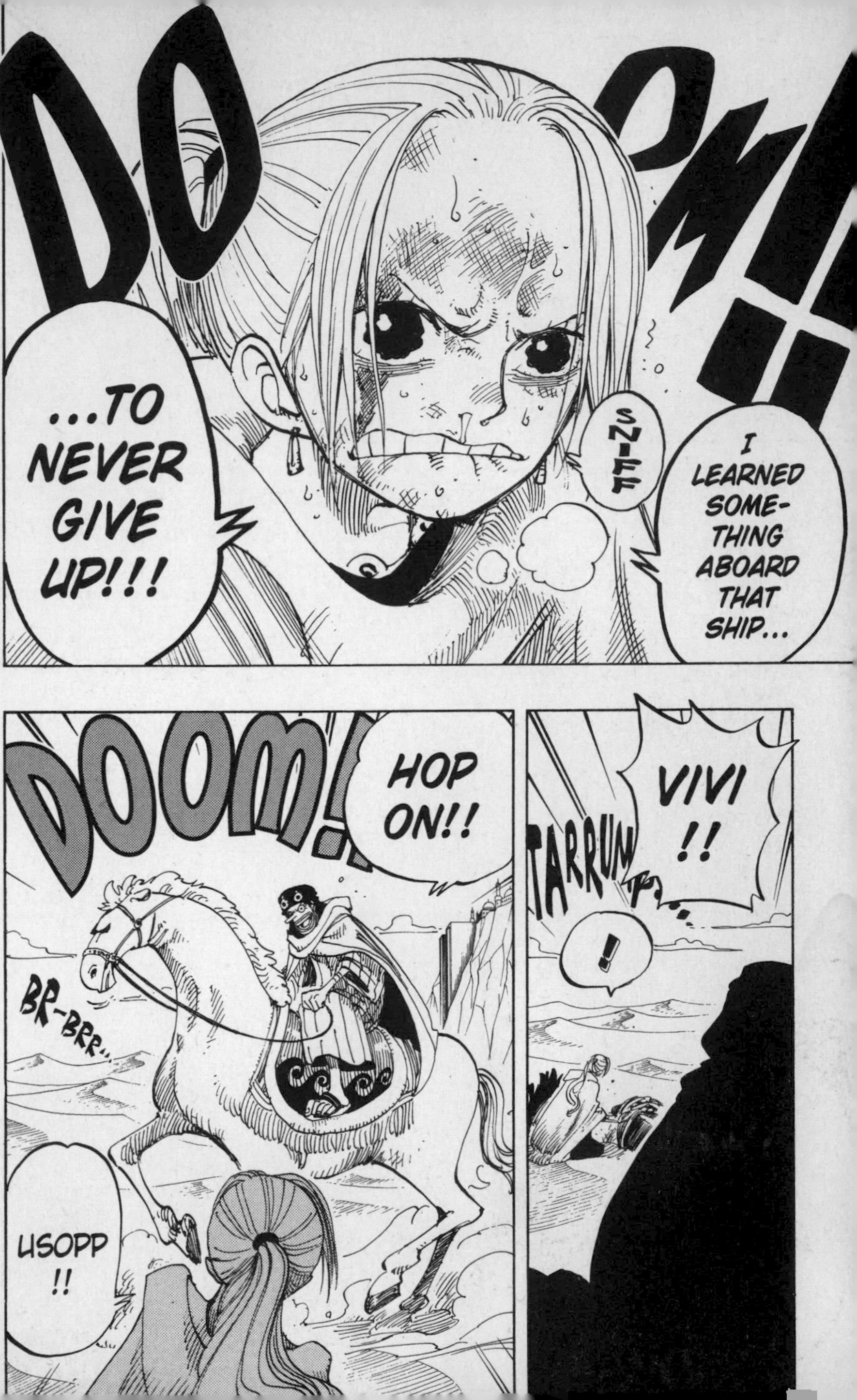
DO
OM!!
I LEARNED SOMETHING ABOARD THAT SHIP...
SNIFF
...TO NEVER GIVE UP!!!
VIVI !!
TARRUMP...
!
DOOM!!
HOP ON!!
BR-BRR...
USOPP !!

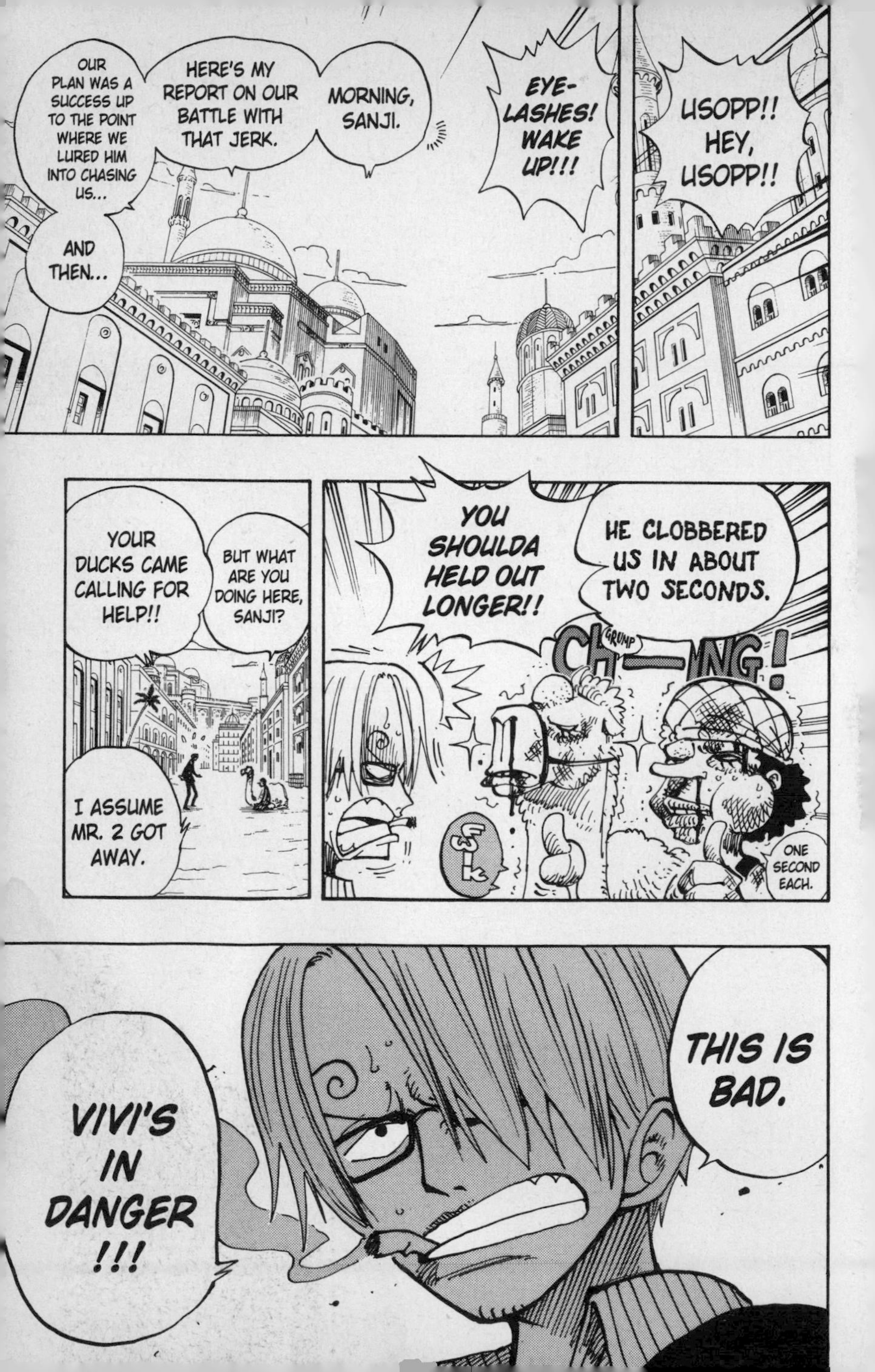
USOPP!! HEY, USOPP!!
EYE-LASHES! WAKE UP!!!
MORNING, SANJI.
HERE'S MY REPORT ON OUR BATTLE WITH THAT JERK.
OUR PLAN WAS A SUCCESS UP TO THE POINT WHERE WE LURED HIM INTO CHASING US...
AND THEN...
HE CLOBBERED US IN ABOUT TWO SECONDS.
YOU SHOULDA HELD OUT LONGER!!
GRUMP
CH—ING!
ONE SECOND EACH.
BUT WHAT ARE YOU DOING HERE, SANJI?
YOUR DUCKS CAME CALLING FOR HELP!!
I ASSUME MR. 2 GOT AWAY.
THIS IS BAD.
VIVI'S IN DANGER!!!

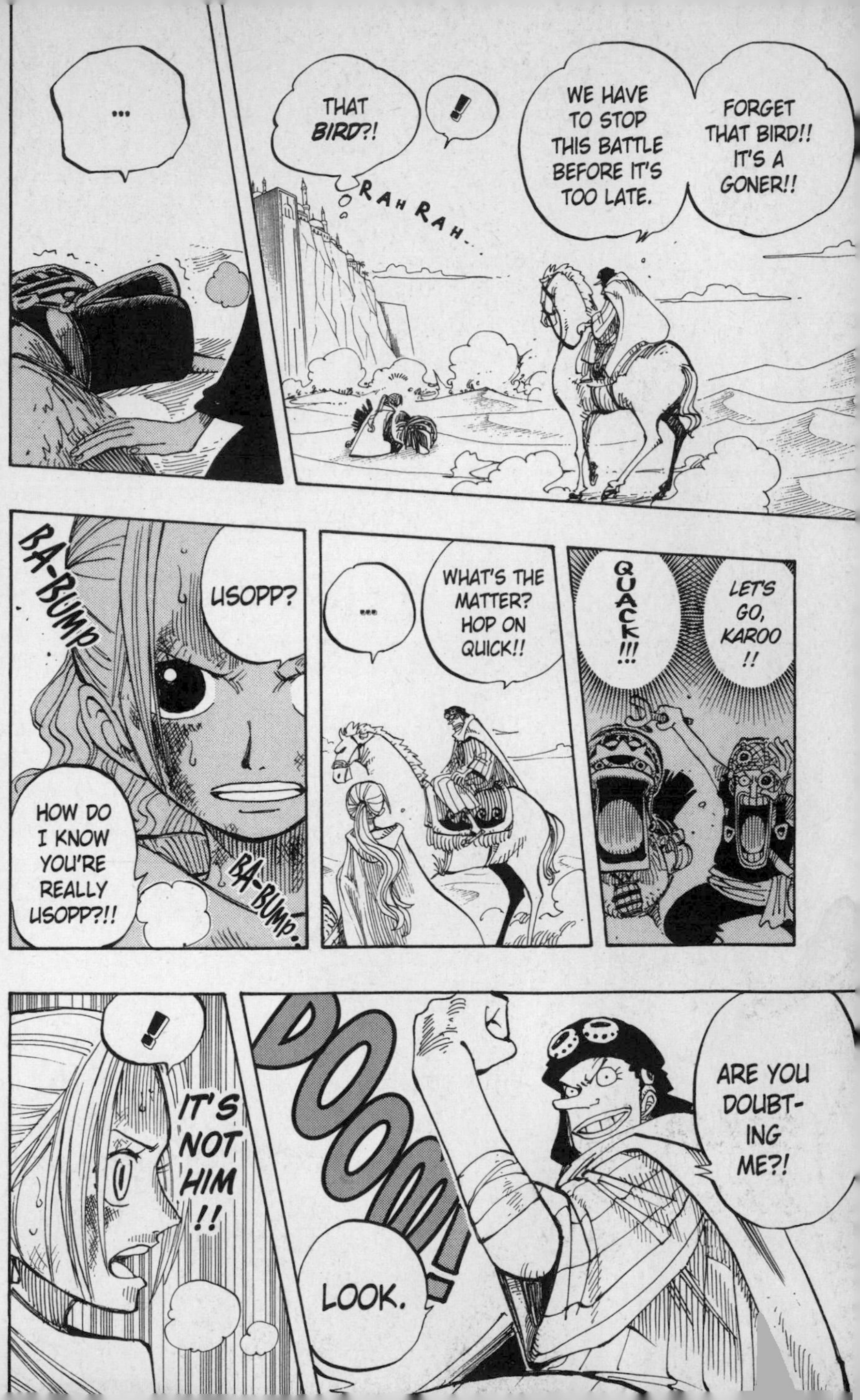
FORGET THAT BIRD!! IT'S A GONER!!
WE HAVE TO STOP THIS BATTLE BEFORE IT'S TOO LATE.
!
THAT BIRD?!
RAH RAH...
...
LET'S GO, KAROO!!
QUACK!!!
WHAT'S THE MATTER? HOP ON QUICK!!
...
USOPP?
BA-BUMP
HOW DO I KNOW YOU'RE REALLY USOPP?!!
BA-BUMP
ARE YOU DOUBT-ING ME?!
DOOOM!
LOOK.
!
IT'S NOT HIM!!

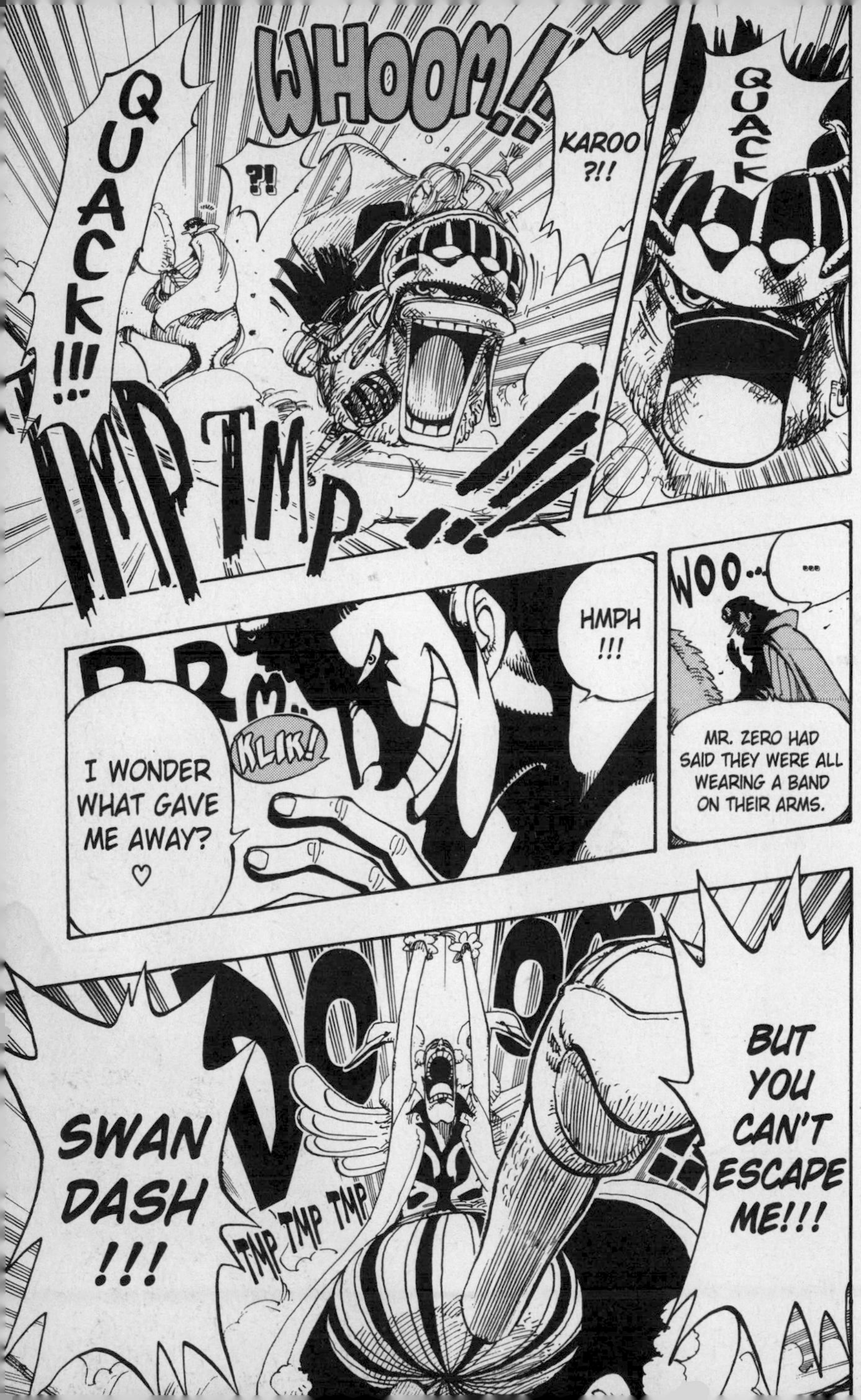
QUACK
KAROO ?!!
WHOOM!!
?!
QUACK!!!
TMP TMP!!!
WOO...
...
MR. ZERO HAD SAID THEY WERE ALL WEARING A BAND ON THEIR ARMS.
HMPH!!!
BRRM..
KLIK!
I WONDER WHAT GAVE ME AWAY? ♡
BUT YOU CAN'T ESCAPE ME!!!
TMP TMP TMP
SWAN DASH!!!

ONE PIECE **STORYBOARD PREVIEW!!** #19

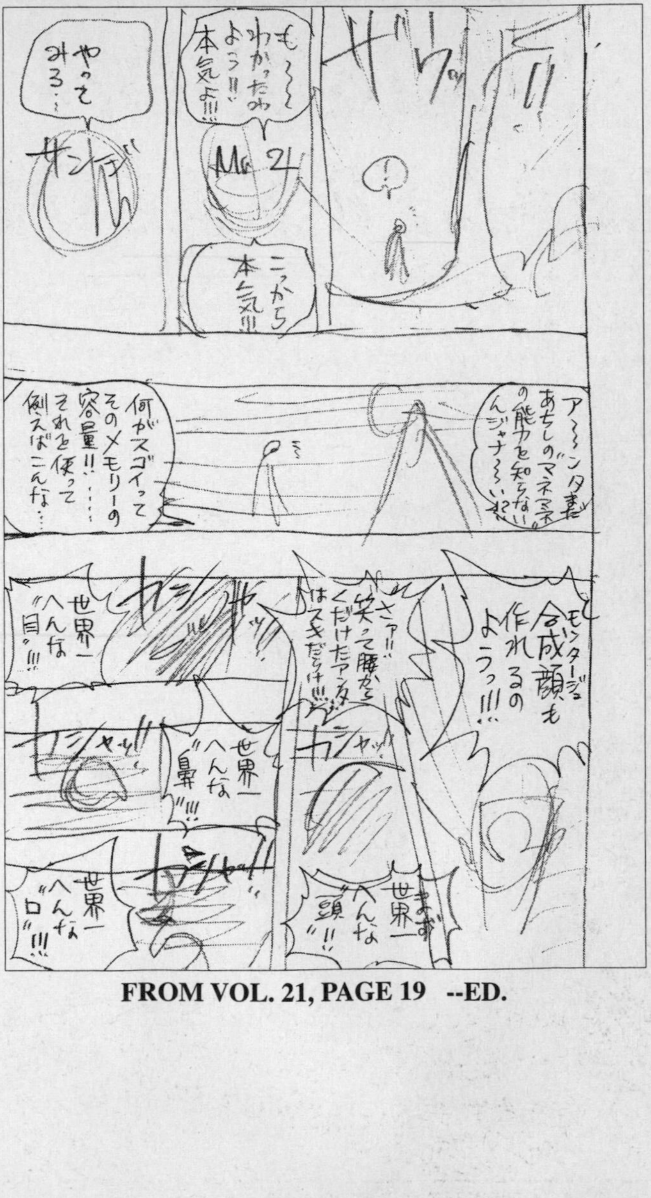
もう〜〜わかったわよう!! 本気よ!!!
ここから本気!!!
やってみる〜
ア〜〜ンタまだあちしのマネマネの能力を知らないんじゃナ〜〜い!?
何がスゴイってそのメモリーの容量!!…… それを使って例えばこんな…
モンタージュ 合成顔も作れるのようっ!!!
カシャッ
まず世界一へんな"頭"!!
世界一へんな"目"!!!
カシャッ
世界一へんな"鼻"!!!
世界一へんな"口"!!!

FROM VOL. 21, PAGE 19 --ED.

Chapter 183:
SQUADRON LEADER KAROO

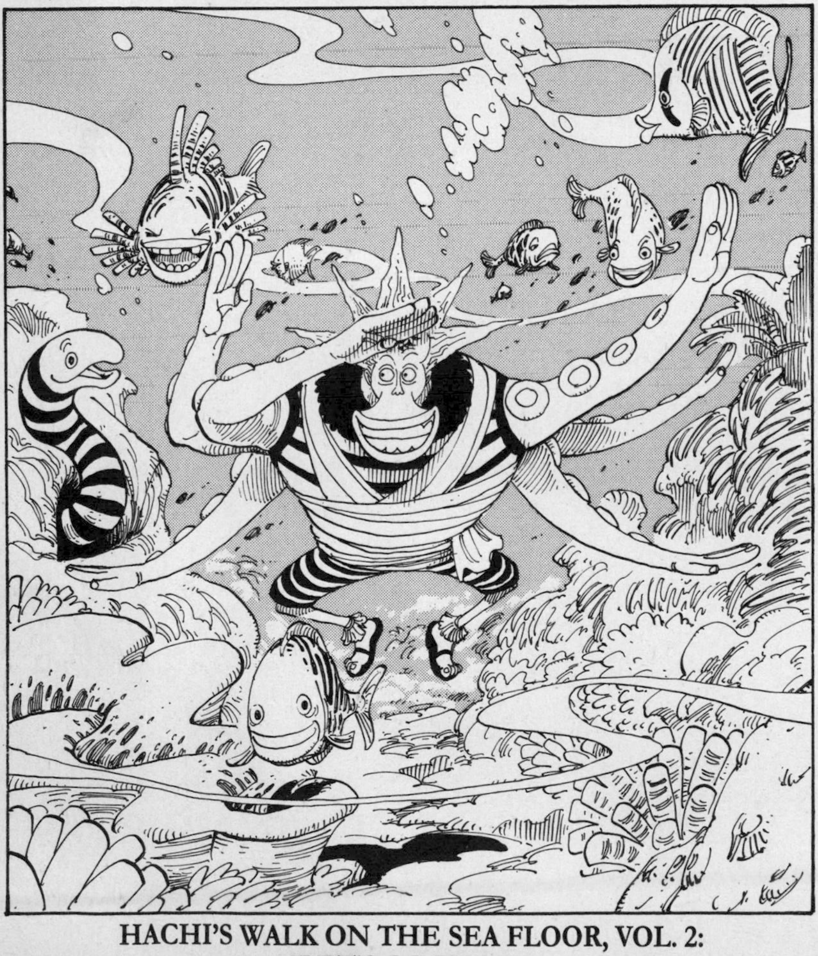

HACHI'S WALK ON THE SEA FLOOR, VOL. 2:
"LET'S GO HOME"

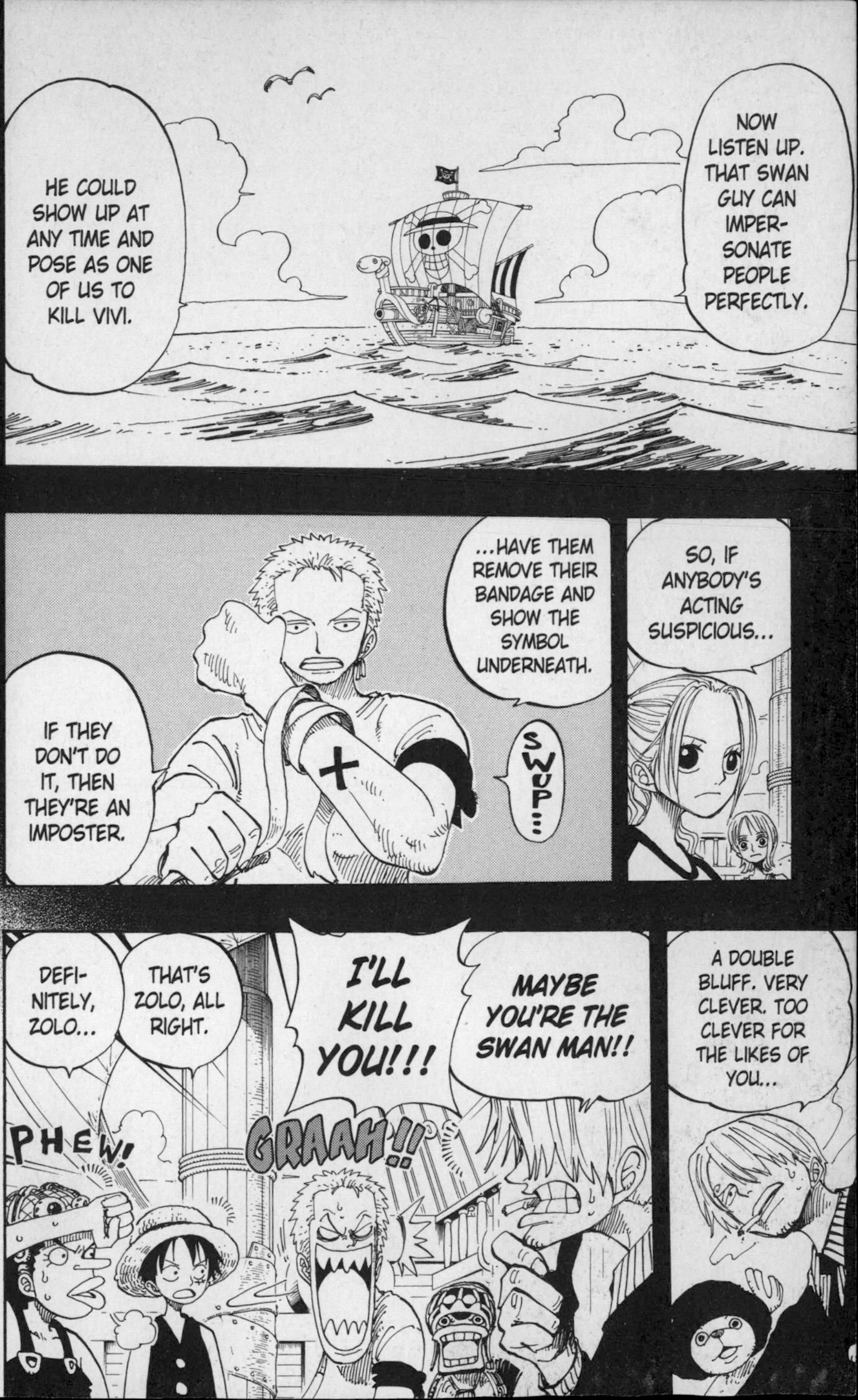
NOW LISTEN UP. THAT SWAN GUY CAN IMPER-SONATE PEOPLE PERFECTLY.
HE COULD SHOW UP AT ANY TIME AND POSE AS ONE OF US TO KILL VIVI.
SO, IF ANYBODY'S ACTING SUSPICIOUS...
...HAVE THEM REMOVE THEIR BANDAGE AND SHOW THE SYMBOL UNDERNEATH.
SWUP...
IF THEY DON'T DO IT, THEN THEY'RE AN IMPOSTER.
A DOUBLE BLUFF. VERY CLEVER. TOO CLEVER FOR THE LIKES OF YOU...
MAYBE YOU'RE THE SWAN MAN!!
I'LL KILL YOU!!!
GRAAH!!
THAT'S ZOLO, ALL RIGHT.
DEFI-NITELY, ZOLO...
PHEW!

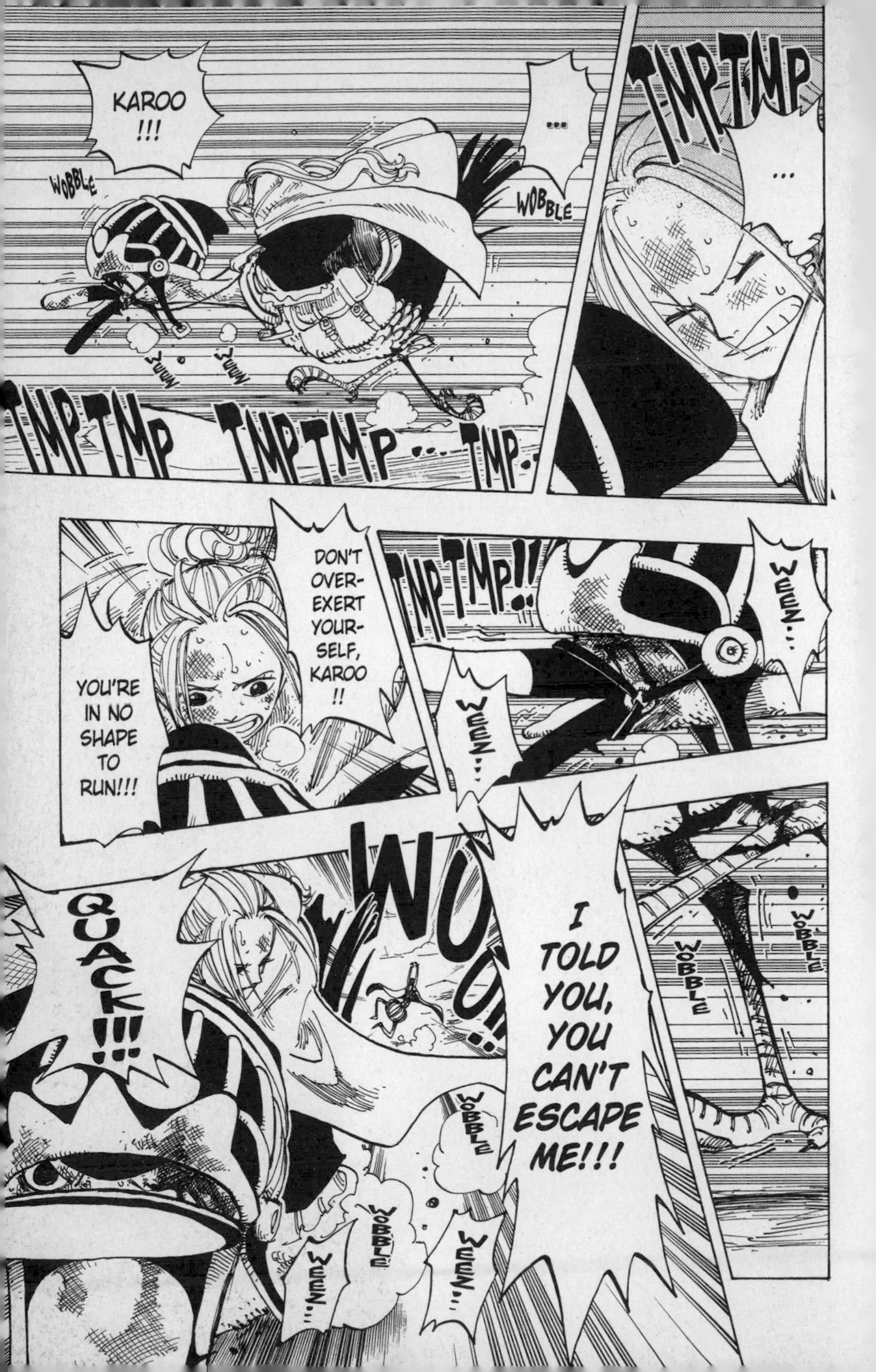
TMP TMP
...
...
KAROO!!!
WOBBLE
WOBBLE
WUUN
WUUN
TMP TMP TMP TMP... TMP...
TMP TMP!!
WEEZ...
WEEZ...
DON'T OVER-EXERT YOURSELF, KAROO!!
YOU'RE IN NO SHAPE TO RUN!!!
WOBBLE
WOBBLE
WOO...
I TOLD YOU, YOU CAN'T ESCAPE ME!!!
QUACK!!!
WOBBLE
WOBBLE
WEEZ...
WEEZ...

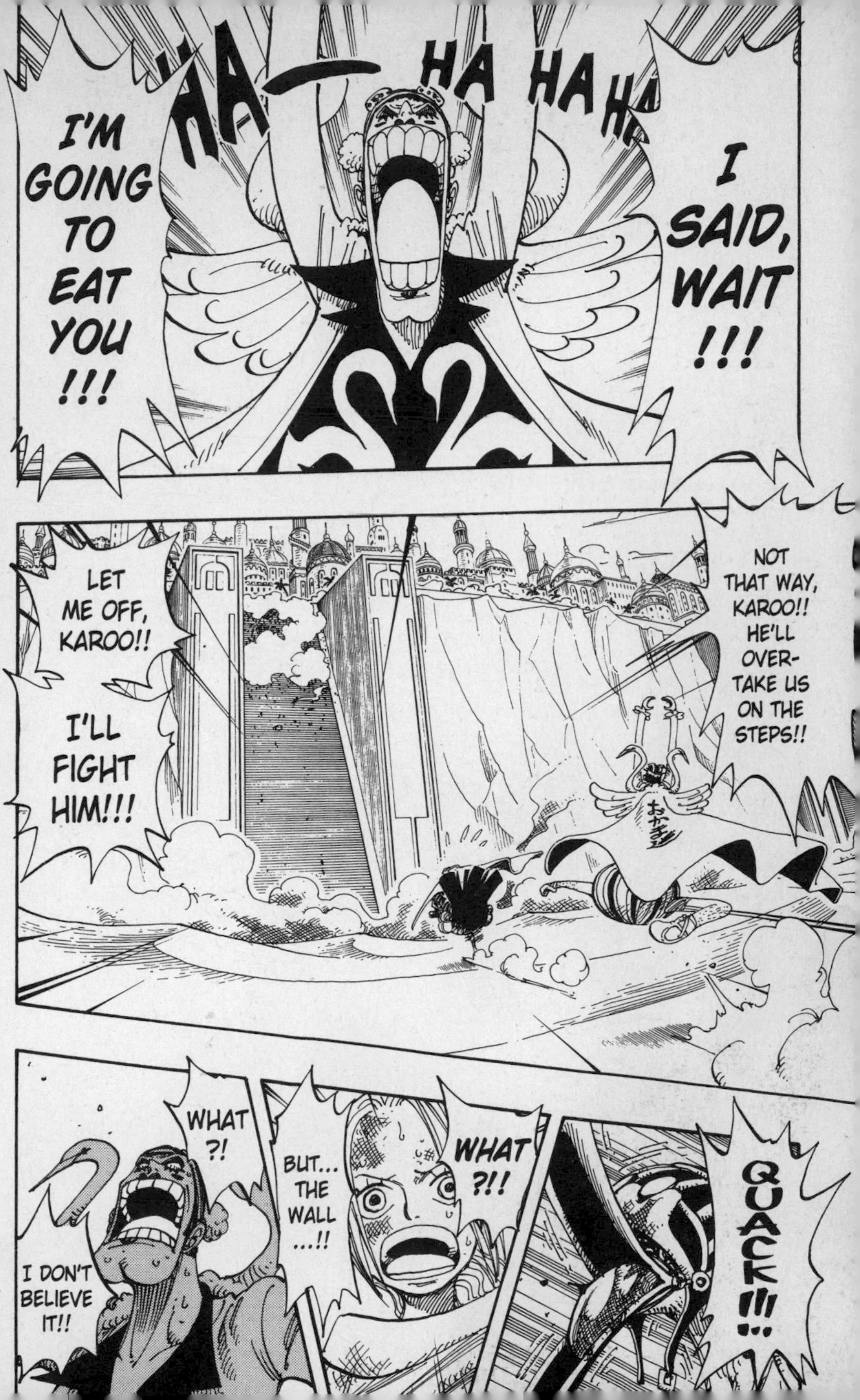
I SAID, WAIT!!!
HA— HA HA HA
I'M GOING TO EAT YOU!!!
NOT THAT WAY, KAROO!! HE'LL OVER-TAKE US ON THE STEPS!!
LET ME OFF, KAROO!!
I'LL FIGHT HIM!!!
QUACK!!!
WHAT?!!
BUT... THE WALL ...!!
WHAT?!
I DON'T BELIEVE IT!!

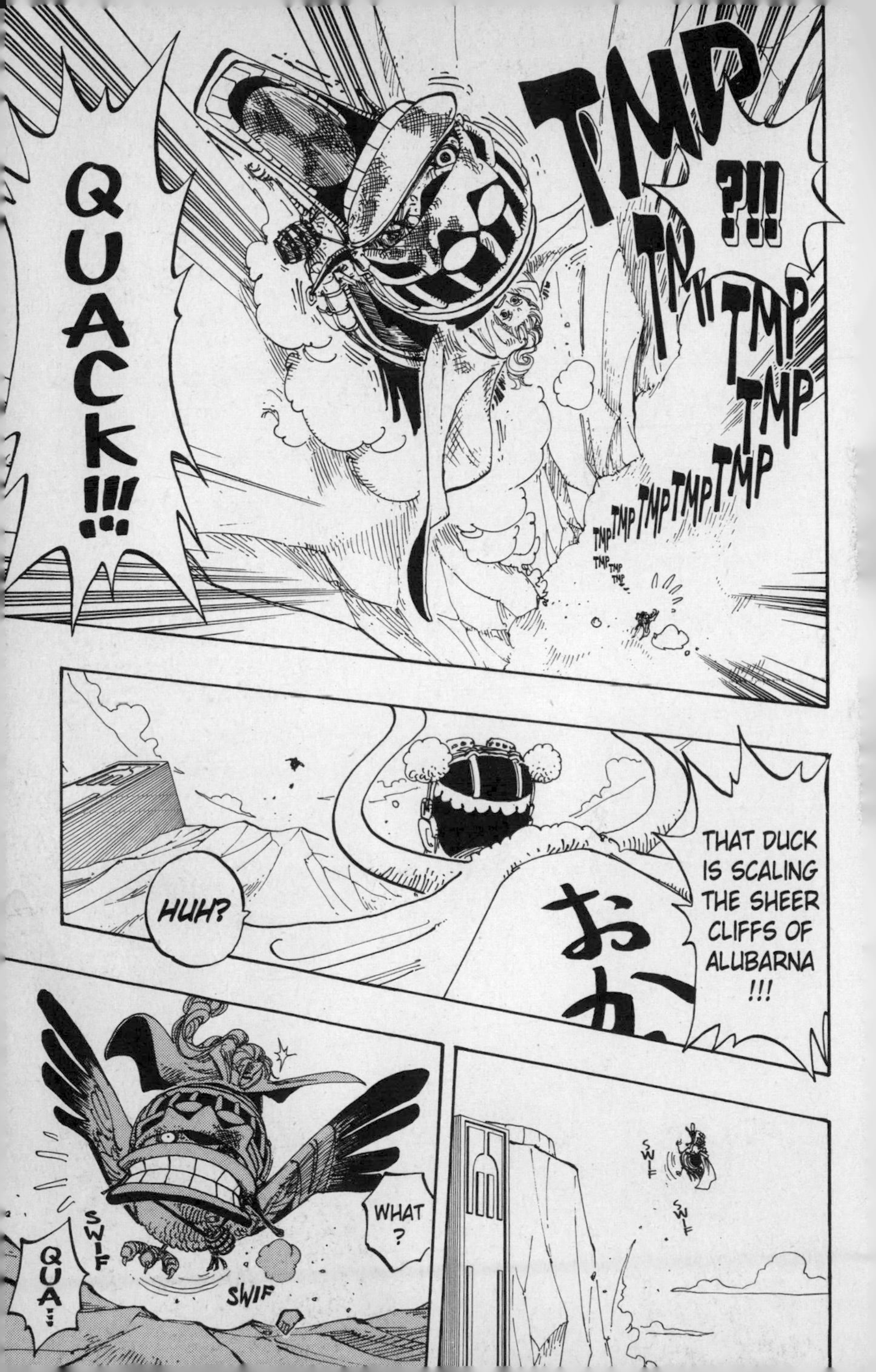

TMP
?!!
TMP
TMP
TMP
TMP
TMP TMP TMP TMP TMP TMP TMP TMP
QUACK!!!
THAT DUCK IS SCALING THE SHEER CLIFFS OF ALUBARNA !!!
HUH?
SWIF
SWIF
WHAT ?
SWIF
SWIF
QUA...

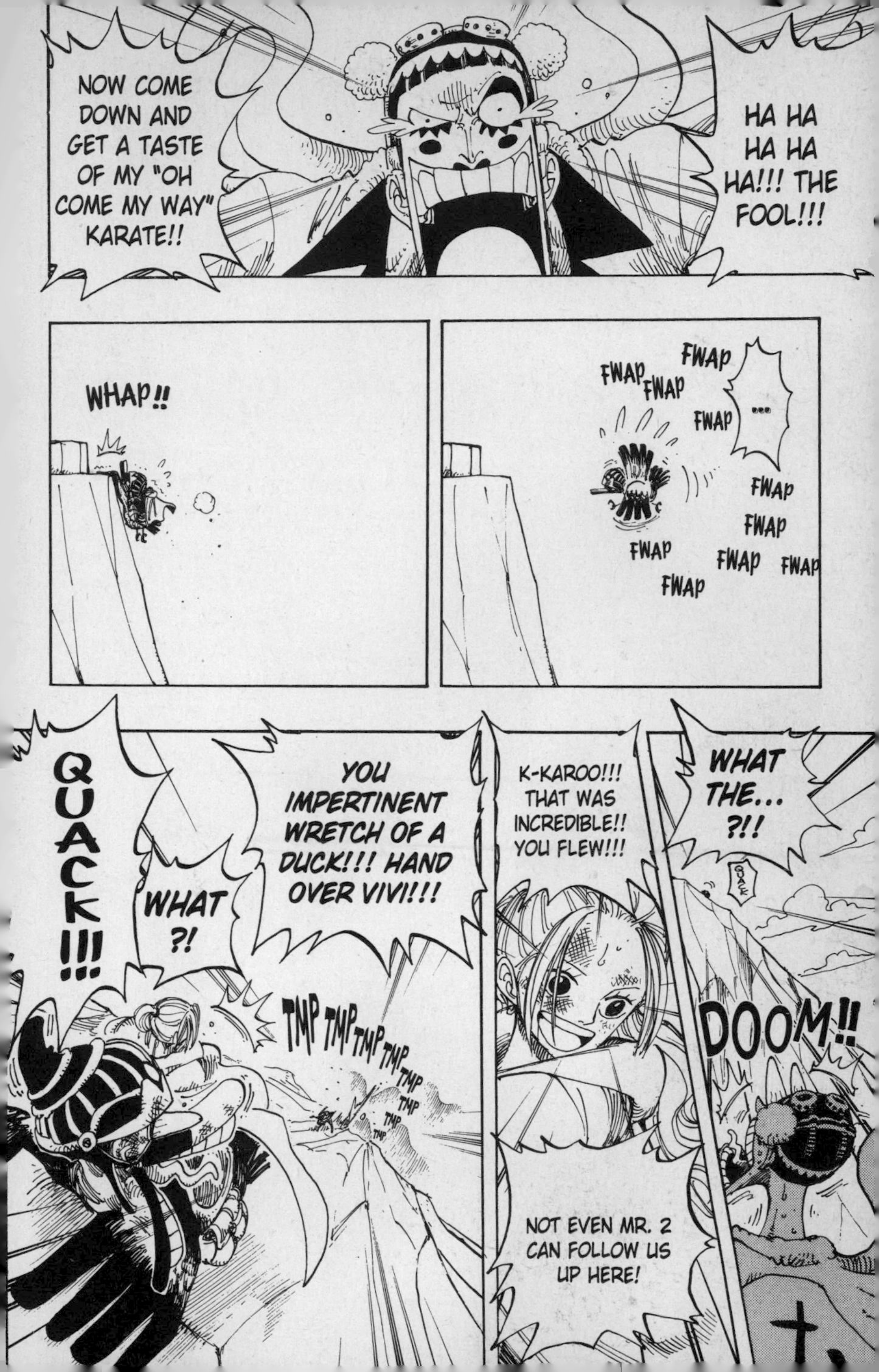
HA HA HA HA HA!!! THE FOOL!!!
NOW COME DOWN AND GET A TASTE OF MY "OH COME MY WAY" KARATE!!
FWAP FWAP FWAP FWAP
...
FWAP FWAP FWAP FWAP FWAP FWAP
WHAP!!
WHAT THE... ?!!
QUACK
DOOM!!
K-KAROO!!! THAT WAS INCREDIBLE!! YOU FLEW!!!
NOT EVEN MR. 2 CAN FOLLOW US UP HERE!
YOU IMPERTINENT WRETCH OF A DUCK!!! HAND OVER VIVI!!!
WHAT ?!
QUACK!!!
TMP TMP TMP TMP TMP TMP TMP TMP

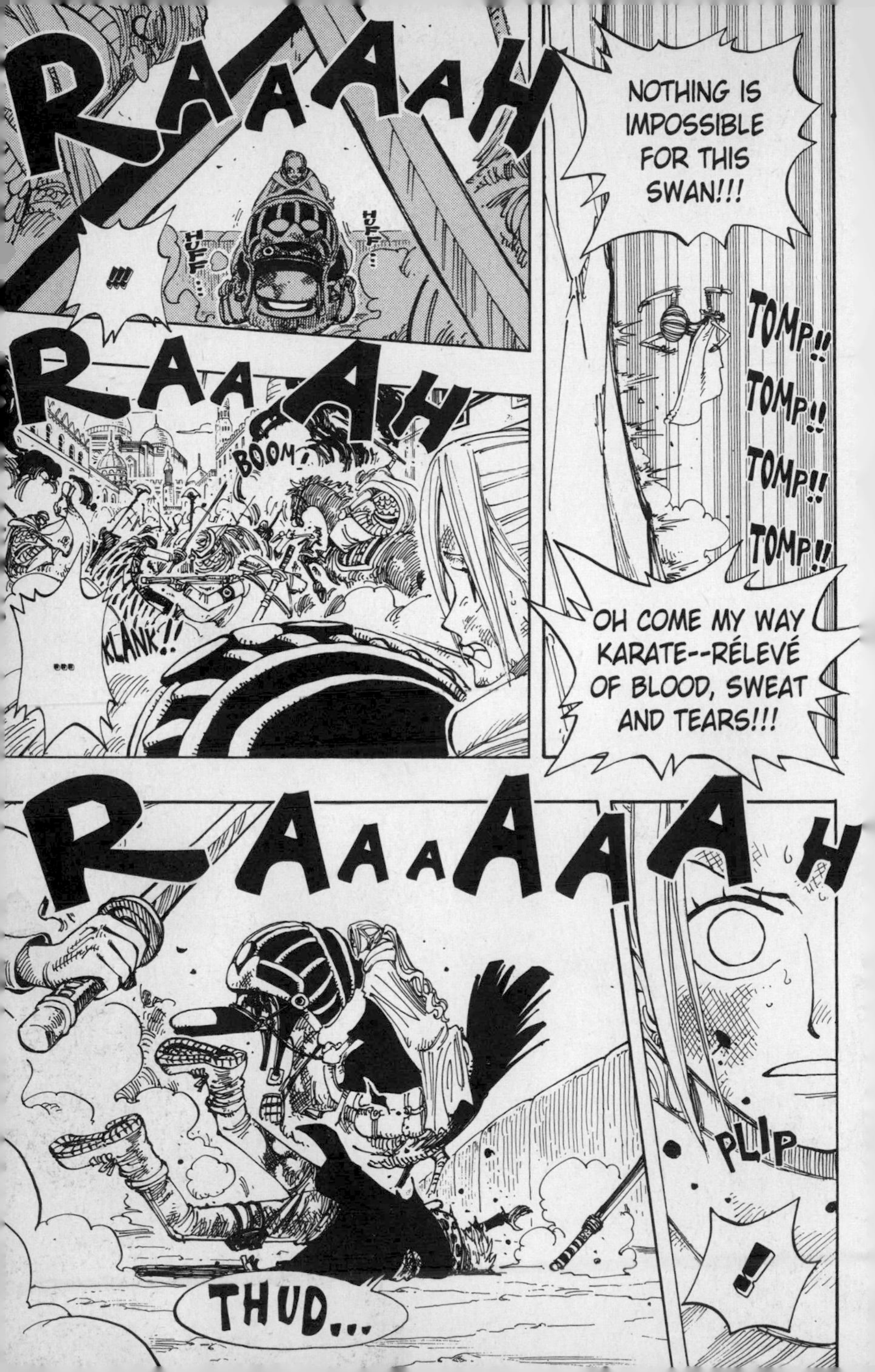

NOTHING IS IMPOSSIBLE FOR THIS SWAN!!!
TOMP!! TOMP!! TOMP!! TOMP!!
OH COME MY WAY KARATE--RÉLEVÉ OF BLOOD, SWEAT AND TEARS!!!
RAAAAH
HUFF...
HUFF...
!!!
RAAAH
BOOM
KLANK!!
...
RAAAAAAH
PLIP
!
THUD...

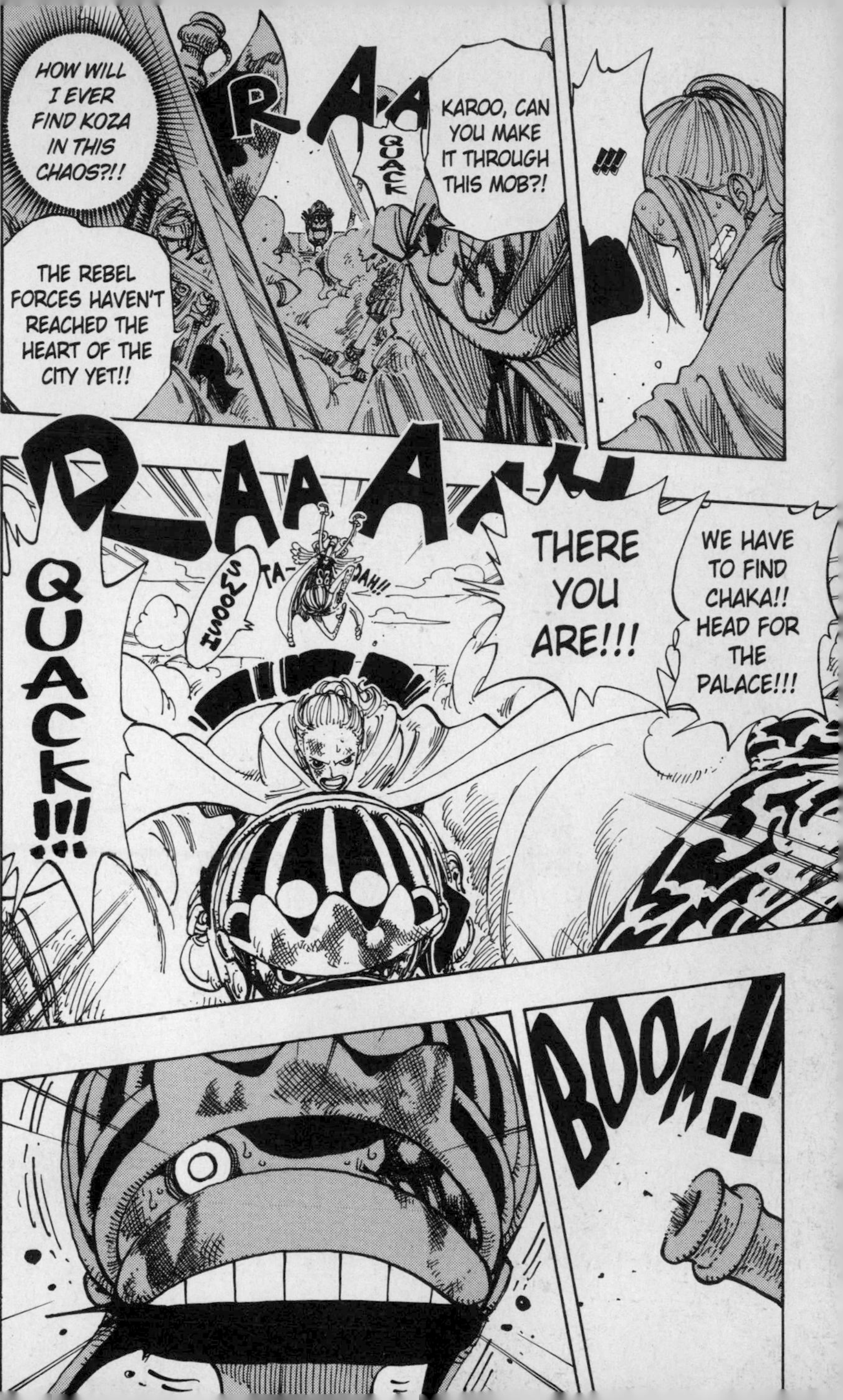
!!!
KAROO, CAN YOU MAKE IT THROUGH THIS MOB?!
QUACK
RAA
HOW WILL I EVER FIND KOZA IN THIS CHAOS?!!
THE REBEL FORCES HAVEN'T REACHED THE HEART OF THE CITY YET!!
WE HAVE TO FIND CHAKA!! HEAD FOR THE PALACE!!!
THERE YOU ARE!!!
SWOOSH
QUACK!!!
BOOM!!

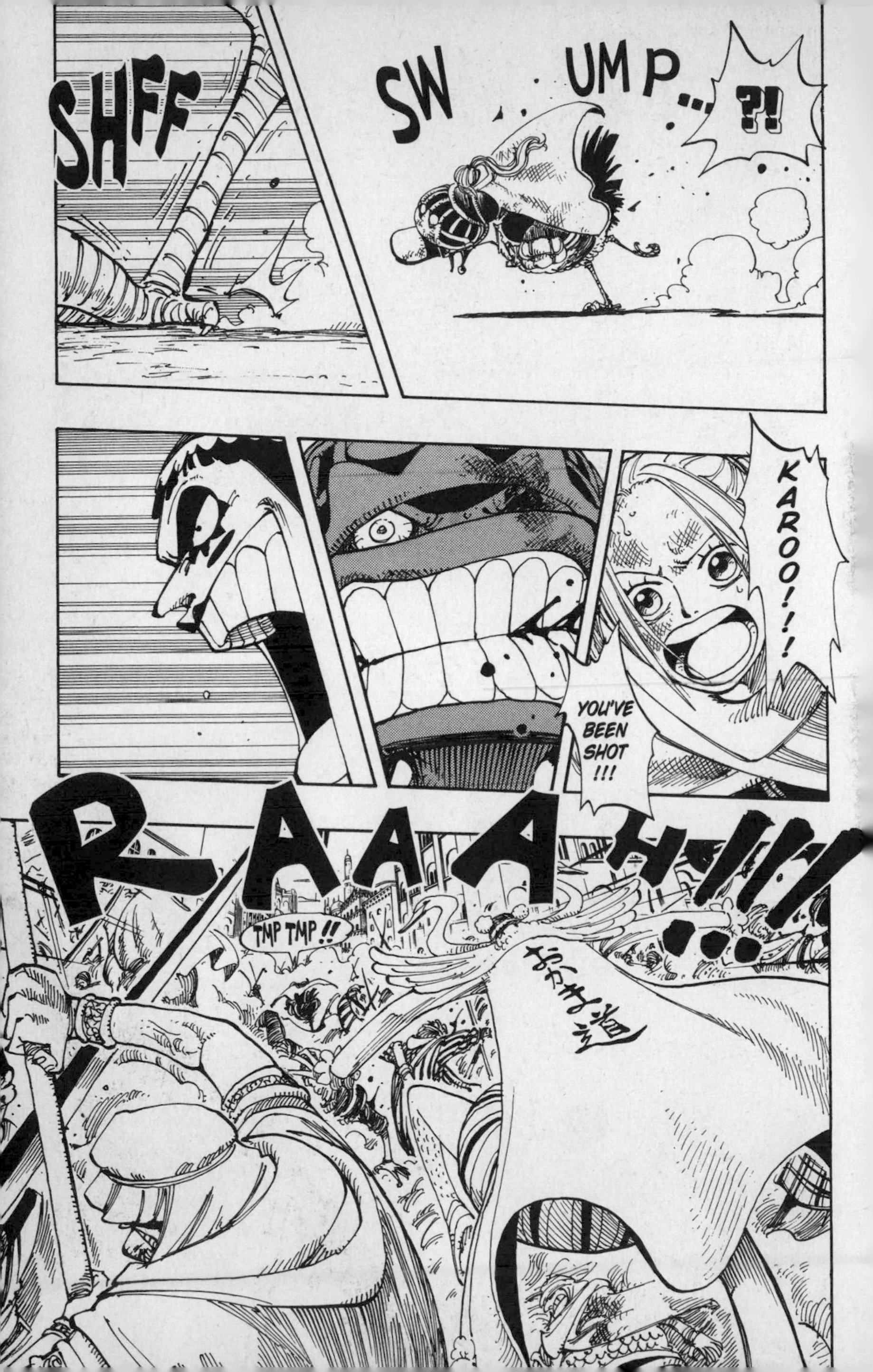

SW . . UMP...
?!
SHFF
KAROO!!!
YOU'VE BEEN SHOT!!!
RAAAH!!!
TMP TMP!!

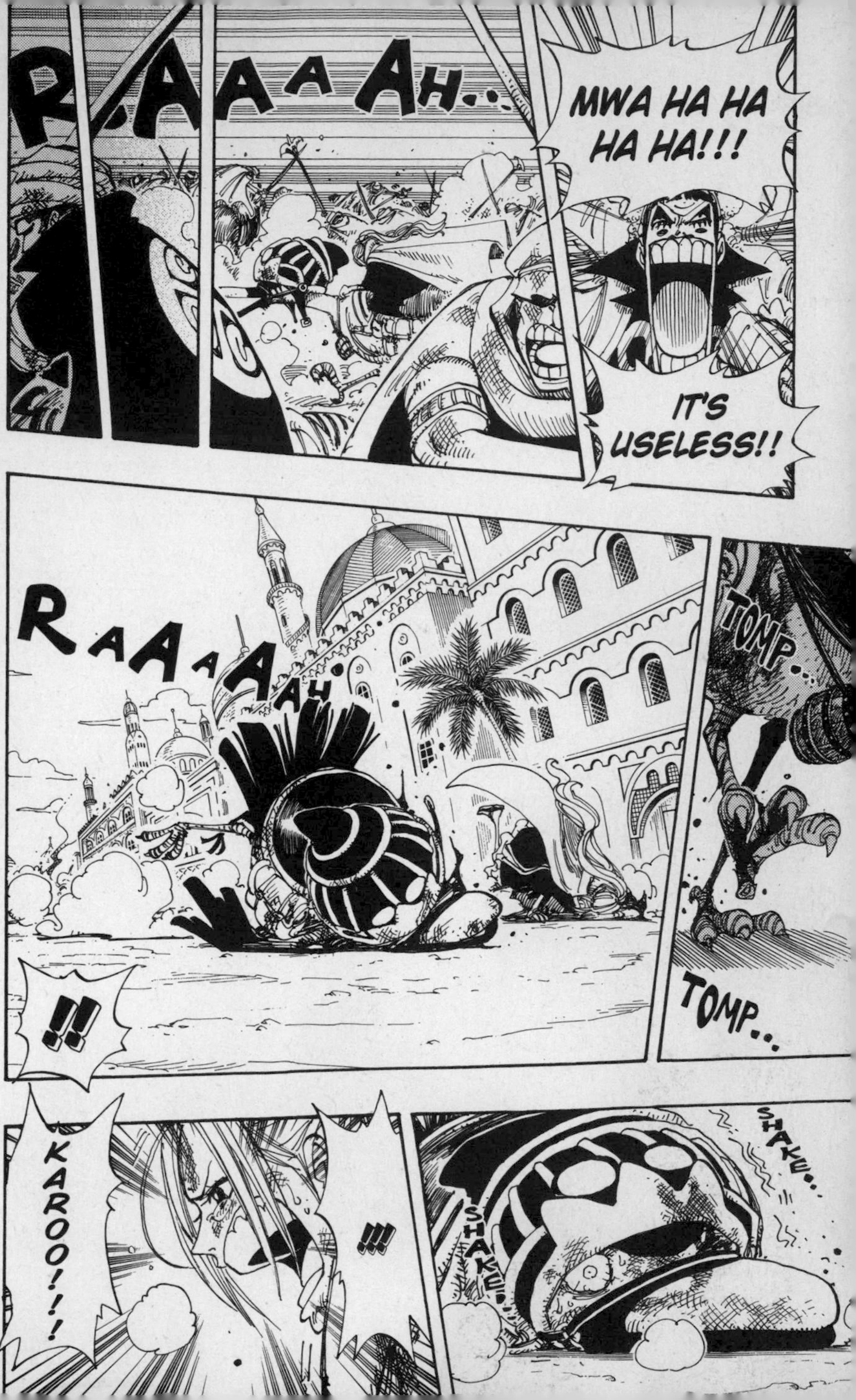
MWA HA HA HA HA!!!
IT'S USELESS!!
RAAAAAH...
TOMP...
TOMP...
RAAAAAAH
!!
SHAKE...
SHAKE...
!!!
KAROO!!!

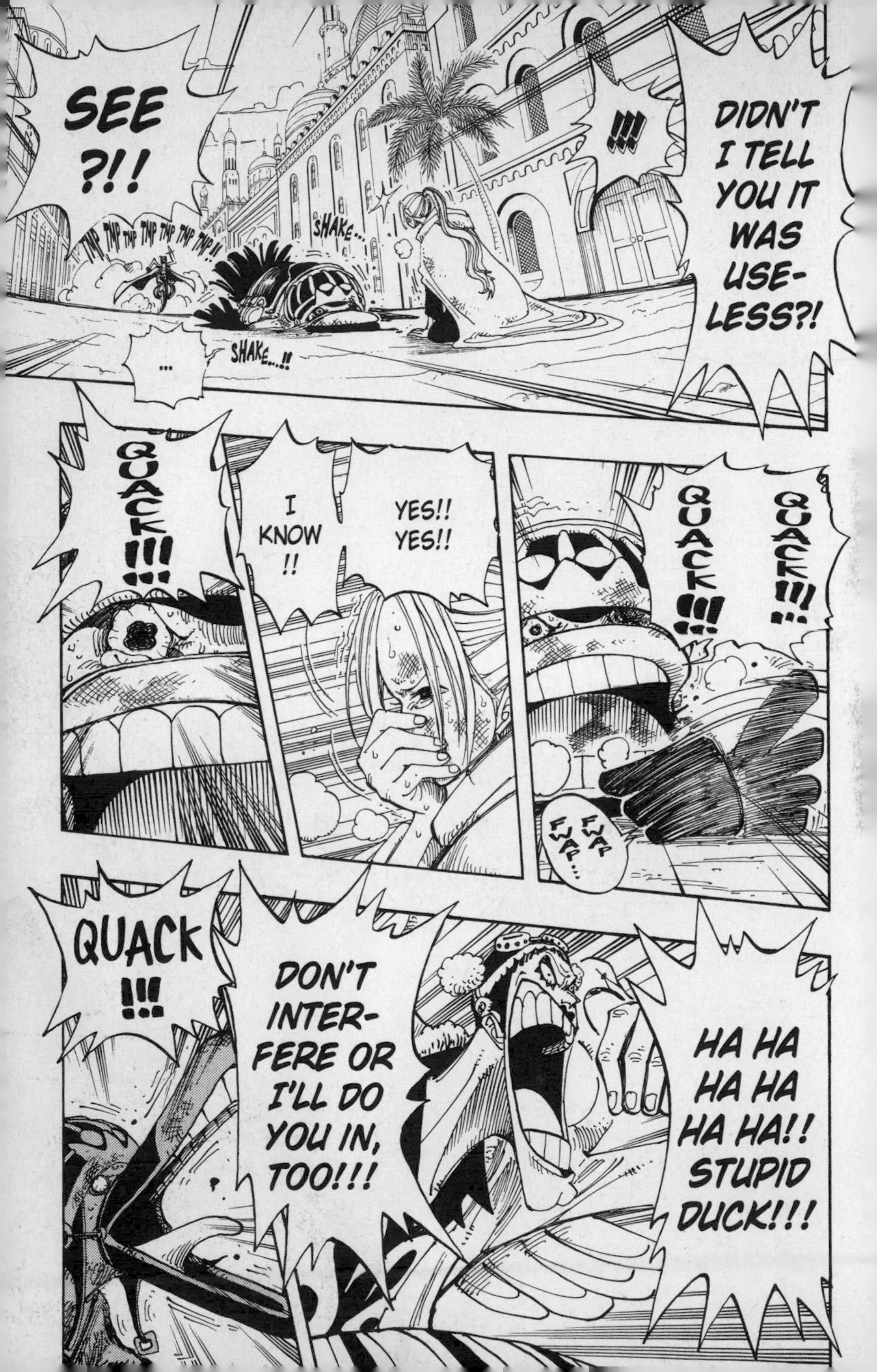
DIDN'T I TELL YOU IT WAS USE-LESS?!
!!!
SHAKE...
SEE ?!!
TMP TMP TMP TMP TMP TMP TMP!!
SHAKE...!!
...
QUACK!!!
QUACK!!!
FWAP FWAP...
YES!! YES!!
I KNOW !!
QUACK!!!
HA HA HA HA HA HA!! STUPID DUCK!!!
DON'T INTER-FERE OR I'LL DO YOU IN, TOO!!!
QUACK!!!

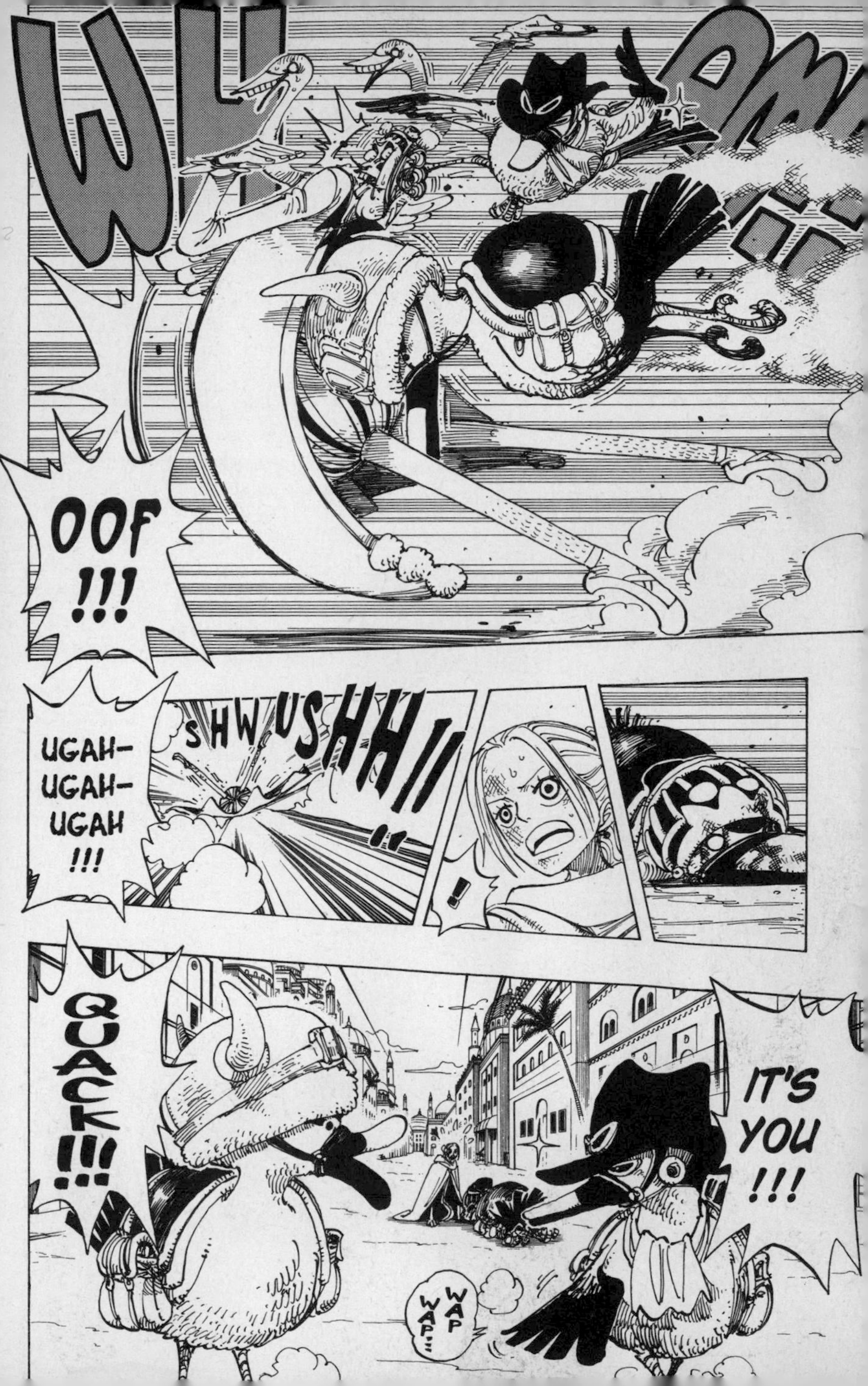
OOF!!!
!
SHWUSHH!!
UGAH-UGAH-UGAH!!!
IT'S YOU!!!
WAP WAP WAP
QUACK!!!

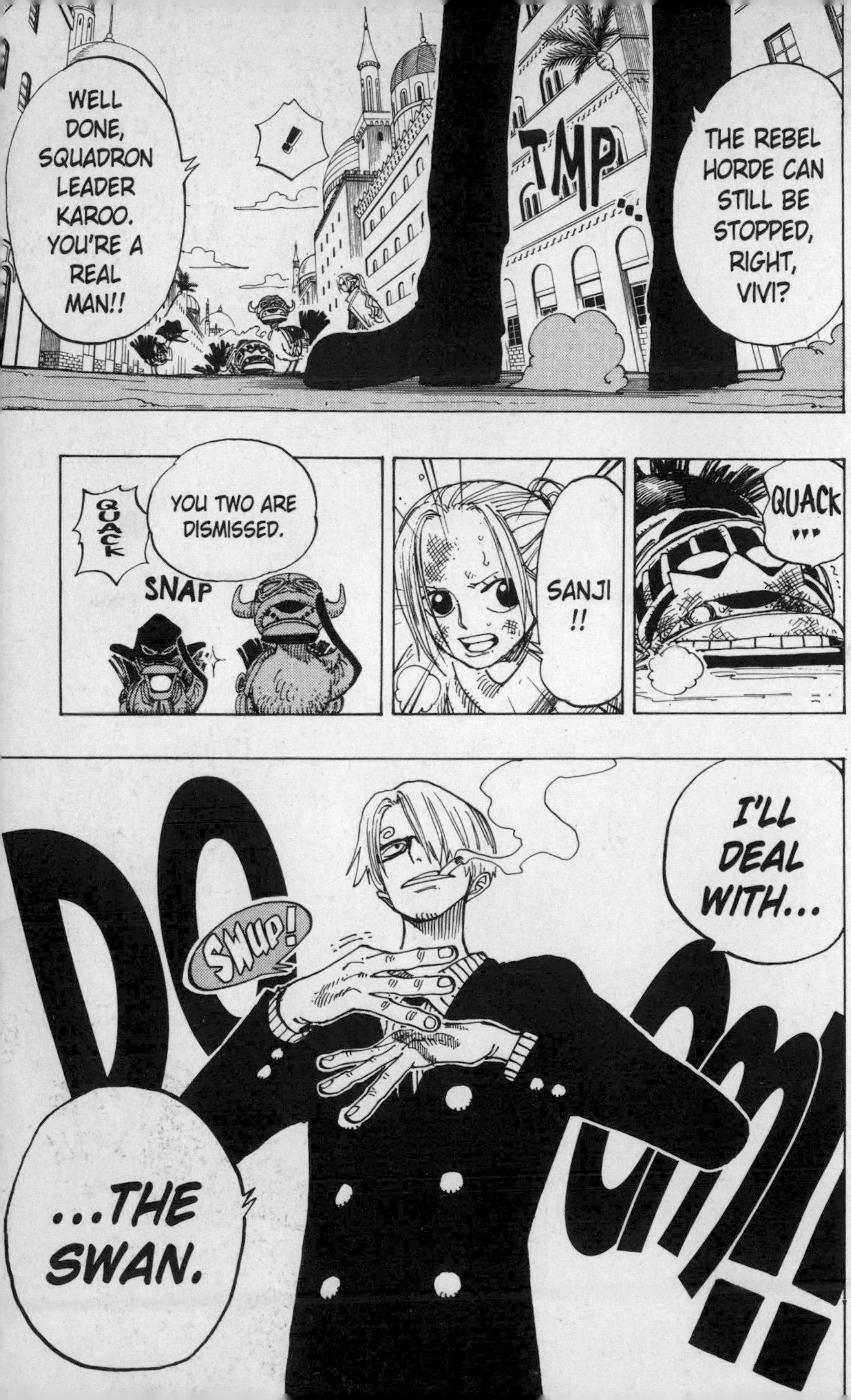
THE REBEL HORDE CAN STILL BE STOPPED, RIGHT, VIVI?
TMP
!
WELL DONE, SQUADRON LEADER KAROO. YOU'RE A REAL MAN!!
QUACK...
SANJI!!
YOU TWO ARE DISMISSED.
QUACK
SNAP
I'LL DEAL WITH...
SWUP!
DOOM!!
...THE SWAN.

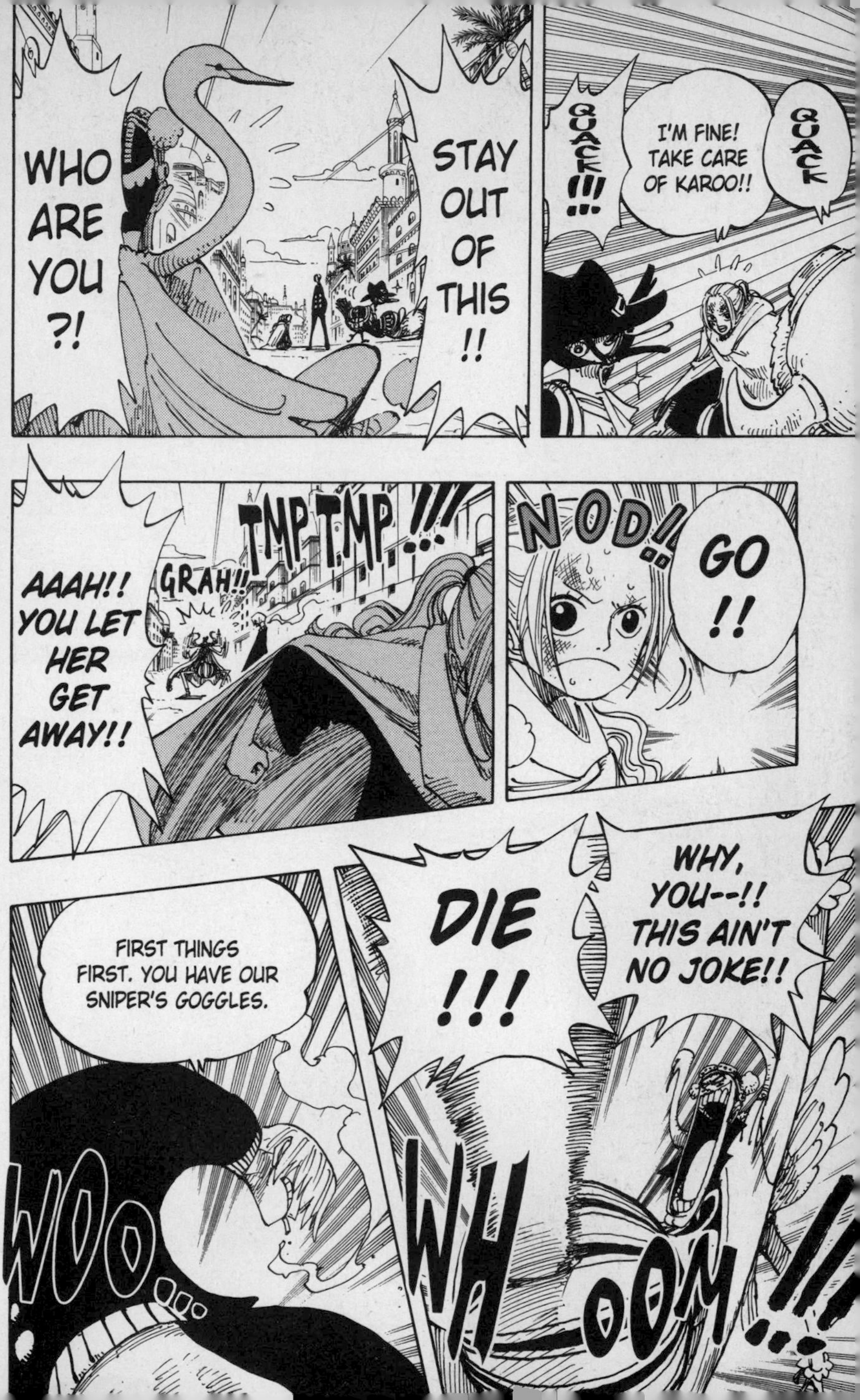
QUACK
I'M FINE! TAKE CARE OF KAROO!!
QUACK!!!
STAY OUT OF THIS!!
WHO ARE YOU?!
GO!!
NOD!!
TMP TMP!!!
GRAH!!
AAAH!! YOU LET HER GET AWAY!!
WHY, YOU--!! THIS AIN'T NO JOKE!!
DIE!!!
WHOOM!!!
FIRST THINGS FIRST. YOU HAVE OUR SNIPER'S GOGGLES.
WOO...

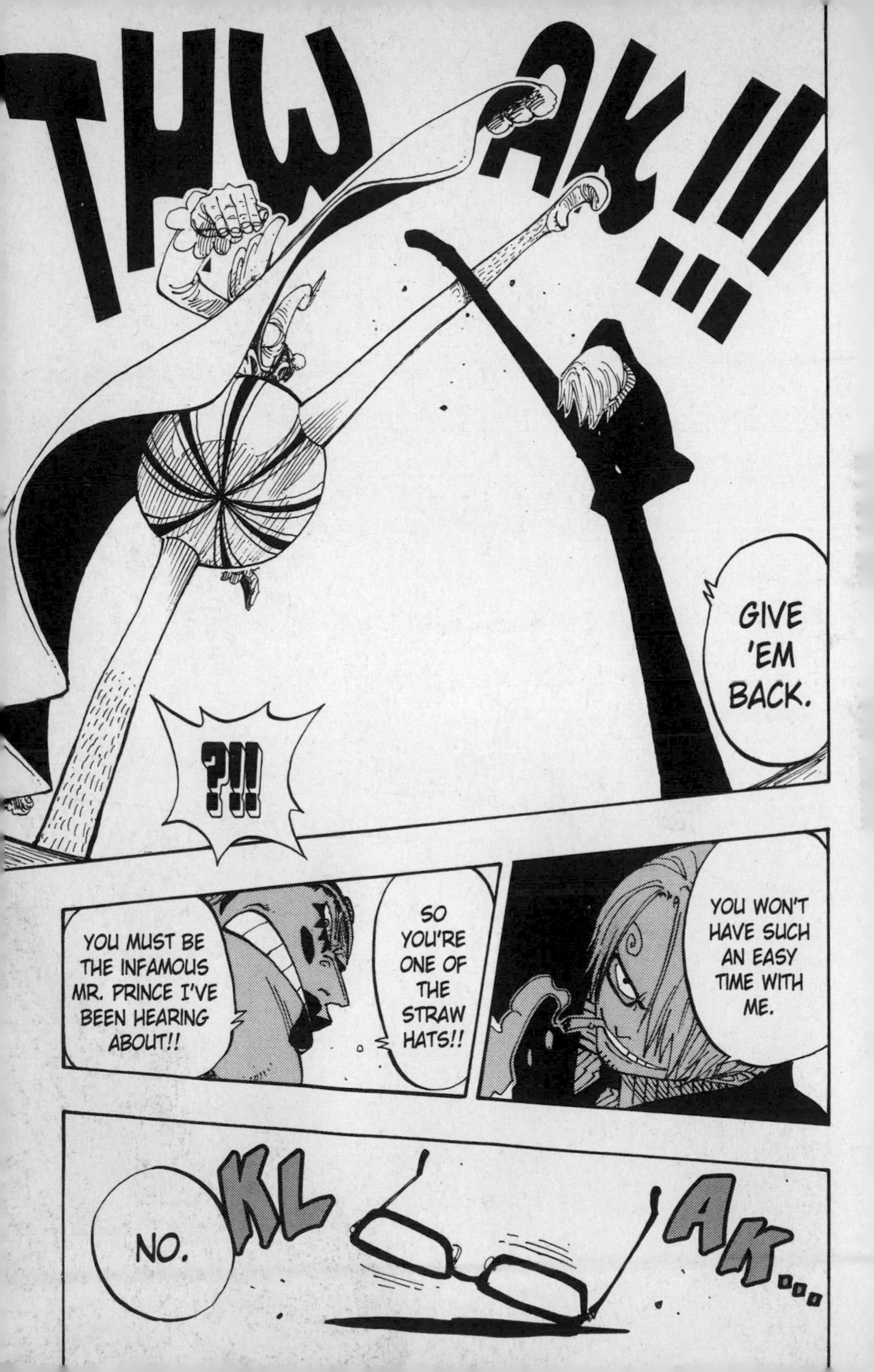
THWAK!!!!!!
GIVE 'EM BACK.
?!!
YOU WON'T HAVE SUCH AN EASY TIME WITH ME.
SO YOU'RE ONE OF THE STRAW HATS!!
YOU MUST BE THE INFAMOUS MR. PRINCE I'VE BEEN HEARING ABOUT!!
KLAK...
NO.

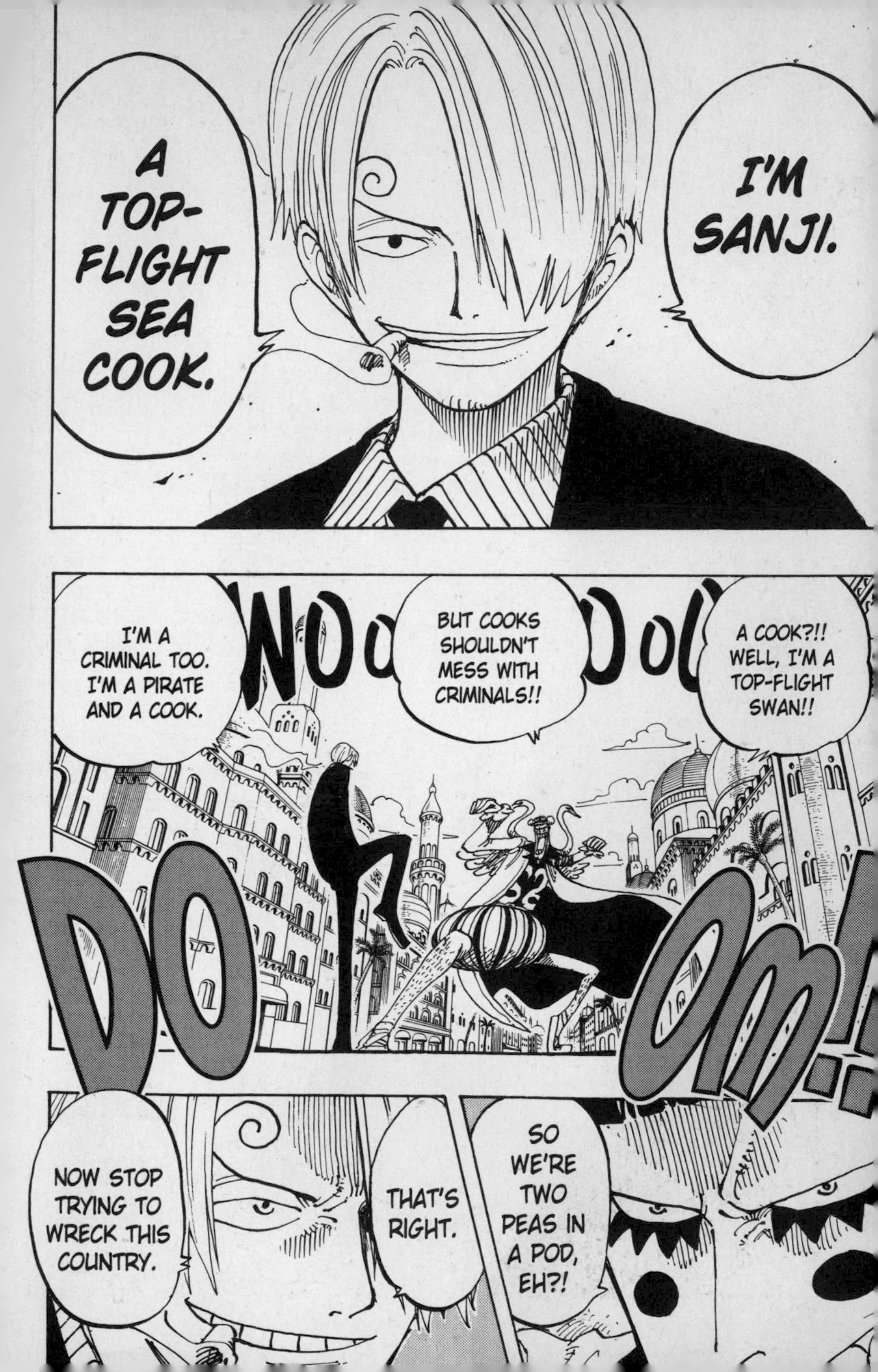
I'M SANJI.
A TOP-FLIGHT SEA COOK.
A COOK?!! WELL, I'M A TOP-FLIGHT SWAN!!
BUT COOKS SHOULDN'T MESS WITH CRIMINALS!!
I'M A CRIMINAL TOO. I'M A PIRATE AND A COOK.
DOOM!!
SO WE'RE TWO PEAS IN A POD, EH?!
THAT'S RIGHT.
NOW STOP TRYING TO WRECK THIS COUNTRY.

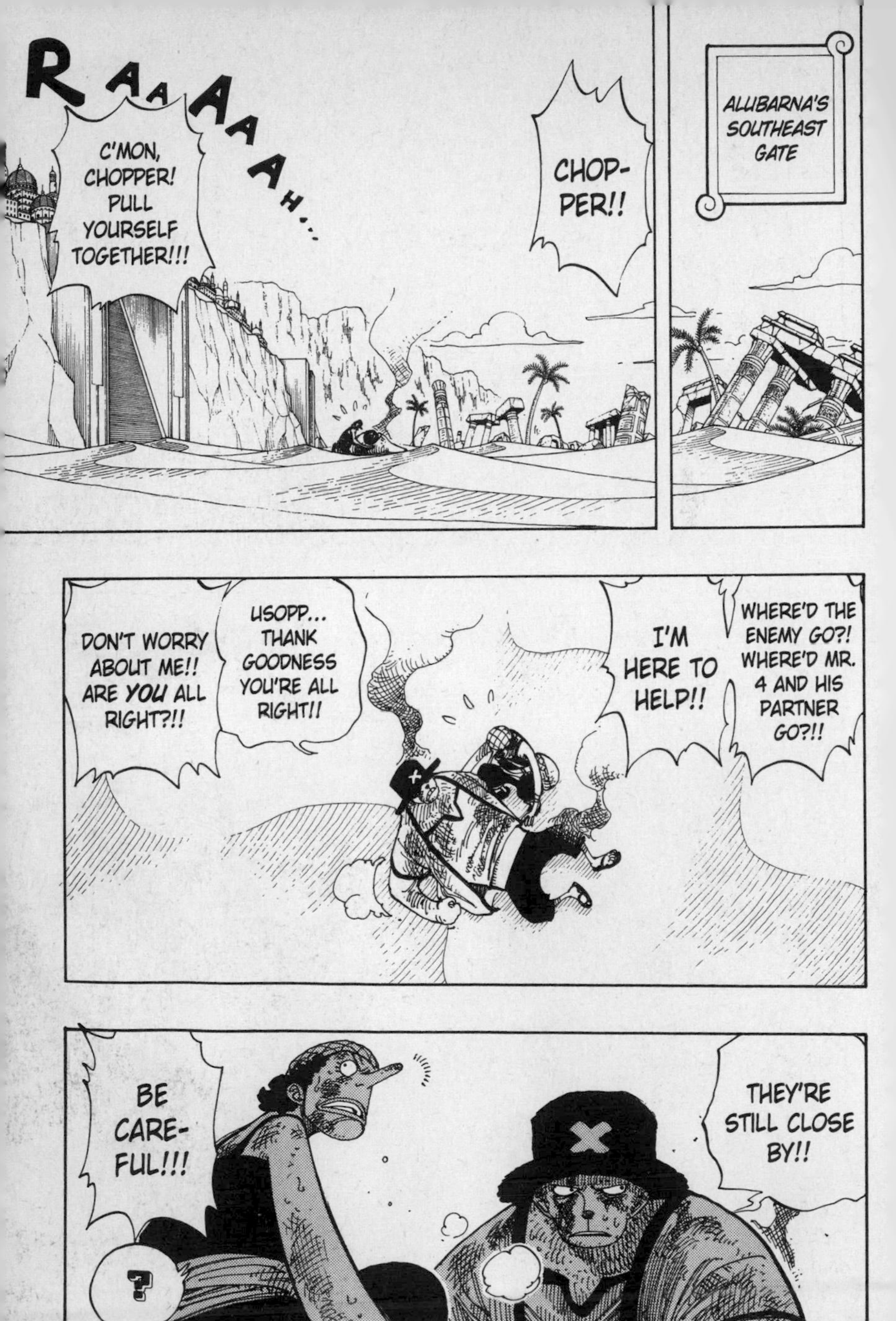
ALUBARNA'S SOUTHEAST GATE
CHOP-PER!!
RAAAAAAH...
C'MON, CHOPPER! PULL YOURSELF TOGETHER!!!
WHERE'D THE ENEMY GO?! WHERE'D MR. 4 AND HIS PARTNER GO?!!
I'M HERE TO HELP!!
USOPP... THANK GOODNESS YOU'RE ALL RIGHT!!
DON'T WORRY ABOUT ME!! ARE *YOU* ALL RIGHT?!!
THEY'RE STILL CLOSE BY!!
BE CARE-FUL!!!
?

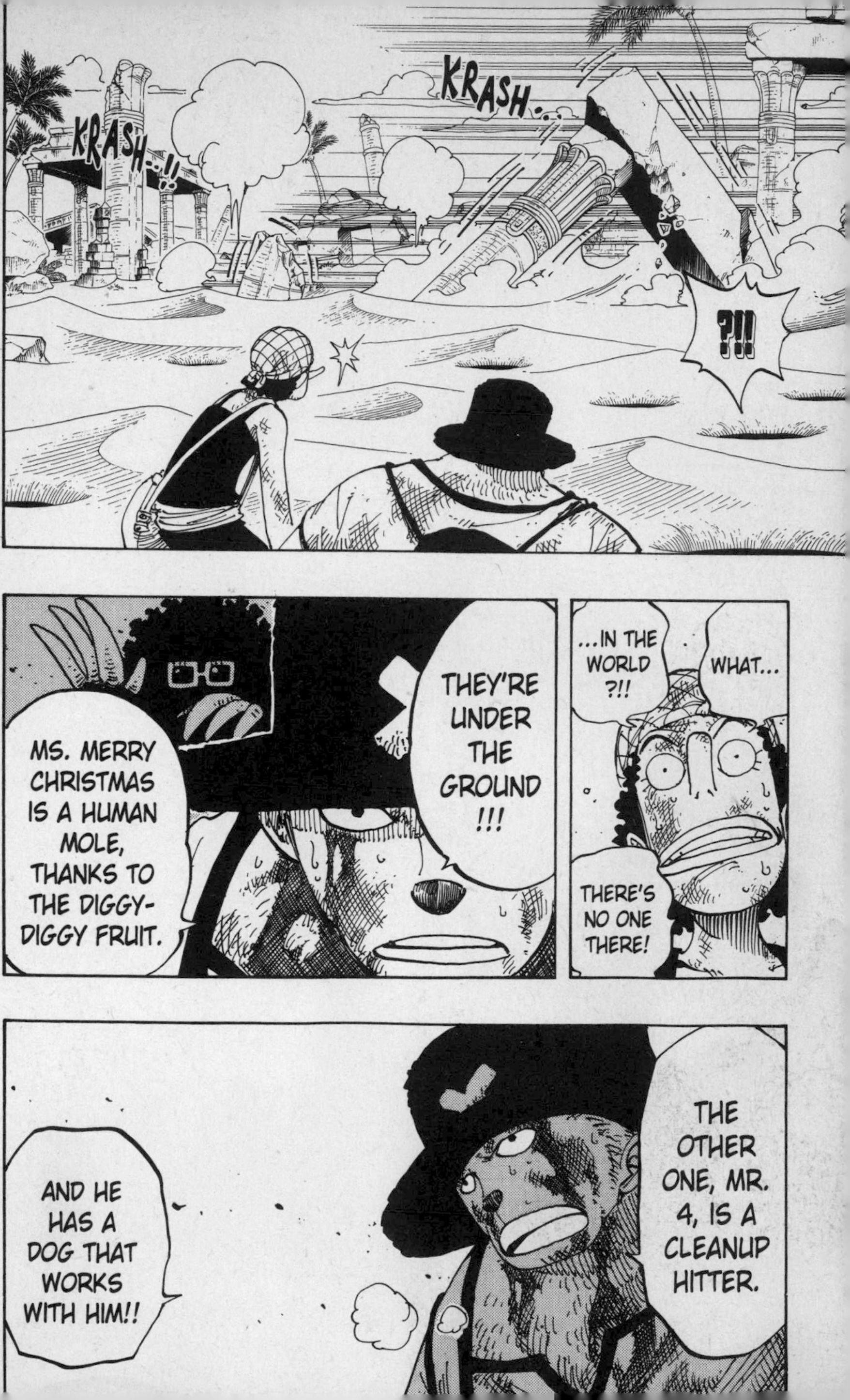
KRASH...
KRASH..!!
?!!
WHAT...
...IN THE WORLD ?!!
THERE'S NO ONE THERE!
THEY'RE UNDER THE GROUND !!!
MS. MERRY CHRISTMAS IS A HUMAN MOLE, THANKS TO THE DIGGY-DIGGY FRUIT.
THE OTHER ONE, MR. 4, IS A CLEANUP HITTER.
AND HE HAS A DOG THAT WORKS WITH HIM!!

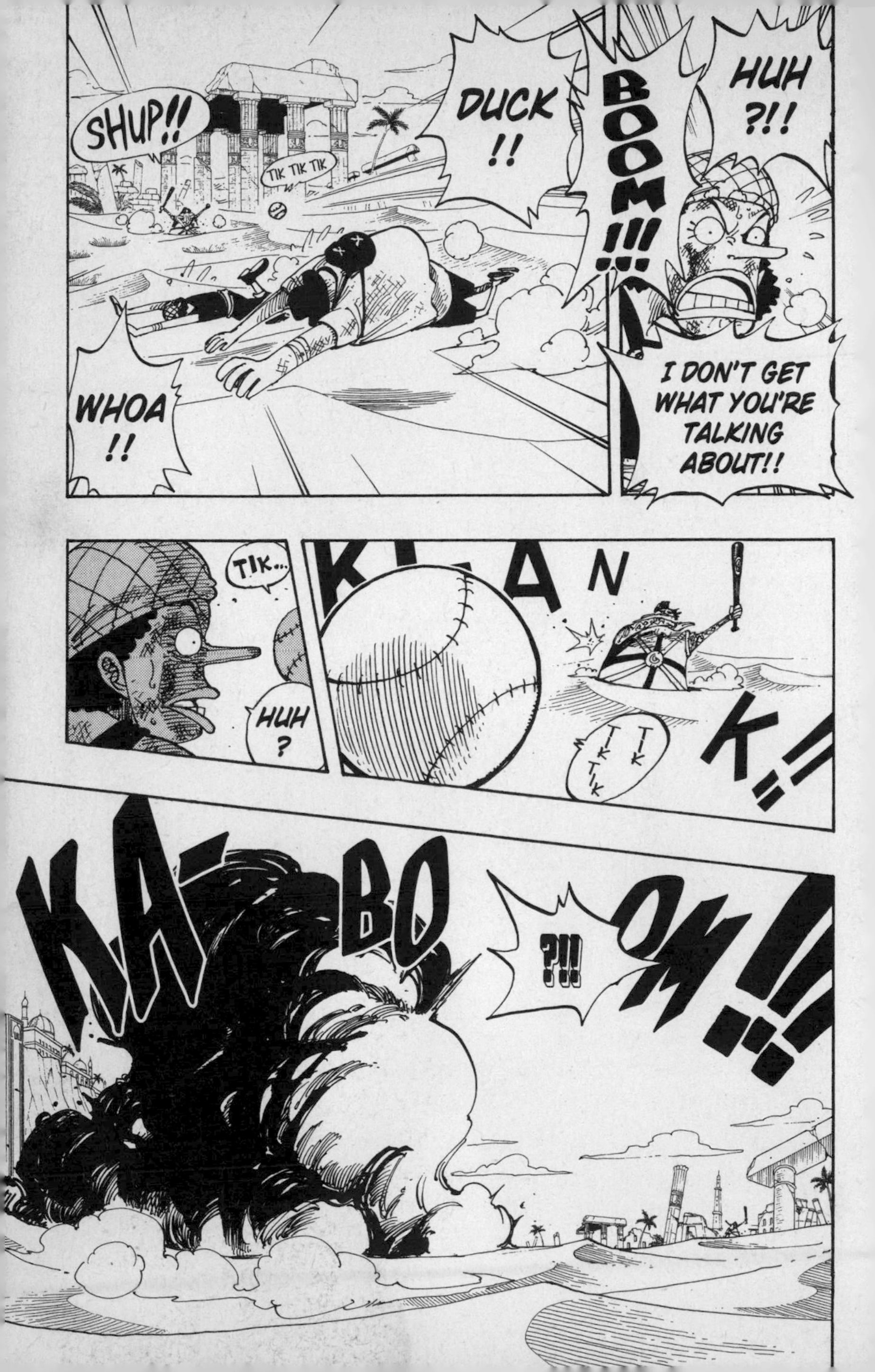
HUH ?!!
BOOM!!!
I DON'T GET WHAT YOU'RE TALKING ABOUT!!
DUCK !!
SHUP!!
TIK TIK TIK
WHOA !!
KLANK!!
TIK TIK TIK TIK
TIK...
HUH ?
KA-BOOM!!!
?!!

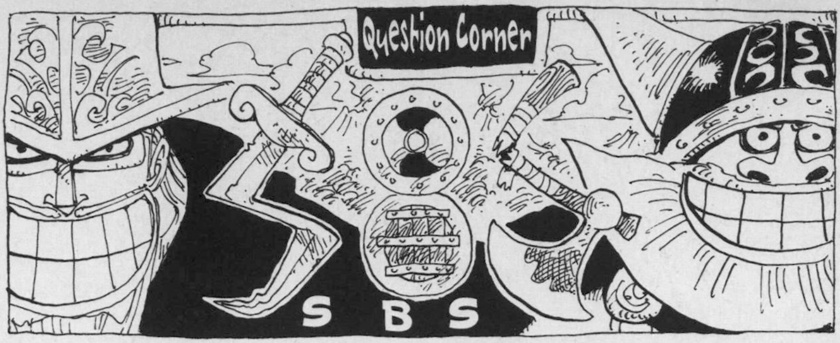
Question Corner
SBS

Q: Well, now, I have something I wanted to ask you, Oda baby. Today I read *WANTED!*, your anthology of short stories, and thought to myself...seems like a lot of your characters pick their boogers.
--Euphoria

A: They do, don't they? They just dig and dig and dig. I wonder why? But they're not the only ones. All characters do it--it's just that other manga artists don't show it. If they didn't dig them out, their nostrils would get plugged up!! Ah! What a gross subject. I get a lot of complaints from female readers when I write about things like that. I'm going to get letters about this too. But guys get a big laugh out of it! Right?! Okay, next.

Q: Good day, Oda Sensei! I know this is sudden, but I have a very serious question. The Spiders Café from volume 18, page 94, looks a lot like director Percy Adlon's *Bagdad Café*. Was that your inspiration? I love that movie, so please do let me know. Please.

A: Wow, you have good taste. You're only 15 years old and you like that movie? Well, you're right. I really loved the feel of that place. But its austere elegance was a bit too far removed from manga, so I just tried to capture a little of that look for my own enjoyment. Readers, see that movie, if you get a chance. It will remain in your heart. *Bagdad Café*...

Q: Oda Sensei, I went to a certain flower shop recently and saw that they were selling crocus seeds. Does this have any connection to the character Crocus?

A: In the language of flowers, the crocus symbolizes "trust."

Chapter 184:
MOLETOWN BLOCK FOUR

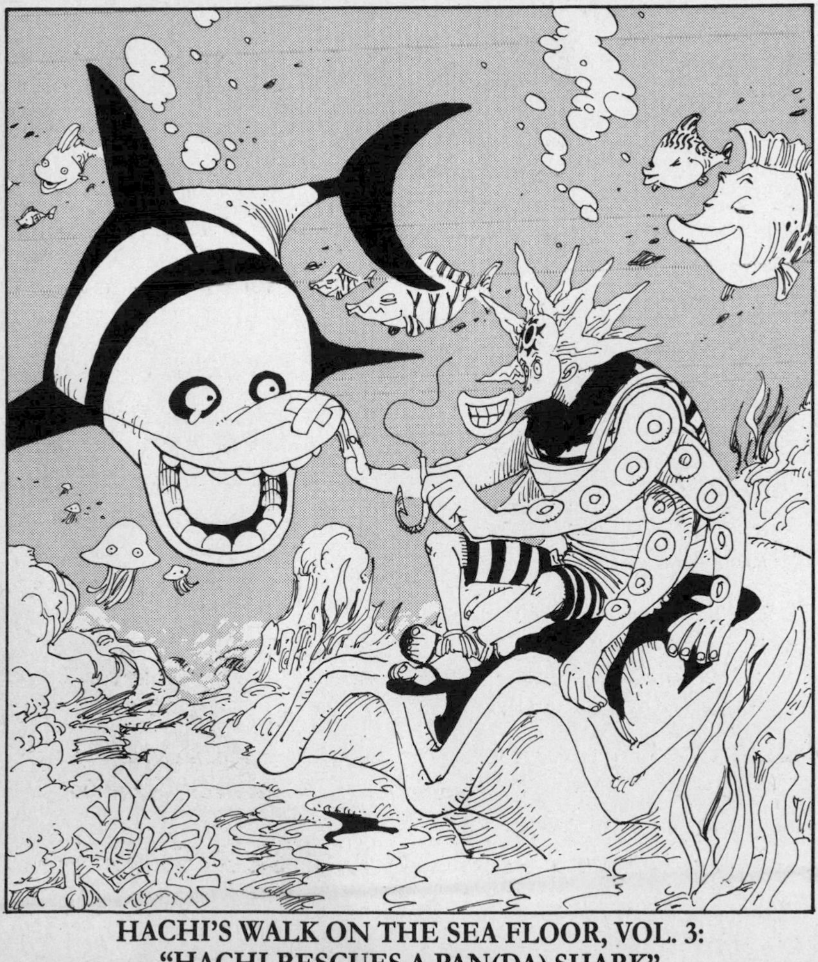

HACHI'S WALK ON THE SEA FLOOR, VOL. 3:
"HACHI RESCUES A PAN(DA) SHARK"

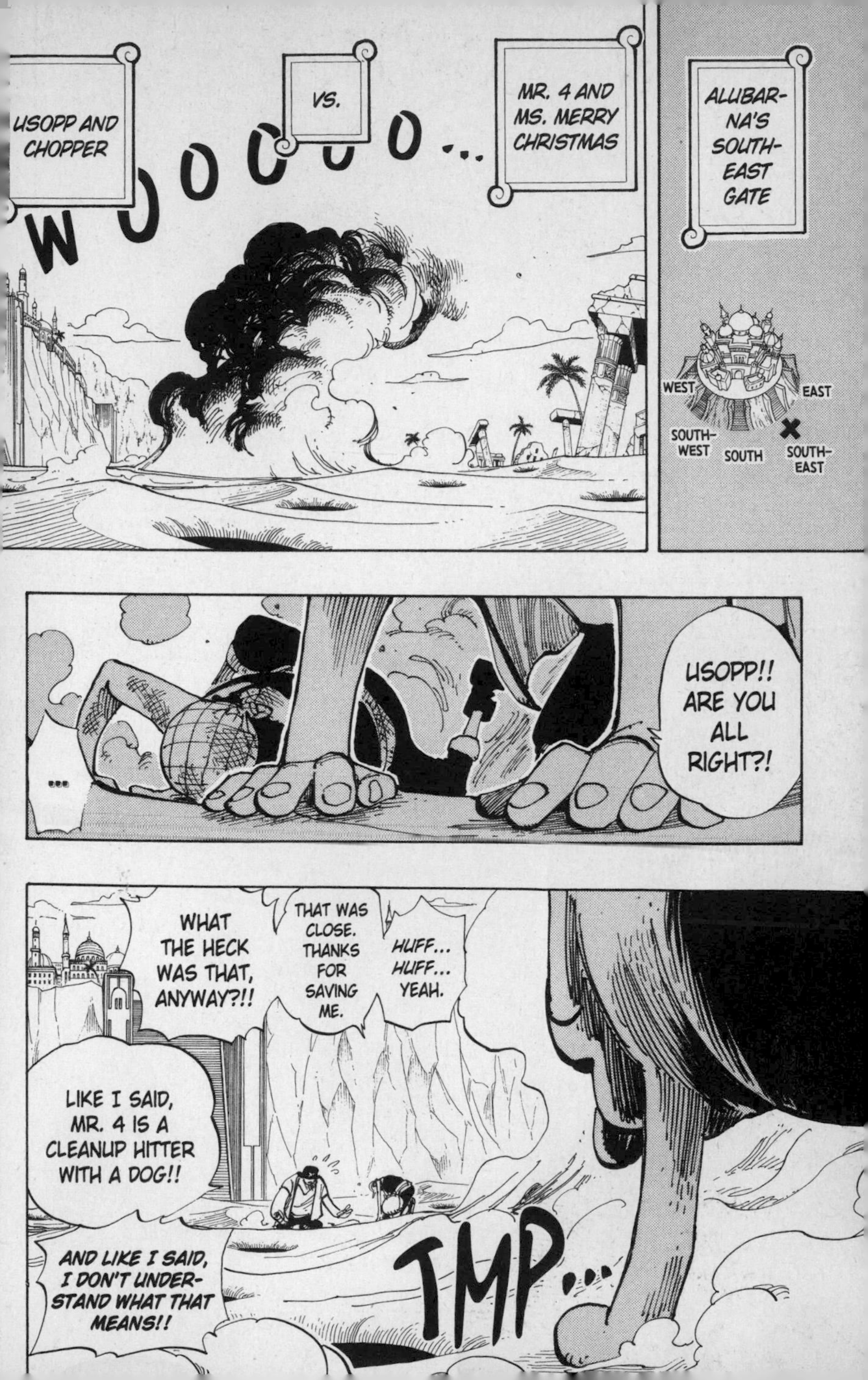
ALUBARNA'S SOUTHEAST GATE
WEST
EAST
SOUTHWEST
SOUTH
SOUTHEAST
MR. 4 AND MS. MERRY CHRISTMAS
VS.
USOPP AND CHOPPER
WOOOOOO...
USOPP!! ARE YOU ALL RIGHT?!
...
HUFF... HUFF... YEAH.
THAT WAS CLOSE. THANKS FOR SAVING ME.
WHAT THE HECK WAS THAT, ANYWAY?!!
TMP...
LIKE I SAID, MR. 4 IS A CLEANUP HITTER WITH A DOG!!
AND LIKE I SAID, I DON'T UNDERSTAND WHAT THAT MEANS!!

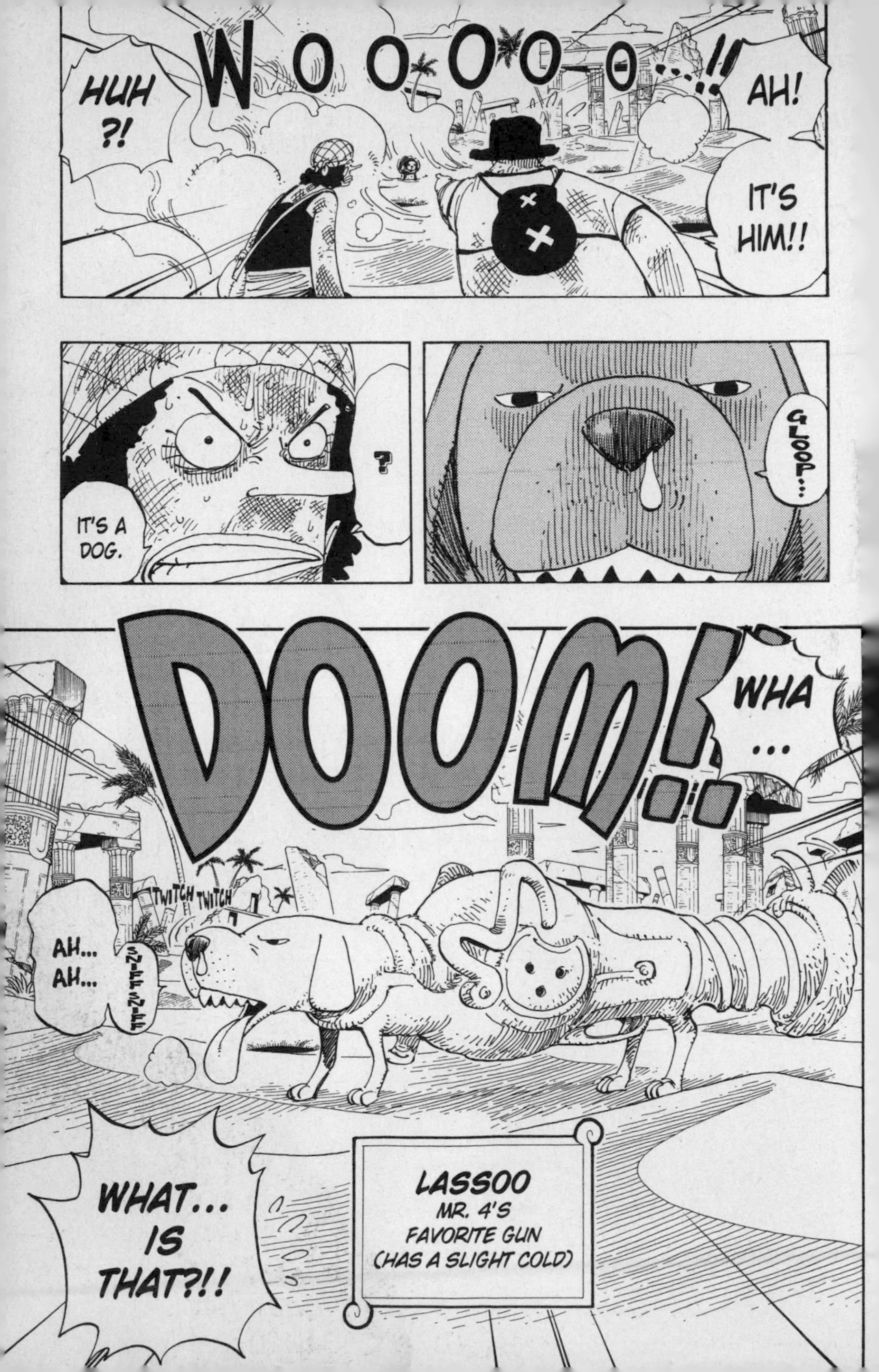
AH!
IT'S HIM!!
WOOOOO...!!
HUH ?!
GLOOP...
?
IT'S A DOG.
DOOM!!
WHA ...
TWITCH TWITCH
SNIFF SNIFF
AH... AH...
LASSOO
MR. 4'S FAVORITE GUN
(HAS A SLIGHT COLD)
WHAT... IS THAT?!!

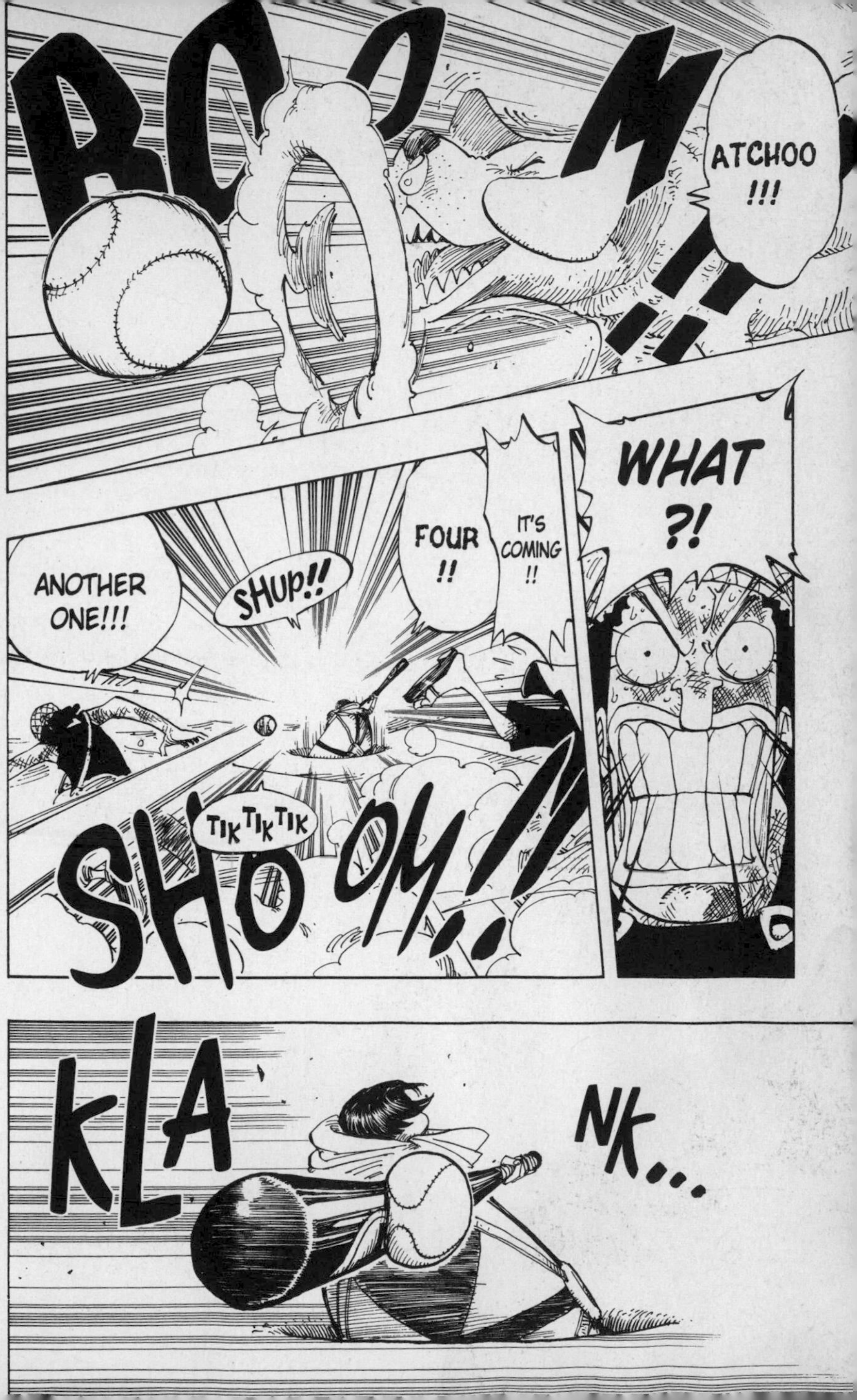
ATCHOO!!!
BOOM!!
WHAT?!
IT'S COMING!!
FOUR!!
SHUP!!
ANOTHER ONE!!!
TIKTIKTIK
SHOOM!!
KLANK...

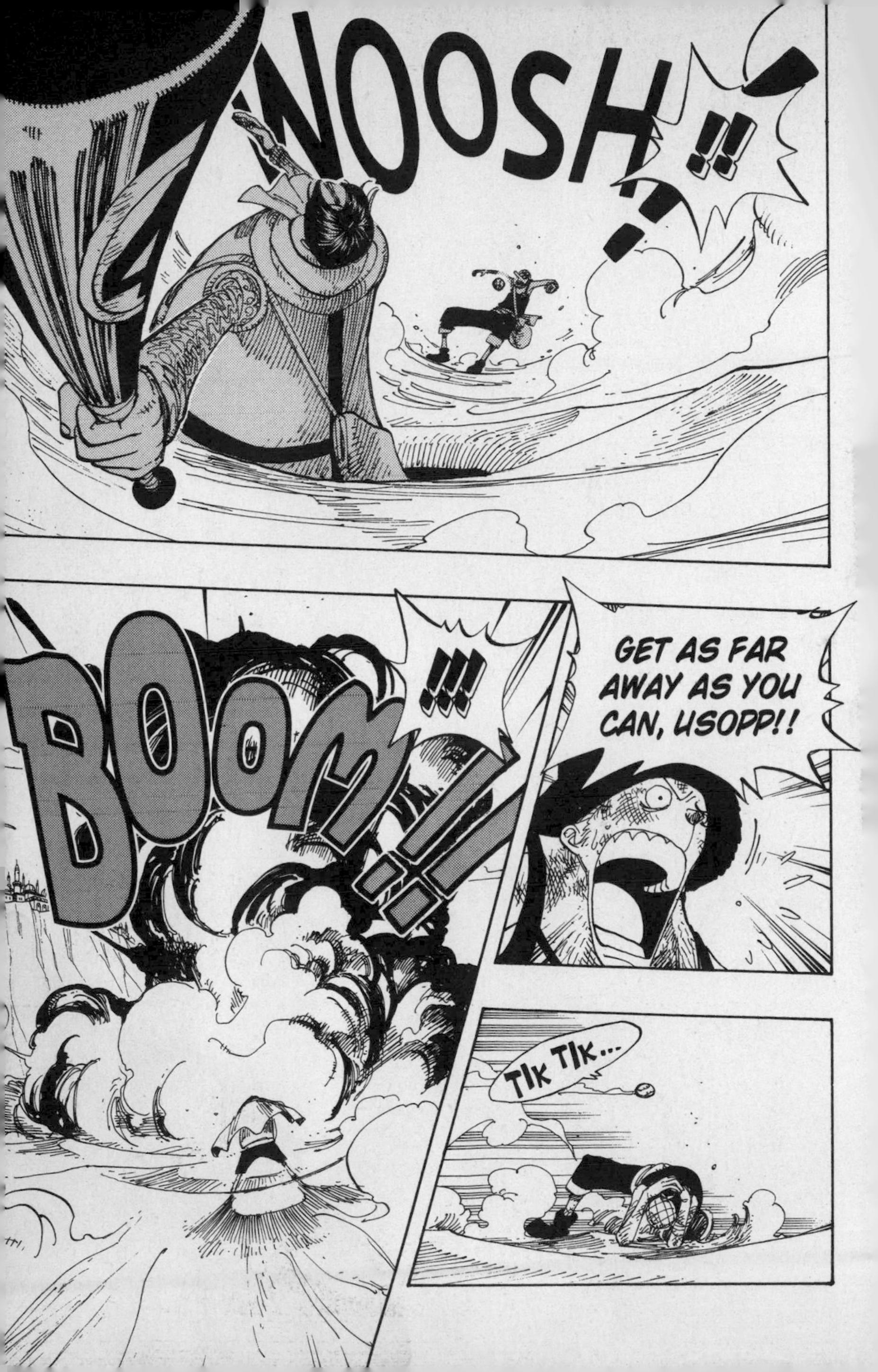
WOOSH!!
GET AS FAR AWAY AS YOU CAN, USOPP!!
TIK TIK...
BOOM!!!

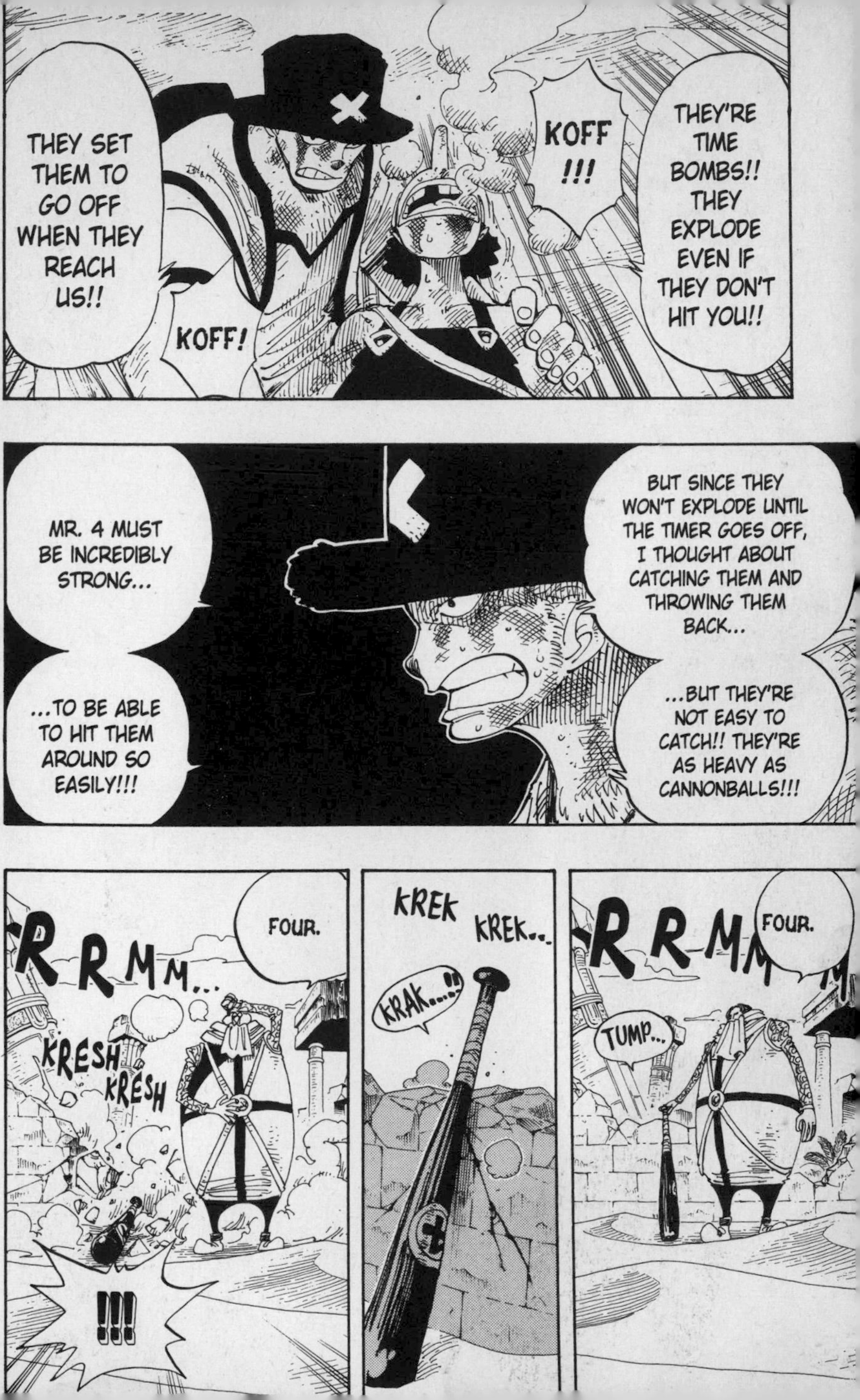
THEY'RE TIME BOMBS!! THEY EXPLODE EVEN IF THEY DON'T HIT YOU!!
KOFF !!!
THEY SET THEM TO GO OFF WHEN THEY REACH US!!
KOFF!
BUT SINCE THEY WON'T EXPLODE UNTIL THE TIMER GOES OFF, I THOUGHT ABOUT CATCHING THEM AND THROWING THEM BACK...
...BUT THEY'RE NOT EASY TO CATCH!! THEY'RE AS HEAVY AS CANNONBALLS!!!
MR. 4 MUST BE INCREDIBLY STRONG...
...TO BE ABLE TO HIT THEM AROUND SO EASILY!!!
FOUR.
RRMM
TUMP...
KREK
KREK...
KRAK...!!
FOUR.
RRMM...
KRESH
KRESH
!!!

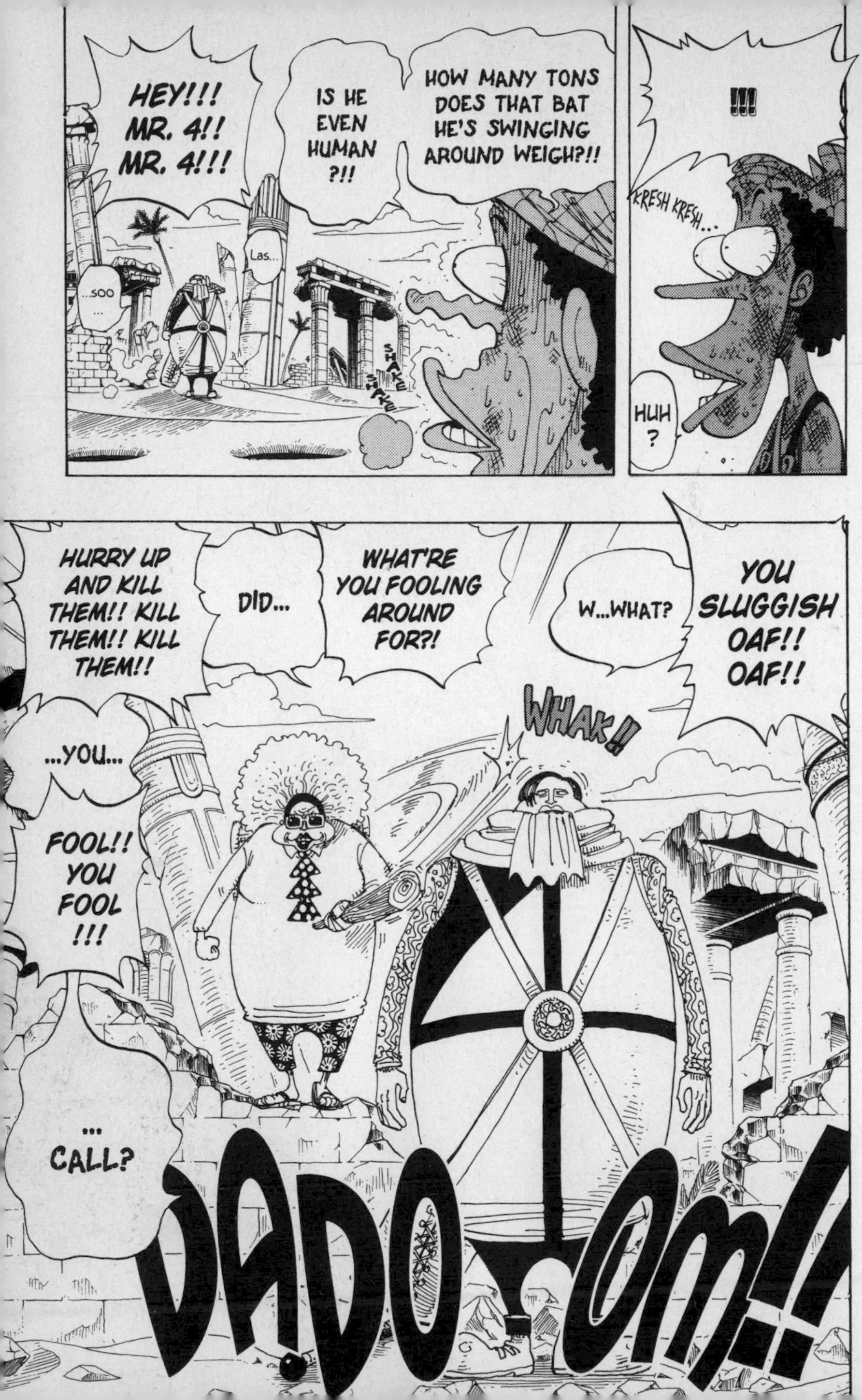
!!!
KRESH KRESH...
HUH?
HOW MANY TONS DOES THAT BAT HE'S SWINGING AROUND WEIGH?!!
IS HE EVEN HUMAN?!!
HEY!!! MR. 4!! MR. 4!!!
Las...
...SOO...
SHAKE
SHAKE
YOU SLUGGISH OAF!! OAF!!
W...WHAT?
WHAT'RE YOU FOOLING AROUND FOR?!
DID...
HURRY UP AND KILL THEM!! KILL THEM!! KILL THEM!!
WHAK!!
...YOU...
FOOL!! YOU FOOL!!!
...CALL?
DADO-OM!!

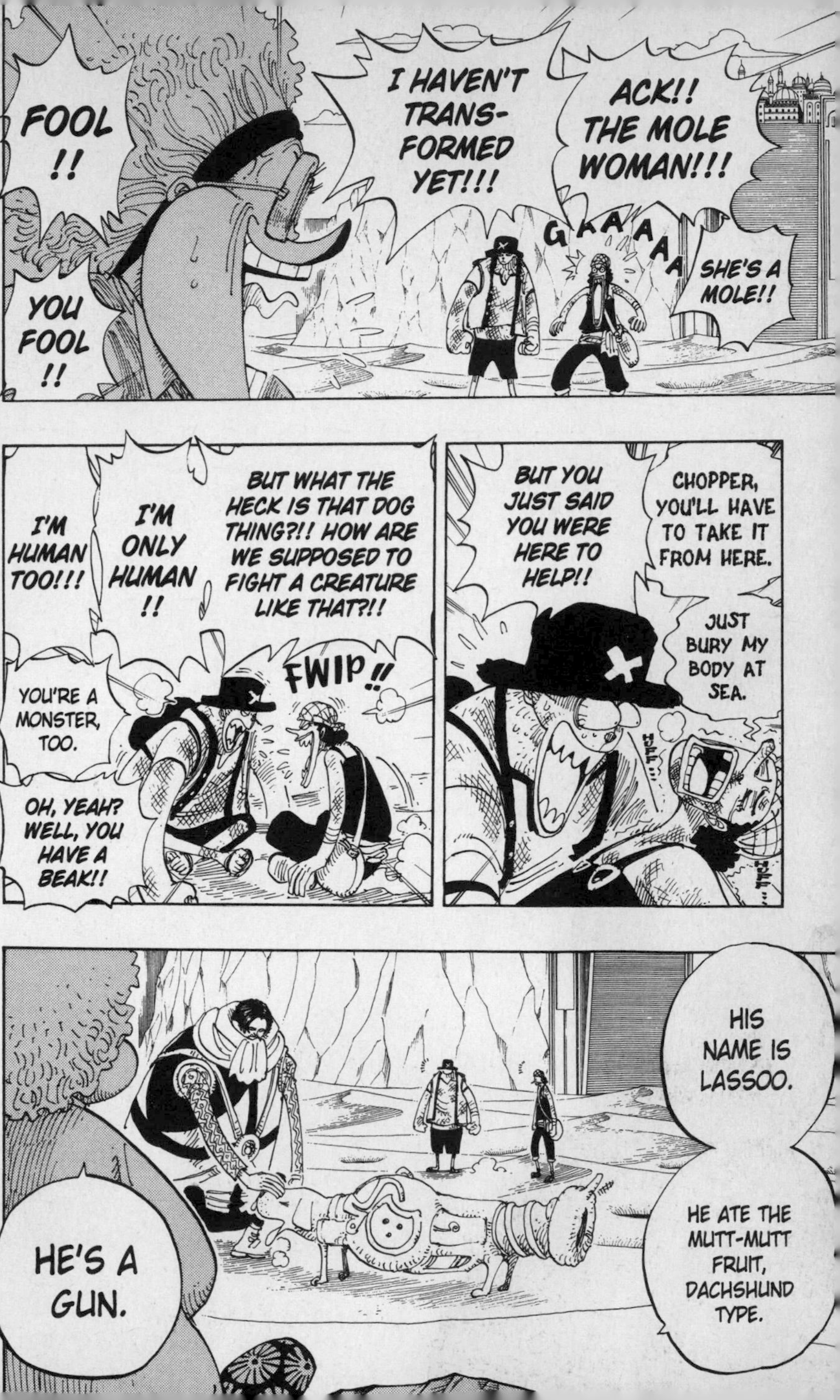
ACK!! THE MOLE WOMAN!!!
SHE'S A MOLE!!
GAAAAAA
I HAVEN'T TRANS-FORMED YET!!!
FOOL!!
YOU FOOL!!
CHOPPER, YOU'LL HAVE TO TAKE IT FROM HERE.
JUST BURY MY BODY AT SEA.
BUT YOU JUST SAID YOU WERE HERE TO HELP!!
HUFF...
HUFF...
BUT WHAT THE HECK IS THAT DOG THING?!! HOW ARE WE SUPPOSED TO FIGHT A CREATURE LIKE THAT?!!
FWIP!!
I'M ONLY HUMAN!!
I'M HUMAN TOO!!!
YOU'RE A MONSTER, TOO.
OH, YEAH? WELL, YOU HAVE A BEAK!!
HIS NAME IS LASSOO.
HE ATE THE MUTT-MUTT FRUIT, DACHSHUND TYPE.
HE'S A GUN.

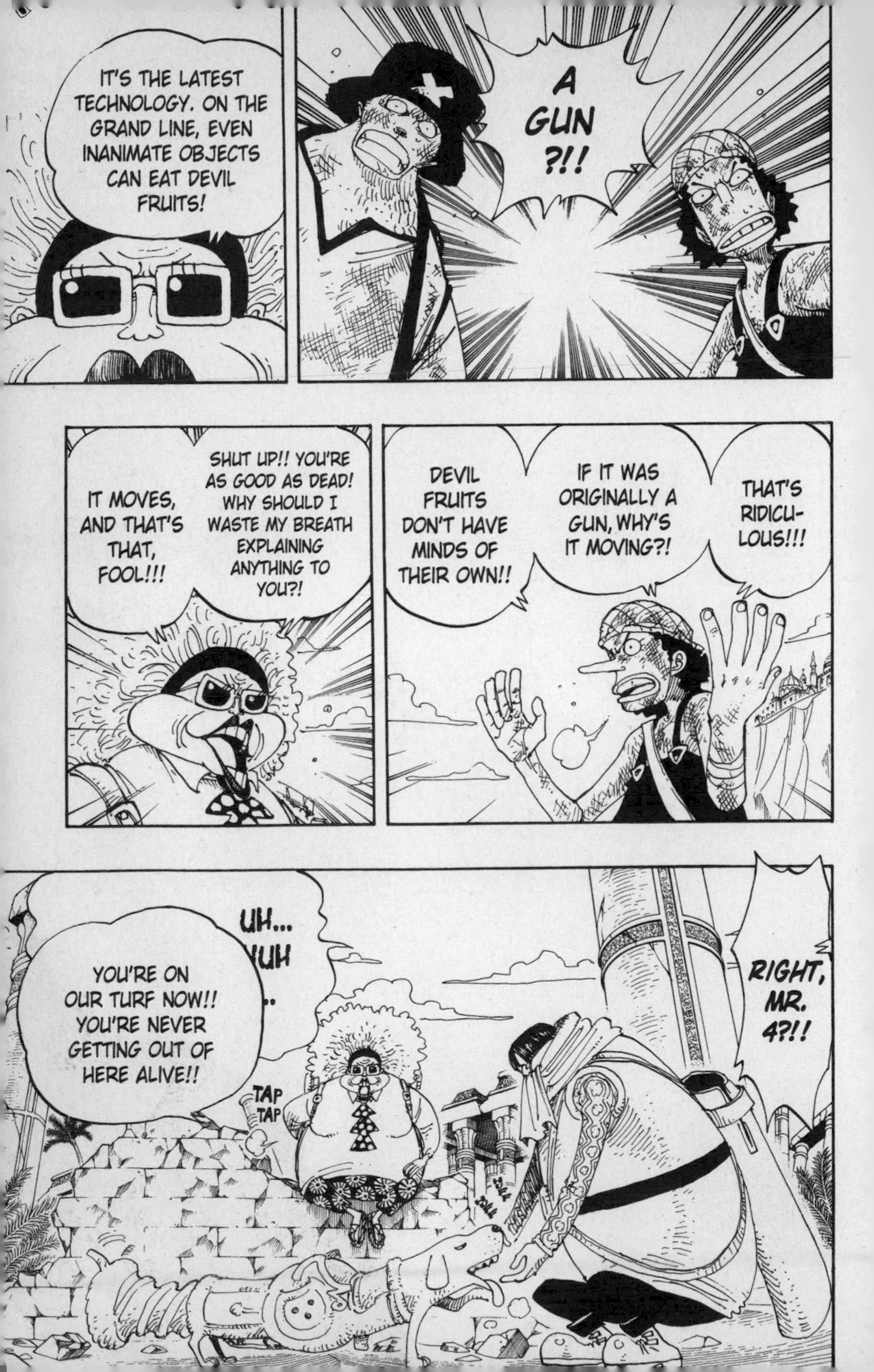
A GUN ?!!
IT'S THE LATEST TECHNOLOGY. ON THE GRAND LINE, EVEN INANIMATE OBJECTS CAN EAT DEVIL FRUITS!
THAT'S RIDICU-LOUS!!!
IF IT WAS ORIGINALLY A GUN, WHY'S IT MOVING?!
DEVIL FRUITS DON'T HAVE MINDS OF THEIR OWN!!
SHUT UP!! YOU'RE AS GOOD AS DEAD! WHY SHOULD I WASTE MY BREATH EXPLAINING ANYTHING TO YOU?!
IT MOVES, AND THAT'S THAT, FOOL!!!
RIGHT, MR. 4?!!
UH... UH ...
YOU'RE ON OUR TURF NOW!! YOU'RE NEVER GETTING OUT OF HERE ALIVE!!
TAP TAP

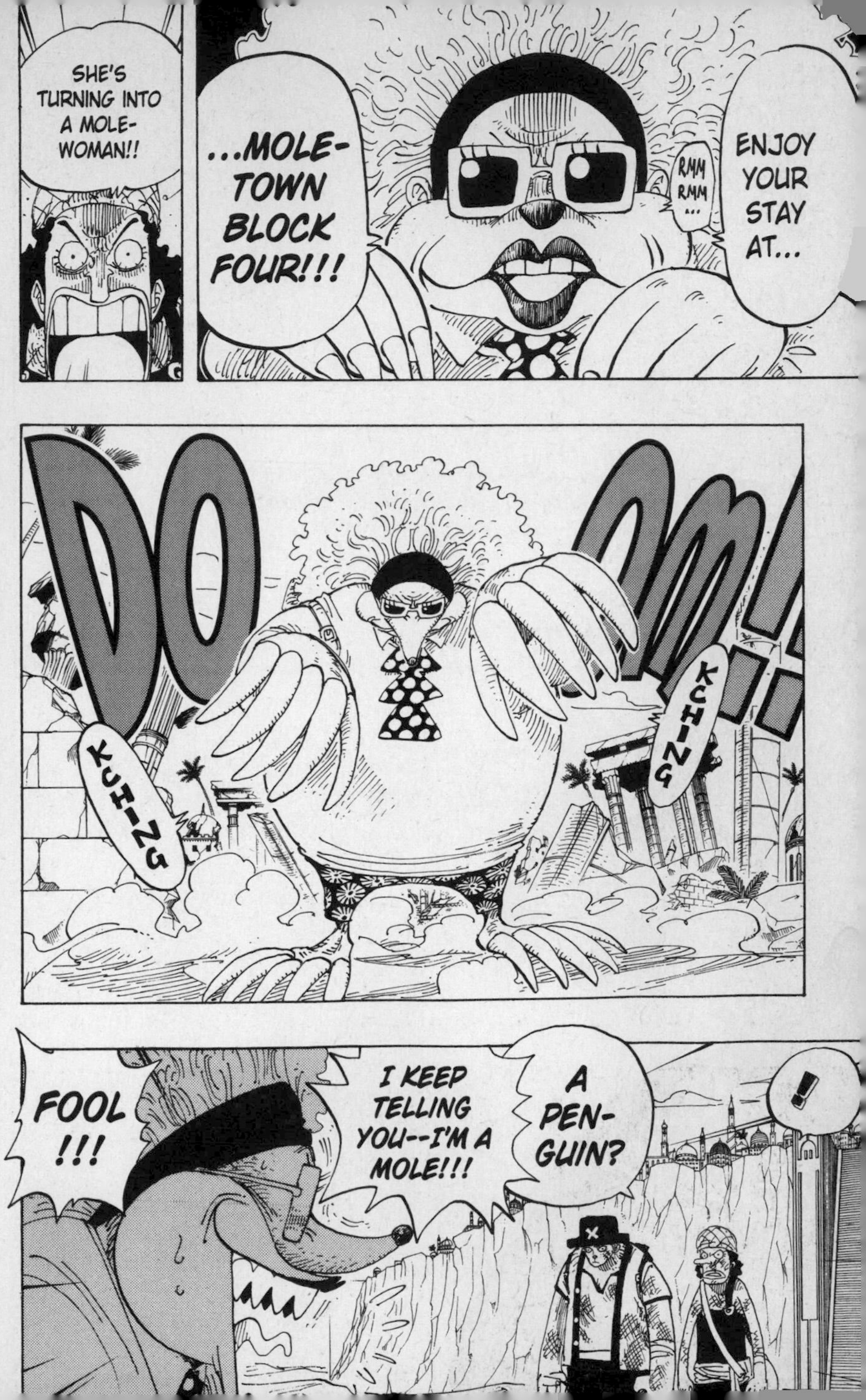
ENJOY YOUR STAY AT...
RMM RMM ...
...MOLE-TOWN BLOCK FOUR!!!
SHE'S TURNING INTO A MOLE-WOMAN!!
DO
OM!!
KCHING
KCHING
!
A PEN-GUIN?
I KEEP TELLING YOU--I'M A MOLE!!!
FOOL!!!

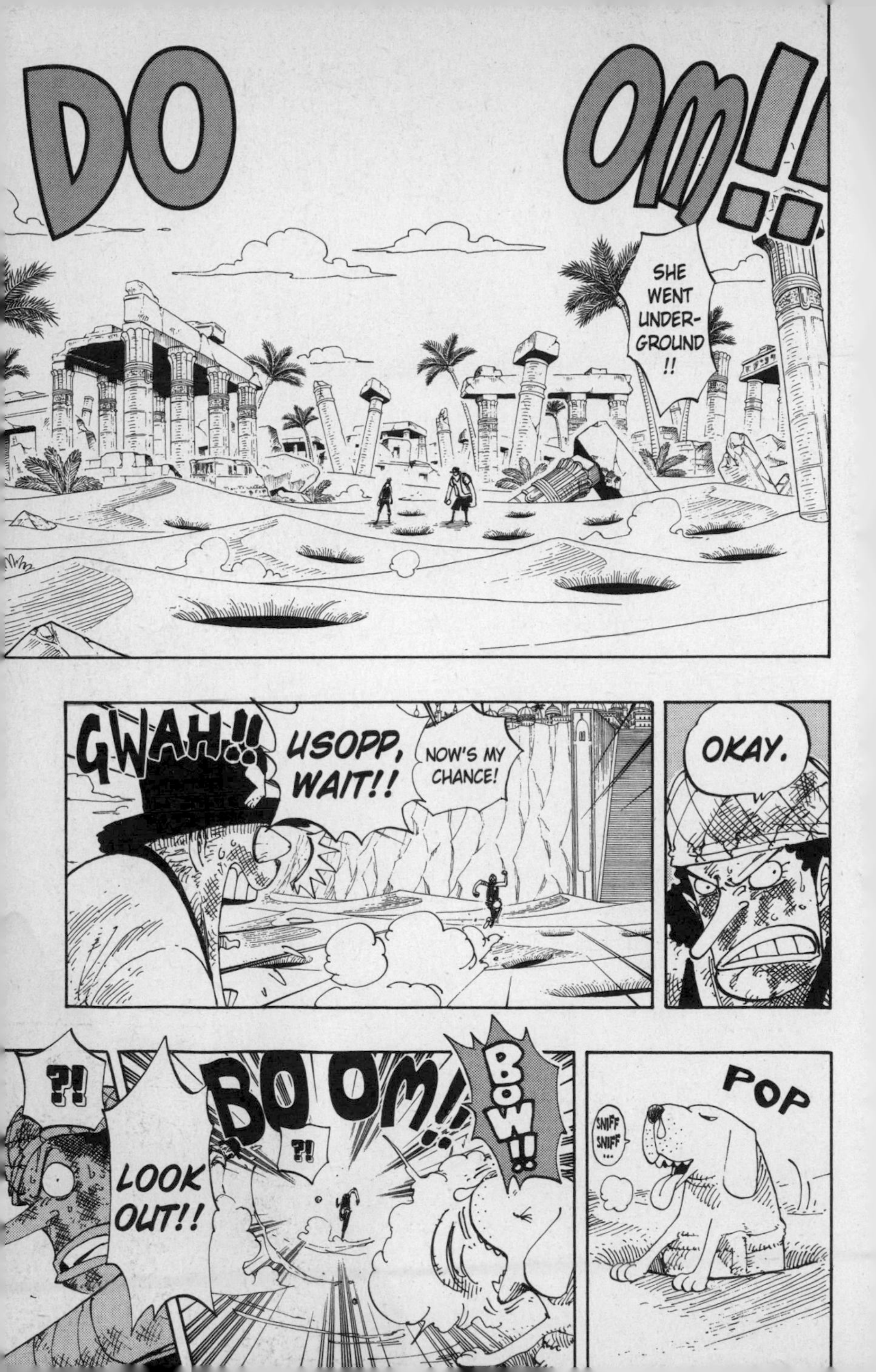
DOOM!!
SHE WENT UNDER-GROUND!!
OKAY.
NOW'S MY CHANCE!
USOPP, WAIT!!
GWAH!!
POP
SNIFF SNIFF ...
BOW!!
BOOM!!
?!
?!
LOOK OUT!!

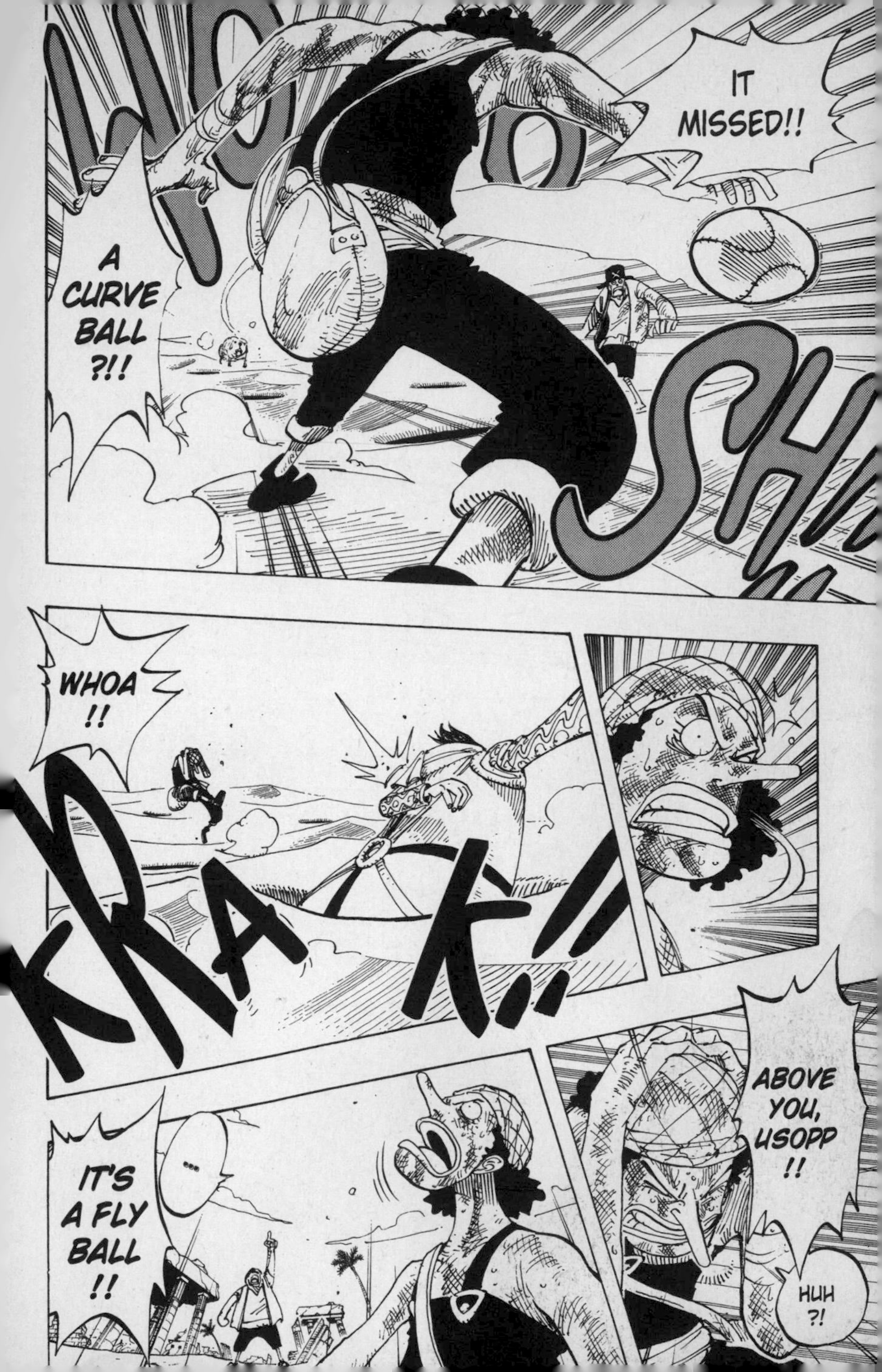
IT MISSED!!
A CURVE BALL ?!!
WHOA !!
KRAK!!
ABOVE YOU, USOPP !!
HUH ?!
...
IT'S A FLY BALL !!

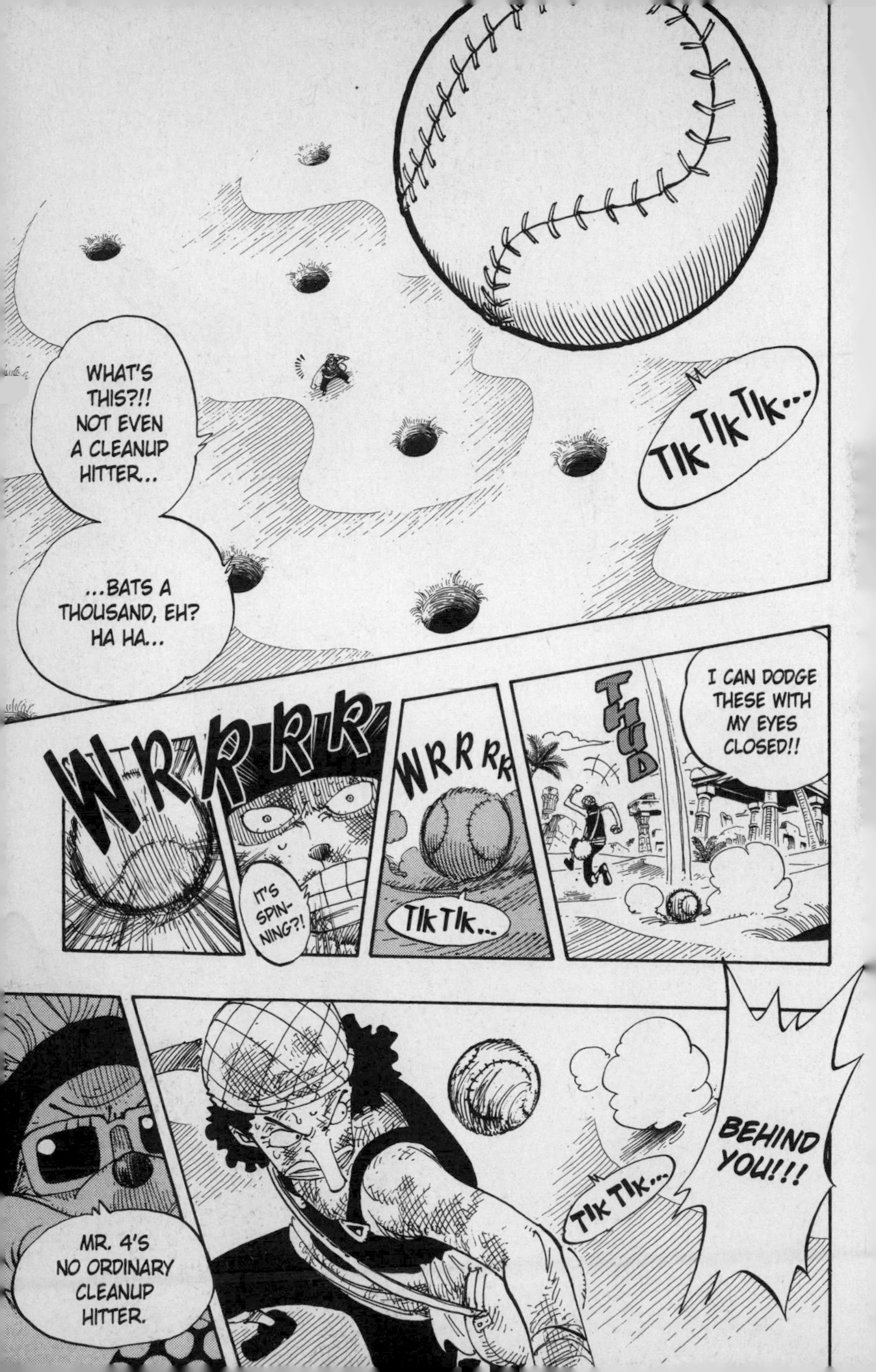
TIK TIK TIK...
WHAT'S THIS?!! NOT EVEN A CLEANUP HITTER...
...BATS A THOUSAND, EH? HA HA...
I CAN DODGE THESE WITH MY EYES CLOSED!!
THUD
WRRRR
TIKTIK...
IT'S SPIN-NING?!
WRRRRR
BEHIND YOU!!!
TIK TIK...
MR. 4'S NO ORDINARY CLEANUP HITTER.

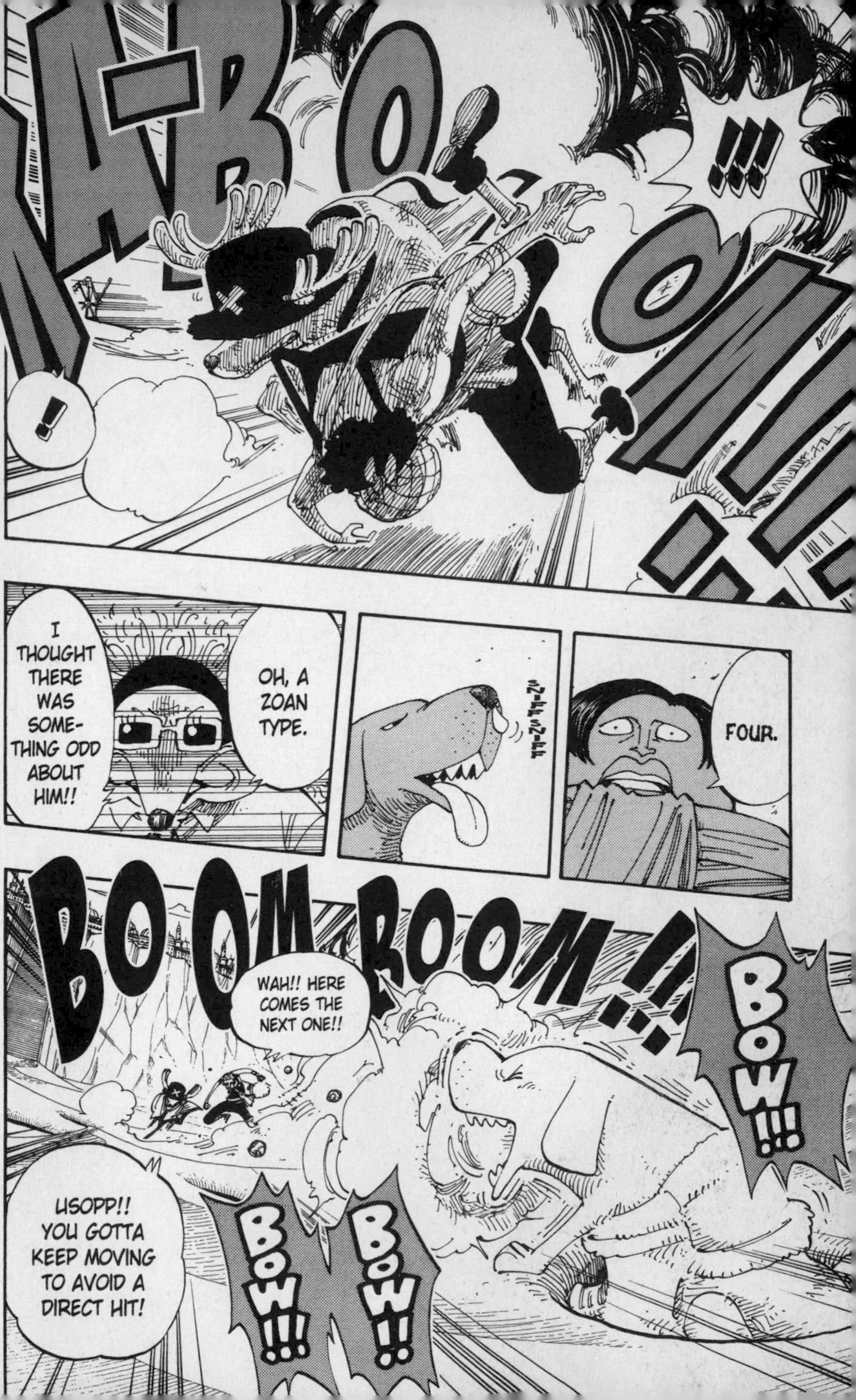
WA-BOOM!!!
!
FOUR.
SNIFF SNIFF
OH, A ZOAN TYPE.
I THOUGHT THERE WAS SOME-THING ODD ABOUT HIM!!
BOOM BOOM!!!
BOW!!!
WAH!! HERE COMES THE NEXT ONE!!
BOW!!
BOW!!!
USOPP!! YOU GOTTA KEEP MOVING TO AVOID A DIRECT HIT!

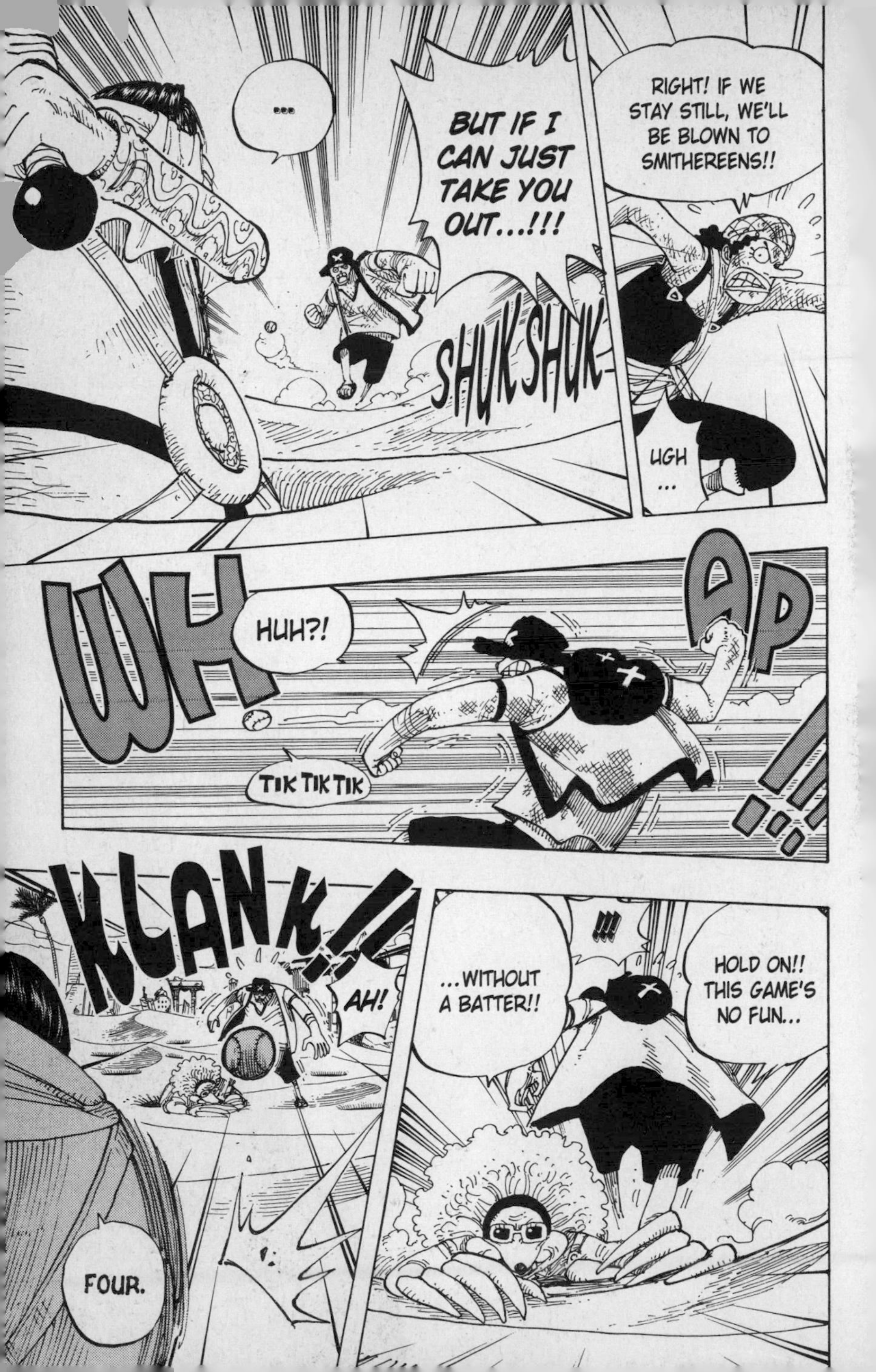
RIGHT! IF WE STAY STILL, WE'LL BE BLOWN TO SMITHEREENS!!
UGH ...
BUT IF I CAN JUST TAKE YOU OUT...!!!
...
SHUK SHUK
AP
HUH?!
WUH
TIK TIK TIK
HOLD ON!! THIS GAME'S NO FUN...
!!!
...WITHOUT A BATTER!!
KLANK!!
AH!
FOUR.

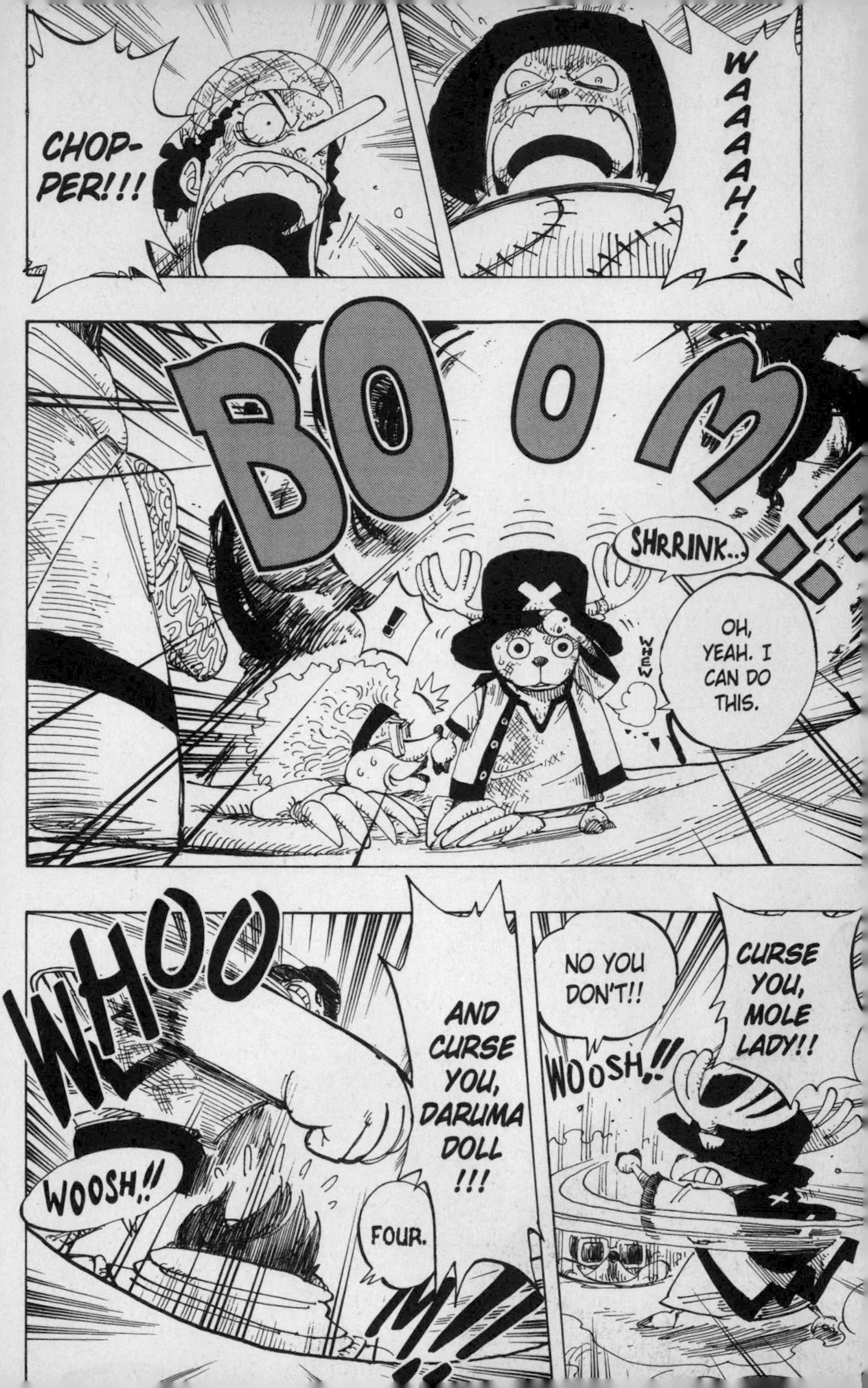
WAAAAAH!!
CHOP-PER!!!
BOOM!!
SHRRINK...
!
WHEW
OH, YEAH. I CAN DO THIS.
CURSE YOU, MOLE LADY!!
NO YOU DON'T!!
WOOSH!!
AND CURSE YOU, DARUMA DOLL!!!
WHOOM!!
WOOSH!!
FOUR.

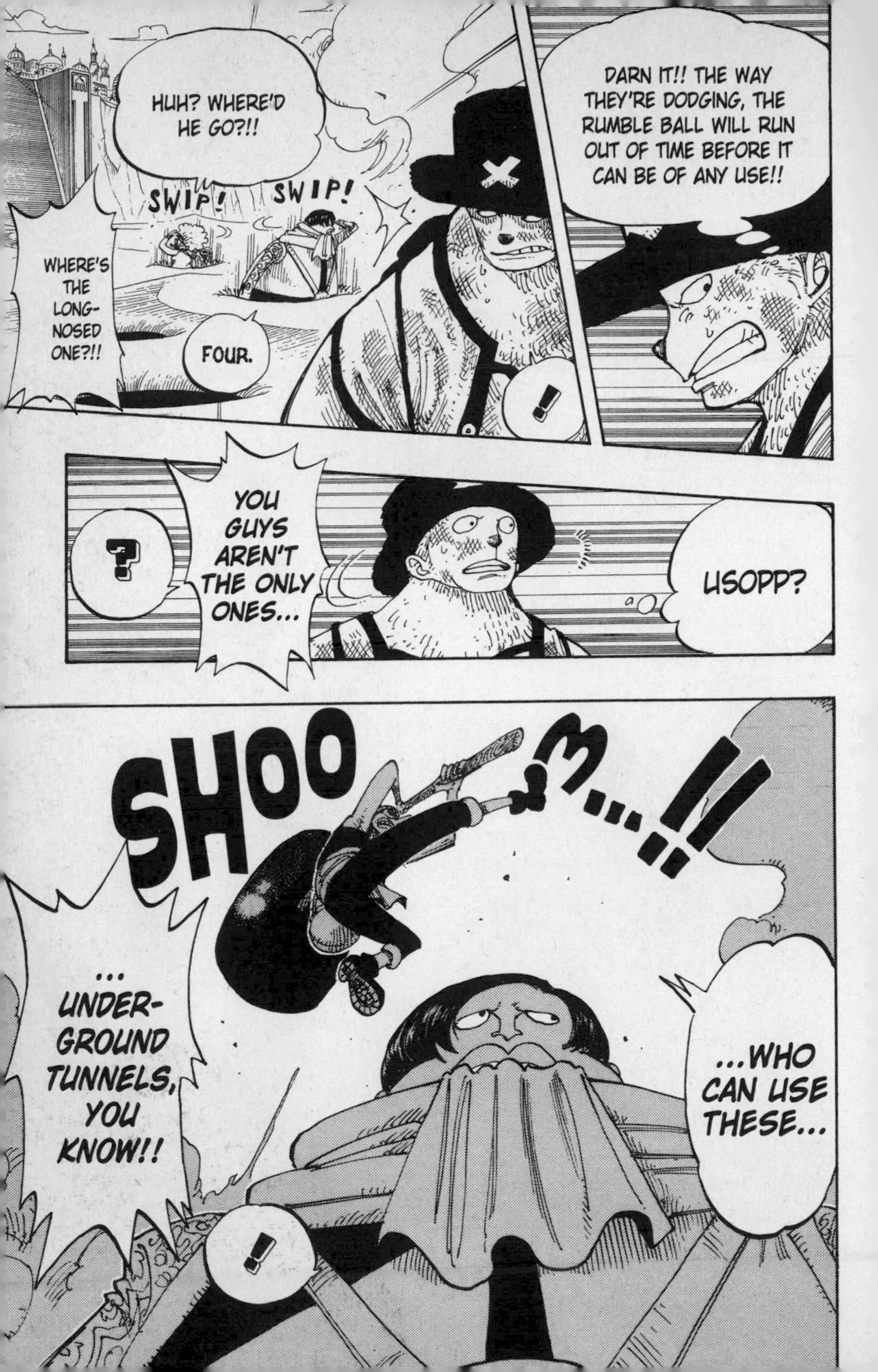
DARN IT!! THE WAY THEY'RE DODGING, THE RUMBLE BALL WILL RUN OUT OF TIME BEFORE IT CAN BE OF ANY USE!!
!
HUH? WHERE'D HE GO?!!
SWIP! SWIP!
WHERE'S THE LONG-NOSED ONE?!!
FOUR.
USOPP?
YOU GUYS AREN'T THE ONLY ONES...
?
SHOOM...!!
...WHO CAN USE THESE...
...UNDER-GROUND TUNNELS, YOU KNOW!!
!

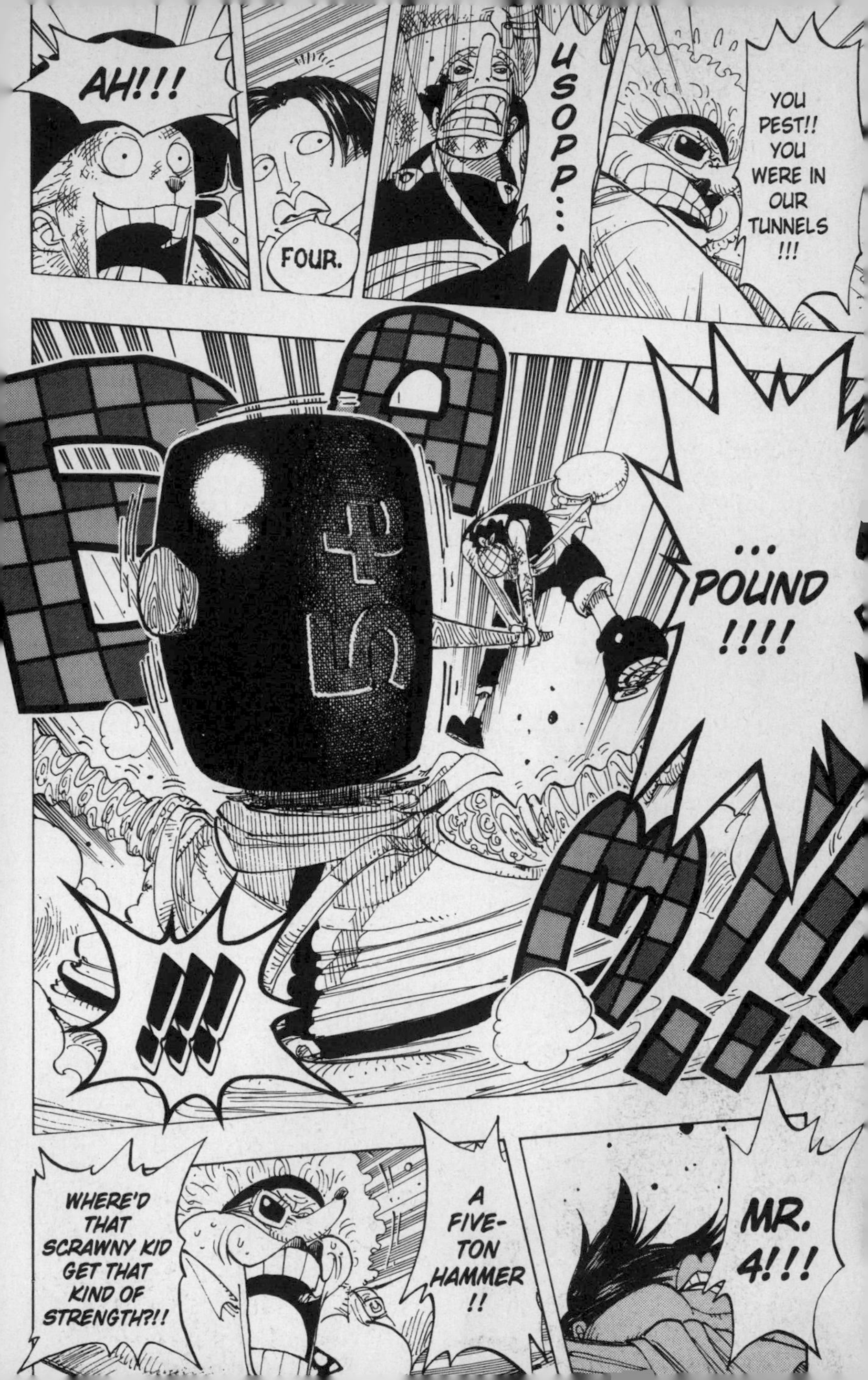
YOU PEST!! YOU WERE IN OUR TUNNELS !!!
USOPP...
FOUR.
AH!!!
...POUND !!!!
!!!
MR. 4!!!
A FIVE-TON HAMMER !!
WHERE'D THAT SCRAWNY KID GET THAT KIND OF STRENGTH?!!

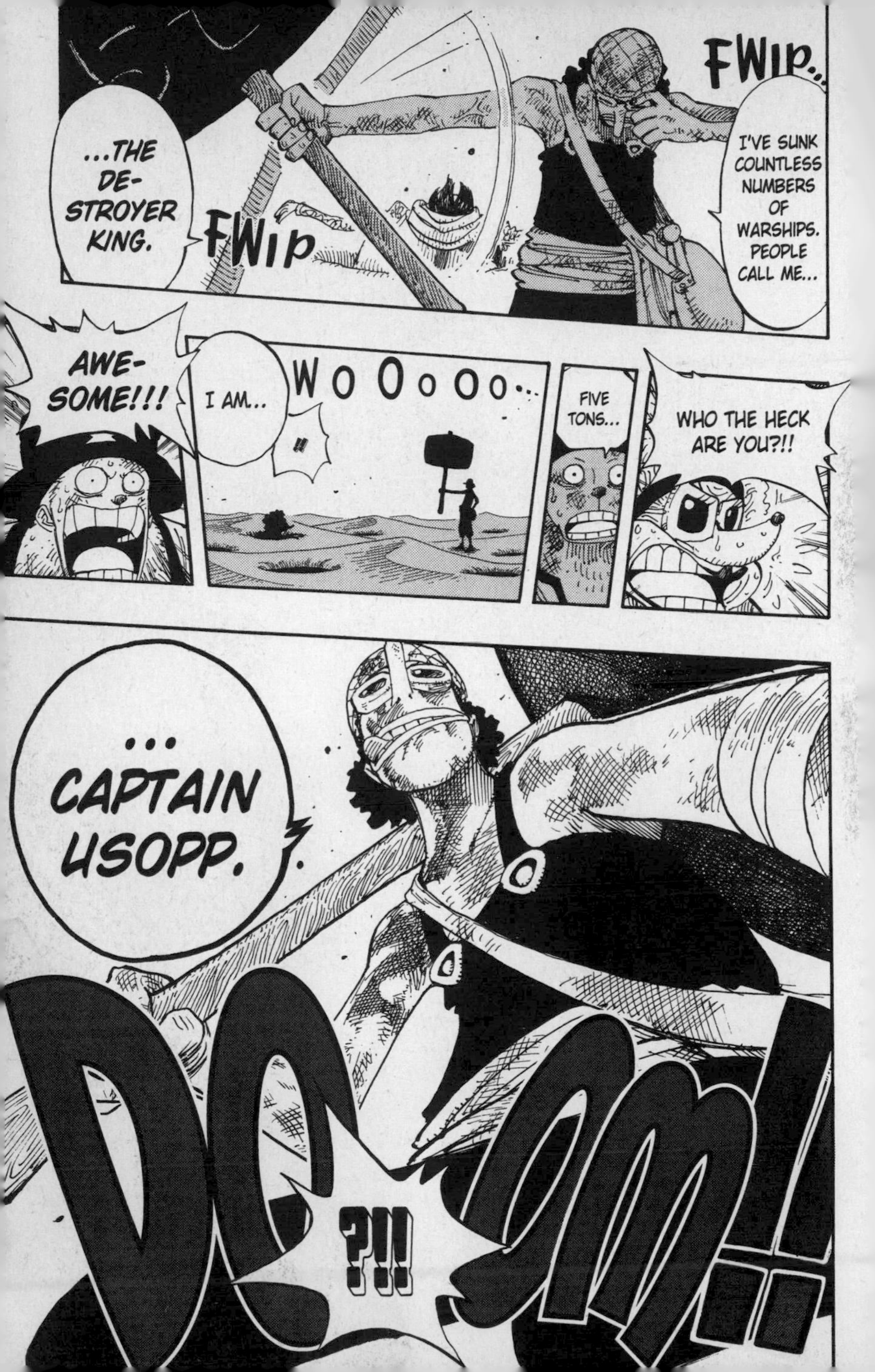
FWIP...
I'VE SUNK COUNTLESS NUMBERS OF WARSHIPS. PEOPLE CALL ME...
FWIP
...THE DE-STROYER KING.
WHO THE HECK ARE YOU?!!
FIVE TONS...
WOOooo...
!!
I AM...
AWE-SOME!!!
...CAPTAIN USOPP.
DOOM!!
?!!

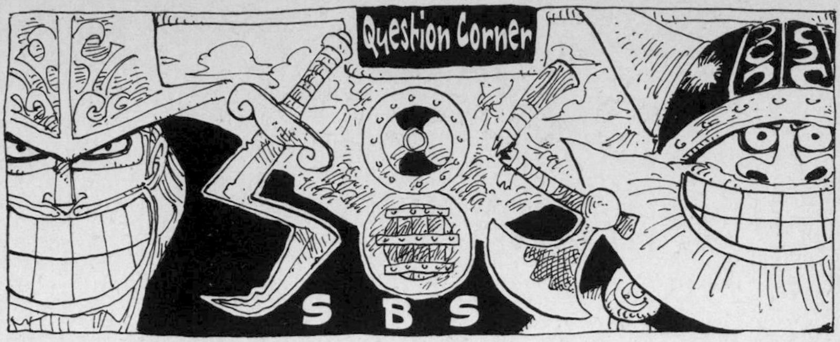
Question Corner
SBS

Q: All the boys at school ever talk about is Nami's body! Tell them to stop it!!

A: Uh... Umm... There was no age written on this postcard, but judging from the writing, I'd guess you're probably in middle school. Middle school boys spend a lot of time thinking about girls. They can't help themselves. I just can't bring myself to scold them. (Hey!)

Q: What would happen if a human ate the Human-Human Fruit?

A: There's a saying we have in Japan: "to become a human" or rather "to come of age." It means to act like an adult or to stop acting crazy--to behave the way a human being is supposed to. Maybe that's part of it. Or not. Well, no. Yes. That's what I mean. (Runs away.)

Q: Mr. Oda!! You have to tell me!! What happened to Sanji's left eye?!

A: Here we go again. I get this question so much that I tended to ignore it. All right. Sanji's left eye is one of the Seven Mysteries of *One Piece*. Let's answer the question at last!! Come on out, Sanji!!

Sanji: **Hey. You called? What? Show them my left eye?! You called me for that? That's stupid. Well, all right, if it'll make you happy. Watch carefully, folks. There.**

Oda: Wow!!! Seriously?!! Holy smokes!! What a finale!! And on that note, this Question Corner is over!! See you in the next volume!!

Chapter 185:

OH... IS THAT SO?

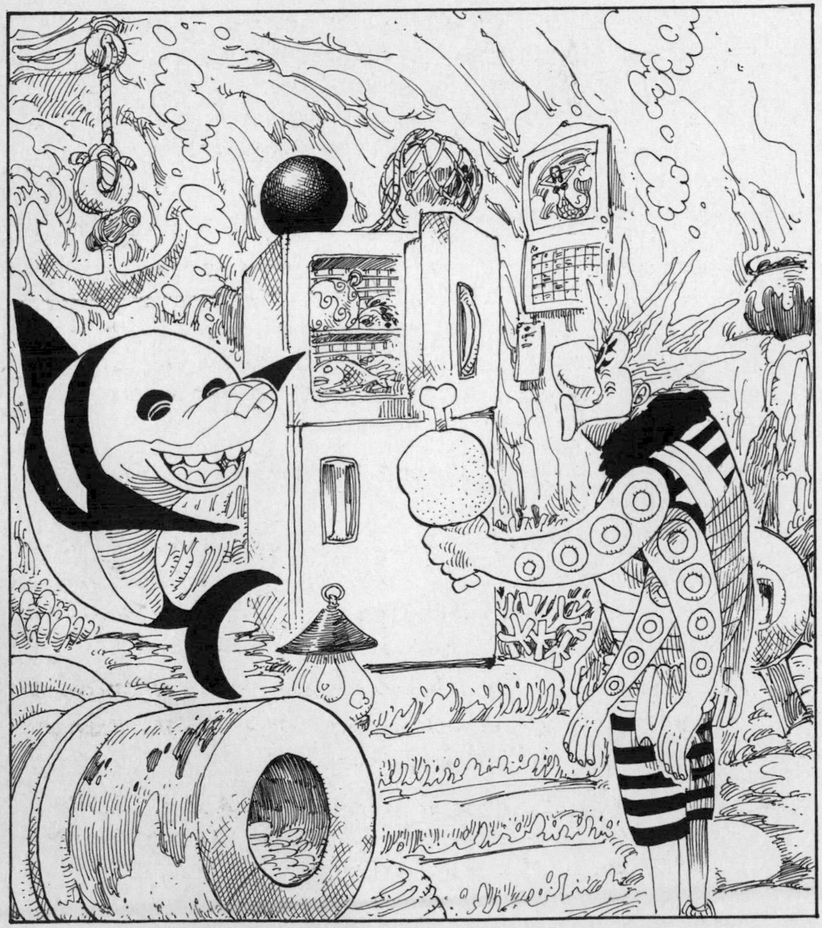

HACHI'S WALK ON THE SEA FLOOR, VOL. 4:
"HACHI RECEIVES A THANK YOU GIFT OF MEAT"

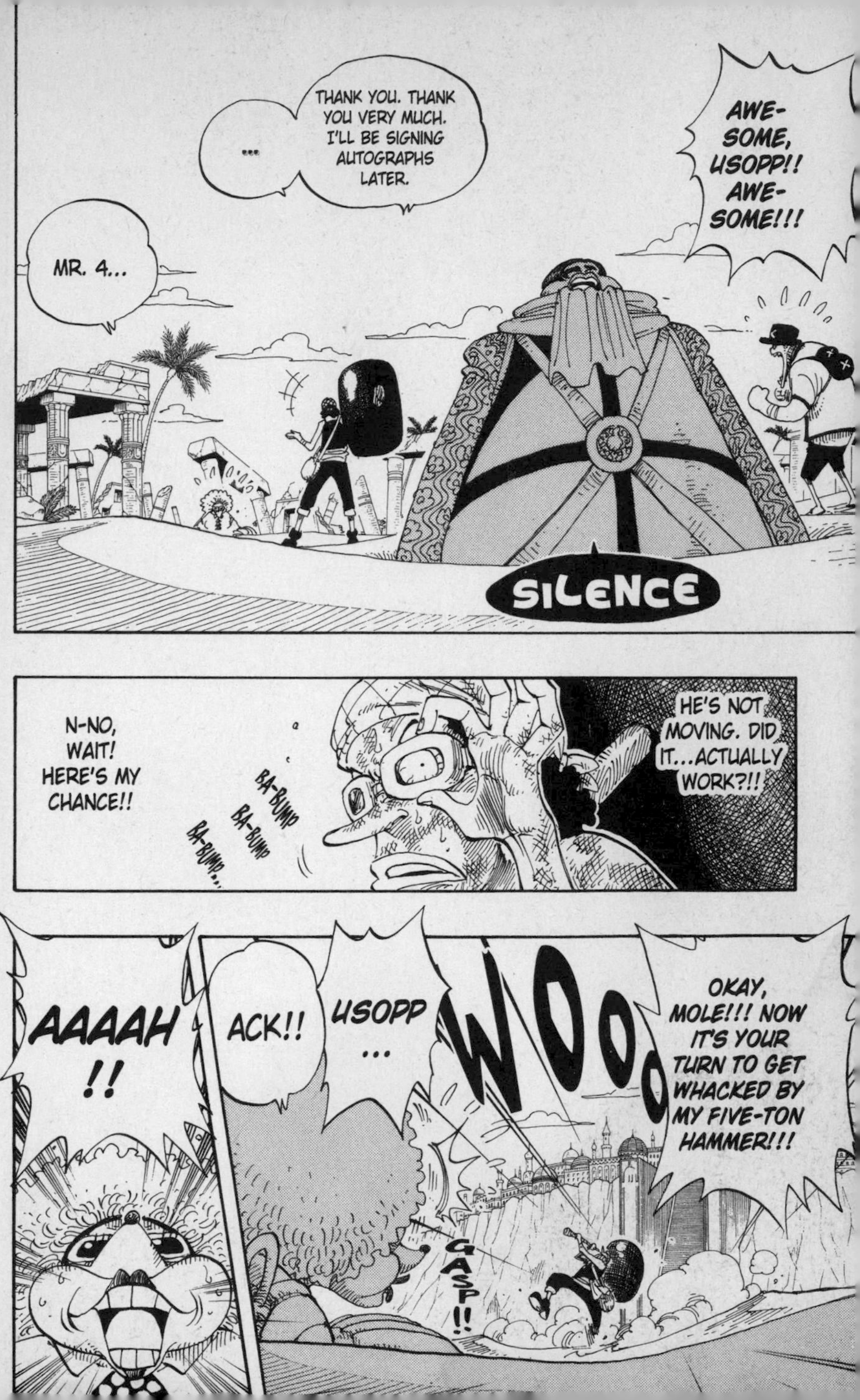
AWE-SOME, USOPP!! AWE-SOME!!!
THANK YOU. THANK YOU VERY MUCH. I'LL BE SIGNING AUTOGRAPHS LATER.
...
MR. 4...
SILENCE
HE'S NOT MOVING. DID IT...ACTUALLY WORK?!!
BA-BUMP BA-BUMP BA-BUMP...
N-NO, WAIT! HERE'S MY CHANCE!!
OKAY, MOLE!!! NOW IT'S YOUR TURN TO GET WHACKED BY MY FIVE-TON HAMMER!!!
WOOO
USOPP ...
ACK!!
GASP!!
AAAAH !!

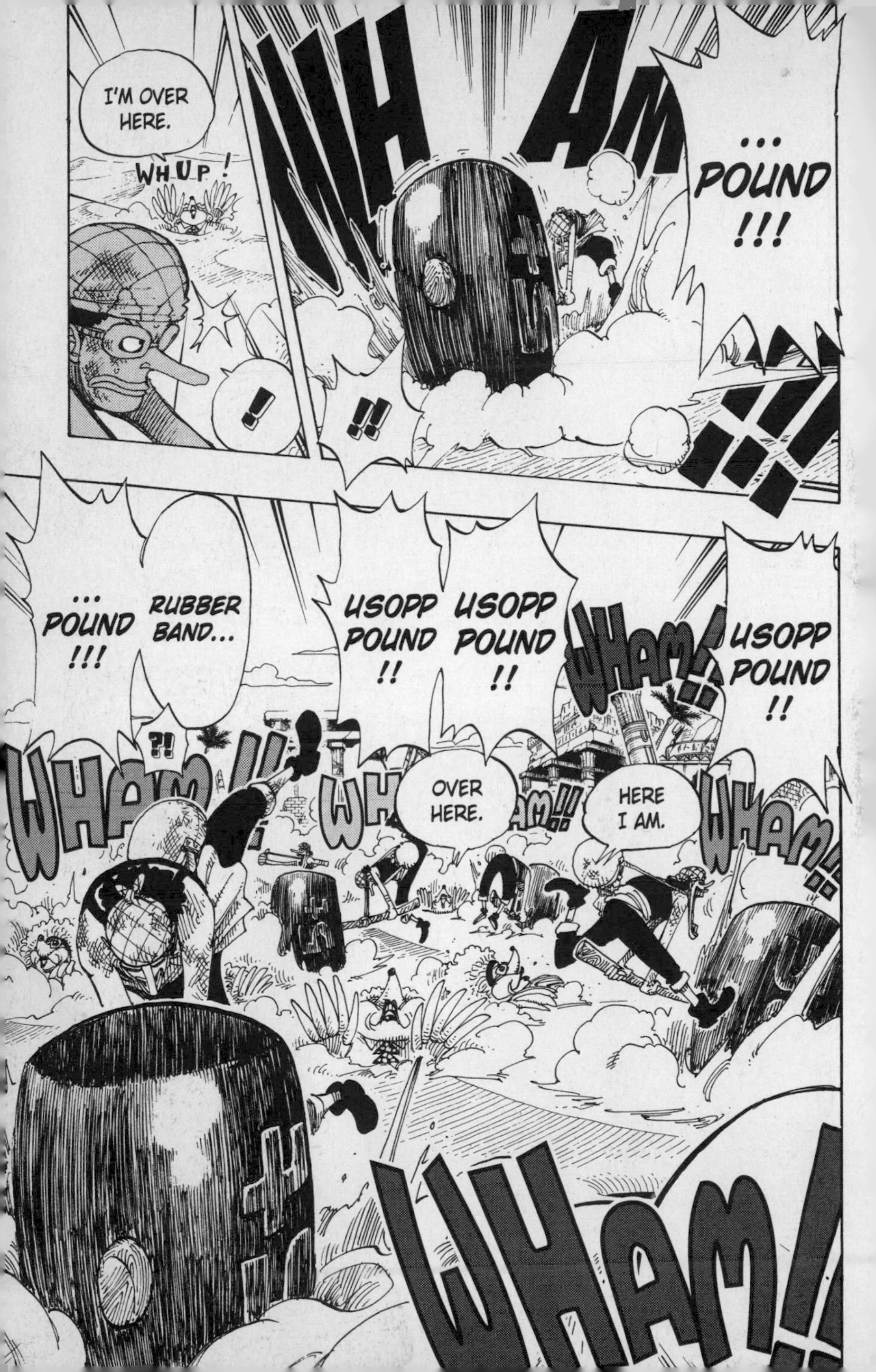
WHAM
... POUND !!!
!!!
!!
I'M OVER HERE.
WHUP!
!
USOPP POUND !!
WHAM!!
HERE I AM.
USOPP POUND !!
USOPP POUND !!
WHAM!!
OVER HERE.
WH
RUBBER BAND...
... POUND !!!
?!
WHAM!!
WHAM!!

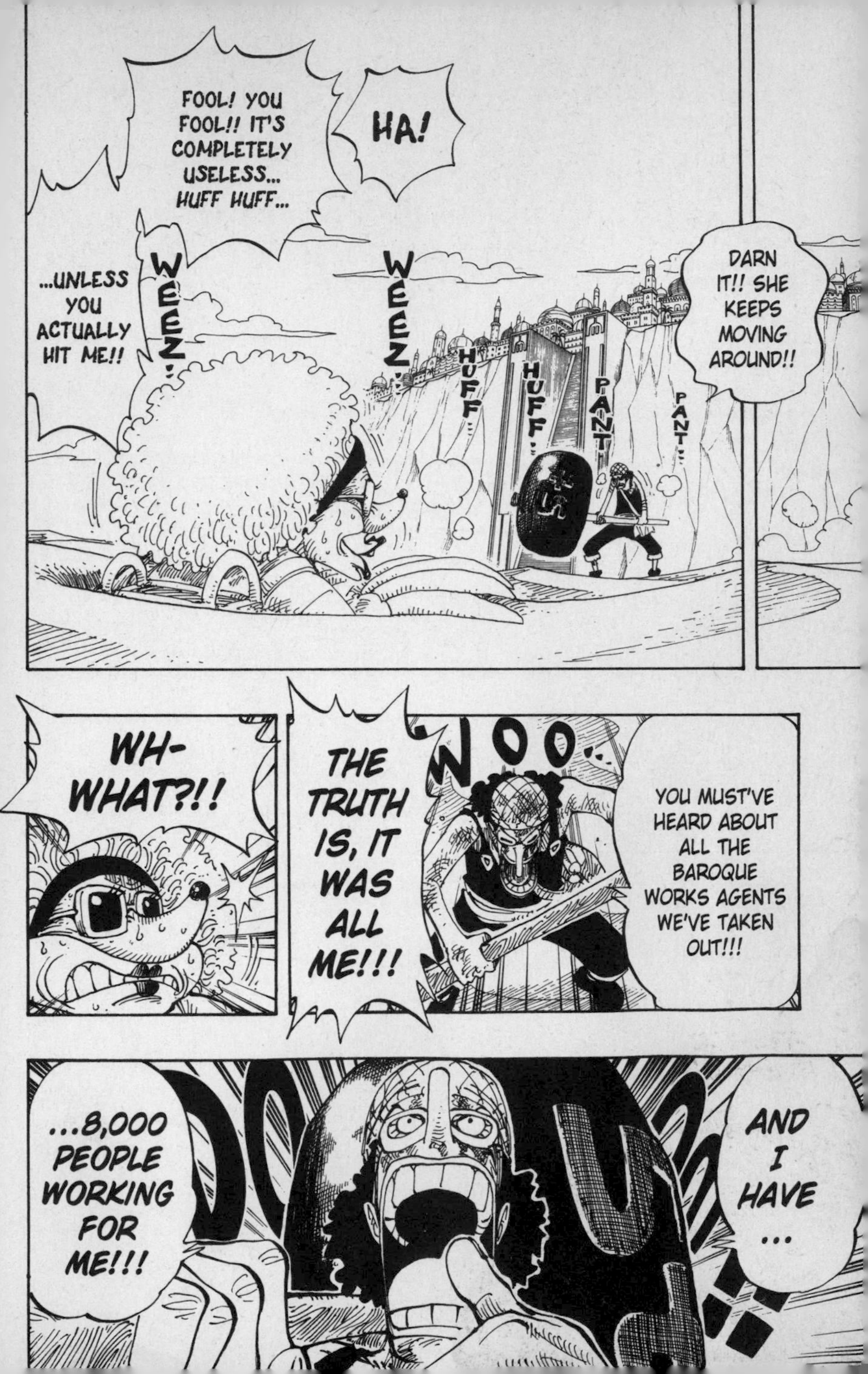
DARN IT!! SHE KEEPS MOVING AROUND!!
HA!
FOOL! YOU FOOL!! IT'S COMPLETELY USELESS... HUFF HUFF...
...UNLESS YOU ACTUALLY HIT ME!!
WEEZ
WEEZ
HUFF
HUFF
PANT
PANT
YOU MUST'VE HEARD ABOUT ALL THE BAROQUE WORKS AGENTS WE'VE TAKEN OUT!!!
WOO...
THE TRUTH IS, IT WAS ALL ME!!!
WH- WHAT?!!
AND I HAVE...
...8,000 PEOPLE WORKING FOR ME!!!

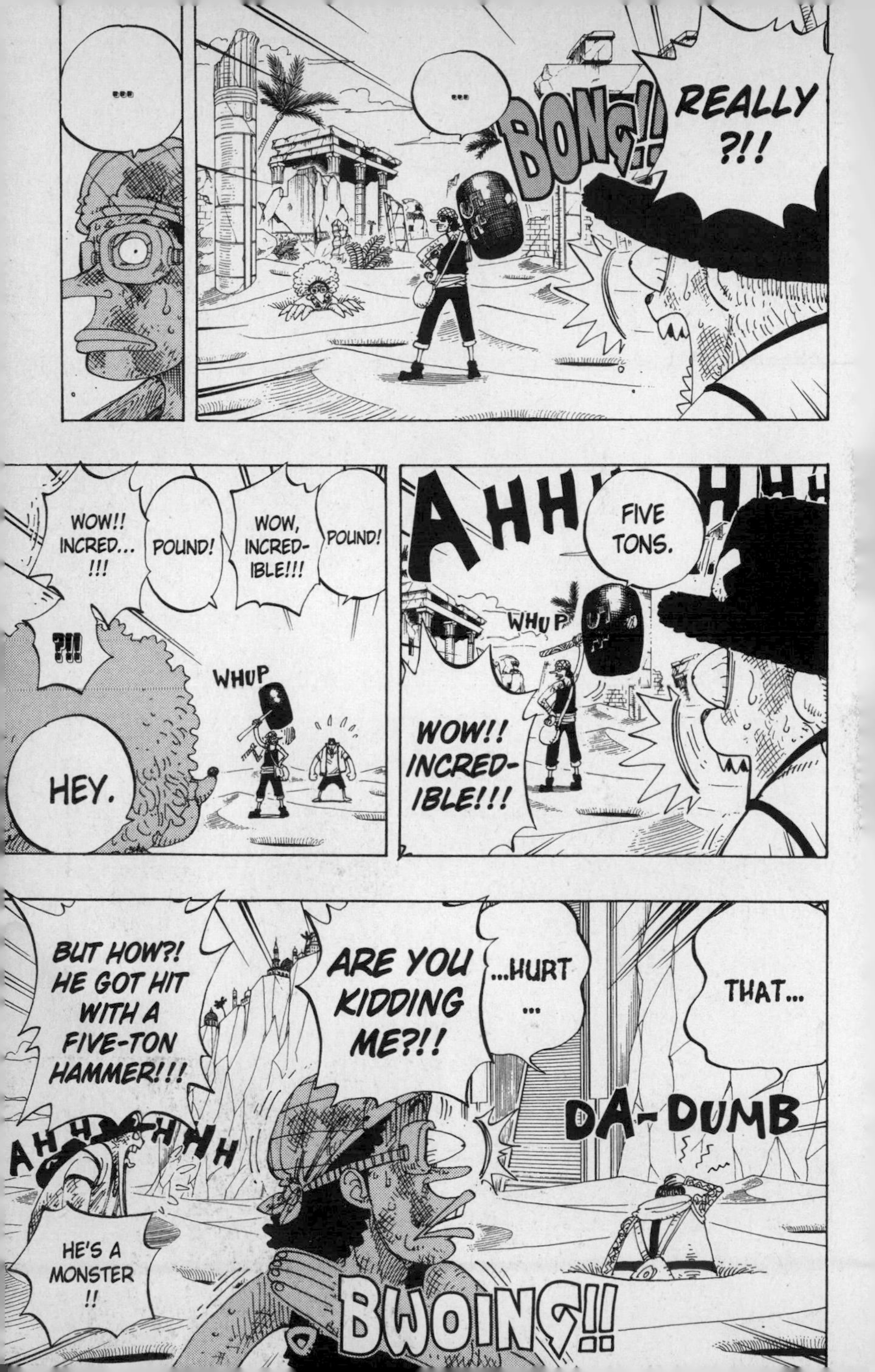
REALLY ?!!
BONG!!
...
...
AHHH
FIVE TONS.
WHUP
WOW!! INCRED-IBLE!!!
POUND!
WOW, INCRED-IBLE!!!
POUND!
WOW!! INCRED... !!!
?!!
WHUP
HEY.
THAT...
...HURT ...
DA-DUMB
ARE YOU KIDDING ME?!!
BUT HOW?! HE GOT HIT WITH A FIVE-TON HAMMER!!!
AHHHHHH
HE'S A MONSTER !!
BWOING!!

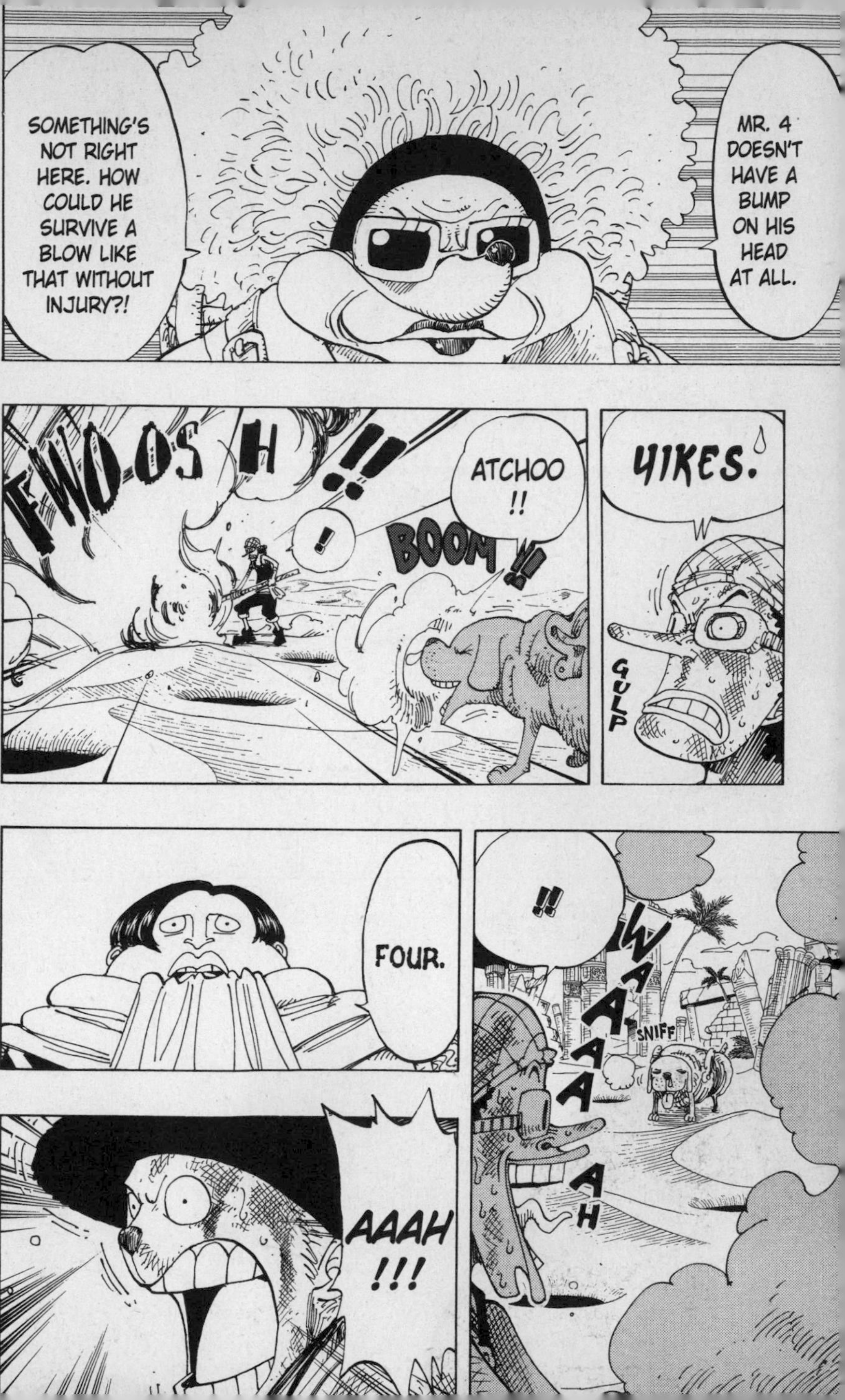
MR. 4 DOESN'T HAVE A BUMP ON HIS HEAD AT ALL.
SOMETHING'S NOT RIGHT HERE. HOW COULD HE SURVIVE A BLOW LIKE THAT WITHOUT INJURY?!
YIKES.
GULP
ATCHOO !!
BOOM!!
!
FWOOSH!!
!!
WAAAAAAAH
SNIFF
FOUR.
AAAH !!!

OF COURSE IT WAS!! YOU THINK I CAN LIFT FIVE TONS?!!

I CAN'T EVEN DO TEN POUNDS!!!

GWAH!

TA-DAH!!

...

IT WAS FAKE!!!

PAPIER-MÂCHÉ!!!

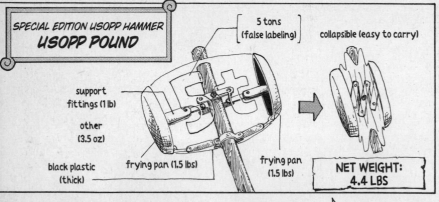

SPECIAL EDITION USOPP HAMMER
USOPP POUND

5 tons (false labeling)

collapsible (easy to carry)

support fittings (1 lb)

other (3.5 oz)

black plastic (thick)

frying pan (1.5 lbs)

frying pan (1.5 lbs)

NET WEIGHT: 4.4 LBS

HOW DARE YOU TRICK ME.

WOO

AAAAH!!!

WHOA!!

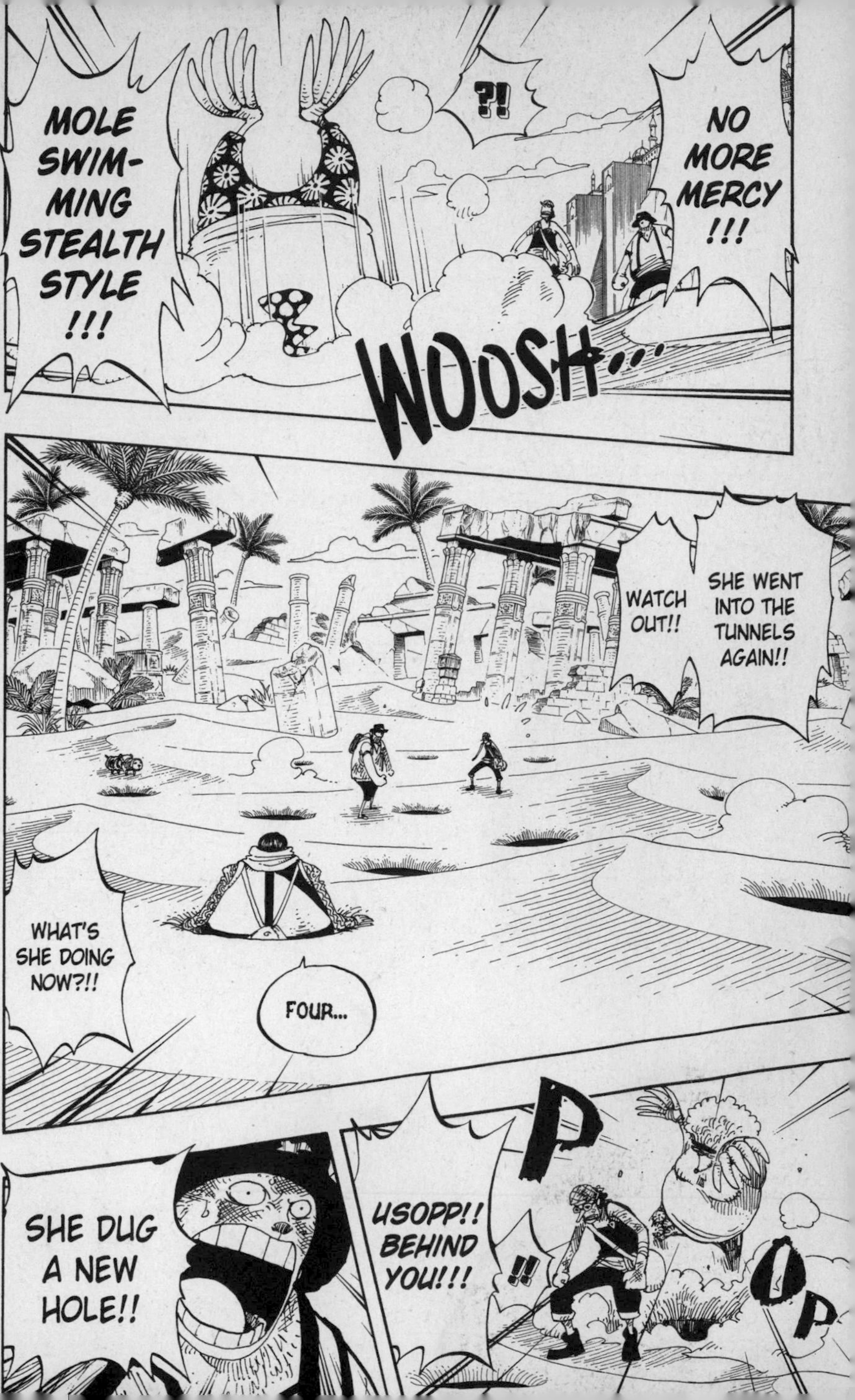
NO MORE MERCY!!!
?!
MOLE SWIM-MING STEALTH STYLE!!!
WOOSH...
SHE WENT INTO THE TUNNELS AGAIN!!
WATCH OUT!!
WHAT'S SHE DOING NOW?!!
FOUR...
P
OP
!!
USOPP!! BEHIND YOU!!!
SHE DUG A NEW HOLE!!

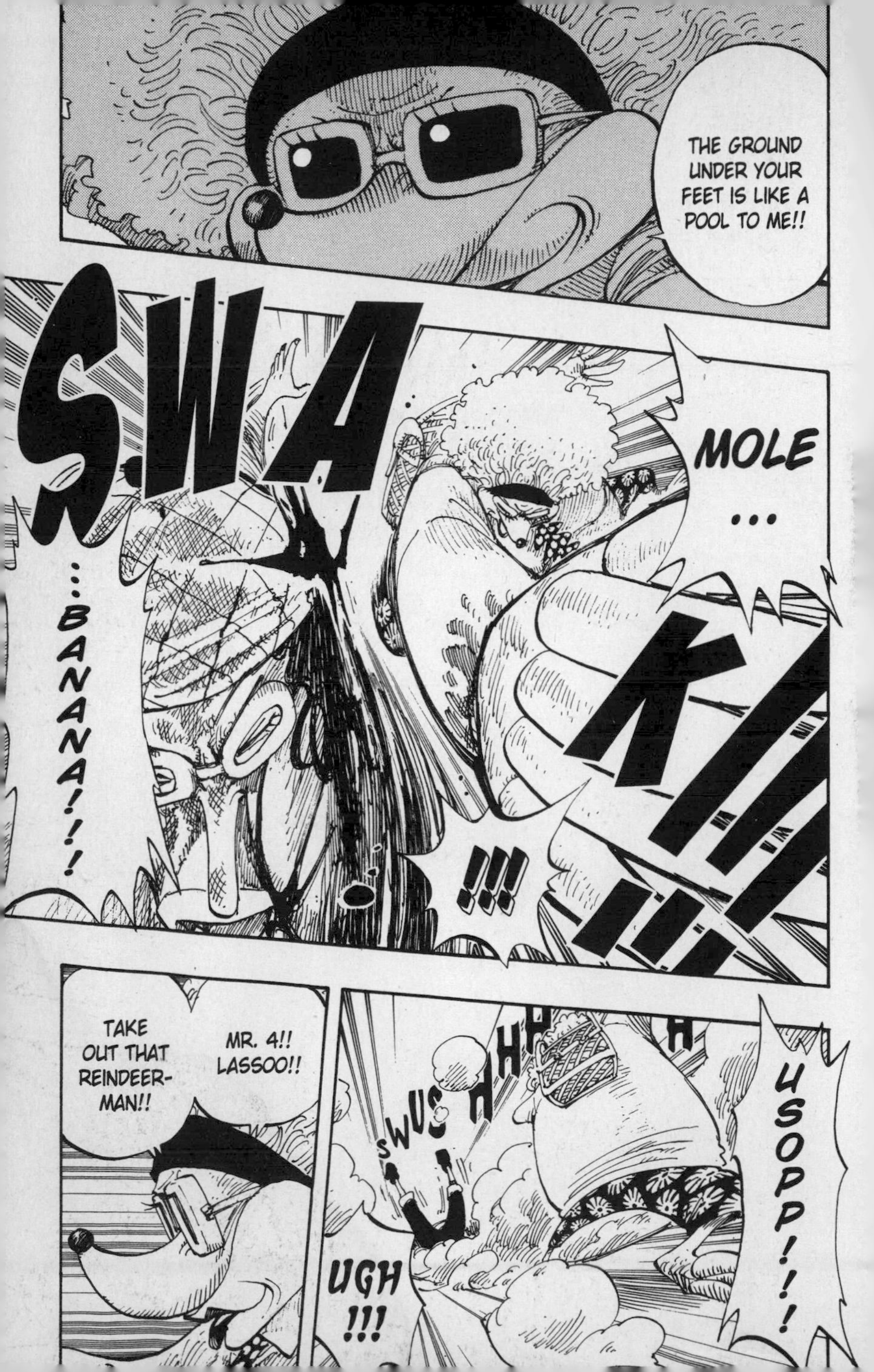
THE GROUND UNDER YOUR FEET IS LIKE A POOL TO ME!!
MOLE ...
KI
SWA
...BANANA!!!
!!!
USOPP!!!
SWUSS
UGH !!!
MR. 4!! LASSOO!!
TAKE OUT THAT REINDEER-MAN!!

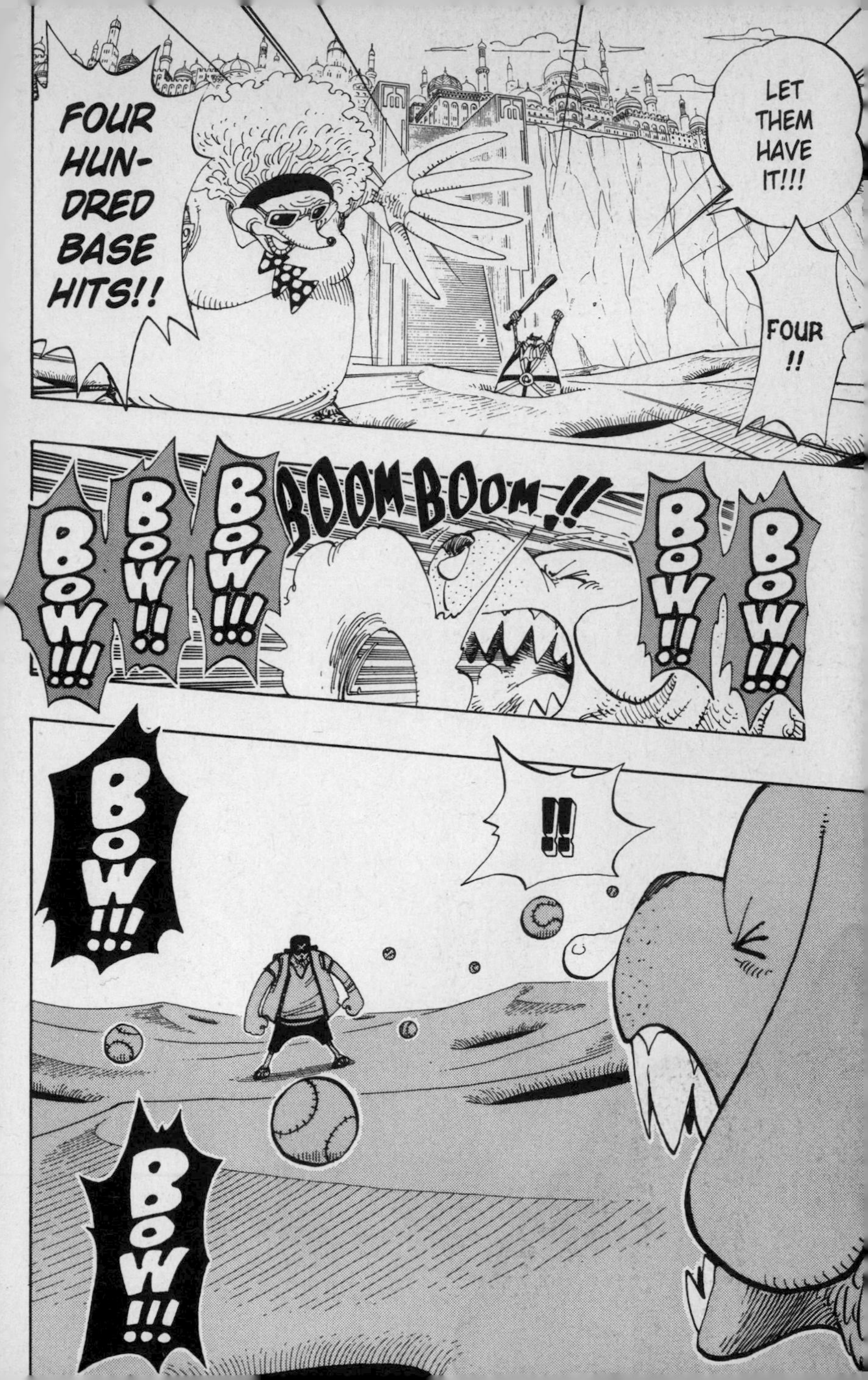
LET THEM HAVE IT!!!
FOUR !!
FOUR HUN-DRED BASE HITS!!
BOW!!!
BOW!!
BOOM BOOM!!
BOW!!!
BOW!!
BOW!!!
!!
BOW!!!
BOW!!!

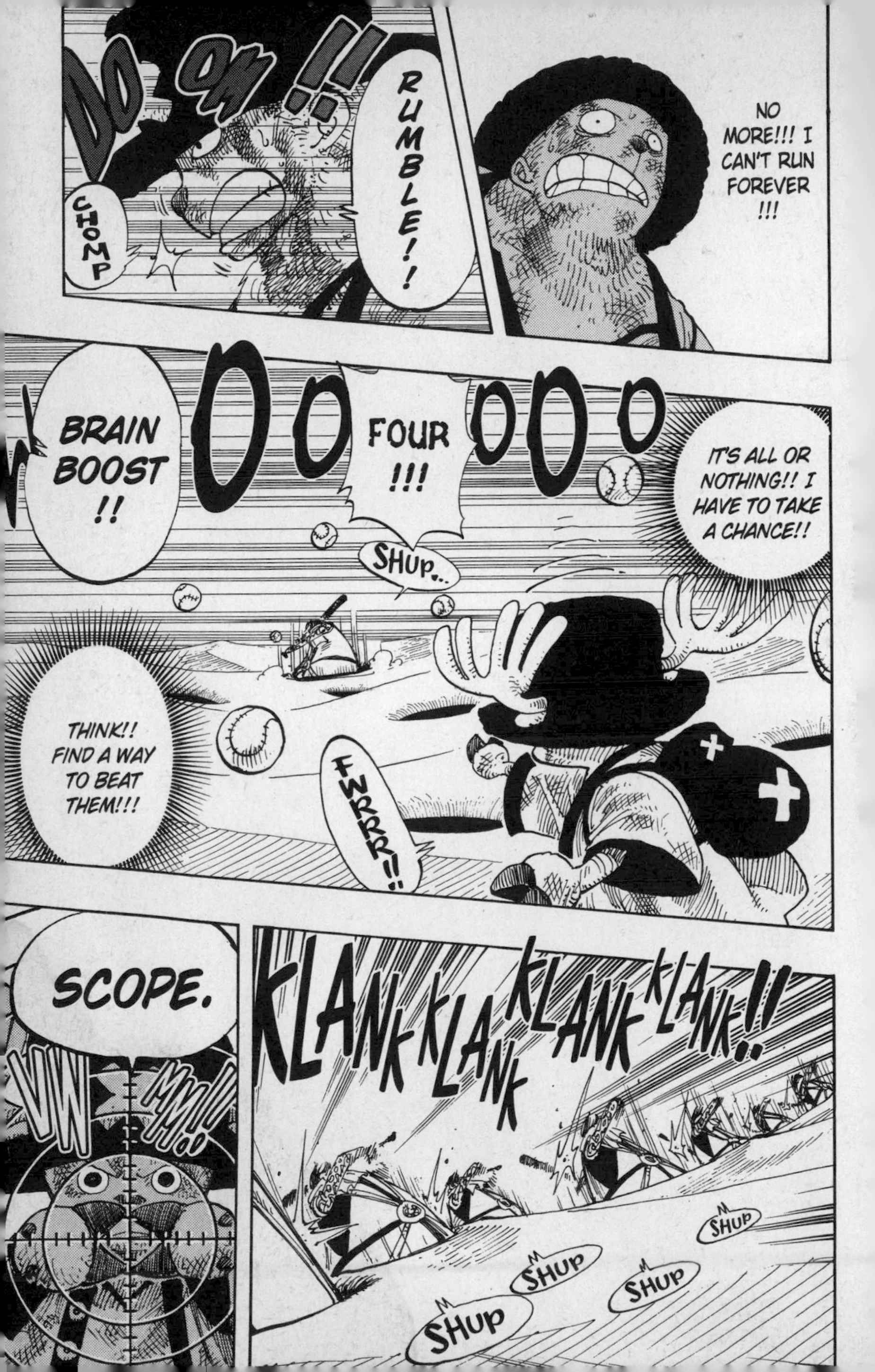
NO MORE!!! I CAN'T RUN FOREVER!!!
RUMBLE!!
DOOM!!
CHOMP
IT'S ALL OR NOTHING!! I HAVE TO TAKE A CHANCE!!
FOUR!!!
BRAIN BOOST!!
SHUP..
THINK!! FIND A WAY TO BEAT THEM!!!
FWRRR!!
KLANK KLANK KLANK KLANK!!
SHUP
SHUP
SHUP
SHUP
SCOPE.
VWMM!!

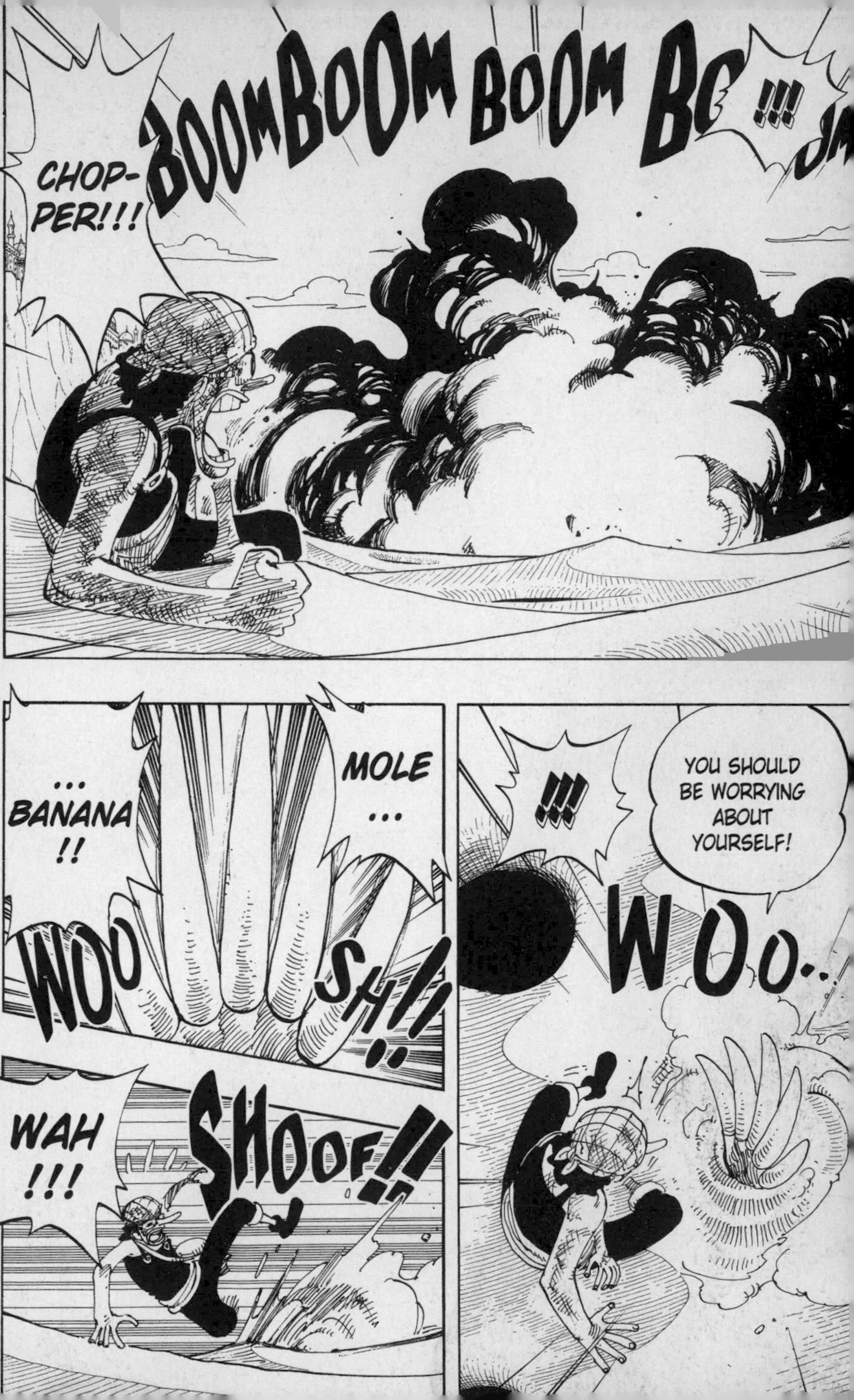

BOOMBOOM BOOM BO !!!
CHOP-PER!!!
YOU SHOULD BE WORRYING ABOUT YOURSELF!
!!!
WOO..
MOLE ...
... BANANA !!
WOOSH!!
SHOOF!!
WAH !!!

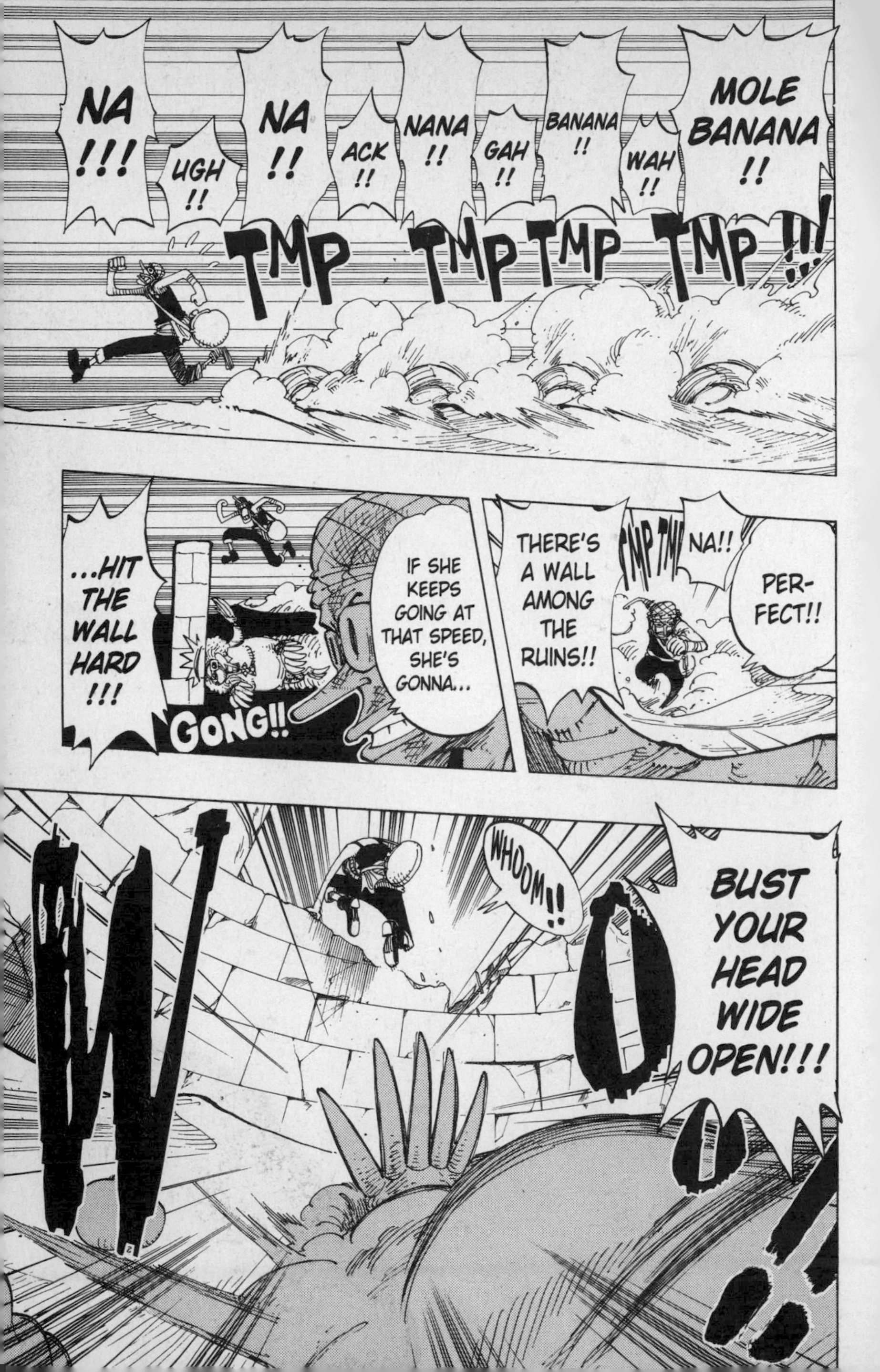
MOLE BANANA!!
WAH!!
BANANA!!
GAH!!
NANA!!
ACK!!
NA!!
UGH!!
NA!!!
TMP TMP TMP TMP!!!
PER-FECT!!
NA!!
TMP TMP
THERE'S A WALL AMONG THE RUINS!!
IF SHE KEEPS GOING AT THAT SPEED, SHE'S GONNA...
...HIT THE WALL HARD!!!
GONG!!
BUST YOUR HEAD WIDE OPEN!!!
WHOOM!!

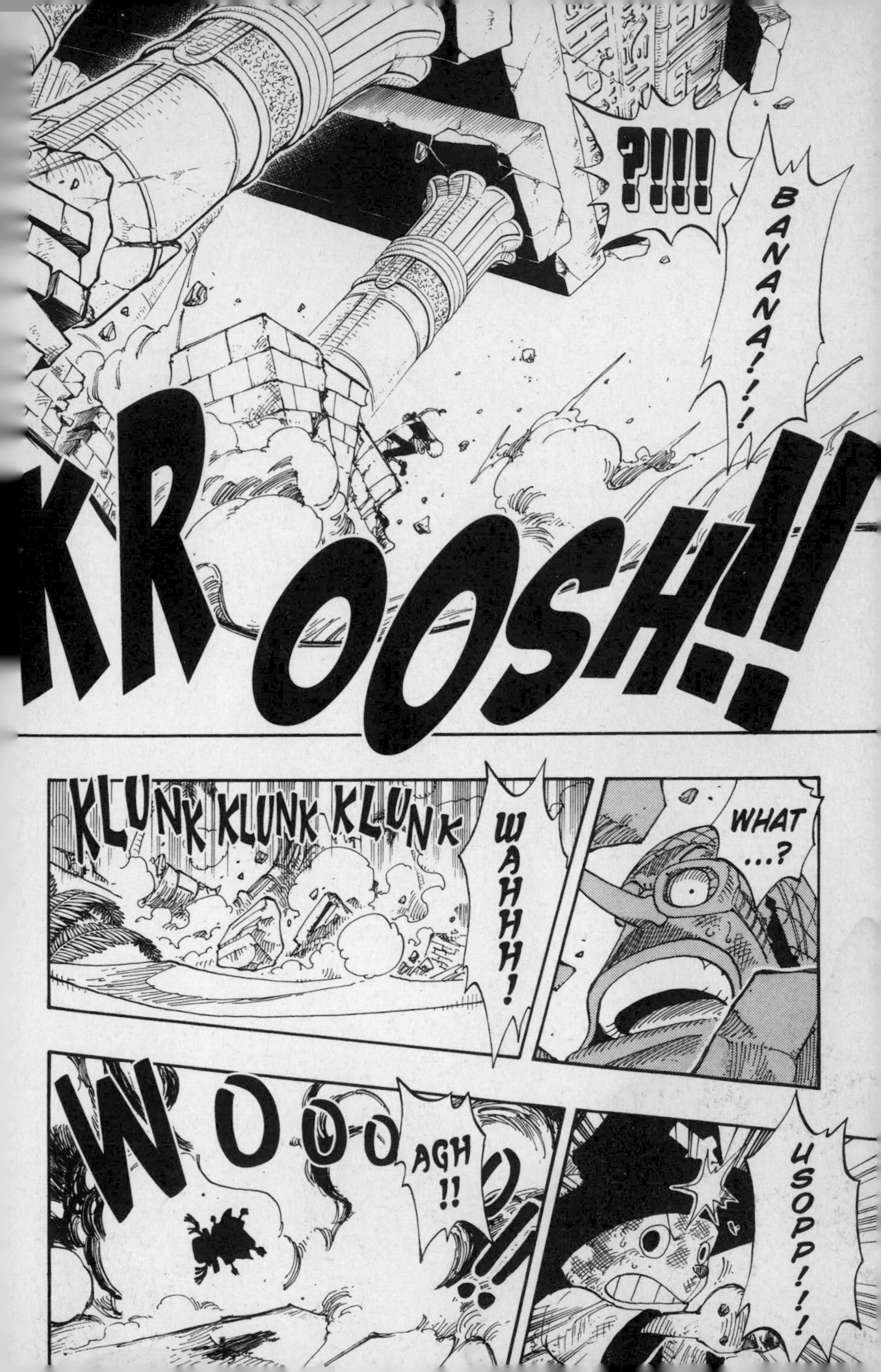
BANANA!!!
?!!!
KROOSH!!
WHAT...?
WAHHH!
KLUNK KLUNK KLUNK
USOPP!!!
WOOOO!!
AGH!!

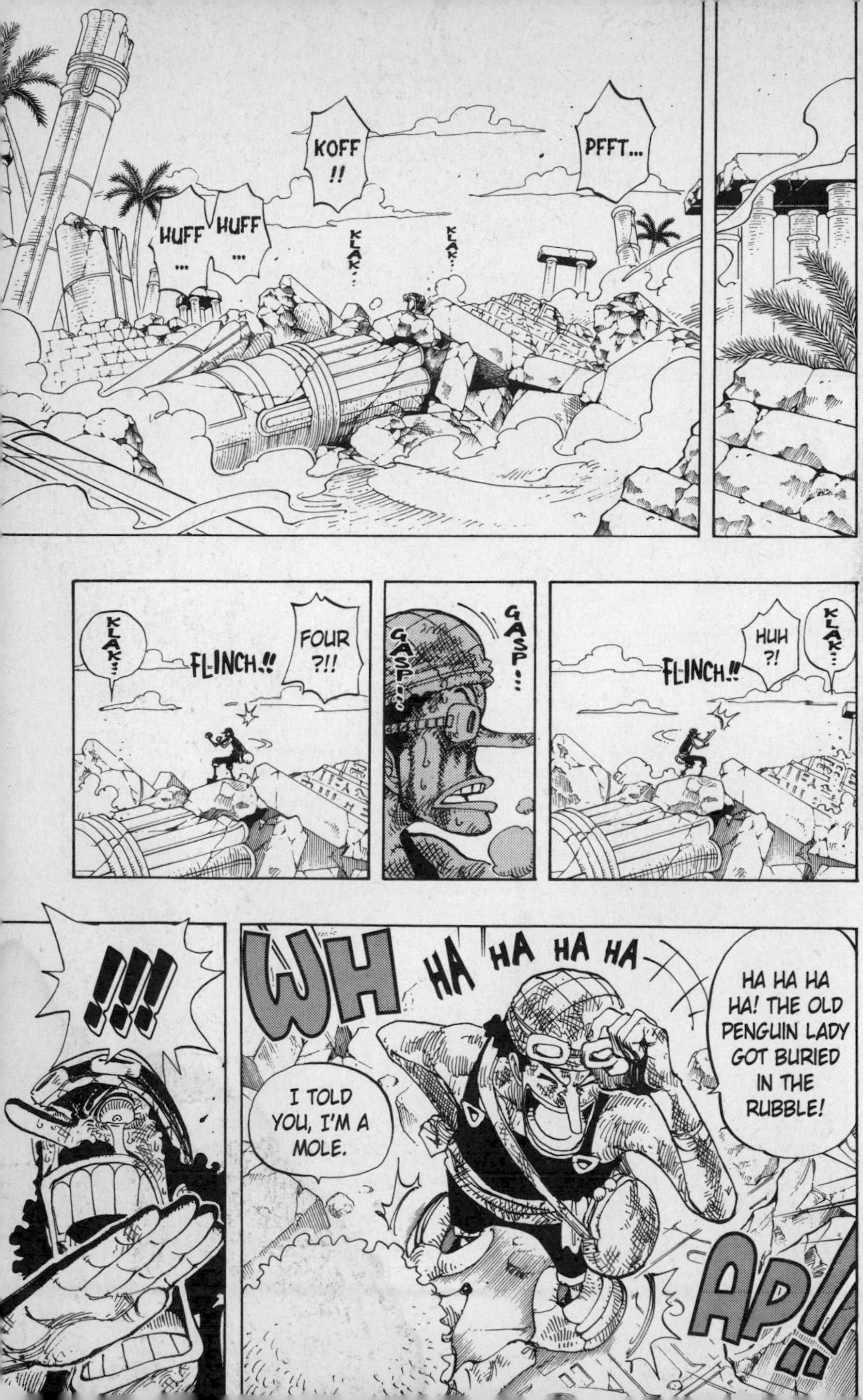
PFFT...
KLAK..
KLAK..
KOFF !!
HUFF ...
HUFF ...
KLAK..
HUH ?!
FLINCH!!
GASP!!
GASP!!
FOUR ?!!
FLINCH!!
KLAK!!
HA HA HA HA! THE OLD PENGUIN LADY GOT BURIED IN THE RUBBLE!
WH AP!!
HA HA HA HA
I TOLD YOU, I'M A MOLE.
!!!

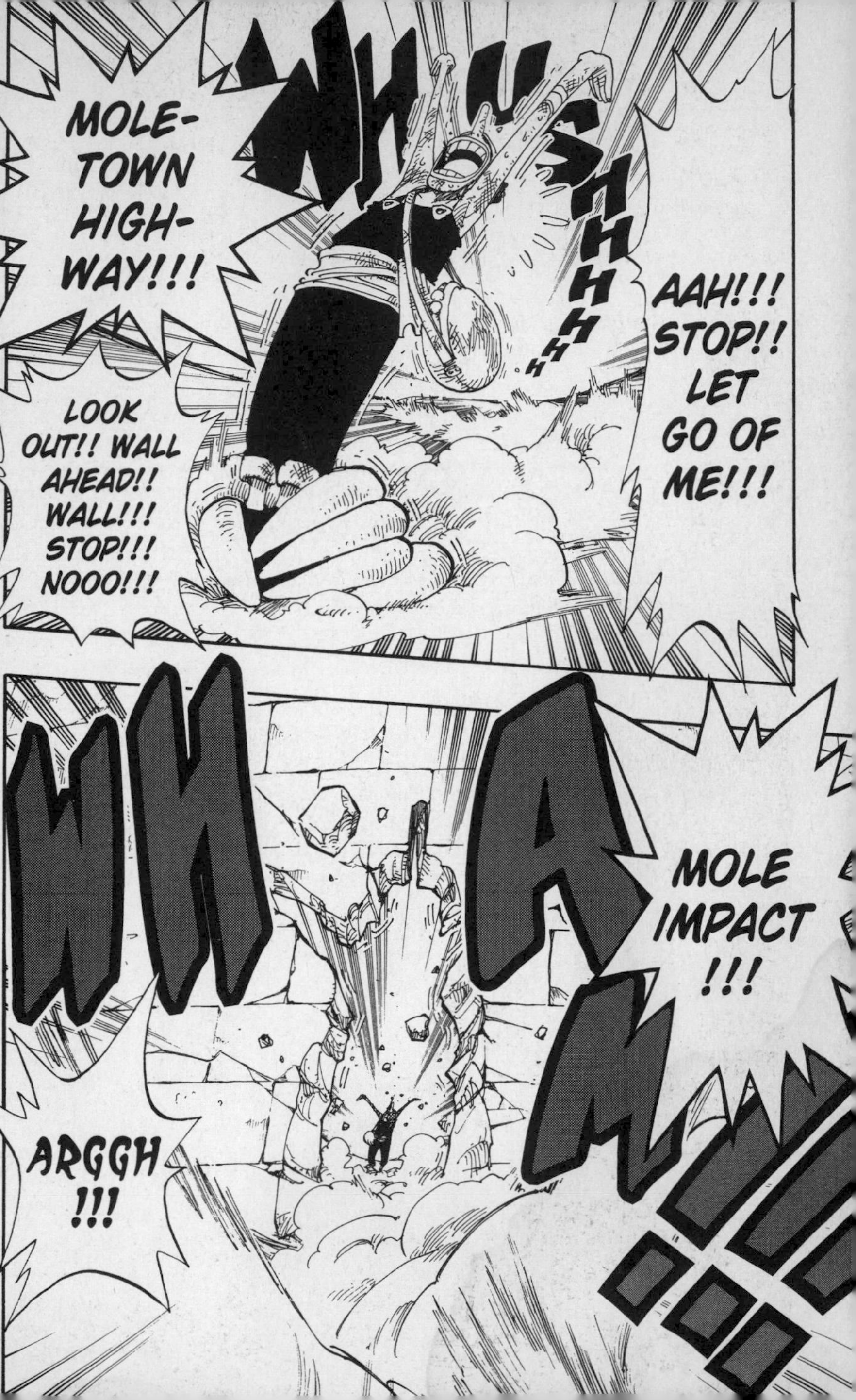
AAH!!! STOP!! LET GO OF ME!!!
MOLE-TOWN HIGH-WAY!!!
LOOK OUT!! WALL AHEAD!! WALL!!! STOP!!! NOOO!!!
MOLE IMPACT !!!
WHAM!!!
ARGGH !!!

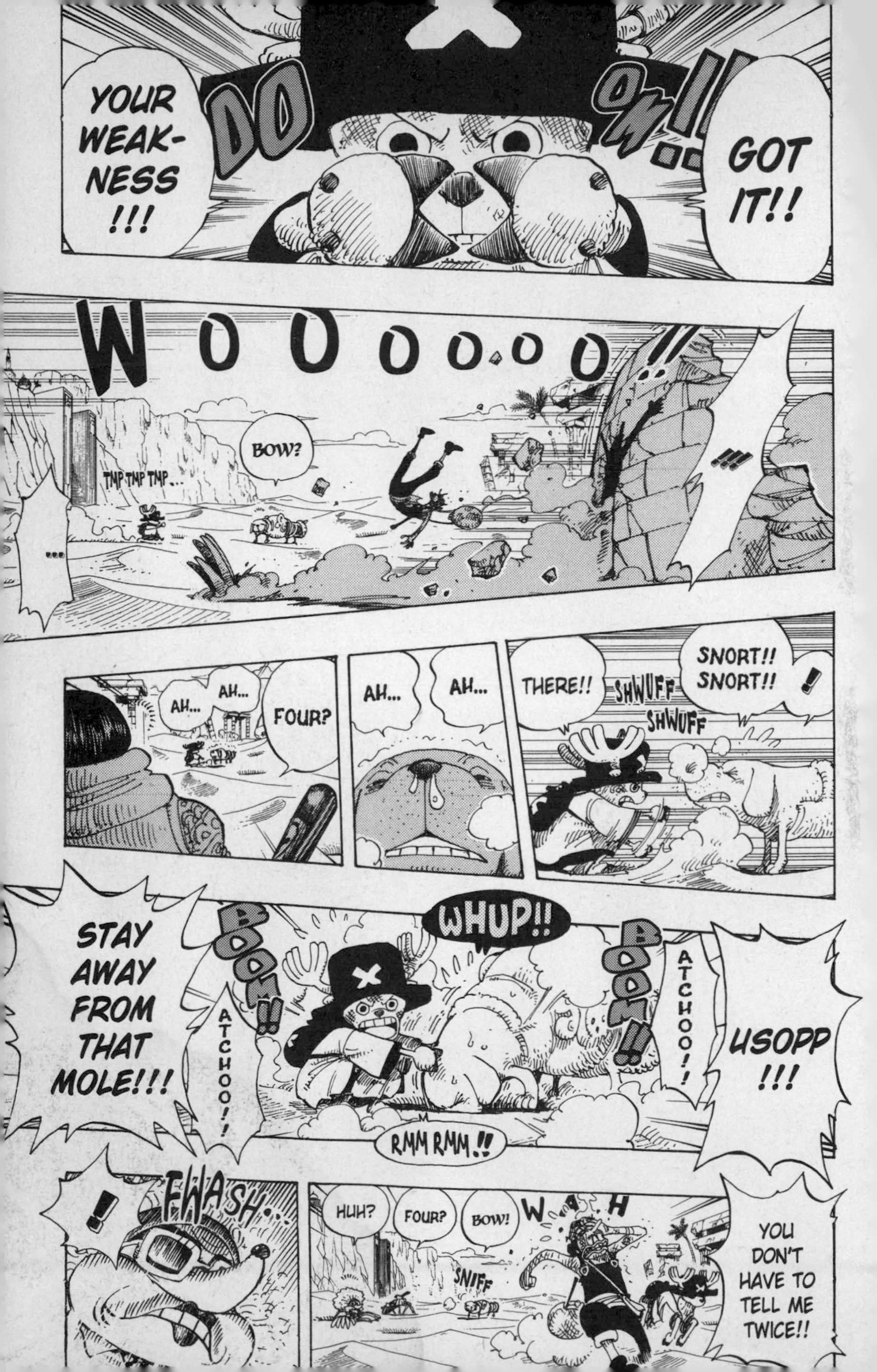
GOT IT!!
DOOM!!
YOUR WEAK-NESS!!!
!!!
WOOOOOOO
BOW?
TMP TMP TMP...
...
!
SNORT!! SNORT!!
SHWUFF SHWUFF
THERE!!
AH...
AH...
FOUR?
AH...
AH...
USOPP!!!
ATCHOO!!
BOOM!!
WHUP!!
BOOM!!
ATCHOO!!
STAY AWAY FROM THAT MOLE!!!
RMM RMM!!
YOU DON'T HAVE TO TELL ME TWICE!!
WAH
BOW!
FOUR?
HUH?
SNIFF
FWASH..
!

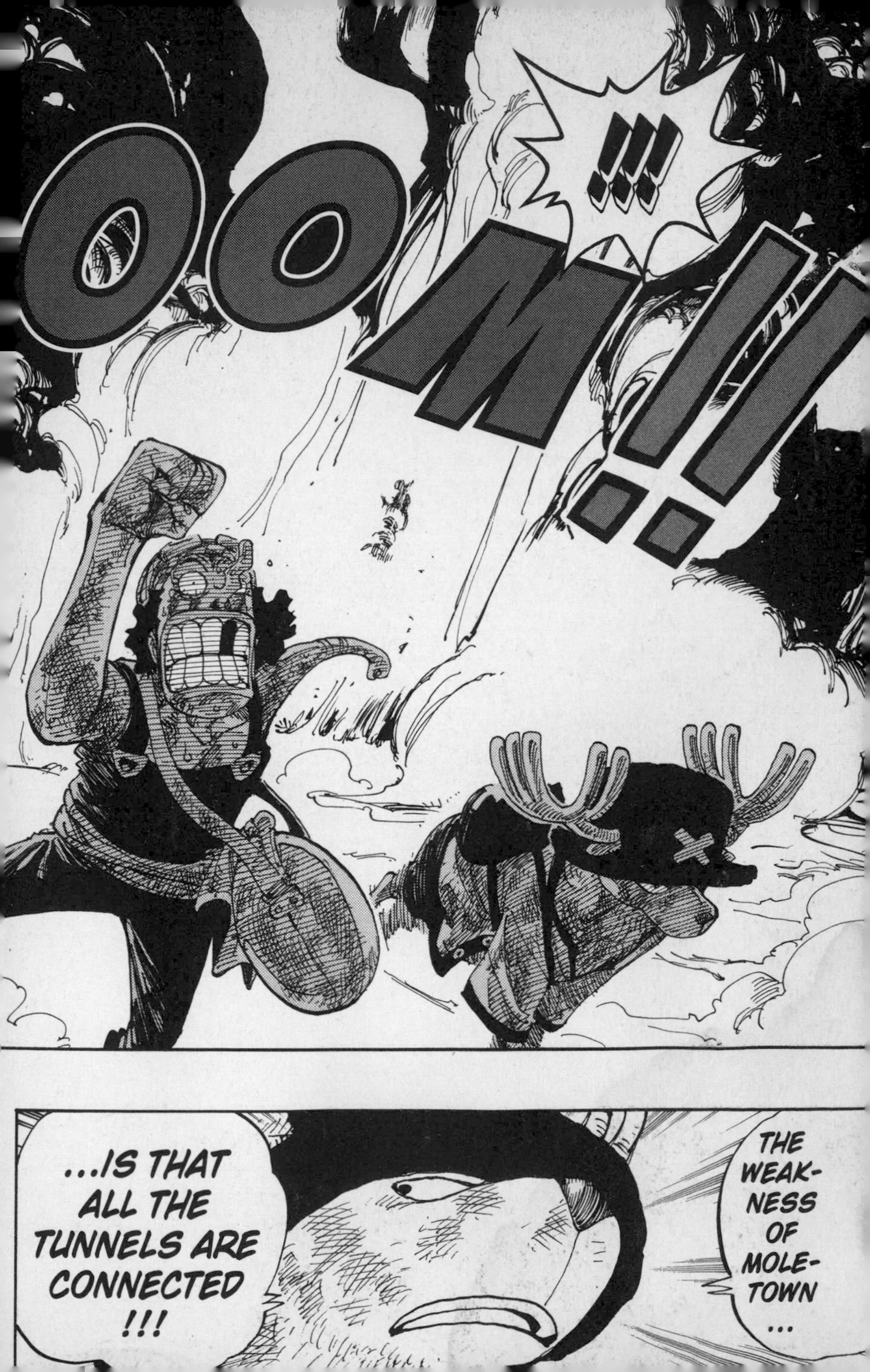
!!!
OOM!!
THE WEAKNESS OF MOLE-TOWN...
...IS THAT ALL THE TUNNELS ARE CONNECTED!!!

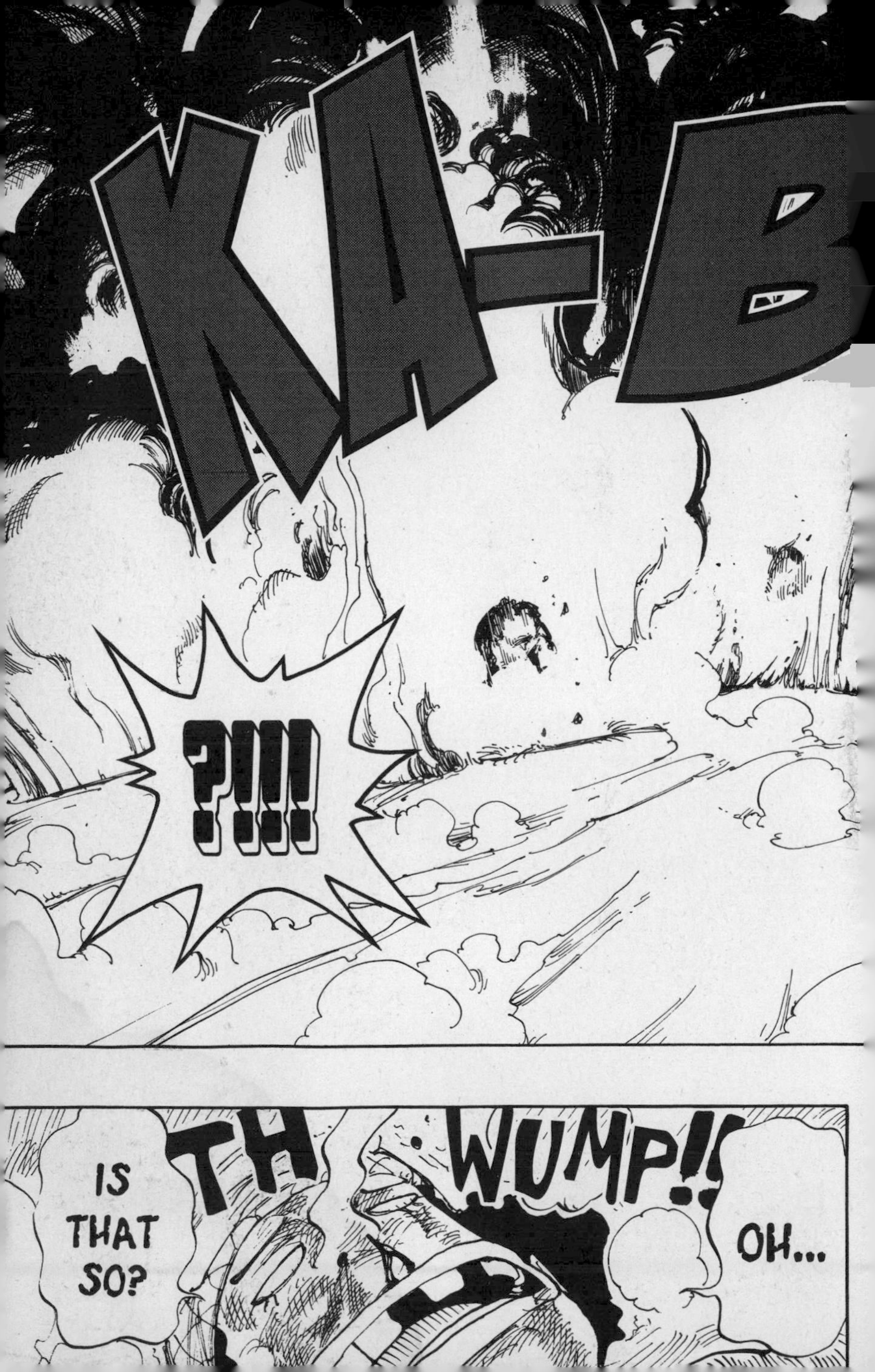
KA-B
?!!!
OH...
THWUMP!!
IS THAT SO?

Chapter 186: 4

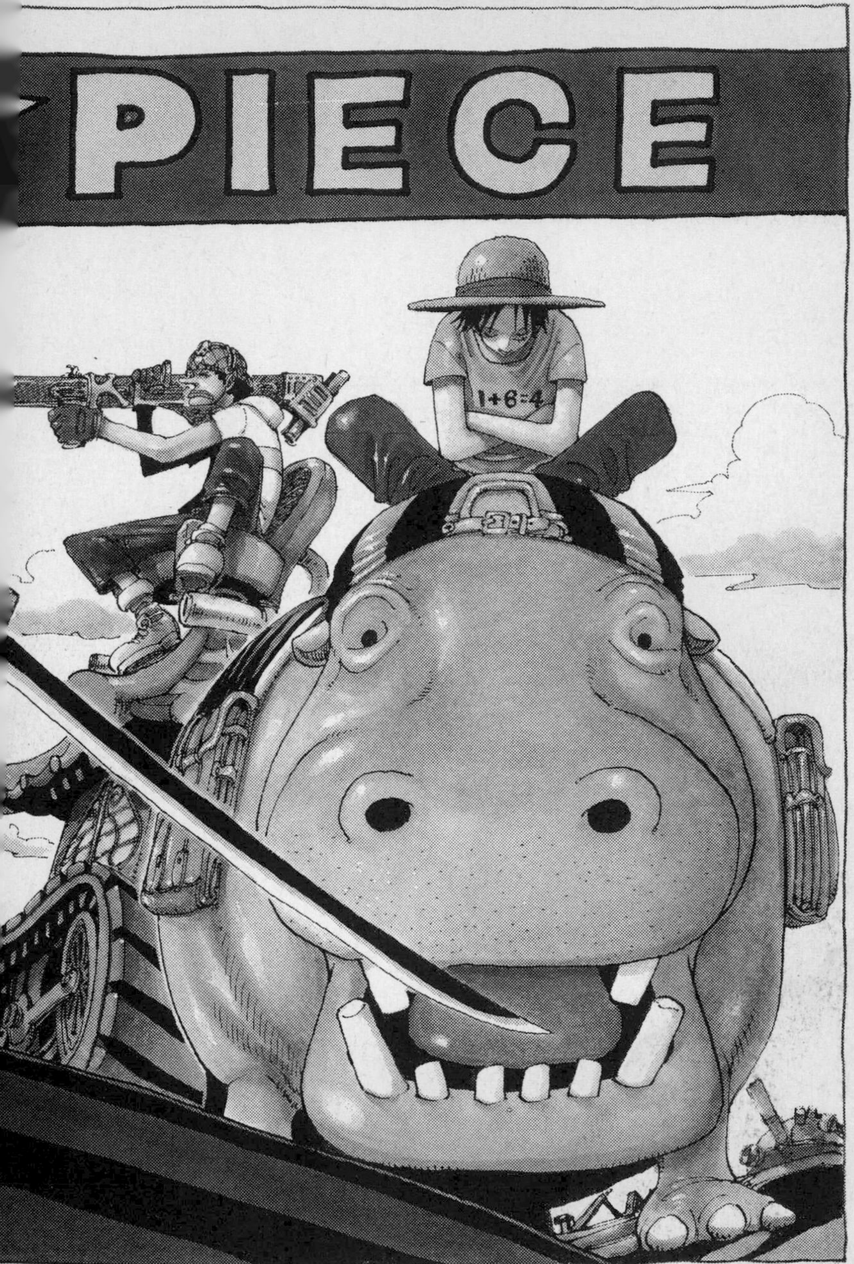
PIECE
1+6=4

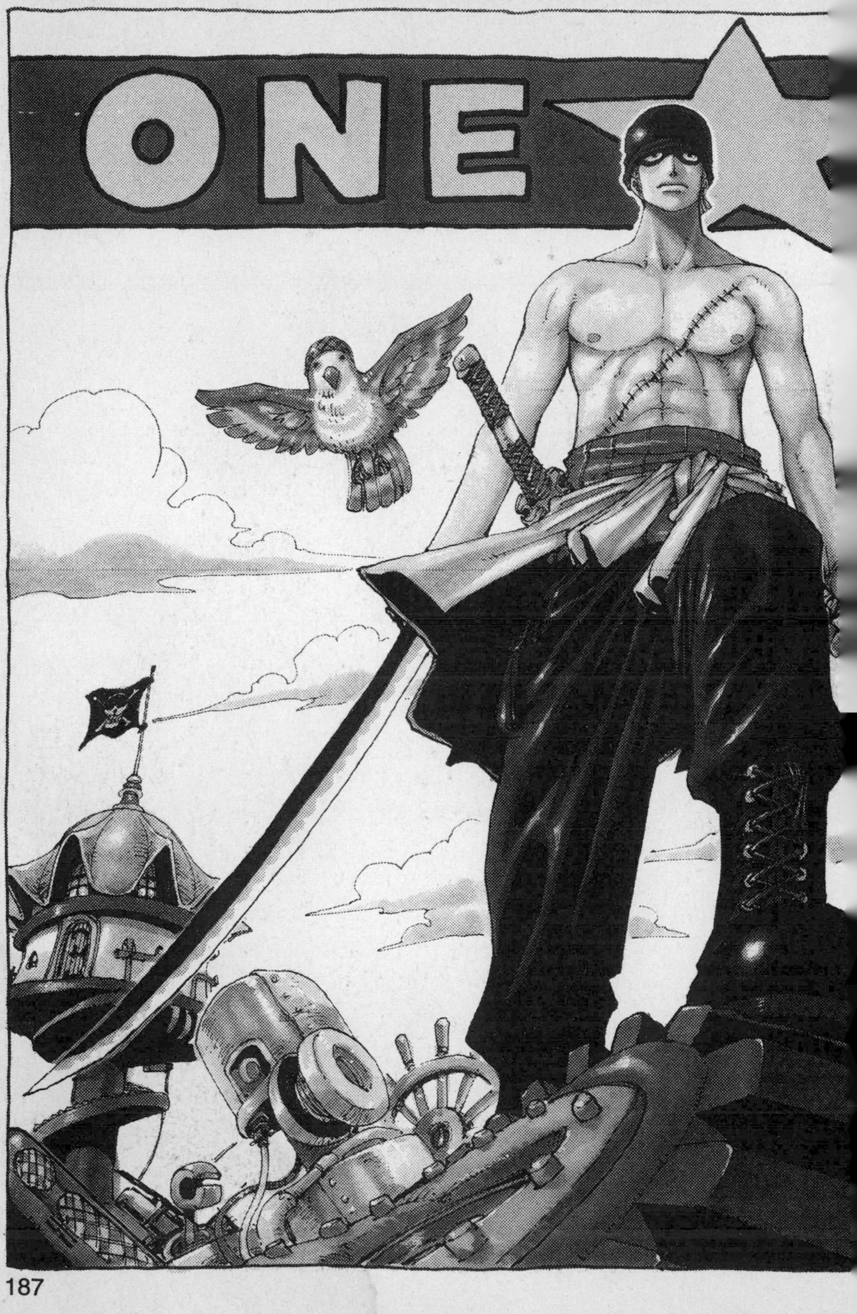
ONE

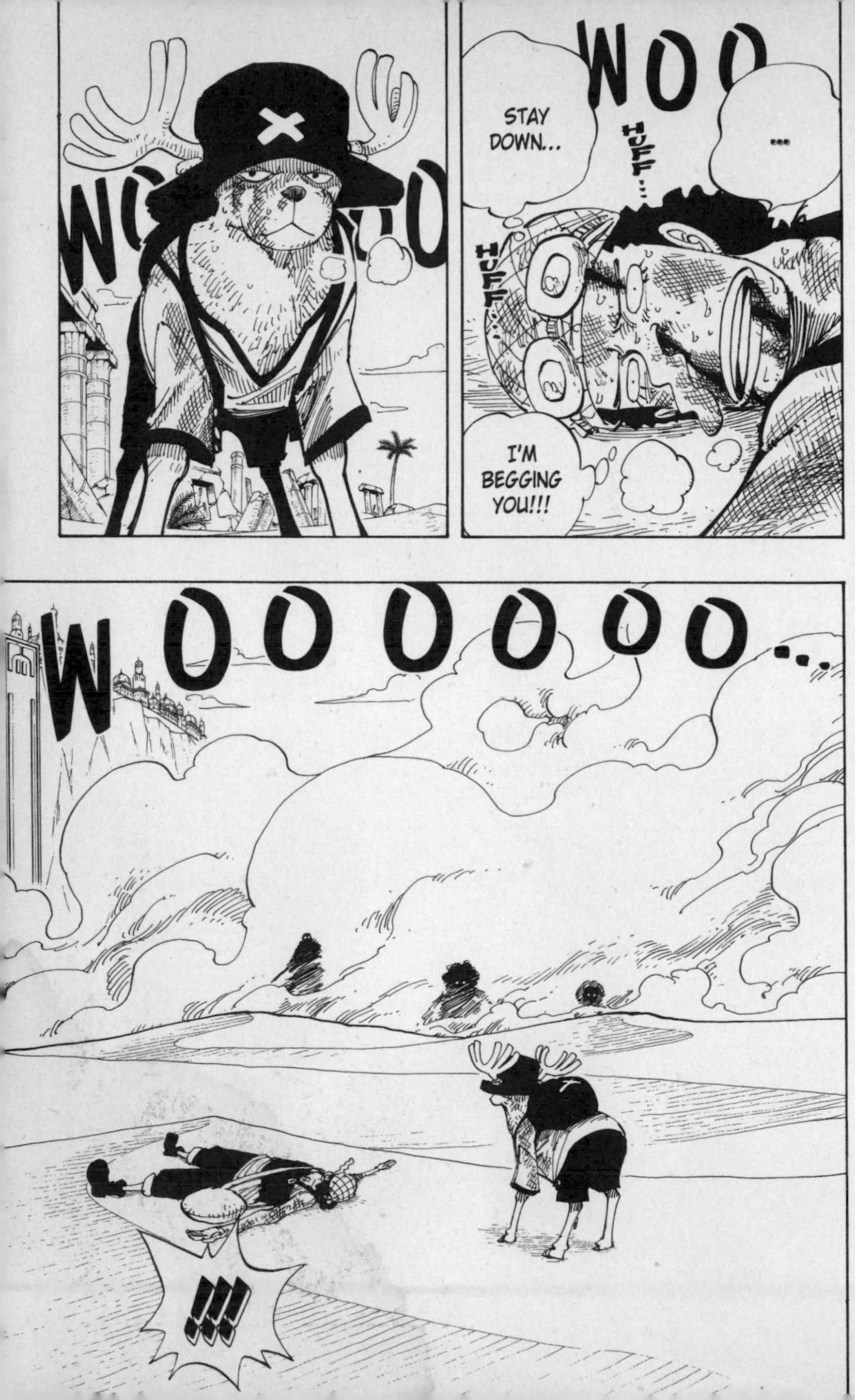

...
WOO
HUFF!!
STAY DOWN...
HUFF...
I'M BEGGING YOU!!!
WO
OO
WOOOOOOO...
!!!

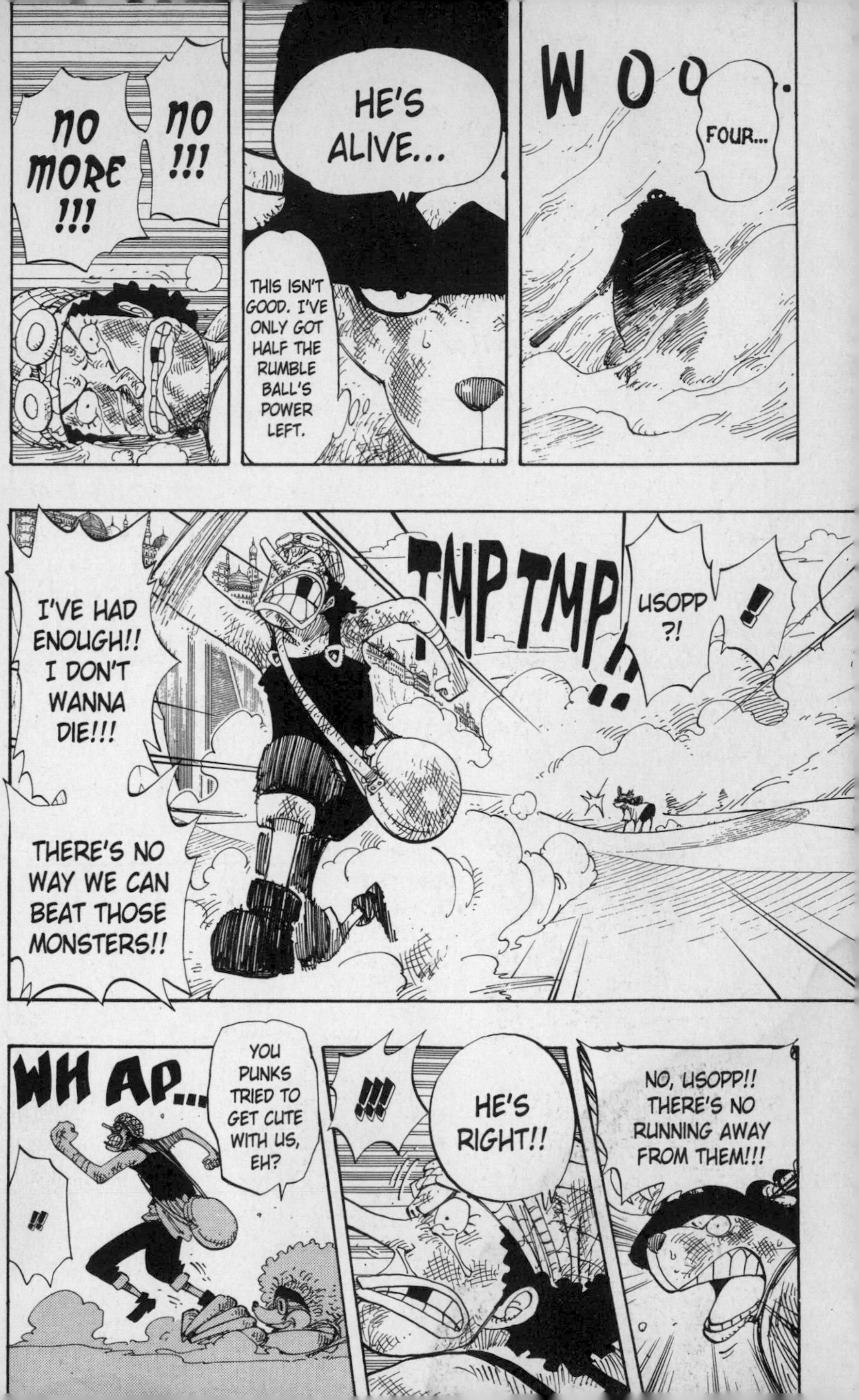
WOO...
FOUR...
HE'S ALIVE...
THIS ISN'T GOOD. I'VE ONLY GOT HALF THE RUMBLE BALL'S POWER LEFT.
no !!!
no more !!!
USOPP ?!
!
TMP TMP
!!
I'VE HAD ENOUGH!! I DON'T WANNA DIE!!!
THERE'S NO WAY WE CAN BEAT THOSE MONSTERS!!
NO, USOPP!! THERE'S NO RUNNING AWAY FROM THEM!!!
HE'S RIGHT!!
!!!
YOU PUNKS TRIED TO GET CUTE WITH US, EH?
WHAP...
!!

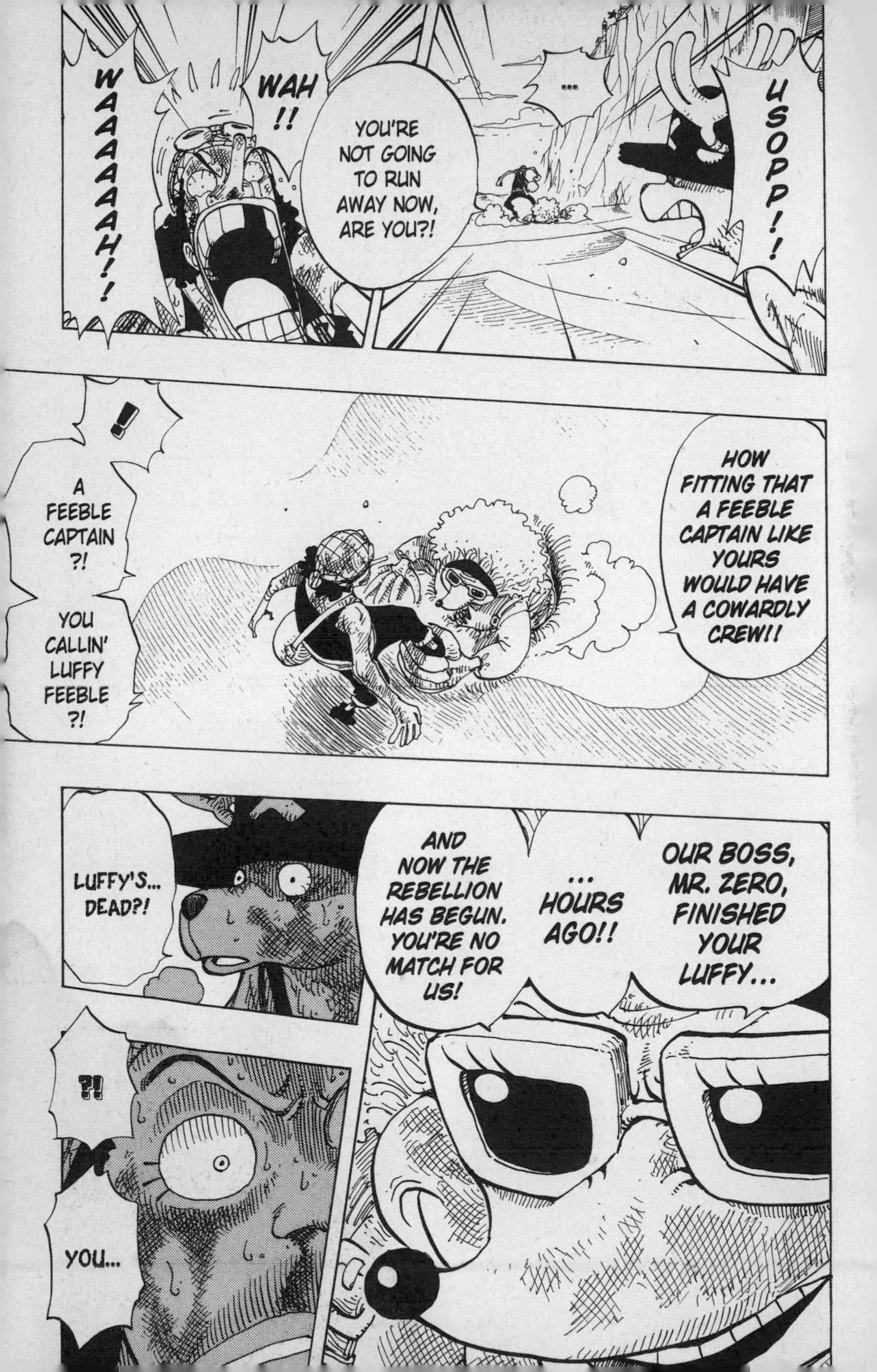
USOPP!!
...
YOU'RE NOT GOING TO RUN AWAY NOW, ARE YOU?!
WAH!!
WAAAAAAAH!!
HOW FITTING THAT A FEEBLE CAPTAIN LIKE YOURS WOULD HAVE A COWARDLY CREW!!
!
A FEEBLE CAPTAIN?!
YOU CALLIN' LUFFY FEEBLE?!
OUR BOSS, MR. ZERO, FINISHED YOUR LUFFY...
... HOURS AGO!!
AND NOW THE REBELLION HAS BEGUN. YOU'RE NO MATCH FOR US!
LUFFY'S... DEAD?!
?!
YOU...

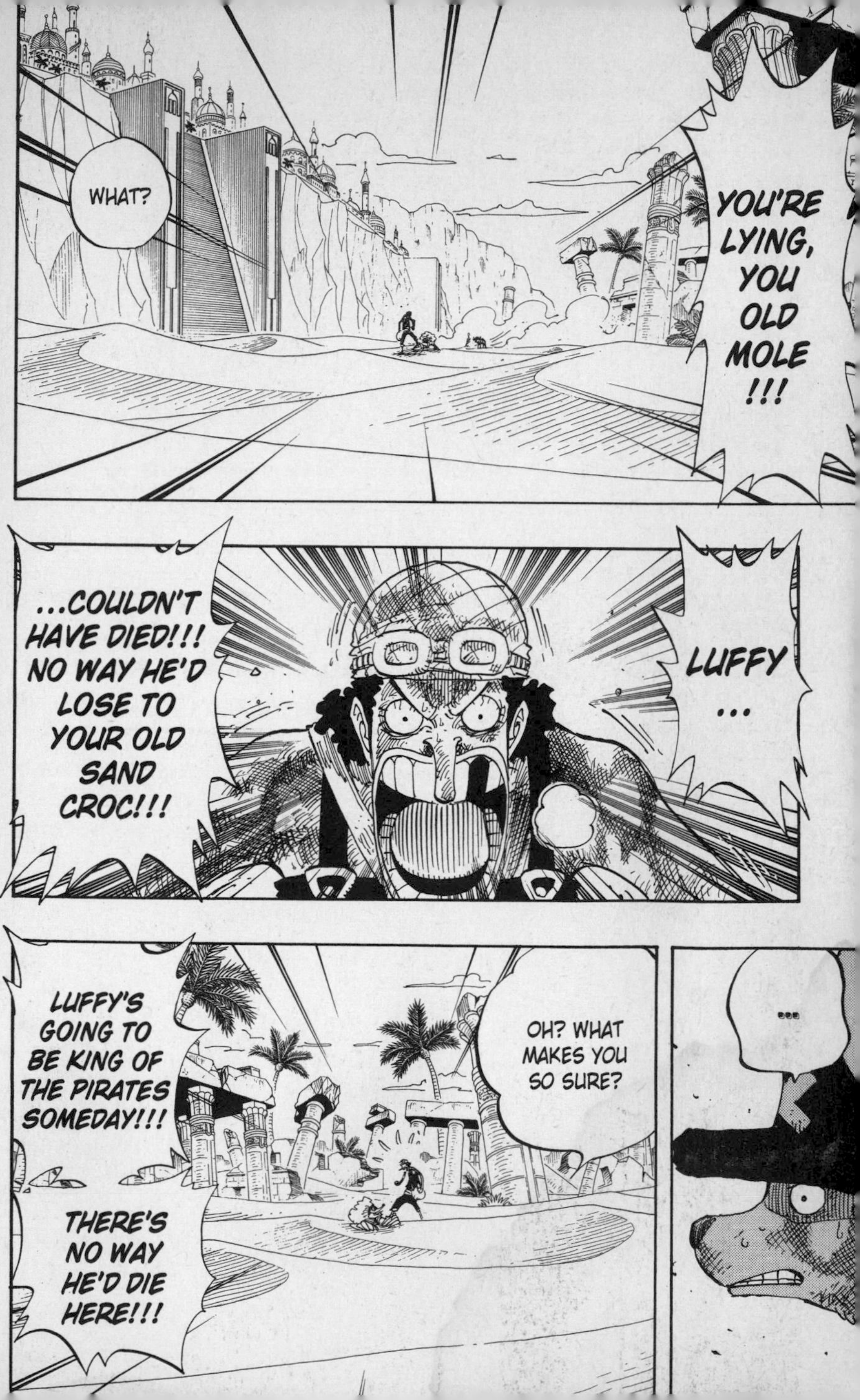
YOU'RE LYING, YOU OLD MOLE!!!
WHAT?
LUFFY...
...COULDN'T HAVE DIED!!! NO WAY HE'D LOSE TO YOUR OLD SAND CROC!!!
...
OH? WHAT MAKES YOU SO SURE?
LUFFY'S GOING TO BE KING OF THE PIRATES SOMEDAY!!!
THERE'S NO WAY HE'D DIE HERE!!!

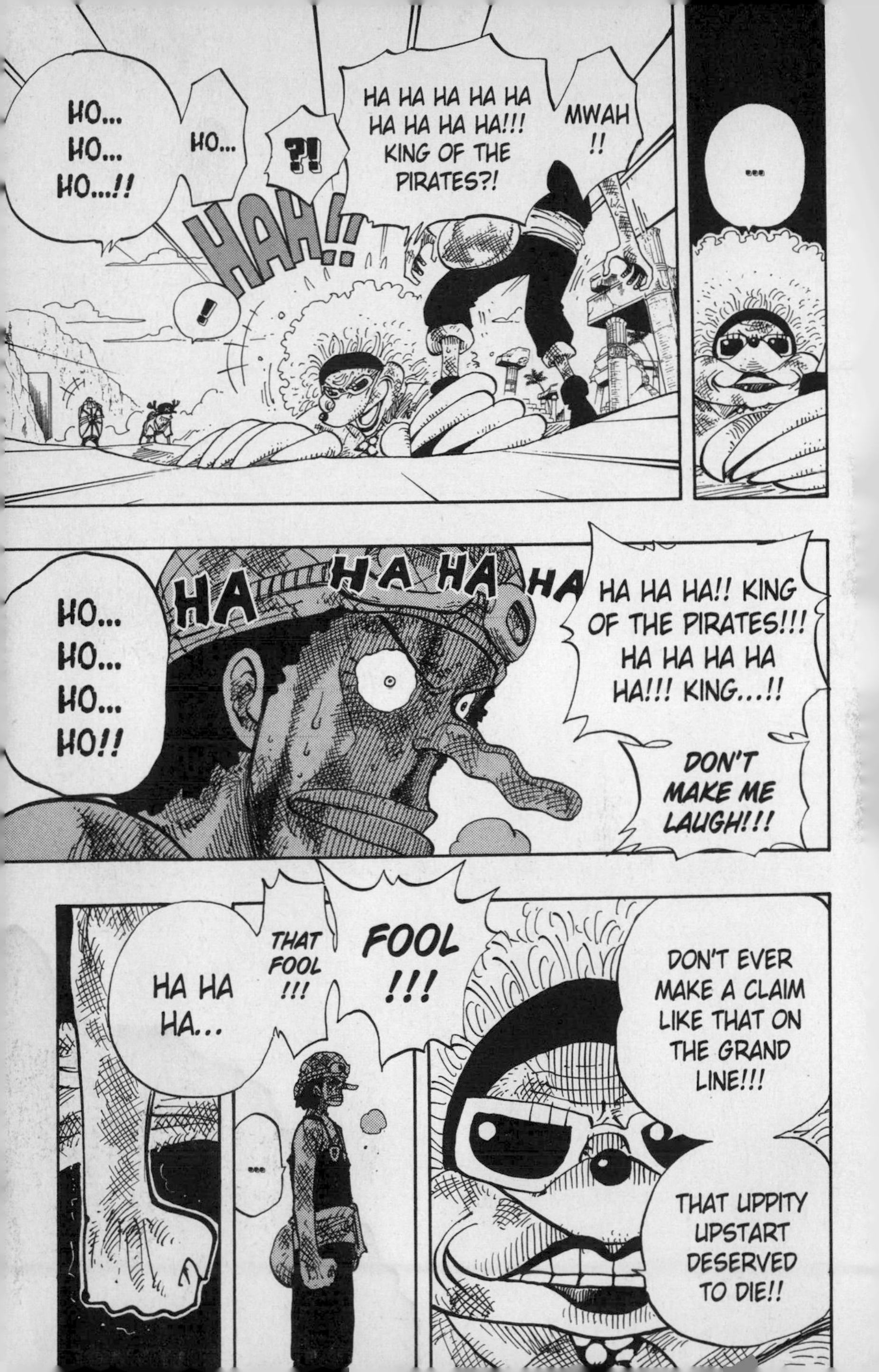
...
MWAH !!
HA HA HA HA HA HA HA HA HA!!! KING OF THE PIRATES?!
?!
HO...
HO... HO... HO...!!
HAH!!
!
HA HA HA!! KING OF THE PIRATES!!! HA HA HA HA HA!!! KING...!!
DON'T MAKE ME LAUGH!!!
HA HA HA HA
HO... HO... HO... HO!!
DON'T EVER MAKE A CLAIM LIKE THAT ON THE GRAND LINE!!!
THAT UPPITY UPSTART DESERVED TO DIE!!
FOOL !!!
THAT FOOL !!!
HA HA HA...
...

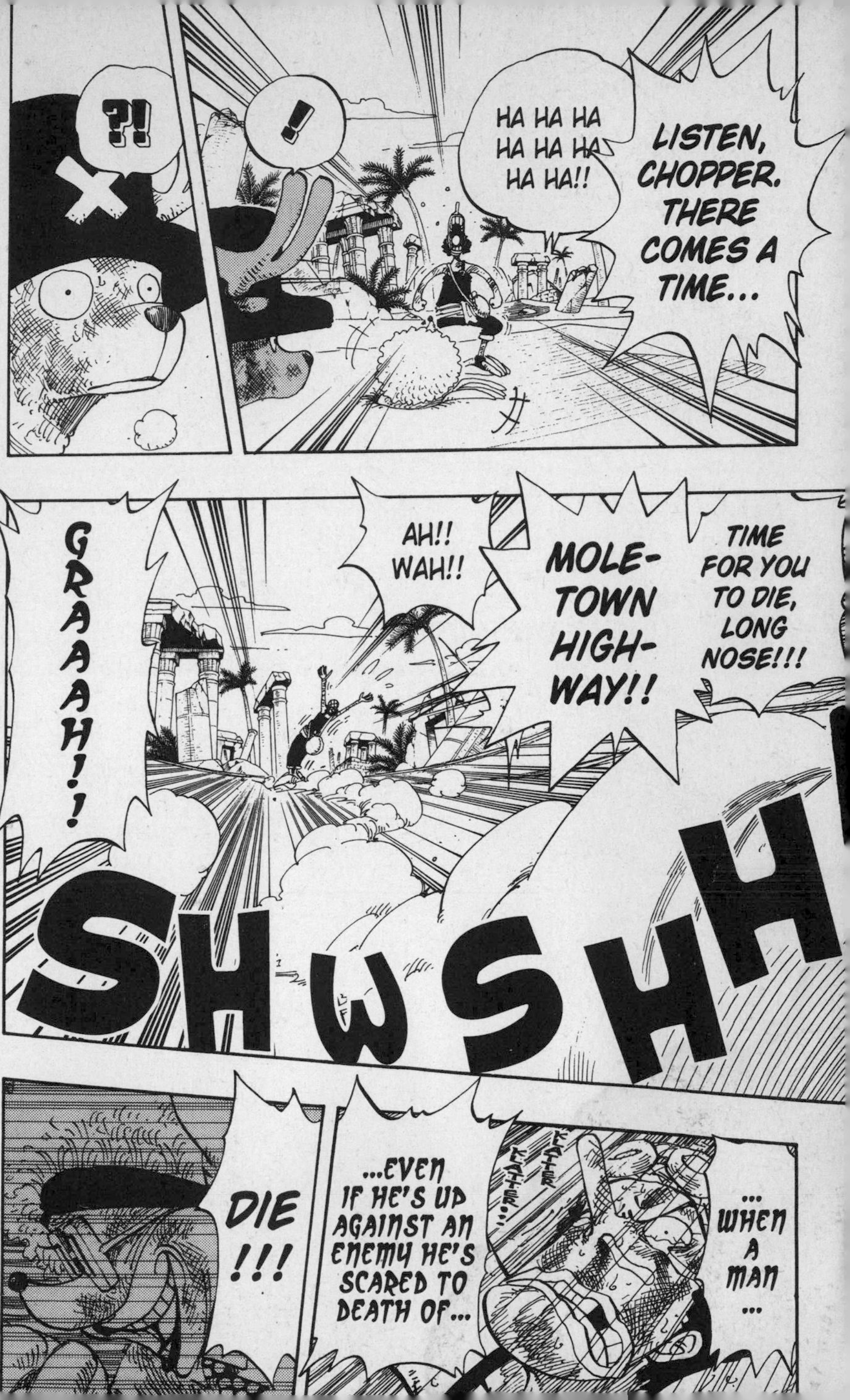
LISTEN, CHOPPER. THERE COMES A TIME...
HA HA HA HA HA HA HA HA!!
!
?!
TIME FOR YOU TO DIE, LONG NOSE!!!
MOLE-TOWN HIGHWAY!!
AH!! WAH!!
GRAAAAH!!!
SHWSHH
... WHEN A MAN ...
KLATTER
KLATTER...
...EVEN IF HE'S UP AGAINST AN ENEMY HE'S SCARED TO DEATH OF...
DIE !!!

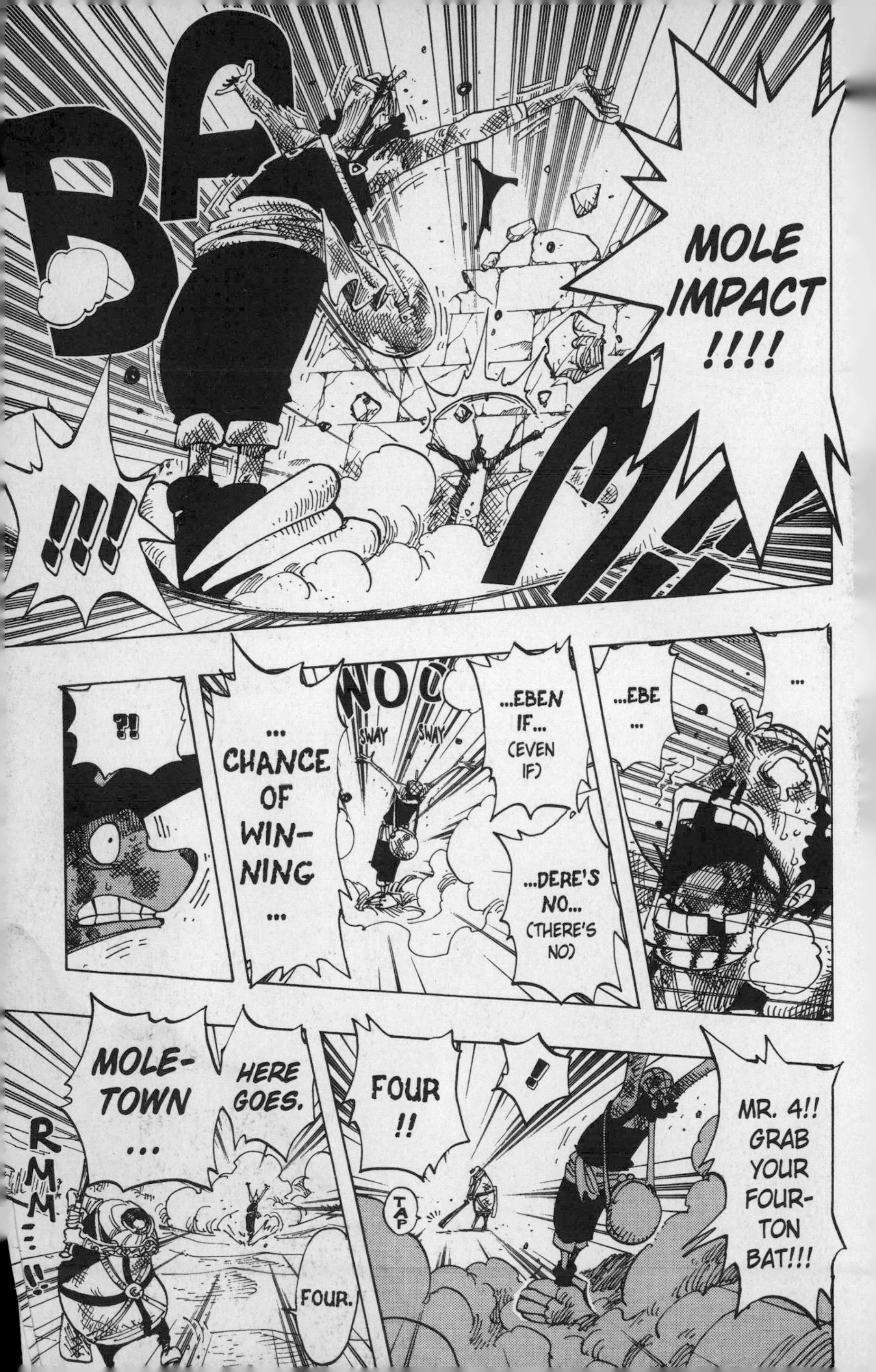

MOLE IMPACT !!!!
BA
!!!
...
...EBE ...
...EBEN IF... (EVEN IF)
...DERE'S NO... (THERE'S NO)
SWAY SWAY
... CHANCE OF WIN-NING ...
?!
MR. 4!! GRAB YOUR FOUR-TON BAT!!!
!
FOUR !!
TAP
FOUR.
HERE GOES.
MOLE-TOWN ...
RMM...!!

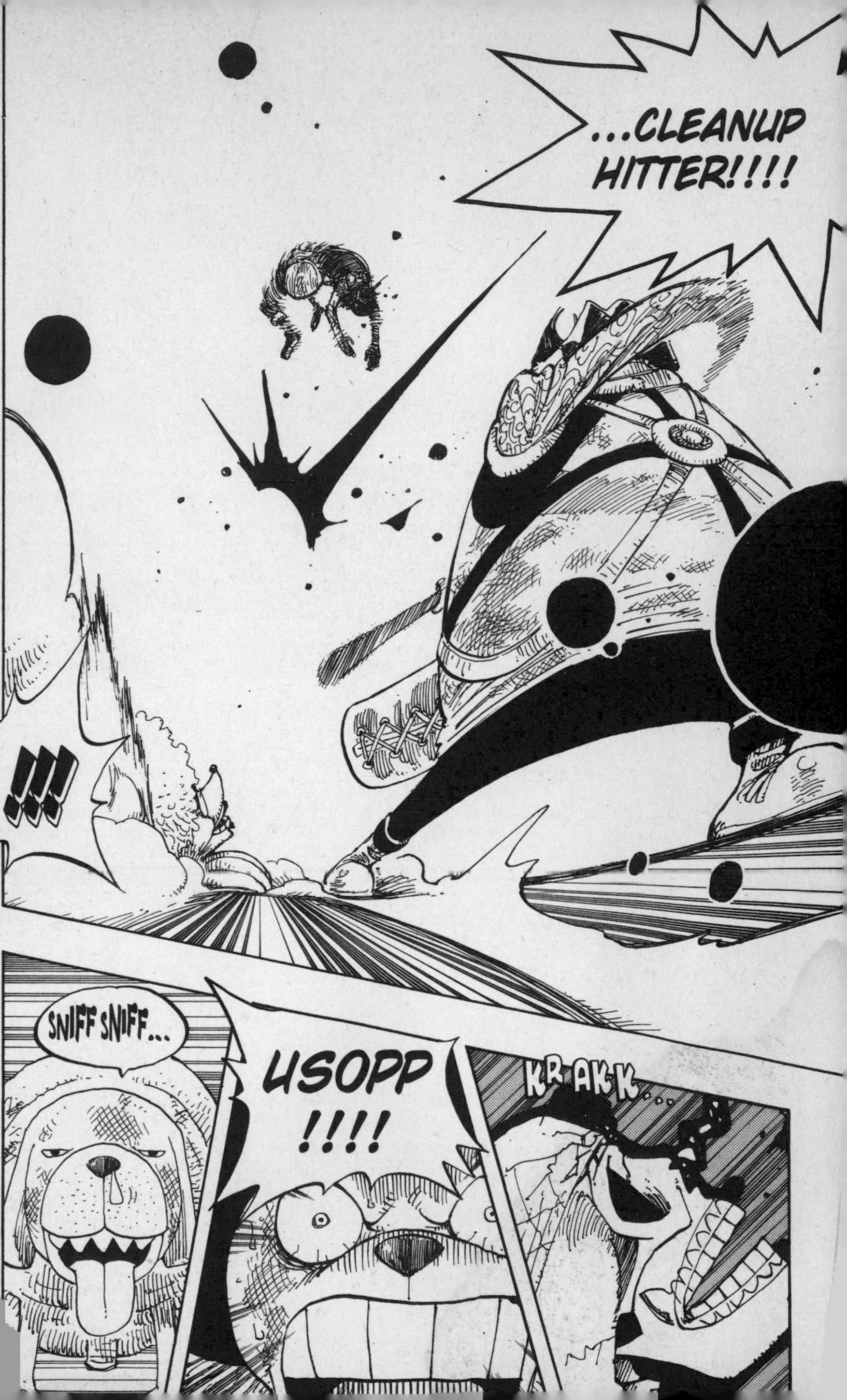
...CLEANUP HITTER!!!!
!!!
KRAKK...
USOPP !!!!
SNIFF SNIFF...

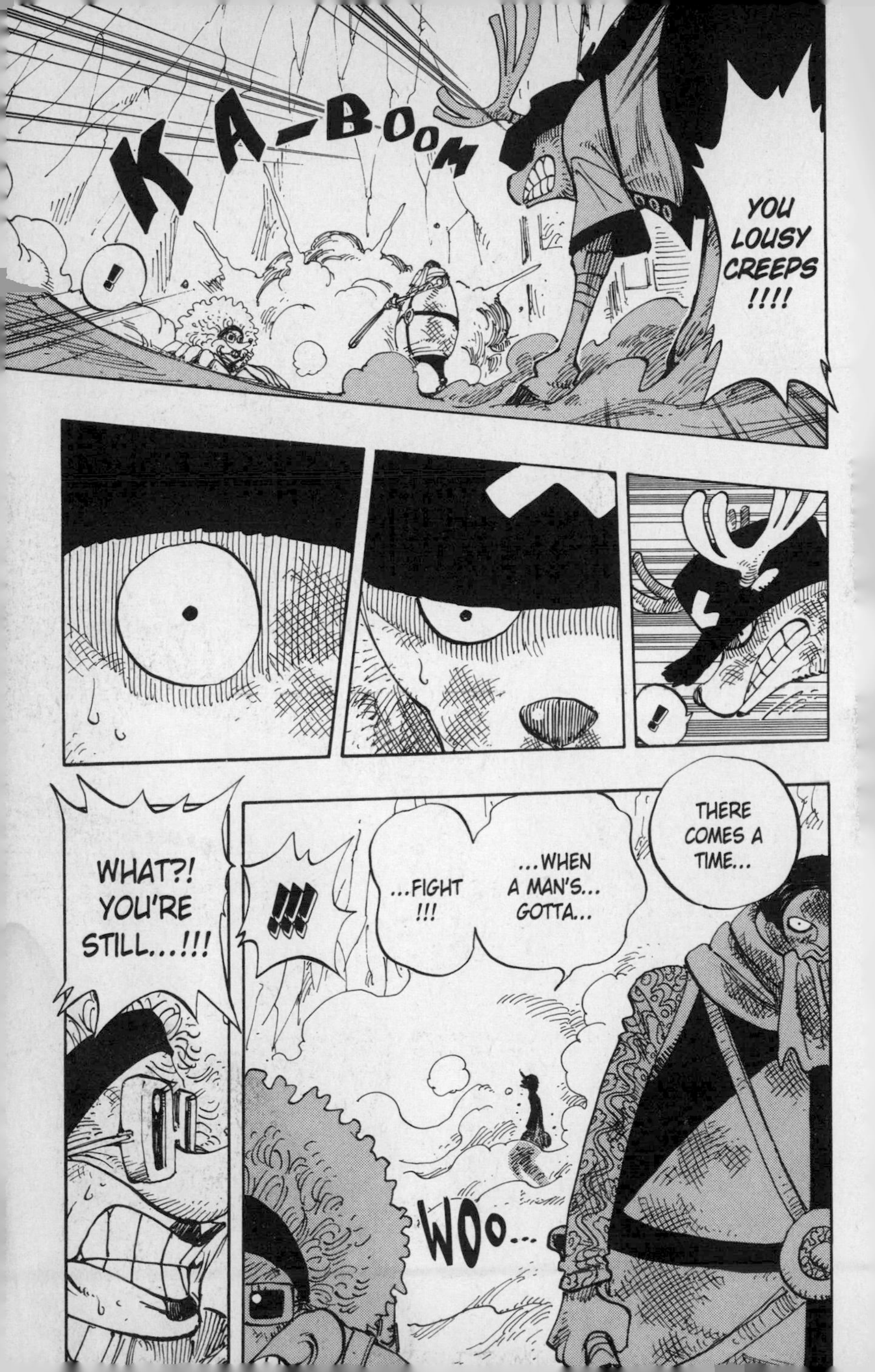
YOU LOUSY CREEPS !!!!
KA-BOOM
!
!
THERE COMES A TIME...
...WHEN A MAN'S... GOTTA...
...FIGHT !!!
!!!
WOO...
WHAT?! YOU'RE STILL...!!!

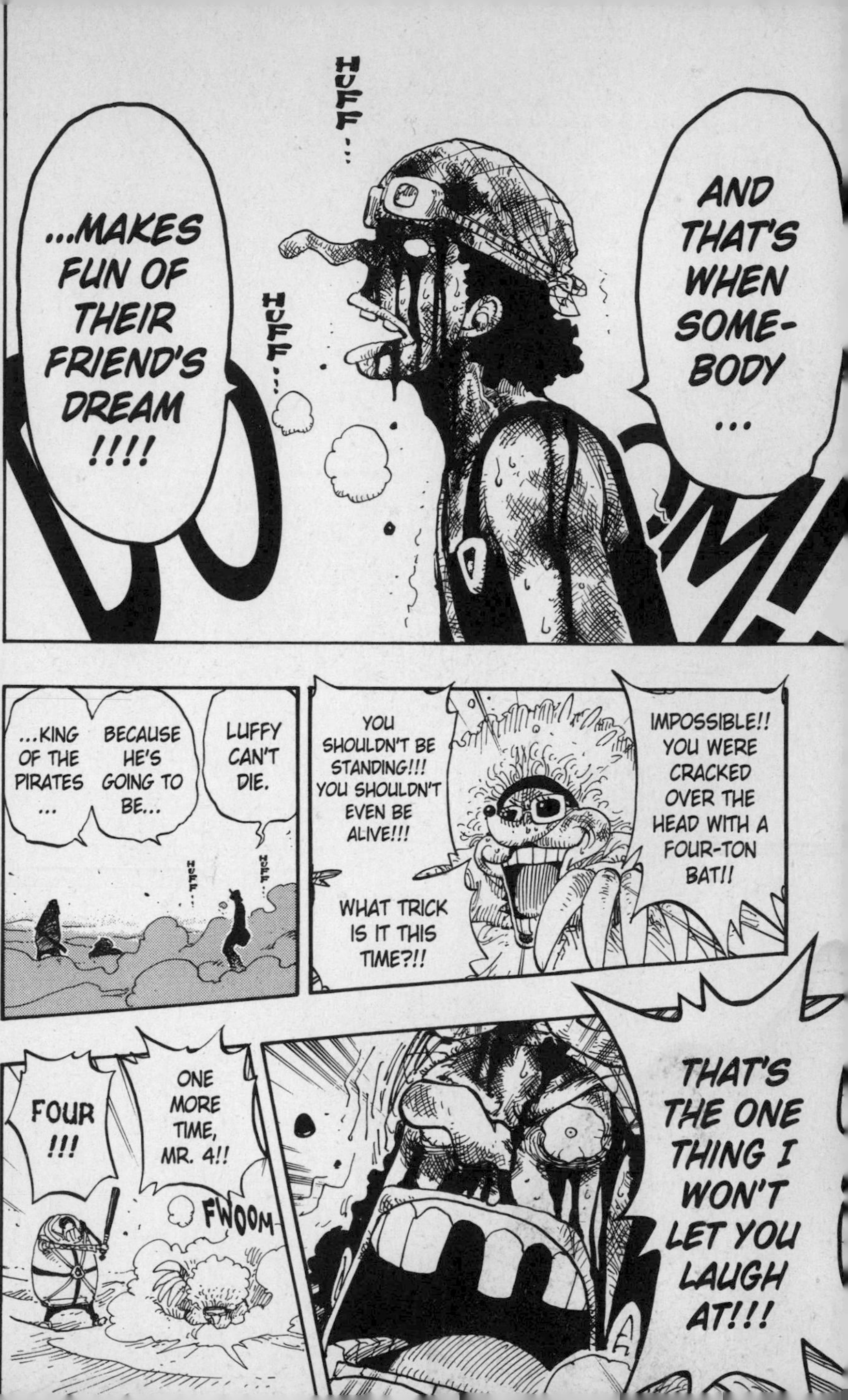
HUFF..
AND THAT'S WHEN SOMEBODY ...
HUFF..
...MAKES FUN OF THEIR FRIEND'S DREAM !!!!
IMPOSSIBLE!! YOU WERE CRACKED OVER THE HEAD WITH A FOUR-TON BAT!!
YOU SHOULDN'T BE STANDING!!! YOU SHOULDN'T EVEN BE ALIVE!!!
WHAT TRICK IS IT THIS TIME?!!
LUFFY CAN'T DIE.
BECAUSE HE'S GOING TO BE...
...KING OF THE PIRATES ...
HUFF..
HUFF..
THAT'S THE ONE THING I WON'T LET YOU LAUGH AT!!!
ONE MORE TIME, MR. 4!!
FOUR !!!
FWOOM

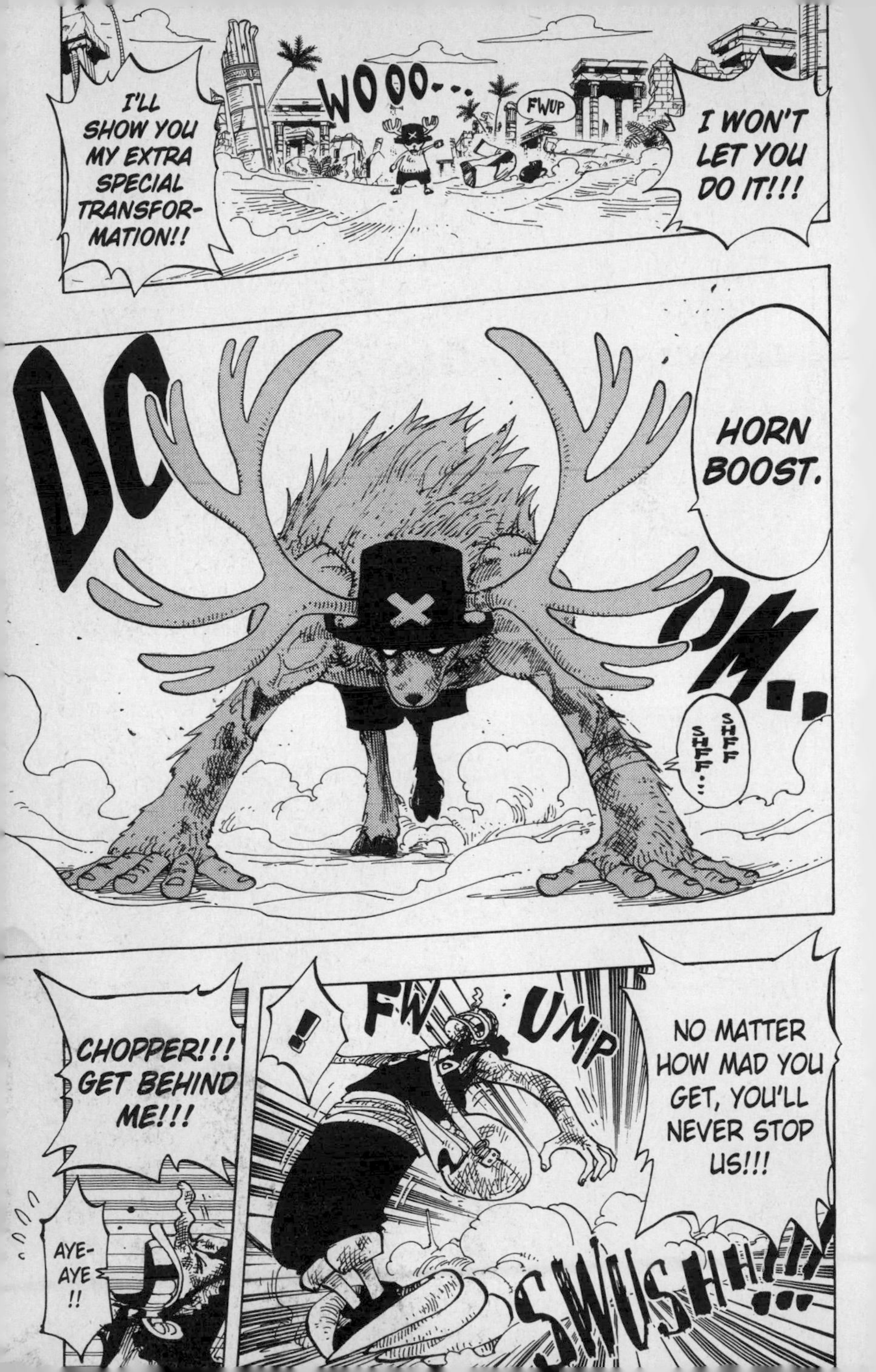
I WON'T LET YOU DO IT!!!
FWUP
WOOO...
I'LL SHOW YOU MY EXTRA SPECIAL TRANSFORMATION!!
HORN BOOST.
DOOM..
SHFF SHFF...
NO MATTER HOW MAD YOU GET, YOU'LL NEVER STOP US!!!
FWUMP
!
SWUSH!!!
CHOPPER!!! GET BEHIND ME!!!
AYE-AYE!!

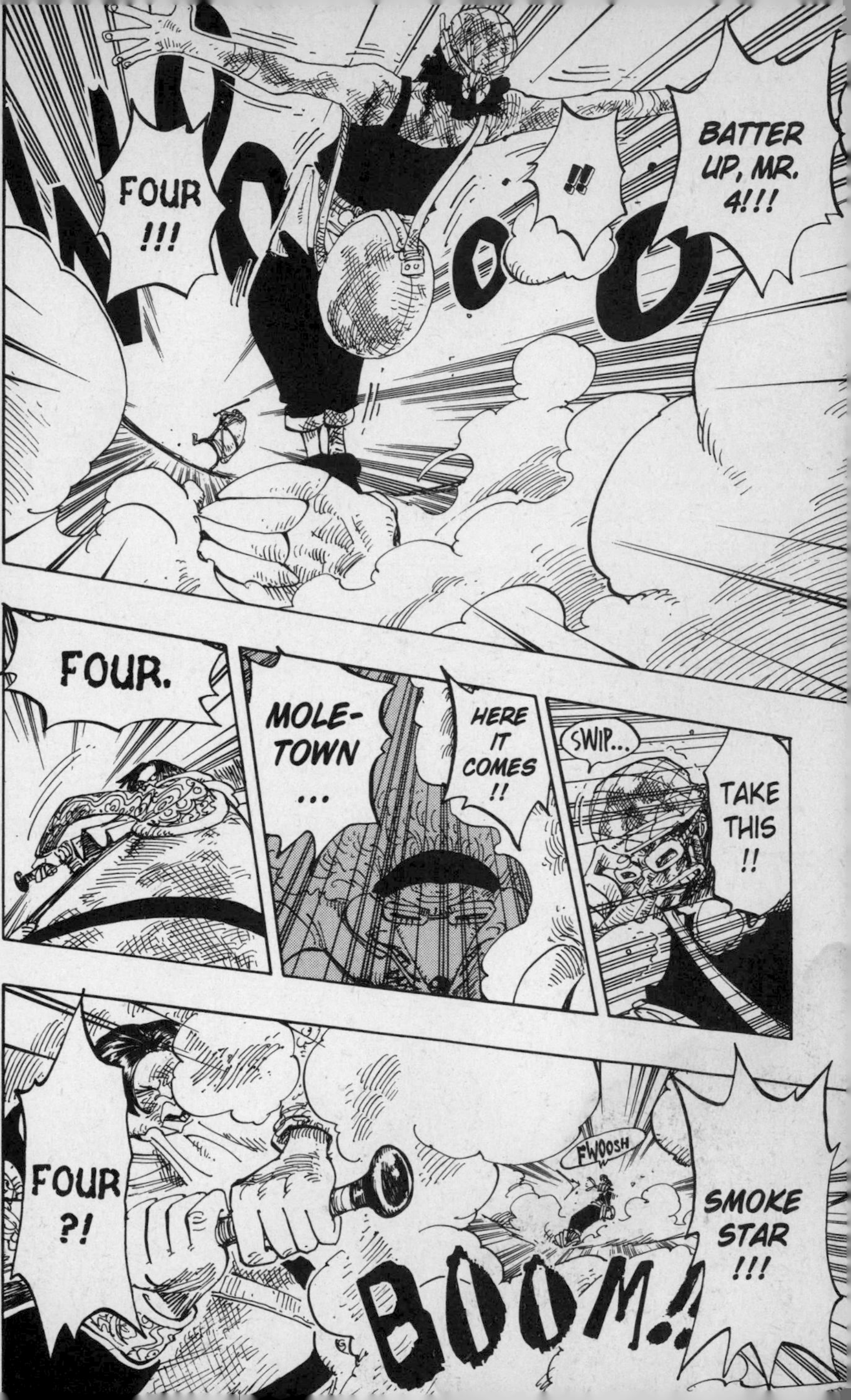
BATTER UP, MR. 4!!!
!!
FOUR !!!
SWIP...
TAKE THIS !!
HERE IT COMES !!
MOLE-TOWN ...
FOUR.
SMOKE STAR !!!
FWOOSH
BOOM!!
FOUR ?!

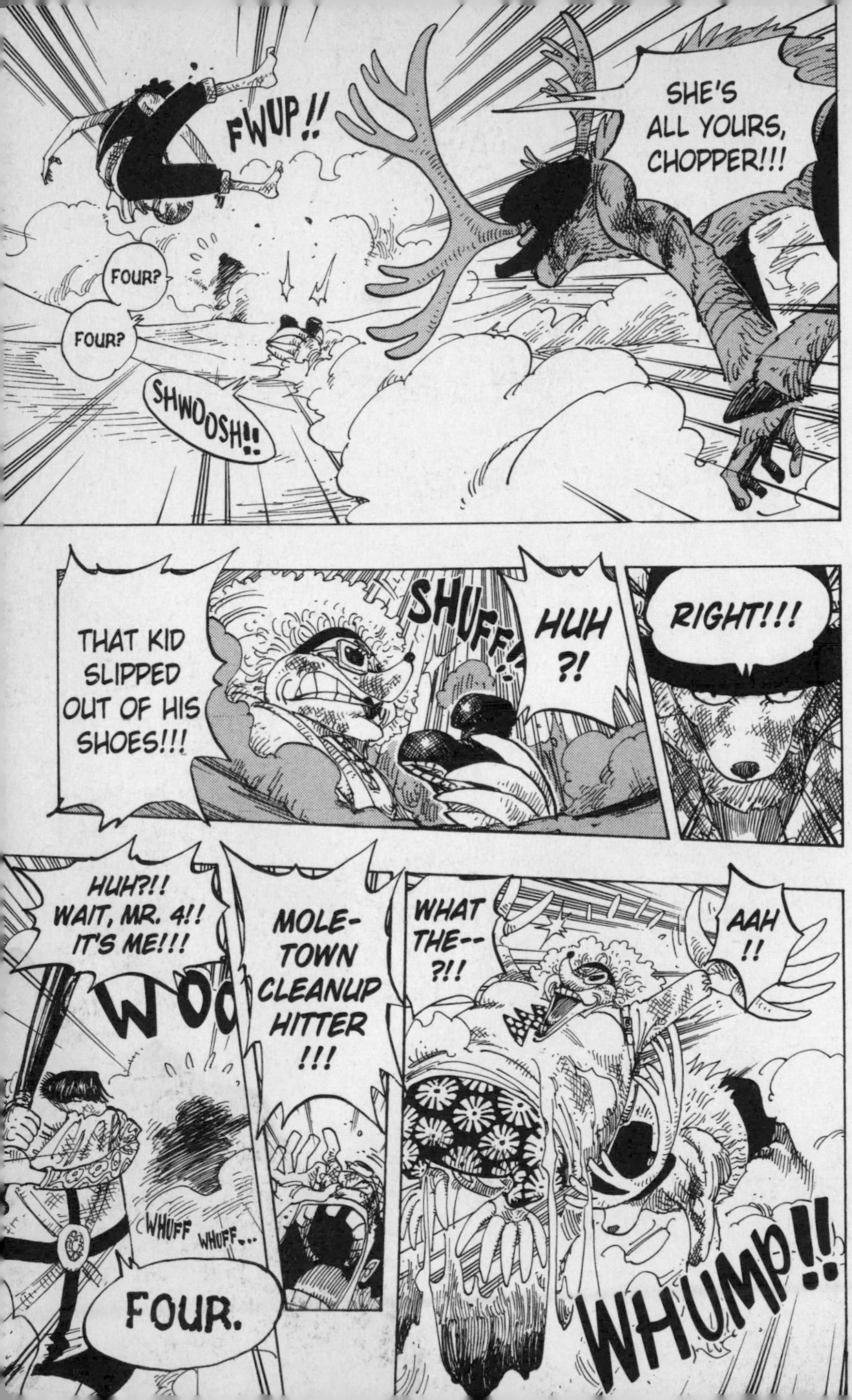
SHE'S ALL YOURS, CHOPPER!!!
FWUP!!
FOUR?
FOUR?
SHWOOSH!!
RIGHT!!!
HUH ?!
SHUFF
THAT KID SLIPPED OUT OF HIS SHOES!!!
AAH !!
WHAT THE-- ?!!
WHUMP!!
MOLE-TOWN CLEANUP HITTER !!!
HUH?!! WAIT, MR. 4!! IT'S ME!!!
WOO
WHUFF WHUFF...
FOUR.

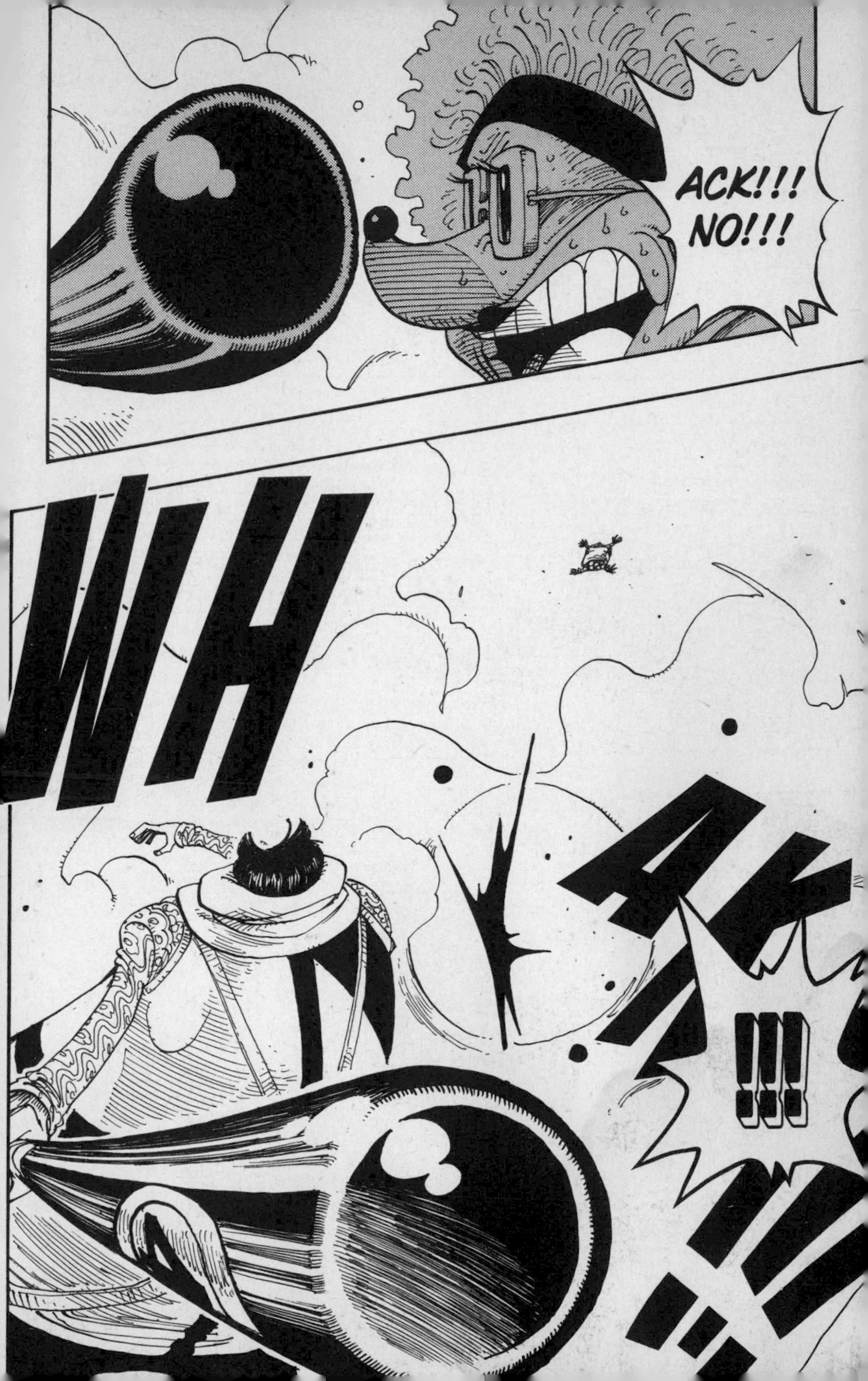
ACK!!!
NO!!!

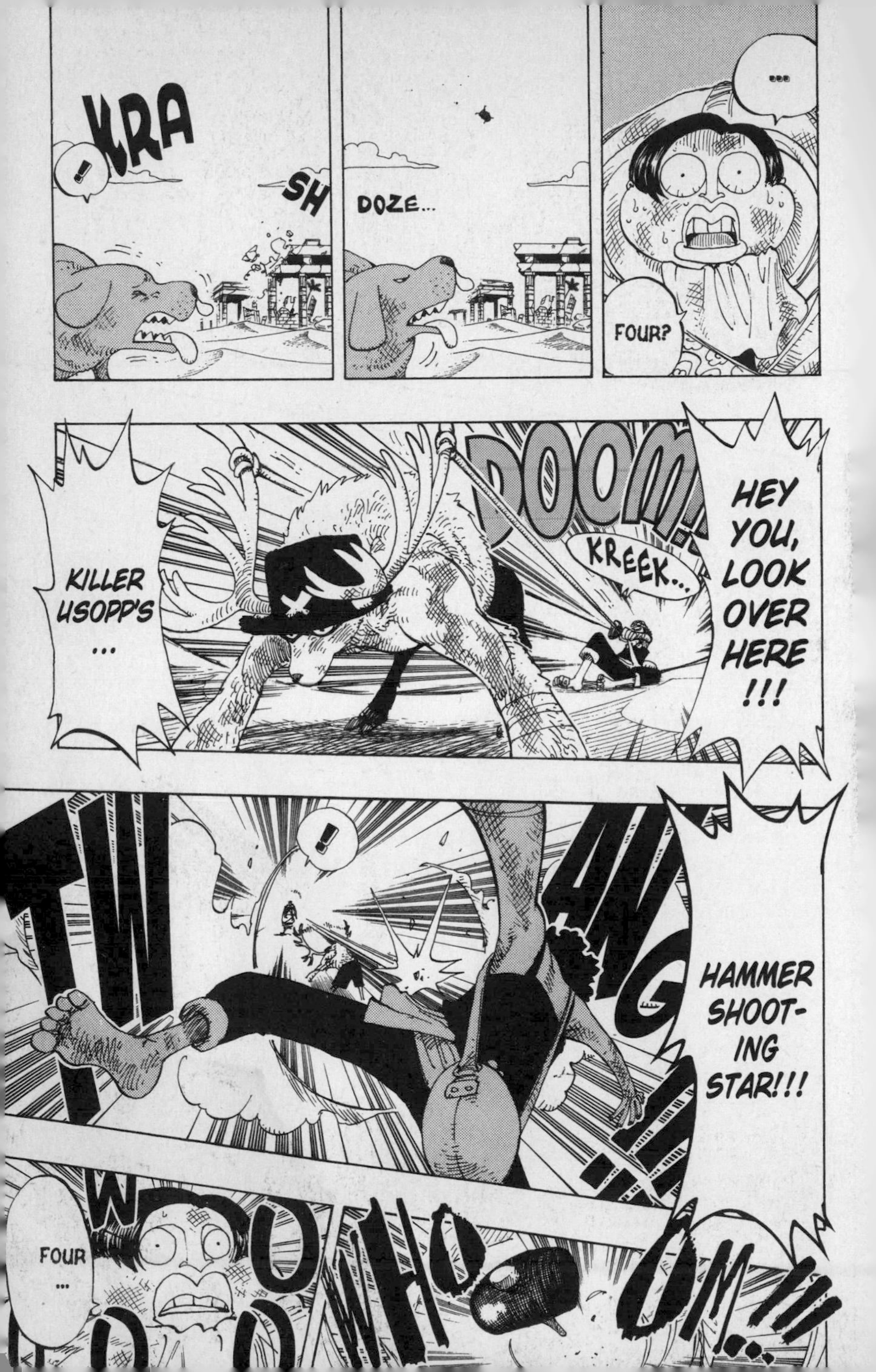
...
FOUR?
SH
DOZE...
KRA
!
HEY YOU, LOOK OVER HERE!!!
DOOM!!
KREEK...
KILLER USOPP'S ...
HAMMER SHOOT-ING STAR!!!
ANG
TW
!
OM!!!
WHO
WOO
FOUR ...

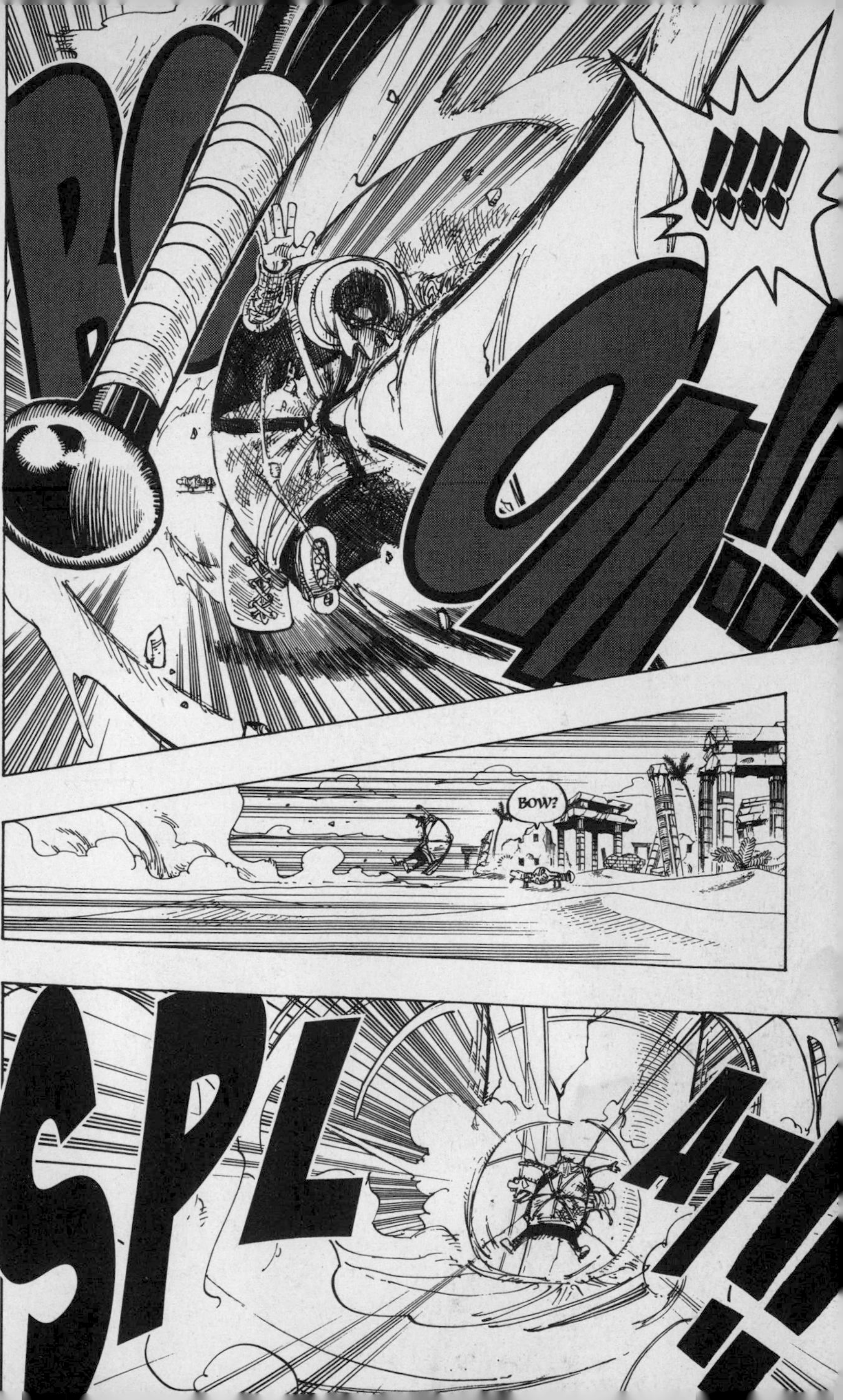
BOW?
SPLAT!!

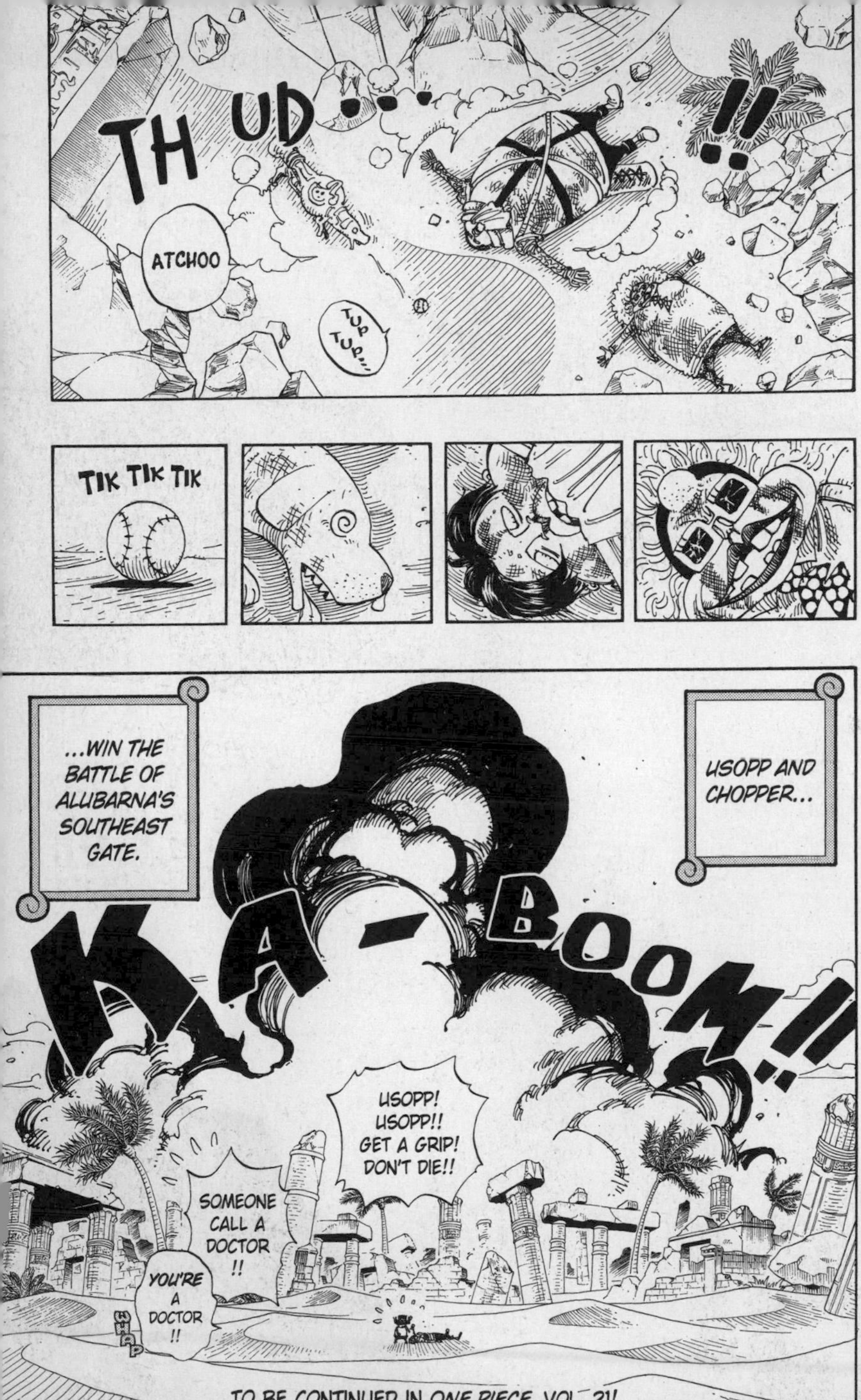
THUD...!!
ATCHOO
TUP TUP...
TIK TIK TIK
USOPP AND CHOPPER...
...WIN THE BATTLE OF ALUBARNA'S SOUTHEAST GATE.
KA-BOOM!!
USOPP! USOPP!! GET A GRIP! DON'T DIE!!
SOMEONE CALL A DOCTOR !!
YOU'RE A DOCTOR !!
WHAP

TO BE CONTINUED IN *ONE PIECE*, VOL. 21!

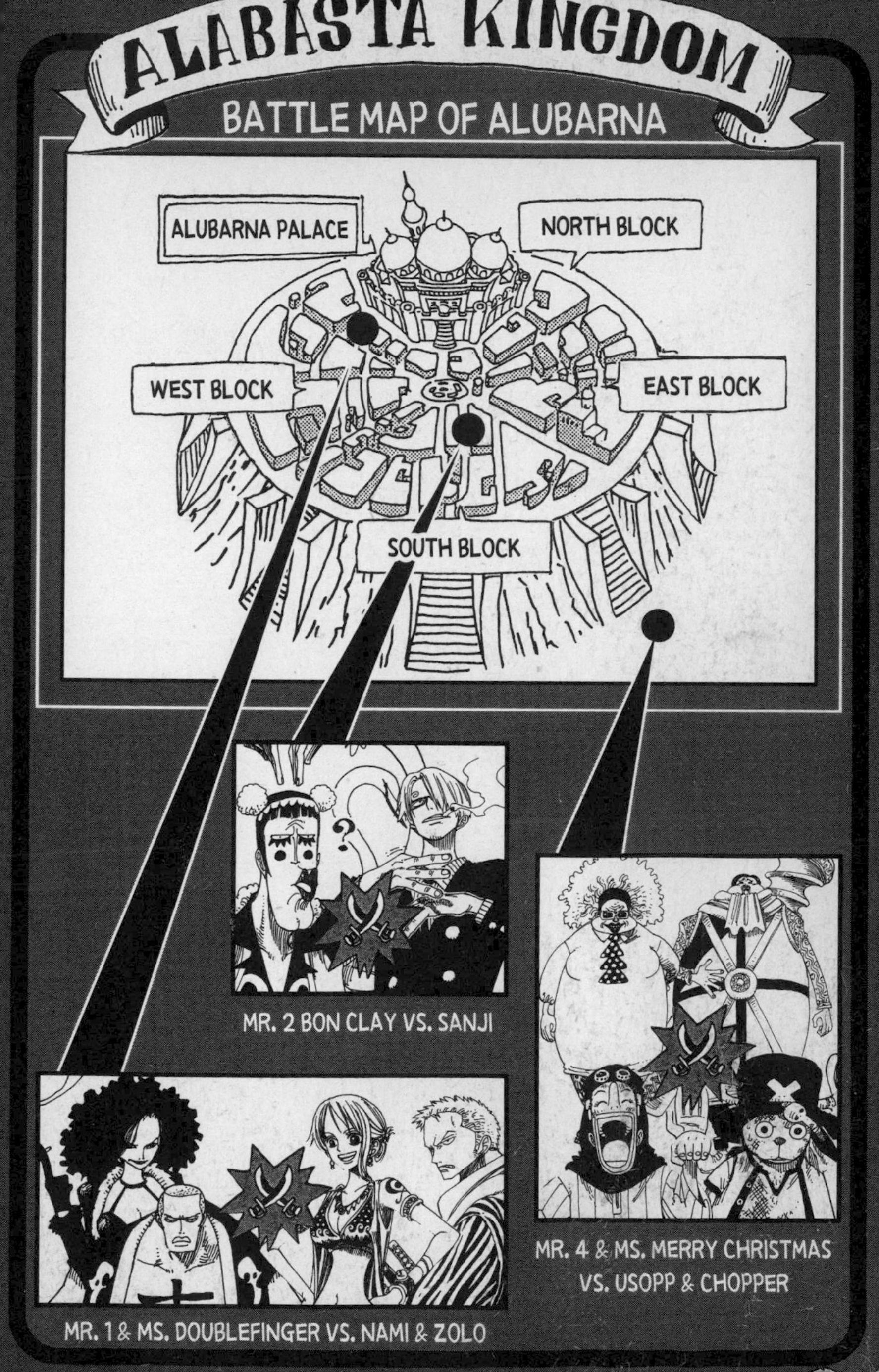

ALABASTA KINGDOM

BATTLE MAP OF ALUBARNA

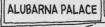

ALUBARNA PALACE

NORTH BLOCK

WEST BLOCK

EAST BLOCK

SOUTH BLOCK

MR. 2 BON CLAY VS. SANJI

MR. 4 & MS. MERRY CHRISTMAS
VS. USOPP & CHOPPER

MR. 1 & MS. DOUBLEFINGER VS. NAMI & ZOLO